GASPAR

The St. Nicholas

Chronicles

Book 1

"... and they bowed down and worshipped Him." May we all be like the wisemen.

—Randy Adamson

By Randy Adamson

Library of Congress Control Number: 2015903904

CreateSpace Independent Publishing Platform

North Charleston, SC

ISBN-13: 978-1508513018 (CreateSpace-Assigned)

ISBN-10: 1508513015

PREFACE

Sixteen years ago I took a teaching job in a small community south of Greeley, Colorado as a keyboarding and drama teacher. During the Christmas season that year, one of the young teachers on staff asked if I would consider playing Santa Claus to her children on Christmas Eve. She told me that two of her neighbors were also interested and that they would pay me well to do it. Needing extra money for my own family's Christmas gifts, I agreed.

One of the boys that I would be visiting was a precocious eight-year-old, who I was told, might try to prove that I was not Santa, caused me a little concern. This caused me enough concern that I spent quite a bit of time studying up on the legend of Santa Claus, trying to ready myself for anything he might throw at me. The more that I got into my study, I became increasingly intrigued with all the stories about the gift givers that had arisen over the centuries around Christmas. I wondered if a person could consolidate all the different legends and true stories to make a novel. The more I thought about it, the more I was able to see a storyline developing. That initial study was the beginning of the story that you will read in the pages ahead. As for my performance to the three households of children, I was told later that all of them were completely convinced that I was not only Santa Claus, but that there is indeed a St. Nick.

2

ACKNOWLEDGEMENTS

My daughters and my wife, Zoe, have been incredibly supportive in this endeavor to write my fictitious history of Santa Claus. I also would like to thank Lindsay Easter and Jasona Brown for reading my initial manuscript and giving me marvelous input. There were times when I did not know where to take the story next, and after a time of prayer, God was always faithful to furnish me with direction.

NOTE

At the end of the book is a Glossary of Characters and Story Information that will help you keep the story straight as you read.

CHAPTER ONE

  Gaspar awoke irritated that his waking preoccupation with the appearance of the new star in the night sky was now affecting his sleep also. He had dreamt that he was standing on a hill on the outskirts of a large city. As he gazed at the star above him it looked to be growing in size. The star was growing, he eventually realized, because it was coming closer and closer to him. Illuminating light was soon enveloping him. His body tingled with its closeness. His initial fear was now being replaced by a warm gladness and peace. Dropping to his knees, he covered his head with his arms as the light continued to intensify. The dream passed and he looked out on the horizon of a Parthian morning that was just beginning to change from black to purple.

  Ever since the rogue star had appeared in the night sky, Gaspar's life had altered. His prayers and recitations at the temple of Ahura-Mazda had become mundane. Something about the new bright star in the sky caused both excitement and foreboding in him. The star did not behave like other stars. It did not circle in the night sky. Instead of moving on a course as other stars did, this star rose out of the west and then halted directly center of the evening canopy of celestial lights and stayed there until the sun illuminated the morning sky. He had always been so sure of his faith in the one true god, Ahura-Mazda. Now, for a reason he could not be sure, he doubted. In some way, the star had altered his ability to believe in the good god. Even though he knew that negative thoughts dampened his chances for him to live in paradise forever, he could not will them away. Other priests had not seemed to have been affected by the star's presence—why was he? Did this star and his dream have any connection, and if so why were other holy men undisturbed? To Gaspar, it seemed that the sureness and sanity of his world was being shaken to its foundation by the forces that ushered in the new star.

  The remainder of the early morning hours were spent tossing and turning. His short snatches of sleep were interrupted, again, by the piercing light emanating from the new star. He knew his fear negated his role in bringing about paradise and aiding the good god in his quest over the evil spirit to thwart his attack on the physical world, but he could not gain control of his thoughts.

Eventually, sleep did come to him only to be awakened by anxious nudging. He opened his eyes to look into the face of his servant and one-time guardian, Balzak. Balzak had always been kind and subservient to Gaspar, but there was an edge of assertiveness that sometimes irritated him about his long-time servant. He had joined Gaspar's family, when Gaspar was but an infant, to be both teacher and caretaker. Training Gaspar in the ways of the magi had consumed much of Balzak's time over most of his young pupil's years growing up, and Balzak made sure he learned everything he had to teach him. Like most youth, Gaspar would have often preferred playing to learning, but he was a quick study when it came to philosophy, religion, mathematics and astrology. The magi were revered all over the known world for their wisdom, their knowledge of the stars, and their mastery of trigonometry. Balzak was reduced to being only a teacher because of his poor family background, but he was much esteemed for his command of the ways of the ancient sect. He had taught other young men, but he had never had as adept of student as Gaspar. Gaspar's intuition to the spirit world, as well as his quick mind, made him a pupil worthy of Balzak's abilities.

"Do you intend sleeping the day away, young master, or do you plan to go to the temple? You must not shirk your duties," said Balzak condescendingly.

"My mind is preoccupied. I had what I believe was a vision last night, and it has consumed my thoughts since then. Please, set out my robes and I will skip breakfast this morning."

Balzak did not make mention of it nor did he show any sign of concern, but he was beginning to worry about Gaspar's apparent lack of attention to his duties. Gaspar, even at his relatively young age, had made a positive impression on the Priest Elders, and he did not want to see his beloved student falter in their eyes.

When Balzak came to Gaspar's family, the House of Bessor, he did so with strong recommendations from the Sheik of Barren Terra—a wise and powerful ruler of the desert peoples. Upon first sight of Balzak, no one would ever guess that he was a man of great prestige. He was scarcely four and a half feet tall, and a great pointed nose stuck out from between his two squinty eyes. Sparse, long hair caught on his nose when he became excited by some teaching that caught his fancy— which was almost everything about which he spoke. He would throw his head and arms about when he pontificated and his untamed hair would catch on first one side and then the other side of his considerable snout. Chattering to himself was a characteristic when he was in deep thought over a lesson or a philosophical issue. Few scholars were his intellectual match, and few servants had his insatiable ambition. He dearly loved what Gaspar could do for him, and the position of power his young master already had acquired.

Balzak was not pure scholar. His skill with a knife made no one safe within his throwing range. Many carried a dagger for protection—Balzak carried two perfectly balanced throwing knives—one on each hip. Keeping up with his skill occupied a portion of each day's routine.

As Gaspar walked from his sleeping quarters, Balzak thought how regal his master had grown. "He has 'the look'," he said aloud to himself. "Yes, someday, my master will be a great magus, and I will aid him in his advisement to kings," he mused as he turned and busied himself setting Gaspar's quarters in order.

CHAPTER TWO

Gaspar came from the temple after his morning prayers angry and frustrated by his lack of attention. Never had he been so clumsy and absent minded in his religious duties. Once, while off in his thoughts, he almost knocked a fire priest over who was hauling sandalwood to maintain the eternal flame of Ahura-Mazda. What had happened to him? Why was it so hard for him to focus? He realized he needed to talk to someone, and he knew he couldn't disappoint Balzak with this kind of information.

"Ah!" He said aloud as he thought of his fellow magus, Melchior. Melchior was fifteen years his senior, and a wise and trusted confidant. He would talk to Melchior about the new star he had seen in the night skies. Each night it seemed to taunt him with its presence. The star had all the characteristics of a sign for their time. Whether this star was a sign for good or for evil no one could know yet. At any rate, the star and his dream the night before had him shaken, and he wanted to get to the bottom of them both.

Melchior was one of the few magi, like Gaspar, who kept a personal home. He had come from a wealthy family and had inherited a great deal. The astrological observatory in Melchior's home was second to none other. It was well stocked with astronomical equipment, astrological charts, and a library befitting his knowledge and influence. Melchior knew the stars and their courses as well as any priest of Ahura-Mazda. If anyone had insight to the new star in the heavens it would be Melchior.

"I am sorry, your reverence, but my master cannot see anyone at this time," Melchior's servant, Moshen, apologized in his gruff manner. "His Reverence has been hold up in his observatory for the past four days, and refuses to see any who comes. If you would like, I could send for you as soon as he makes himself available again."

This was unsettling news on two counts for Gaspar. He was dismayed because he thought Melchior could shed some light on his own disconcerting dream, and he would now have to wait. Secondly, he knew that the star had Melchior concerned as well or he would not have shut himself off from the rest of the world.

"The star must have even greater significance than I had originally thought," said Gaspar distractedly. Turning back to Moshen, "Please tell Melchior that I would like to see him as soon as possible."

As Gaspar turned to leave, he was scared out of his wits by Melchior's booming voice echoing down from his observation tower. "Send my young friend up immediately." The hair on his neck stood on end as he received the edict from his friend.

Moshen indicated that Gaspar was to follow him to his master's study.

The spartan furnishings of Melchior's home spoke of his desire to eliminate the clutter of physical possessions from his life. There were few rugs on the stone floors, and only the barest of furnishings. Except for the observatory and the library, there was nothing noteworthy in Melchior's residence.

On the highest hill overlooking Seleucia sat Melchior's house. This gave him an unimpeded view of the night's sky without any hindrance from night fires in the city. His observatory was the pinnacle of the enclosed tower that rose alongside his modest, but comfortable home.

The climb up the steep spiraling stairs was easy enough for Gaspar, but for Moshen, who was old enough to be Gaspar's grandfather, it was a rigorous climb to the top. Before either man could knock, an excited voice from within beckoned Gaspar to enter.

A powerfully built man behind a large wooden table filled with scrolls met Gaspar's eyes as he entered the room. Melchior's observatory was circular with windows lining the walls on every side. Beneath the windows were shelves holding an untold number of map scrolls that marked the courses of all the known stars along with the writings of scholars from all over the known world. On each of the four sides of the observatory were double doors that opened out to a balcony that encircled the entire tower. Centered in the room was a large table with scrolls, some old and some newly scribbled upon. A plate of food left untouched on one side of the table had a large slice of bread, poultry, figs, and goat's cheese that were beginning to dry out in the arid climate. The goblet of wine that accompanied the meal sat empty on one of the scroll cases.

"Gaspar! I was just going to send for you. By Ahura's goodness, you are here already. I have so much to tell you, my boy.

"Please, I am a bad host, have a seat. Moshen! Send Daniel with something refreshing to drink and eat."

Melchior was not the quiet scholar that most people associated with the magi sect. Many magi believed that if Melchior had not been one of them, he would have been a desert bandit—his temperament being much better suited to the latter.

"I am sure that you are aware of the new star that appeared five nights ago," Melchior boomed.

Gaspar nodded his head.

"There is an ancient Persian prophecy that says,
> When the heavens are
> illumined by the brilliance of a new
> star that rises out of the west, men
> will follow it to find he who will be
> ruler over all.

"Each night I have watched and seen the star with increased interest. The star behaves like no other star in the heavens. As you must have noted yourself, the star rises in the west and proceeds to the center of the sky and stays there until morning. It is not particularly brilliant, but I do believe that it heralds the coming of a great world ruler. Surely, this is a sign sent from Ahura-Mazda."

"I don't know what to say, Melchior. This is all so fantastic. No one, in my studies, has ever reported seeing such a thing."

"My, boy. I want to check this with an old friend and fellow priest. He will be able to confirm or dismiss my theory."

"Who is this man?" Gaspar queried surprised that Melchior would seek anyone else's counsel in astronomical matters.

"His name is Balthasar. Have you heard of him?"

"No."

"He is a magus who was sent to the temple in Nippur over twenty years ago. He and I were very close in my younger years, and I have kept in contact with him these many years. If you have nothing better to do, why don't you join me on this trip. It is but a few days travel and we will be back within the fortnight. It will give you and me time to catch up."

"That would be good. There is something I want to talk to you about, and I would like your undivided attention when I tell you."

"You young men today. You are always so sure that what affects you is of grave importance," clapping Gaspar playfully on the back, almost knocking him off his balance. "Very well! I value your company, and you shall have my ear. Shall we plan to leave tomorrow?"

"Tomorrow?"

"Is there a better time to leave than the present when curiosity and adventure mix to rouse one's desire to know the truth?"

"But it will take time to get provisions and to put things in order at my own residence."

"I have already made all of our travel plans. Balzak runs your household very well, and there is no better businessman in all of Parthia than your servant Cephas. There is nothing you can say that can keep you here unless there is a young woman you have not told me about?"

"No, Melchior there is no woman. How did you know that I would go with you?"

"I knew because I knew of your great desire for the truth."

CHAPTER THREE

What was early to Gaspar and early to Melchior were two different times. Gaspar usually awoke just after the sun had risen in order to perform his daily rites to Ahura-Mazda and to say the required prayers. By that time, Melchior had done all of that, read for at least an hour, bathed and eaten a simple breakfast. So when Gaspar was roughly shaken awake by his friend, he was surly for a good while until he had eaten a hasty breakfast of fruit and bread.

Balzak enjoyed Melchior's robust personality and appreciated the rugged male presence he brought into Gaspar's life. To be well-rounded, thought Balzak, Gaspar needed the influence of many people. He did have concern, however, that Melchior's independent ways could lead Gaspar down the wrong road, so Balzak, like the good mother hen that he was, kept a close watch on Melchior's effect on his pupil.

Melchior went out to make sure that all of Gaspar's personal items were properly loaded on the camels. Balzak used the time of Melchior's absence to question Gaspar about this hasty trip that he was about to embark upon.

"Young Reverence, do you think that this is the best time for you to leave? This new star has the elite of the city in a quandary. Your presence could present you with an opportunity to rise in their esteem if you were to be called upon for answers. Besides, this is a time when the king needs his most able advisors around him, and you have caught his eye as a magus in whom he can lay his trust."

"I appreciate your concern Balzak, but I would not be taking this trip if it were not absolutely necessary."

"I must learn to give you room to become a man," smiled Balzak—betraying his inner disagreement. "I will not press you on your decision. Being left out of your decision hurts my pride, but you must make your own choices when you feel fit to do so. I will watch over your affairs here until you return. May the good god protect you. I am sending Cyrus and Amehlech with you. They are strong young men and hard working. Amehlech is a gifted storyteller, Cyrus has a good sense of humor, and they will serve you well on your trip."

Grabbing Balzak's shoulders firmly in his hands, Gaspar acknowledged, "You always have thought of what is best for me as your own concern. I will be careful."

"Are we to go, or are you two going to cackle like hens?" boomed Melchior entering the room. Gaspar regarded Balzak good-naturedly and then left with the big magus.

Mounting their camels, both men sensed adventure in the air. Whenever one takes a trip there is always anticipation, but this feeling was heightened for the two magi. Both Melchior and Gaspar could feel what a hunter feels just before he is ready to shoot a trophy quarry—their senses were alert and their minds were sharpened.

As adventure quickly fades into the monotony of the journey, their excited chatter was eventually reduced to each man caught up in his own thoughts. Eventually, the rhythmic sound of the camels' padding feet and swaying motion was disturbed by Melchior.

"So, my young friend, what did you wish to tell me?" Smiling, he said, "I have nothing to do but listen to you."

"For several days I have wished to talk to you about the new star in the sky, but just the other night I had a dream that was so real I cannot shake its reality. At some point, I want to discuss the star with you, but as my trusted friend, I want your impression of this dream of mine."

Melchior was a man who enjoyed being playful with those he loved, but he could see that this was no time to poke fun at his friend. He knew Gaspar well. What the young magus had to tell Melchior was obviously troubling him a great deal. He only nodded, and smiled as a gesture to continue.

"In my dream," Gaspar began as he looked into the distance, "I was standing on a mountain top outside a large city I have never seen before. It had few of the characteristics of our Parthian cities. I was observing the new star when all of a sudden I realized that it was coming closer and closer to me. At first, I thought that it was growing bigger, but it was definitely coming nearer to me. This frightened me initially, but there was a calming effect as the light surrounded me. The light became so dazzling that I could no longer keep my eyes open. I put my arm across my eyes to shield them, and it was at that time that I woke up. What do you think, Melchior?"

Those who found Melchior overbearing and pompous accused him of never failing to have an opinion on anything. The truth was, he rarely gave flippant responses. His quick mind could sift through the minutia of a concept, make sense of its affect on the big picture, and then make a rational response on anything that was presented to him. It was also not below him to admit that he did not know what he thought, or to say that he needed more time to think something over. So when Gaspar asked him what he thought, Melchior did not reply immediately. Gaspar had learned to let his friend process information. Again, the two men swayed in silence to the rhythmic gate of their resolute bearers.

Gaspar smiled as he thought about the first time he had met Melchior. The prominent holy man had been a dinner guest of his father, Arioch, when Gaspar was but a boy. He remembered thinking how unlike his father was the big magus. His father was every inch the aristocratic intellectual. His physical bearing and mind presented the image of grace, charm, propriety and punditry. The graying at his temples and his tall lean stature only enhanced the perception of high Hellenism. Melchior, on the other hand, was rough, abrasive, and built like an ironsmith. The two were intellectual matches and the most unlikely of friends. But Melchior had loved Arioch like a brother and grieved greatly when he died unexpectedly on a return business trip from Jerusalem. Somewhere in the deserts of Arabia were the remains of Arioch. Melchior was the one who came to Gaspar's home to relate the tragic news that Arioch had died. Melchior held Gaspar in his powerful embrace as they both wept openly. Diana, Gaspar's mother came into the entryway, found the two weeping and knew immediately what had happened. She collapsed on the slate floor. Her life had been wholly wrapped up in her husband and their love for one another. Diana lived but one more year and then followed her husband to paradise. Fortunately for Gaspar, Arioch had hired Balzak the year before his death. Balzak had handled all the affairs of the household from that time to the present. In many ways, Balzak became Gaspar's father, mother, and teacher. Arioch had been a trusting man, and when a close associate advised him to hire Balzak to school his son, he did so not knowing the extensive impact that decision would have on his son.

Gaspar blinked back to the present and was caught in Melchior's gaze and smile. Sometimes when Melchior looked at him, he could swear the man knew what he was thinking. He always felt this unnerving.

"What do you think?" Gaspar asked again wondering if Melchior really could read his mind.

"I believe you have seen into your own future, but I do not know anything beyond that. I am almost certain that what you described was not of your own imagination. Only time will tell us what it all means. I will be interested to see how all of this works into your life. Does the dream bring fear or excitement?"

"I feel dread at the thought of it, but I do not know if that comes from the unknown the dream presents or a danger I have manufactured in my own mind."

"Ahura-Mazda speaks in many ways to us. In this case, I believe, you will be given more information as time goes on. It is not good to fear what will ultimately happen to us. The good spirit would not give you a vision of an impending calamity that you could not deter from its course. I believe I give you good counsel when I tell you to not fear the vision. Be aware of it and recognize it when it comes to fruition so that you can use it to your good."

"Do you have a sense as to whether the images I saw in the dream are symbolic or actual?"

"The fact that the setting of the dream is unfamiliar to you makes me think that your dream is not one solely of symbolism. Symbolism needs reference points to make sense. If the dream contained objects that were familiar to you, but were misplaced in their settings, I would be more obliged to consider its symbolic qualities. I think your dream is a picture of a future reality. Having said that, the star drawing closer to you with its blinding light is symbolic, I believe, and represents growing awareness—maybe new understanding—or possibly spiritual insight."

"I believe you have given me sound discernment. Already I see the dream in a new light. What kind of travels might I encounter that would make such a reality possible?"

"Only Ahura-Mazda could answer that question."

At mid-day the small caravan stopped for a meal and the feeding and watering of the camels. Intuitively, Gaspar knew that although the star had greatly agitated Melchior, he was not ready to talk about it. So lunch and the rest of the day's journey was spent in happy conversation about casual life occurrences and laughing at the jokes and antics of Cyrus and Amehlech. Balzak had made the appropriate choice for their journey in sending the two servants who kept up everyone's spirits.

That evening the tents were placed and the evening meal was prepared. The shamal wind that was ever present during this time of year was but a gentle breeze this particular evening. Though it had a drying effect that made the land brittle as baked clay, it was cooling once the sun had gone down and the stars began to settle themselves in the night sky. The shamal made everything dusty and gritty. Melchior's servants had made gallant attempts to shield the cooking from the wind, but no matter what they did, the grit was present in everyone's food. It made no difference to the consumers—food prepared in the open air after a long day of travel always tastes better than it is.

"You look well fed," Melchior said standing over Gaspar.

Smiling, Gaspar responded, "I am satisfied, and the meal was delicious. You are a generous host even on the road."

14

"Your father will not forgive me when I get to paradise if I do not adequately care for his son. I have no wish for him to lash me with that eloquent tongue of his. He was my only match when it came to verbal reproach."

"I cannot imagine you fearing any man for any reason, Melchior, but I will not argue with you where my father is concerned." Both men mused in their own recollection of Arioch.

"I want you to come walk with me to the top of that near hill over beyond the twin date trees. I would like to discuss the star with you as it rises. It should be doing so soon."

As they walked to the hill, Melchior chuckled anew as he talked about the capers of Gaspar's servants. Nothing gladdened Gaspar's heart more than to hear his friend's hearty guffaw. Melchior was one of those who laughed with his whole being. The young magus sniggered more at Melchior's laughter than at his retelling of the servants' antics.

Reaching the top of the hill, Melchior began to reveal what had been on his mind. "This star puzzles me, Gaspar. It does not behave as other stars do in the sky. Look, now! It is rising in the western sky. See how quickly it moves to its place and then it will move no more. It has no course like any other star. It is small and would not be noticed except for the likes of us. Truly, this small star is a portent of a coming great king or leader of men."

"Melchior, you have mentioned this possibility before. Do you think that truly this is the star foretold to us by the old prophets? Could this star be the one that ushers in he who will bring all men to himself? Melchior, what you say sends waves of anticipation up my spine. This is incredible."

"Hold on, my young friend. I have only made a possible observation. This could be no more than a passing star that is seen and then is seen no more."

"This star is not a momentary falling star. You said yourself that it behaves like no other heavenly body you have seen."

"I said 'no other star'. If this is a star, and I think that it is, it has the possibilities of which I speak. I need to broach this subject with Balthasar before I can know with more certainty. No matter what, it is good to live in the expectation of a great thing —is it not?" Melchior laughed his great laugh and clapped Gaspar on the back, sending him sprawling in the grass.

"I wish that you would give me notice before you do that. You almost knocked all sense and excitement out of me," said Gaspar looking up from his hands and knees glad that no one else was around. "When will we be in Nippur," he asked standing and brushing himself off.

Helping Gaspar to his feet, Melchior said, "Two days, I

should think. We are making excellent time."

"Even my meditations to Ahura-Mazda will not make the day go quickly enough for my liking. I have much to learn in the ways of patience."

"Don't we both. Come, it is time that we returned. We do not want to tempt the lions and jackals any further with our presence. It is time for sleep and dreams."

Gaspar's sleep was filled with stars and an unknown city. Instead of fear he felt joy in what the future would bring. He felt that his destiny lay unfettered before him. The star and his dream were somehow tied together. He would not mention it to anyone for a long time, but he knew that along the path of the star and his dream lay his own destiny.

CHAPTER FOUR

Nippur was a city that had known greatness and seemed willing to settle for basking in the past. The pace of life here was much slower than in Seleucia. The city was kept surprisingly clean in spite of its worn walls and buildings. What Nippur lacked in modern aesthetics, it made up for with trees and shade —a practical commodity in a desert climate. The vegetation gave a venerable air to the ancient city. The temple was on the highest hill in the center of the city. At one time, like much of the Hellenized world, the city lay at the foot of the temple mount, but over the decades, houses and commercial buildings had grown up the hillside and around the hill. Although Gaspar had traveled some with his father on his shorter business trips, he had never before been to Nippur.

Beggar children nipped at the feet of the travelers asking if they had food or money they could give. Their dirty faces and ragged clothing were always more than Gaspar could resist. He gave each a coin and bade Cyrus to give each a date.

Melchior laughed heartily at all of this, "You will only encourage more of them."

"Better to encourage more than to let them starve, old friend," responded Gaspar.

"You are a purse that is too easily plucked."

The small caravan wove through the streets to the foot of the temple mount. At this point, Melchior began to laugh, jumped from his camel, and ran down the street. Gaspar watched in obvious amazement. What could Melchior be doing? In the distance, Gaspar saw a small, older priest walking towards them. Insight dawned in Gaspar as he realized that this must be Balthasar. What a coincidence, he thought, that Balthasar should be coming down the street at the same time that they were arriving. In spite of themselves, Gaspar and the whole caravan began to laugh at the sight of Melchior behaving in such an undignified manner. Upon reaching Balthasar, Melchior embraced his old friend. The two were quite a picture. Melchior's great size completely enveloped the diminutive, older Balthasar. The whole crowd stopped to see the sight. Tears streamed down the crevices of the ancient priest's face, while bright, young eyes shown out from behind the mask of his old age. The two men stood hugging unashamedly as the caravan caught up to them.

"Come, Gaspar, meet my oldest friend," and turning to Balthasar he said, "And this is my youngest friend. It is good that the two of you finally meet."

"Melchior has written of you much over the years. It is a joy to finally meet you. I had tremendous respect for your father. He was a good man."

"You honor me with your words, Balthasar. I too am honored to meet you. What a coincidence that you were coming down the street at the same time that we were arriving."

At this Melchior grinned and said, "That, my friend, was no coincidence. Balthasar knew that we were coming."

"You sent word ahead?" Gaspar queried.

"No, Balthasar sees things that are coming before they happen. He has always been like this, and it was this ability that caused him to be sent to Nippur. We shall talk of this later."

Melchior loved to open a topic and then leave it unresolved until a later time. It was an occurrence that always made Gaspar a prisoner of curiosity. If Melchior had not been such a tormentor, Gaspar would take these times as lessons in patience by the older Magus, but there was no such teacher in him.

"You're not going to say anymore about this, are you," said an annoyed Gaspar.

Melchior smiled and said, "Another time."

Balthasar saw the obvious amusement that this situation gave Melchior and the irritation it caused Gaspar. Laughing, he put his arms around each man directing them up the hill, and said, "Come. I know that you are tired and hungry. We shall feast tonight and answer all mysteries. I have good news for us all," he said looking at Melchior. Now it was time for Melchior to wait for the answer to an implanted thought.

They reached the temple where servants met them with cool water and a bounteous supply of grapes. Balthasar ushered them into baths that were cool and relaxing. They talked of families and carefree reminiscence of long-time friends.

The living quarters of Balthasar were the opposite of Melchior. Fine rugs covered the floors and comfortable furniture greeted visitors and beckoned them to linger. Potted plants and flowers, thoughtfully placed, added character and warmth to the stone walls. Double doors led out on to a spacious porch that in turn overlooked a sprawling garden. Everything about Balthasar's apartments invited one to rest and to be at peace.

A feast was presented in honor of Balthasar's guests as they lounged comfortably propped up on pillows around a table filled with food and drink. Nothing makes one quite so happy as a meal befitting his hunger. Balthasar's banquet was all that.

The three men moved to the sitting area of the apartment sipping sekanjabin, a sweet refreshing drink made with honey, cucumber, lime, vinegar and mint.

"I don't know that I have ever enjoyed a meal as much as the one this evening," commented Gaspar gratefully. "If I were a cat, I would purr."

"You honor me Gaspar. Thank you." Hesitating a moment, looking to Melchior with his hands clasped together in a single fist pointing with two steepled index fingers, Balthasar spoke again, "Shall we move our conversation toward the topic for which you have come to me? I know that you seek an affirmation to your theories on the new star. Would you like to begin our conversation?"

"If you don't mind, I would prefer that you tell us what your thoughts are. I am anxious to learn of any insight that you may have," countered Melchior.

"Very well, I will begin, but I too desire to hear all that you have conjectured up to now.

"As you know, Melchior, I have long been a student of the Hebrew prophets. Conjointly with this star is, I believe, their expectation of a deliverer. They speak of a coming Messiah who will deliver the Jews from tyranny. The name for their God, which they do not utter, is written Y-h-w-h. The prophecy states that God will send a messiah who will rule over the people of Israel and establish them as a force in the world. I believe this star is the herald of the coming of this king of the Jews."

There was silence in the room as Balthasar alternately looked at the other two holy men. Gaspar moved as if to speak, and then said nothing.

"If what you say is true, how will this king of the Jews appear?" queried Melchior.

"I do not know. There is much that I still have to research. There is a community of Jews here in the city. I would like to speak with their rabbi, or teacher, about these things. "

"That a star would signal the coming of a Jewish king is remarkable," said Melchior. "It means that this is not just a regional god alerting his people to an important event, it means that his powers transcend the borders of the people who worship him."

"Do you know what you are saying?" gasped Gaspar. "If what you say is true, then what of Ahura-Mazda? What is his place in the scheme of things if Yhwh is God? What does this do to what we believe?"

"Ah, you have hit upon the alarming aspect to my speculation," smiled Balthasar. "Your insight is excellent. We magi are first and foremost seekers of truth. If we have been worshipping the wrong deity all of these years, shouldn't we correct that? To be true to who we are as men of religion and science, we must be willing to admit when we have been mistaken."

"But the two of you combined have spent almost a hundred years worshipping and teaching the ways of Ahura-Mazda. Don't you think that you would have found a different way before now if there were some other god than Ahura-Mazda? Wouldn't this other God have corrected you in your error before now? Wouldn't he have corrected another of the magi over the years?" Gaspar seemed to almost be pleading with Balthasar now.

"I have not said that I agree with Balthasar yet," interjected Melchior. "I too am hearing this for the first time. My mind has not worked through this sufficiently yet. Besides, Balthasar has not said that Ahura-Mazda does not exist, he is only positing that the reality may be so. If our faith cannot hold up under scrutiny, then it is not worth believing—nay should not be believed."

"I realize that this is the first time that I have ever considered that what I believe may be wrong," Gaspar conceded. "It unsettles my faith foundation when I hear men such as yourselves entertain such notions."

Balthasar stood, walked over and knelt down in front of Gaspar. "Gaspar, we believe that there is only one true god and he is Ahura-Mazda. The Hebrews believe that there is only one true God, and He is Yhwh. Could it be that we believe in the same god, but only know him by a different name. Isn't it possible that he revealed himself to we Parthians in different ways to match our culture and societal sensibilities? This is not so very big a step away from our own faith. It only enlarges who god is."

Nodding his head, Gaspar said, "I must think this through. I just need time to think. Please excuse me, my friends. I will be in the garden." Within a moment the two older Magi were alone. Melchior, holding his bearded chin in his hand, sat staring at the floor. Balthasar looked at the door through which Gaspar left with a faint smile still on his lips.

Melchior's thoughts were taken back to a time and place in Balthasar's and his past. It was thinking like this that had caused Balthasar to be sent to Nippur in the first place, thought Melchior. Balthasar was the kindest and wisest of the magi, but he was also the one who was most likely to share ideas that caused turmoil in others. Tonight should have been predictable, but who would have thought that Balthasar would talk about heresy to their faith. Gaspar had every right to be concerned. Those who were of other faiths were not well tolerated in the present political climate. Even the Hebrews who had proven in the past to be loyal and good citizens of the empire were looked at with a jaundiced eye. This was no time for second thoughts about the faith. Magi, who were seen as something between intellectuals and wizards, would be in a most serious predicament if they were to start espousing another way of faith. With the spiritual preferences of King Phraataces on the throne of the king of kings, Balthasar's talk was much more than intellectual exercise, it could be seen as treason.

"You have been quiet a long time, my friend. Have my thoughts frightened even the belief of the great Melchior?" said Balthasar in a cordial, teasing manner.

"I had no idea that you would bring this kind of conversation to the table. The Hebrews are primitive, and their God is an angry and wrathful god. To suggest that theirs is the true way is a little hard to swallow. I know you and love you like few men in my life, but you have gone too far. This borders on preposterous."

"If we go searching for this new king sent by God and find that he is who I say that he may be, what would you say to that, Melchior?"

"Who could denounce it? If it is right, it is right, and must therefore be proclaimed as such."

"It has been quite some time since you and I took a trip like this together. I have one, last long trip left in me before I go to the next life. Would you indulge me and come with me on an adventure to where the new star directs? It would be a good trip for Gaspar too. He needs time to sift through more than just this one issue. Come with me."

"There is much happening right now. King Phraataces is afraid that Rome may be trying to amass a new offensive on our empire. I don't know that he would be willing to let us leave the realm. But yes, my heart is ready for a new adventure and the one that you suggest would be an exciting one. When would we leave?"

"I could be ready to travel within the month, and what better excuse for us to leave the country than to say that we are studying this new star and that we would be willing to collect intelligence for the king."

A smile stole across Melchior's lips. "You have involved me once again in one of your escapades. Are you not getting too old for this kind of behavior?"

"May it never be so."

As laughter filled the room and great plans were being made, Gaspar sat on a bench in the garden gazing at the star that seemed to be as dreadful now as any nightmare he had ever experienced. The night was destined to slowly crawl along until sometime early in the morning fatigue overtook Gaspar, and he found rest in the quarters that Balthasar had prepared for him.

CHAPTER FIVE

All the next day Gaspar listened to Melchior and Balthasar as they looked through scroll after scroll trying to gain a better understanding of the star's purpose. Much of their discussion, he felt, bordered on treason. If King Phraataces could hear their talk, he thought, they would already be hanging from crucifixion poles. The whole day, Gaspar scarcely made any contributions to the magi's conversation. He listened and felt himself growing more irritable with each new discovery.

The night before, while Gaspar was out in the garden, Balthasar explained to Melchior that their analysis of the star might be difficult for one so young who has tied his future to a theological belief system that might possibly be proven to be false.

"I have no problem searching for truth, why should he?" countered Melchior.

"Yes, but you have lived with the reality that our belief in Ahura-Mazda has not proven to answer many of life's difficult questions. You may be ready to hear the truth. Our young priest may have to battle against notions he may have never challenged before."

"I see what you mean. What do you suggest we do?"

"Give him his space. Whatever we discover in our research will not change the fact that there is a deity or deities that caused the reality in which we now live. We Parthians have a king who is over regional kings. It may be possible that we discover that there is a god over regional gods. We cannot make him think a particular way; he is too intelligent for that. We must let god have time to reveal the truth to him."

"You have spoken wisely," Melchior said smiling at Balthasar in respect, "I can only hope that time blesses me with wisdom as it has with you."

"Time can only achieve so much, my friend," Balthasar said mockingly.

Melchior did a double-take and both men laughed heartily.

Out in the garden Gaspar heard their laughter and wondered if the "two wizened priests" were laughing at the young, imprudent magus.

The journey back from Nippur was unbearable for

Gaspar. It irked him that Melchior seemed to be as enthralled with the trip to follow the star as was Balthasar. The two magi talked Gaspar into going along on the trip but he now wished he had not agreed. What would the king think? How could he explain this to Balzak? Balzak was not going to like any of this talk at all. He still had several days travel to think what to say to his servant, but as yet he had no idea what that would be. He should have listened to him in the first place, he thought, and none of this would have ever happened. He vowed, when he got back to Seleucia, he would reestablish his discipline to Ahura-Mazda. Surely the good god would not allow him to struggle with these doubts much longer if his devotion was unyielding. He was a magus after all. He determined he would not stoop to apostasy.

Looking at Seleucia's gates, he was never so glad to get back from a trip in his life. To be honest, the young magus was glad to get away from Melchior. Their friendship seemed now strained and without emotional attachment. He was irritated with his friend and did not stop to think why. Gaspar only wanted to get away from him for a few days and think his own thoughts. He longed for the days when he did not have these lingering doubts, when the universe and his life seemed to fit nicely together. Why did he feel like he was at such a crisis point in his life? All he really needed to do, he told himself, was to believe what he had always believed. He tried to push out the thought that he had doubts before he left on the trip, placing the blame for his reservations on Melchior, Balthasar, and the star. If only there was something outside of himself to blame, he thought, he could more easily move back to what he had believed in the past when life made more sense to him.

Melchior and Gaspar had separated their provisions that morning so each could go to his home when they reached sight of Seleucia. Melchior had dropped back to divide the caravan into two groups as he would be branching off before they actually reached the city. He now came riding up to Gaspar to say his parting words.

"This has been a trip that both of us will look back on as a turning point in our lives. I know that you are feeling anxious about the upcoming expedition to the land of the Hebrews, but we will gain answers to our questions as a result. Do not let your impatience for the truth drive a wedge between us. I love you as a brother. I will be in contact with you." Before Gaspar could respond, Melchior had whipped his camel into a gallop and was off down the road to his home.

It was just as well, thought Gaspar, he really had nothing to say that had not already been communicated. As he entered the gates to the city, there, astride a pony, was a dour Balzak.

"Welcome home, master. I have been impatient to hear about your trip, and there is also much to tell you."

CHAPTER SIX

On the way back to the villa, Gaspar informed Balzak about all that had happened on their trip. As he spoke a cloud came over Balzak's expression. He did not respond—thinking it better to wait before conveying his thoughts.

It felt good to be back in his own surroundings. Balzak had told Gaspar that he had much to tell him, but the magus was glad that he had not unloaded the information on him just at that time. Right now his thoughts were overwhelming to him, and he felt that his mind would explode if he had to think about one more thing. That night, as he slept, he dreamed about the star shining so brilliantly that all he could see was its brightness. Once gain, his dream had become his tormentor.

The next morning Gaspar woke wearily and went about his morning prayers and cultic duties. He asked Ahura-Mazda to give him counsel and direction concerning his doubts. He felt a lifelessness in his prayers. They seemed to be coming from someone else and he was just mouthing their words.

His father's warehouses were always a good place to distract him, so he decided that he would go there to see what new merchandise had arrived. Maybe there would be something there that would catch his interest. When he entered the gate, the workers ran to greet him and welcomed him back home. He was always amazed at how fast news traveled in even a big commercial city like Seleucia. Dismounting his horse, Yalda, he was joined by a smiling Cephas, the overseer of all Gaspar's holdings. His father had bought the man as a servant when Cephas was but a young boy. His abilities became more and more evident as he grew. He was just a young man when Arioch gave him a strong hand in all their business dealings. Faithfulness was something neither Gaspar nor his father had ever questioned in the man.

"Master, I see Balzak gave you my message to come and see me. It is good to have you home. You must see the newest silks just received from the orient."

This must be what Balzak had delayed telling him until Gaspar had settled in, he surmised. Sensing Cephas' excitement, Gaspar again had that pang of regret wondering what it would have been like if he had gone into the family business. Instead, he had turned all of its workings over to Balzak and Cephas as his father had done.

26

The warehouse was full of the purchases of two separate expeditions. The one, as Cephas had already mentioned, had returned from the orient, and the other had returned the week before from Egypt. Trade within the Roman empire was always fluid, and at this particular time tensions had eased between the two empires giving Parthian merchants access to eastern Mediterranean trade routes. Rome needed trade routes through the Parthian empire for its needs. To have that, it had to allow Parthian traders free access through her empire.

"We have buyers for all of our merchandise," said Cephas. "We will have most of it out within the month. This is going to prove to be a very good year for us. Most merchants work a lifetime for this kind of return. Ahura has smiled most warmly on his most favored son."

Gaspar hated it when Cephas spoke like this. He couldn't help thinking that this kind of talk would cause the god to turn his back on the person who was foolish enough to make such a presumptuous statement. It also made him feel guilty that he did not have as much faith in the god Cephas called upon. Did Ahura-Mazda know that he did not have as much faith as his servant?

Shaking off these thoughts, Gaspar said, "Show me the trove that you have collected for me. There may be something that catches my own fancy."

Cephas eagerly showed his master all that he had acquired. Two different expeditions had arrived within days of each other. One from the east and the other from the west. After seeing all that had been purchased, Gaspar thought that the goods would bring even more than Cephas had revealed. Truly his warehouse held a king's ransom in assets.

"What kind of guard do you have set up to protect the warehouse, Cephas?"

"We have our regular contingent of twenty-four, and I have hired another ten from our most trusted business associates to reinforce on the inside walls what we normally have along the top of the walls. Does that please his eminence?"

"Why don't we make it an even twenty, and I will sleep better tonight. And don't be stingy with their pay," Gaspar said with a wink.

"As you have spoken, it will be done."

That night at supper Gaspar could see that Balzak could no longer wait to give him whatever news he had to give. He smiled to himself thinking that he knew what Balzak had to say. Gaspar was amazed at how Balzak could patiently wait until an appropriate time to tell whatever information he had to tell—no matter how exciting the information. This time, Balzak could not wait, his excitement was obvious from his fidgeting and poking at his food.

"Balzak, tell me what you have to tell me. If you wait any longer, you will explode."

"While you were away, King Phraataces sent a seneschal with an order for you to appear before him in two days. The messenger said that the king desires your expert opinion on a matter that has him confounded. This is a well-timed opportunity for you to move up in favor at court."

"This is what we have worked toward, I know, but I do not welcome the challenge with as much anticipation as I once would have."

"You cannot let this opportunity pass you by, Reverence. Occasions like this do not happen frequently. You must take advantage of it while you can. I know that you have been experiencing inner turmoil, but do not let momentary questions destroy a chance of a lifetime." Balzak spoke with characteristic calculation and manipulation which did not escape Gaspar's attention. He hated the condescending tone Balzak used when someone did not agree with him. If he were just a common servant, he would have considered having him beaten for insubordination.

"I will not allow myself to let this opportunity pass if I so choose it," Gaspar began. "I want to remind you who is the servant and who is the master here. But you do speak wisely, and I can always count on your insight and knowledge of what is best for both of us. I will not let either of us down when I appear before the king."

Both men glared at each other for a moment. Gaspar broke the uneasy silence, "I spoke to you with the frustration I have been bottling up for the past few days. Please forgive my out burst."

Allaying some of Balzak's fears concerning his audience before the king, Gaspar then told him everything that had been happening to him the past few weeks. Balzak listened carefully as Gaspar recounted his dreams, the star, the trip to Balthasar's, and the longer trip that Melchior and Balthasar were planning with him.

"Do you think that it would be wise to undertake this trip to Palestine at this time. It would take you too far away and reduce your influence with the king. You've just made a huge inroad and now you're removing yourself from the influence you have sought." Then with desperation slipping into his voice, "This trip could ruin everything for you."

"I know that what you say is true, but my life is upside down at this point, and even though I do not necessarily want to go on this expedition, I feel like there may be answers for me in taking the trip. I am also concerned how effective I will be if I don't get myself under control."

Balzak had been slowly losing patience with Gaspar, and now his cool countenance broke. "Do you hear yourself? I do not forget my place, but because of the affection I feel for you, I must say you are not a slave who can afford the luxury of self-doubt and self-pity. You are a Magus. You are capable of being the highest nobleman in the kingdom, second only to the king himself. You must be the man your father desired for you to be. Just because you don't feel something does not make it unreal. It is time for you to think like a man and lay claim to your beliefs whether you feel them or not."

Shaken by his verbal foray, but still desiring Balzak to understand him, Gaspar shot back at him, "You have touched on the point! I'm not sure I think our system of belief makes sense. The star directs me toward truth—I feel it—I fear it. I know this without being able to prove it, and it unsettles me." He was formulating his beliefs as he spoke. "Ahura-Mazda has never brought to me the sense of his presence. Somehow I know that my destiny lies more in the path of that new star than it does in the knowledge I have acquired as a magus."

Balzak sat mouth open in disbelief. He would have never imagined that his greatest pupil would ever betray the faith that he had worked so hard to foster in him. Even more, he saw his chance for power and position melting away with every word Gaspar spoke.

"I don't say this to hurt you," Gaspar continued. "What I have expressed to you is the truth of my wrestling with my beliefs."

Balzak only sat visibly shaken by Gaspar's comments.

CHAPTER SEVEN

Ezri was sixteen years old when the mysterious star appeared in the heavens. In upper Galilee, in the town of Gischala, his father worked in the olive groves of a man named Levi. Green valleys and forested mountains were the backdrop to his early life. In the spring those same mountains would burst forth in a cacophony of color. Purple and white coral peony's, spiny bushes of european wolfberry jealously protecting blossoms of violet and deep purple, tiny white trumpets of bosthom, tall green stalks of Mesopotamian iris topped with brilliant displays of purple and gold, and black-leaved mullein branches, raised in praise, adorned in bright splashes of yellow petals all spread their color over hill and valley.

As a boy, Ezri was mischievous, as many boys are, and his mischief often took him beyond the bounds of acceptable boyish devilry. His other friends might pull a girl's hair and run, or steal an unwatched bread cake from atop a neighbor's oven, or bonk someone in the head with a dried goat pellet. Ezri's pranks were more of a criminal nature.

His mother had died giving birth to him. And even though people told his father, Abirami, to find a new wife, he never did. He had loved Miriam completely, and his shattered heart never mended. Abirami worked hard in the olive groves of Levi Ben Yaakov. As Ezri got older, he had too much time to participate in his favorite activity—petty larceny. It was unfortunate that he was never caught because it just encouraged him toward more theft. "People are too stupid to catch me," he frequently thought to himself.

In an age when it was not uncommon for a woman to lose her life in childbirth, there were those children who went on to live lives that seemed unaffected by the loss of a mother. Although Ezri could not identify his feelings, he was one who angrily fought back against an unfair world that would take the life of his mother. Each year that he physically matured into manhood, the more he played out his unperceived revenge. He lashed out at seemingly everyone and everything with his father being his favorite target. He was never able to connect the loss of his mother with his behavior that pushed away everyone who tried to befriend him. No one wanted to be closer to Ezri than Abirami, and so Ezri's anger was displayed most viciously against him.

It was at age sixteen that Ezri finally held his hand too long in the fire and got burned. He had become friends with Levi's son John. Abirami was over-joyed with the relationship, hoping that his boss' son might have a good influence on his own. Levi was less than pleased, but trusted his son's integrity. One day Ezri showed up at John's house with a white horse. Seeing his friend atop the creature, he ran out into the field to meet him.

"Where did you ever get that animal?" John asked.

"I've been doing work for a widow-woman west of town, and she let me borrow her husband's old horse to get to and from work. I thought you might be impressed," he said carelessly.

"Are you sure you didn't steal it?" John asked.

"How stupid do you think I am?" Ezri said with false indignation. "Who would steal something this big and then prance around with it in plain sight?"

"All right then, let me saddle my horse, and we'll go for a ride."

John was an expert rider with years of experience. He handled his own mount with precision. Ezri had been on a horse only a few times and it was evident. The horse and Ezri did not even approach moving as one. It was difficult to tell who was in control—the horse or the rider. Horses know when they have a rider who is not sure of himself, and will take advantage of him. John spent a good deal of their ride instructing Ezri in the equestrian arts. After about an hour some of John's instruction began to sink in and Ezri was beginning to look like he had been on a horse before.

About that time, a Roman patrol came riding up over one of the hills behind them. When the commander saw the two, he immediately ordered his men into a gallop to overtake them. The boys heard the hoofbeats behind them, and turned to face the soldiers. Ezri, seeing the approaching patrol, kicked his horse into a run while pulling on the reigns to turn him. Unfortunately, his lack of skill on a horse showed itself most humorously as he turned to flee. Turning the horse to make his get-a-way, he lost his balance. The horse's forward acceleration sent him feet over head off the rear end of his mount. He lay there flat on his face as the soldiers drew up. John watched all of this in confused surprise.

"Where did you get these horses?" the officer asked gravely.

"This horse is my own," said John, "And the other one was loaned to us?"

Ezri got up spitting and wiping grass and dirt out of his mouth. Two of the soldiers in the rear of the patrol sneered at his untrained antics. Ezri could feel the blood of shame and anger rise to his face.

"Where do you live?" the officer queried.

"I live up over that hill," John pointed, "and my friend lives in town."

"There's a widow-woman who lives west of Gischala who said her horse had been stolen that matches the description of this other fellow's horse. I think it's best if we go back to your house, and see if we can work this out."

"Sir," Ezri said in mock respect, "I only borrowed the horse. She gave it to me to use to get to work and back. I left her house early today because I was done with all of my chores." One of the soldiers snickered and rolled his eyes.

"Cavalryman, that will be enough. Come on, we'll go by your home," the commander said again to John, and then to Ezri he said, "Mount up and come with us. I suggest that you don't try to outrun us as we have already witnessed your skills as a horseman."

Ezri got on his horse with one soldier taking the reins and leading him while the rest of the soldiers followed. John rode up front with the officer. He could not understand what could have been going on in Ezri's mind. Why would he do something like that to a widow, he wondered.

When they got back to John's house, his mother came running out with half of the house staff. Levi had just come in from the fields with Abirami and a handful of other workers. Fear was written all over John's mother's face—gloom marked Abirami's.

"This boy yours?" the Roman asked Levi.

"Yes he is. What has he done?"

"Nothing that I can tell yet. Is this horse his?"

"Yes. We gave it to him on his twelfth birthday," Levi responded.

"This other boy. Does anyone know if his story is true about having been lent the horse to ride to and from work?" asked the officer. "Otherwise, it looks an awful lot like the description of a horse that was stolen from a widow woman west of town.".

"What have you done?" his father began. "He only works for me around our house. There's no way he could have been lent that horse," he said to the soldier looking at Ezri disapprovingly. Ezri met his gaze as though the day's incident had no effect on him.

"Well, the horse answers the description. You know stealing horses is an expensive crime for a young man," said the officer.

"I know," said Abirami.

"If I might interrupt, I think that I may have a solution to all of this," said Levi.

"What's that?" asked the commander.

"Ezri, tell your father and me the truth. Did you steal the horse?"

Ezri looked first at Levi and then to his father realizing there was no easy way out of this mess by lying. Meeting Levi's eyes, he said, "Yes."

"The law says that you must pay twice the amount of the item stolen, commander. Whatever you say is a fair price for that horse. I'll see that the boy returns the horse, works off the debt, and pays that woman's fair price on top of it."

The officer rubbed his chin looking off into the distance for a moment. Looking back he said, "I think that will settle the matter. I'll be back through in a month, and we'll be checking with the widow-woman to see that all has been done as was agreed." Having said that, he led his patrol off at a cantor.

John's mother let out a deep sigh and ran over and hugged her son, leading him into the house.

"Wait, Judith, I still need the boy," Levi told his wife.

Abirami walked to his own son and said, "What possessed you to do something so foolish?"

"It seemed like a fun thing to do at the time, and I figured I'd have him back before she ever missed him."

"You will work off this debt, take the money yourself to that woman, and beg her forgiveness," said Abirami. Turning to Levi, he said, "Forgive me for bringing any shame on your house because of this disgraceful matter, and thank you for settling this for us. You have always been generous with me."

"You are a good man, Abirami. Sons are not always the reflection of their fathers, but they can always learn." A sour expression crossed Ezri's face as he glared at Levi.

Abirami smiled weakly, looked with disappointment at his son, and started walking home by himself.

"I expect to see you at sunrise tomorrow, young man," Levi said to Ezri.

Ezri shrugged and followed his father. Levi watched him leave. Shaking his head he said to John, "Tomorrow morning, I want you to take the horse back to the woman who owns it and tell her that I will make sure she gets what's coming to her." Then as an afterthought he said, "I would like it very much if you didn't spend anymore time with Ezri."

CHAPTER EIGHT

As Balthasar rolled out one of the old Jewish scrolls that contained the writings of the Jewish leaders and prophets. His mind returned to thirty years prior, before he was sent away to Nippur, where he had stumbled across some of the old manuscripts penned by the Hebrew prophet Daniel. The prophet's writings had interested him and he had investigated other Hebrew writers of the time. That trail had led him to the library in Seleucia where he discovered a chest filled with the scrolls of many of the books of the Hebrew Bible. It had been untouched for as long as anyone in the library could remember. There was a very strong chance that the scrolls were decades old. Getting a few of the temple servants to help him, he had "borrowed" the scrolls and never returned them. He had figured that no one would miss them anyway. He was right. No one ever asked him about them or asked for them to be returned to the library. Taking one of those same scrolls, Balthasar gently spread it out on the table of his personal library so that each side of the scrolls was about the same size. Then he began to roll up the right side until he came to the book of Zechariah. Balthasar had gained a fondness for the Hebrew prophet. He, like him, was a priest, and the old wiseman had gained this affinity through the years of reading his book.

Something he had read a few weeks prior had plagued his thoughts. An idea in Zechariah was needing his mental refreshment. Near the middle of the book he let his finger move line by line down the sheet. Finding what he was looking for, he read out loud, "*And speak to him, saying, Thus says the Lord of hosts, saying, Behold the man whose name is The Branch; and he shall grow up out of his place, and he shall build the temple of the Lord: Even he shall build the temple of the Lord; and he shall bear the glory, and shall sit and rule upon his throne; and he shall be a priest upon his throne: and the counsel of peace shall be between them both.*"

"Most peculiar," he said out loud again. "This man will become both a king and a priest. Most unusual."

Rolling up that scroll, he took out another. He unrolled it until he found the book of Numbers. About two-thirds the way through he found another passage, "*I shall see him, but not now: I shall behold him, but not nigh: there shall come a Star out of Jacob, and a Scepter shall rise out of Israel, and shall smite*

the corners of Moab, and destroy all the children of Sheth."
Sitting back in his chair, he said, "Our star! It has to be the
herald of a new world king, or, at the very least, a new king of
Israel."

Melchior leaned over the rail of the balcony of his
observation tower watching the new star. He wondered what he
and the other magi had not yet discovered about the star. He
knew neither he nor any of his fellow priests had ever seen it
before. It rose out of the western sky and settled, as usual, west
of center of the night sky. Then it struck him, "How far away is
it? What a fool I am. How far away is it?"

He ran back into his study to begin making calculations.
After a few minutes he sat rubbing his chin in disbelief. He went
over his figures and came up with the same answer.

"This cannot be accurate," he said.

CHAPTER NINE

For a few weeks Ezri was faithful in showing up for work and doing whatever Levi asked of him, but the work was hard and he came home every night exhausted. Abirami warmed back up to his son after a few days and enjoyed the company as the two walked to and from work together. He loved the time spent with his son, but Ezri's sullenness never subsided.

One day walking home from work Abirami commented to his son, "You are so angry. Are you troubled about the affair with the horse?"

"No," Ezri said.

"Do you not like the work that you do?"

"I don't like work, period," he snapped. "I want to be free to do what I want to do."

"What do you want to do?" Abirami asked.

"I want to travel. I want to find something interesting to do with my life. I don't want to be cooped up in Gischala my whole life. I want to meet interesting people," he hesitated, and then said, "I want to leave Gischala, and never come back."

Abirami, wearing the hurt he felt on his face said, "I would miss you, son. I have greatly enjoyed working and being with you these past few weeks. It is what I always dreamed of."

"Not much of a dream, father."

"It's a father's dream."

"But not a son's"

Shaking his head Abirami said, "It takes money to do what you want and you've only paid a portion of the debt you owe. Your dream is a fool's dream with no purpose." As soon as the words were out of his mouth he wished he had not said them. He braced himself for his son's retort.

"I am no fool. You are the fool working your whole life trudging up and down the same road every day. I hate this!"

"Son, I misspoke. I know you are no fool. I just want you to consider. . ."

"No. You said what you thought. I have plans and I am going to go through with them. Then we'll see who is the fool."

Abirami had no comeback. They walked along together, but they were miles apart.

CHAPTER TEN

Cyrus ran up to grab the reins of Melchior's horse that he rode in a gallop up to the entrance of Gaspar's residence.

"Where is your master?" Melchior asked, not stopping for the servant's reply.

"He's in his study reading," Cyrus called after Melchior who burst through the doors.

Tala, the chief house servant, chased after him saying, "The master is in his study and does not want to be disturbed. May I announce you?"

"He'll want to stop whatever he's doing to hear what I have to say," he said as he opened Gaspar's door.

Gaspar was standing looking over the documents he had spread out on his work table. Looking up without smiling he said, "You have something to tell me that is more important than my own work?"

"We are too long friends, and we love each other too much for you to hold on to your anger. Come. I have important news to share." Behind the two men, Tala shut the door.

"Is it about the star," Gaspar said in exasperation.

"It is. I was so foolish not to have made these calculations prior to this, but the ramifications are staggering. I can't believe we didn't think of it before."

"Melchior, I'm not interested. I have pressing matters here, and I'm not even sure I can go on this wild excursion with Balthasar and you."

Melchior's eyes grew wide as he sucked in a room full of air. "What?" he bellowed.

"The king has need of me, and I don't want to miss this opportunity. I have to start thinking of my own future and the future of those who depend on me," Gaspar said.

"Don't you realize what you're giving up?"

"I know what I won't give up."

Calming himself to a fatherly tone, Melchior said, "Gaspar, we have never experienced anything like this heavenly body. We have reason to believe nothing like this has ever happened before. What could be more important than the possible arrival of a great king from God?"

"Of which god do you speak?"

Melchior stood dumbfounded. All the enthusiasm

instantly left him. He stood there in the middle of the room like a disciplined school boy. Lifting his head as if to speak, he dropped it again, turned and walked slowly to the door. Turning to face Gaspar he said, "Let me know if your mind changes."

Balzak had been listening outside the door and had heard the whole conversation. Hearing Melchior's voice getting closer to the door, he slipped silently down the hallway to his quarters. A smile spread across his face as he thought, "The boy has regained his control."

CHAPTER ELEVEN

Hebrew Bible scrolls were spread all over Balthasar's tables. He had had one of the servants bring in another table so he could more easily search multiple scrolls. He had been hunting through book after book of the Bible to find any information he could about this priest king he had discovered in Zechariah.

In Isaiah he read, *Of the increase of his government and peace there shall be no end, upon the throne of David, and upon his kingdom, to order it, and to establish it with judgment and with justice from henceforth even for ever. The zeal of the Lord of hosts will perform this.* So, Balthasar reasoned, this king will be a descendant of King David and will rule forever in absolute peace. He continued to search.

Toward the end of Isaiah, he came to a passage that caused him to wonder at its meaning. It read, *Behold, my servant shall deal wisely, he shall be exalted and extolled, and be very high. As many were astonished at thee; his features were so marred more than any man, and his form more than the sons of men.* "This cannot be about the one for whom I am searching," he thought. He studied it for awhile and then determined that it must be speaking metaphorically about the Jewish people and not a single man. The Jews had suffered a great deal over their history, and surely this must be about them as a people and not the priest king.

Balthasar rolled up his scrolls and began putting them back in their places. He took his notes, called for a servant and said, "make a copy of these and have a messenger deliver them to Gaspar in Seleucia."

He laid down on his couch, closed his eyes, and began to meditate on all that he had read that day about the priest king. There was much he did not understand. He needed time to think through all that he had read to make any connections and sense out of it all.

CHAPTER TWELVE

Gaspar went to bed even more angry with Melchior than he was before. He did not see why his friend could not accept his decisions. He had a great opportunity to advance himself in every way: position, power, and wealth. He lay there thinking over the schism that had arisen between him and Melchior and thought that he was now seeing how Balzak had his best interests at heart. Maybe Balzak really was the one he needed to have influencing him at this stage of his life.

Sleep finally came fitfully. He would doze and then have to readjust to get comfortable. Sometime in the early morning he settled into a deep sleep, and dreamt of the star and that it would change everything he knew to be true.

Balzak found that he too could not sleep that night, and after spending a time in tossing and turning, he went to the warehouses to check on the watch. Arioch had built two long enormous buildings that sat parallel to each other for his warehouses. Made of stone, each had double sliding doors at either end with a wide aisle down their middles. Branching off on either side were row upon row of shelves to hold merchandise that was brought in from time to time. A wall surrounded the two structures with guard towers every twenty yards. On the inside of the wall was a walkway that ran around the entire perimeter of the wall. The value of the wares inside determined the number of guards within the walls. From the outside, an observer could always see a guard on duty at each of the five front and five rear towers, and seven on either of the side walls. Inside, the number of guards varied with the expense of the merchandise being housed. Behind, beyond the wall, were stalls and barns that housed the hundreds of camels and mules necessary to transport the finery from all over the world to Gaspar's warehouses.

To Balzak's surprise he found Cephas there.

"You couldn't sleep either I see," said Cephas.

"There are so many good things happening for us all that it overly occupies my mind. We have great opportunities awaiting us, my friend."

"That we do," said Cephas not looking up from the ledger with which he was working.

"I am distracting you. I came only to check on the guard,

but I should have known that you already had your hand upon it. I won't bother you anymore," Balzak said as he moved further into the warehouse. He thought that he might look for material that would make robes for future audiences he presumed his master would have before the king.

There were wool fabrics from central Asia, an array of colored silks from the far east, and cool, fine linens from Egypt. He wanted his master to look spectacular, but not more spectacular than the king. He spent some time looking through the different choices of fabric and colors, and then decided to let Tala the next day use her feminine eye to choose the right fabrics. Feeling that he could return to his quarters and finally find sleep, he said good night to Cephas who was just finishing up his own work.

Gaspar woke with a start and looked around his bedroom. The half-moon sky cast an eery blue hue in the available light, making long shadows out of objects in the room. It took a few moments to orient to his surroundings. There had been a person in his dreams this time. A man with very average features, a beard, and white robe had said something to Gaspar with a voice that seemed to vibrate through his very being down to his soul. "What was it that he said. Why can't I remember?" Scratching his head with his fingers, he reached for the pitcher of water on his nightstand and poured it into a cup. He took a few sips of the water staring at the floor.

Silently, almost like a dream, a voice said, "Gaspar."

At first Gaspar thought that he may still be dreaming. Shaking his head, he knew he was awake. He put the cup down, rubbed his eyes, and blinked several times deliberately. And then. . .

"Gaspar."

"Who calls my name?" The voice sounded familiar, so he said, "Melchior are you playing a game with me?"

Again the voice, "Gaspar, he has need of you. Why are you running from him?"

Gaspar now recognized it. It was the voice in his dream. "Who is it that I am supposed to be running from?" It dawned on Gaspar to whom this must be—Ahura-Mazda. "It is the good god, wisest of all."

There was no answer. The room had gone silent. There was an owl outside somewhere hooting. No other sound was heard. Gaspar waited again for the voice, but he did not hear another word from whomever spoke to him. He returned to his bed eventually drifting off to sleep once again. This time there were no dreams only the deep, dreamless sleep of a tired man.

CHAPTER THIRTEEN

Next morning, Balzak was busying himself around Gaspar's room laying out the robes that he would wear for his audience with the king. He wished he had had more time to have new robes sewn for his master, but it was not like the ones he had showed signs of wear. Today Gaspar would be resplendent, looking every bit the wise magus he was. Balzak had already contacted Tala the night before to have the master's breakfast brought to his room shortly after daybreak. He began waking Gaspar just as she brought in his breakfast.

Thanking Tala for his meal, he fingered a diced piece of sweet melon and popped it in his mouth. Along with the melon was warm flatbread with a scrambled egg and crisp diced radishes, cucumbers, and onions. She took the water pitcher from beside his bed, replaced it with a new one, and left the room.

"Today is your big day, sir," Balzak beamed.

"That it is, Balzak. I wish I had some idea why the king is summoning me. It would be nice to be able to prepare ahead of time."

"You are intelligent, wise, and a fast thinker. You will be brilliant," Balzak reassured.

"I will settle for not making a fool out of myself," he said sheepishly.

Balzak smiled knowing that his master would not let him down. He had seen Gaspar in action too many times. The young man always seemed to be able to rise to any situation that presented itself. The higher the stakes, the better he performed. Besides, he felt the favor of the good god on Gaspar. He was a man destined for greatness.

Audiences with King Phraataces were notoriously behind schedule. People had been known to be kept waiting for days to see the king only to be told that he no longer wished to see them. Phraataces enjoyed his position as ruler of the Parthian Empire. He was in no way a humble man, but he was fair and a competent administrator. Because Gaspar was first on his docket that morning and the king wanted to see him, he was issued into the throne room exactly on time. Gaspar was now glad that Balzak had made a fuss about his being a little early.

42

Balzak had advised taking the ferry across the Tigris, from Seleucia to Ctesiphon. It did take some time, but it was infinitely faster than taking the road and bridge into the empire's capital. He did not want his master to keep the king of kings waiting.

One could say that the throne room of the Parthian empire was lavish, but the word would not do it justice. The room itself was a large rectangle with two rows of twenty foot marble columns supporting a barrel-vaulted ceiling ending in a domed exedra covering a raised dais where the throne itself sat. Atop each column was a Corinthian capital revealing the hellenic influence that once dominated that part of Parthia. An ornate frieze encircled the entire room with carvings of the military victories of the empire's history. Four-foot square marble slab floors were polished to almost mirror-like luster with one inch bands of gold inlaid between each square. Semi-circular arched windows ran down either side of the lengths of the great rectangle. The exedra was framed in crimson silk drapes that hung from ceiling to floor. The throne itself had two gold lions for the arm supports while carved ivory was artistically sculptured with an antelope and deer leaping arch-wise forming the back of the chair. Advisors to the king stood to the sides of the dais in beautiful flowing robes adding the final touch of grandeur and majesty to the whole effect.

Gaspar, though he had appeared before the king previously, was schooled by the king's seneschal in the proper etiquette while in the monarch's presence which only made him more nervous about the audience. One entered the throne room through two massive brass and bronzed doors opposite the throne which were opened by two guards during each audience. There was an inlaid high-gloss black marble walkway down the center, two meters wide. On entering the throne room he was to take two steps inside, stop, and bow waiting for the king to motion him forward. When he came to the end of the walkway, several meters in front of the dais, he was to stop again and bow down on his knees careful not to speak until his majesty beckoned him to do so or spoke to him. For no reason was one ever to advance past the walkway unless the king directed him to do so. Further, the king should only be addressed as *your majesty, your royal highness,* or more desirably, *king of kings,* or *lord of all.*

If a person did not follow this routine, and the king was in an ill humor, it was not uncommon for that individual to be hauled out and beheaded. Parthian kings were absolute monarchs with power to grant riches or death. No one, in the presence of the king was ever to draw his sword. To do so, meant instant death for the transgressor. Following the etiquette of the court was a wise move for anyone—priest of Ahura-

Mazda or slave.

Bowing after he took his requisite two steps, Gaspar heard a joyous king say, "Enter priest of the good god. We have been looking forward to your visit. Come."

Startled by Phraataces' candor, for he was not known as an overly friendly monarch, Gaspar was taken back in no small measure. The king's reaction to the magus' presence made him even more unsettled than he was before.

"It is always good to be in your presence, king of kings," he said with as much control as he could muster.

"Come, come, sit," said the king as he motioned for a chair to be placed on the dais. This was highly irregular for this king, and Gaspar could not help noticing the raised eyebrow and flash of anger that crossed Zand, the high priest's face. Phraataces motioned for Gaspar to sit again when he reached the dais before he had time to fall on his knees before the king. Again, Zand's countenance flashed displeasure at the favor Gaspar was receiving from the king. Waiting for Phraataces to sit, Gaspar did the same.

"The high priest tells me that this strange star is a good omen of our reign and that it signals a long and successful rule. You, young priest, we have been told, have met with both priests Melchior and Balthasar to discuss the star's appearance. Is that true?"

"Yes, your majesty, it is true," said Gaspar glancing again at Zand unable to read his expression. It always amazed him how much intelligence the king was able to gather. Even on something like this that seemed of no concern to his majesty, he had been informed.

"Do your reverences agree with our learned high priest?" queried Phraataces. Zand's eye lids and eyebrows lifted slightly. Gaspar did not want to make the high priest his enemy, but he also did not want to show stupidity to the king. He knew he would have to choose his next words wisely.

"The high priest is a gifted astrologer, my king. I would not presume to argue with his interpretation. The other two magi and myself do perceive another possibility, however. Your majesty should know that our understanding of the star's occurrence is just that, a possibility."

"Yes, yes, yes. We know that we have placed you in a difficult situation. The high priest is a valued member of our personal council. Your disagreeing with his conclusions will not alter his standing with us. We want to know what you think." Zand's face seemed to relax under the king's assurance.

Gaspar began slowly, "Because the star rises out of the western sky unlike any star we have ever been able to observe to date, and it is a new star, it definitely is a portent by god of a great happening. My associates and I believe that it has more to do with writings we have discovered in Hebrew mythology about a star that will foretell the coming of a ruler who will come out of the land of the Jews. The Jews, I believe, refer to this personage as messiah, the anointed one. That is all that we really know. Melchior and Balthasar have invited me to go on an expedition to Palestine to see if their interpretation of the star's presence is accurate. I have not determined whether or not I will accompany them." Gaspar did not want to tell the king or have the high priest perceive that this whole study around the star had deeply affected his faith in Ahura-Mazda. He tried to sound more objective than he felt.

"With all due respect to our subordinate priests, your majesty, I. . ." began Zand, but before he could finish, the king raised his hand for him to stop.

"We want you to learn all you can about this star and the mystery surrounding it," Phraataces said to Gaspar, and then to Zand he said, "We do not want you to interfere with their reverences in any way. Your position here will not change no matter what they find to be true. Do you understand me, high priest?"

"Yes, lord of all," Zand said bowing while retreating a step.

Back to Gaspar the king said, "We want you to go on the expedition with the other magi. This will be a royal enterprise. The crown will pay for expenses and a small detail from our personal guard will protect you along the way. Consider this a great favor to ourself. We desire to have you leave before the end of next week. We will send a cavalry detail to Nippur to inform Balthasar and to bring him to Seleucia so no time will be lost. Now go, priest, and bring us back what news you can." Phraataces rose and signaled his seneschal to send the next audience in. Bowing lowly, Gaspar departed the king's presence.

Outside in the hallway Balzak had been waiting for Gaspar to finish his audience with the king. His body language did not hide his excitement to hear all that had been discussed. Balzak rushed to his master's side tapping his fingertips together with his eyes as wide as he could make them. The look of confusion on his master's face caused some degree of concern, but he still was filled with anticipation. Gaspar motioned him to wait until they were outside the palace grounds. Once safely out of earshot of anyone in the palace, Balzak said, "What happened?"

"The king wants me to go on the expedition with Melchior and Balthasar," Gaspar told his mentor succinctly. "He's as interested in the star as they are."

45

Balzak's mouth dropped. For a rare moment he was speechless. Regaining the power of his tongue he said, "This is the worst thing that could happen," his thin hair catching first on one side of his nose and then the other as his head bobbled excitedly. "You will not be here to influence the king for months. We must find a way to get out of this career crushing catastrophe. Did you encourage this?"

Gaspar was surprised at Balzak's response but said, "That's an awfully negative response to the situation, and, no, I didn't have a chance to say anything about it at all. I don't see how you could see this as anything but an opportunity to ingratiate myself with his majesty."

"You'll be gone for months. Others will have the opportunity to move into the position you and I have worked so hard to foster. This is a calamity."

Attempting to calm Balzak down with a soothing tone, Gaspar said, "Look. I can't lose. I'll come back with a boon of information that we don't have now, the king will be satisfied, and he'll see it as a performance of great service to his royal person."

"And if you fail to bring back the expected *boon* of information?"

"Balzak, it won't happen that way. Besides, the king is funding the whole adventure with provided security, no less. Now that my choice has been made for me, I'm beginning to regain some of my initial excitement."

"Oh, no," groaned Balzak.

CHAPTER FOURTEEN

Ezri had tried several times over the next few months to rekindle some of the friendship he and John once experienced, but John would have no part of it. There was always some errand that he needed to perform for his father. Several times Ezri offered to help and said that they could do whatever John had to do together, but John's task was always something he had to do on his own. John had been humiliated in the incident of the stolen horse, and he did not want to be caught in a situation even vaguely resembling that fiasco. Levi had warned his son not to spend time with Ezri— John never needed the advice.

"Here comes the criminal," said Uri, a neighboring farmer's son. The comment immediately set Ezri's temper flaring.

"Leave him alone," said John, "It's best to leave him to his own business." Uri grinned at Ezri with hurtful intent. Although seething inside, Ezri let the slight pass.

"It's people like him that give Jews a bad name," pursued Uri.

"Look, Uri, I said let it go. It's best to just ignore him as if he was never there."

Though John meant to be indifferent towards Ezri, his statement cut Ezri deeper than Uri's.

Ezri saw John pursuing other friendships, stinging his pride. He couldn't help thinking that John had been his friend once but now wanted nothing to do with the *hired hand's* son. John was not vain, but in Ezri's mind that was what he became. More and more Ezri felt loathing for his old friend. Rather than try to change his own ways and apologize for his behavior, which would have healed the relationship with both John and Levi, Ezri chose to simmer. He became more and more difficult for his father to relate to at home. At work, he emotionally pushed everyone away until he was truly an angry loner. Ezri perceived everyone's avoidance of him as their attempt to punish him.

One evening, when everyone was working late in the olive groves, Ezri stole back to the stables, slipped a saddle on John's horse, Raven, and rode away. He had not completely worked off what he owed for the first stolen horse, but it made little difference in his mind—*they* all deserved what *they* were getting.

CHAPTER FIFTEEN

Zand had slipped into a sour disposition once he was back in his chambers after Gaspar's audience with the king. Two of his close confidants stood by quietly knowing better than to speak when the high priest was in one of his moods.

"If not for the great wealth of his family and his father's influence with the king's father, that upstart would never have even been known by Phraataces," Zand said throwing his hands in the air as he paced. "It's infuriating to have to stand by and watch as his majesty treats this boy as an equal. I have never been invited to sit in the presence of the king, and I am the high priest. I must deal with this boy before he gets a chance to gain more status with the king." He flung himself into a chair exhausted by his tirade.

He was only seated for a moment when the patter of sandals running in the corridor outside his chambers was heard. Seconds later a voice called playfully, "Father, I'm coming to see you and you must not be busy."

Slowly Zand's scowl was replaced by a broadening smile. Zand's two trusted priests looked at one another and gave expressions of relief.

A tall, dark haired, dark eyed beauty popped into Zand's inner chamber bursting with youthful energy. Bowing her head to the two priests she said, "Good day Farrokh and Daba. Father, is now a good time to have a word with you? Or should I come back?"

"You should be more formal with the priests of Ahura-Mazda."

"Eminence, she is like a niece to us. She honors us with her familiarity," said Daba. "May we have your leave to go?"

To the priests Zand said, "Thank you, my friends. You have my leave." To his daughter, Rachel, he said, "We were just discussing one of our young priests. Why do you come to see me?"

Paying no attention to his question, she said, "Father, I heard you raising your voice. Did Farrokh and Daba upset you?"

"It is of no consequence. Why have you come?"

Not wanting to let him off the hook nor able to contain her own curiosity, she pursued Zand, "Father, what upset you?"

Pretending to be exasperated he said, "You are so much

like your mother," and then smiling added, "You will never tell why you came until I tell you what angered me, will you?"

"I'd say you've got everything about right, Father."

"I was in on the audience his majesty had with the young priest, Gaspar, today. The king seemed to behave in a way that was unseemly, that's all."

"Gaspar met with King Phraataces?" Rachel's interest was elevated at the mention of his name. "Did he anger the king?"

"Much the opposite. The king called him to his presence and bade him sit with him."

Rachel smiled, not able to contain herself she asked, "The king showed favor toward Gaspar? Why would that upset you?"

"No one sits in the presence of the king. Especially a pretender to the priesthood. The only reason he was admitted to the priests of the good god is because of his father's wealth and standing with the king. The boy is too sure of himself. He does not know enough of the deep secrets of our faith to enjoy so much of the king's benevolence."

Smiling at her father, Rachel asked, "Were you a little jealous of Gaspar's attention from the king?"

"You go too far, daughter. The king was very clear that my standing with him is unshakable. My concern is for the boy's welfare and what is proper."

"As you say, Father," Rachel demurred. "May I tell you why I came?"

Relieved to be off the topic of Gaspar and the king, Zand nodded his head.

"Mother and I have been invited to lunch with the queen next week, may I buy something new at the market to wear when we appear before her majesty?"

Pleased that he would be well represented to her highness, Zand immediately said yes. While it was difficult to gain the ear of the king, gaining influence with the king through the queen was a much easier task. No woman in the realm was better at representing her husband to the royal family than his wife, Nazli.

Leaving, Rachel peeked back through the door and said, "You know all the girls of Seleucia speak of no one more than the handsome, wealthy Gaspar?" And before Zand could react, Rachel bolted down the hall.

Zand sat at his chair staring at the entrance that his daughter had just quitted—his scowl returning.

Gaspar had not seen Melchior since the big priest had left after their last encounter, and he was unhappy with the rift in their relationship. The outcome of his audience that morning with King Phraataces had been far different than he ever imagined it would be, and he wanted to be the first to tell his friend what had transpired. He felt sheepish about returning to Melchior only to tell him that he had once again changed his mind about what the star might mean from a theological standpoint. Why could he not just see this whole thing as a big adventure, Gaspar wondered? Why did it have to take on the proportions of which god was the true god?

Some of the pagan countries surrounding Parthia believed that every realm had its own god or set of gods. Why should Parthia be different? Maybe Ahura-Mazda was the god of Parthia while Zeus and Marduk were, respectively, the chief gods of Greece and the old Babylonian empire. Was it only important because so much was riding on the answer to the question of the *why* of the star? The ramifications of the star heralding in a king who would overthrow all other kingdoms could make him out to be a traitor to the man who was his present king. If the gods ruled realms as did men, how could one god, say the God of the Jews, cross boundaries to send signs to those who were priests of another god? The more he wrestled with the idea, the more confused he became.

"I wish I could treat this whole expedition as an adventure and leave all the concerns about which deity is the true one out of the equation," he said out loud. In his heart of hearts, he knew that he was pulling for the god of the Jews, and maybe that was what was so unsettling about this whole affair.

Striding across the room to the servant gong, he gave it a quick rap. Tala instantly appeared.

"Your reverence," she said.

"Have Cyrus ready my horse. I won't be home until late this evening."

Changing into his riding clothes, Gaspar smiled thinking how Melchior would take in all that he had to tell him. Then it occurred to him that Melchior had never told him what it was that he had come to tell him, nor did he ever explain what he meant about Balthasar's being able to see things before they happen.

"He really can be irritating," he said shaking his head as he walked out of his quarters.

As Gaspar was riding out of the courtyard of his home, he saw a rider coming up the road at a fast pace. Gaspar reined his own mount to the side of the road to give the rider room to bring his own horse to a stop.

"Pardon my haste, eminence, but I have urgent news from my master the priest, Balthasar of Nippur. He is anxious that you should read what he has written and to give him feedback when he arrives." The messenger handed Gaspar a small leather pouch used to carry scrolls, and then said, "He has also told me to bid you to have the magus Melchior read it too."

Cyrus had come running up when he saw his master pull to the side of the road to make way for the rider.

"Cyrus," Gaspar said, "see that this man receives our full hospitality before he begins his return trip."

"You are most generous, your reverence," the rider said.

Cyrus led the courier into the courtyard. Gaspar unfastened the pouch's cover to look at the scroll. He went to unroll it and decided that he would wait to read the contents with Melchior.

CHAPTER SIXTEEN

Making his way to Caesarea Beneath Panion had taken Ezri the better part of two days. Hellenists referred to the city this way, and those whose loyalties were Roman called it Caesarea Philippi. He had traveled about twenty miles through hilly terrain leading John's horse, Raven, around rock escarpments that slowed his travel. Staying off the main road, so he wouldn't have to answer any difficult questions of any persons of authority, had tested his directional skills to their limit. His desire to distance himself from anyone who might recognize him had trumped his desire for food, but now he wished he had also stolen a few denari so he could buy some. Rounding Mount Hermon, Ezri found a cave outside the city where he could leave Raven until he returned.

Outside the city, atop a rocky cliff, Ezri saw another cave where water was cascading down the face of Mount Hermon into the Jordan River. On either side of the cave were carved out niches in the stone where statues were placed of Pan, Hermes —his father, Echo—Pan's companion, and various other gods of the Greek pantheon. Ezri had heard stories about this place, never believing them. Now that he was here, he felt an eerie fascination for it. This cave was where the Greeks said Pan was born and the entrance where many of the fertility gods traveled to the underworld during the winter months only to come back to the over-world once spring came. Many pagans thought of Pan's cave as the gates of Hades.

Ezri quickly made his way to the city. Caesarea was part of the Roman Empire in the region of Paneas located twenty-four miles north of the Sea of Galilee in Palestine. Historically, it was part of the northern extension of Ptolemy's portion of the Alexandrian empire. Here, Greek pagan culture exerted greater influence than in lower parts of Palestine. Pandering to the gods and participation in all sorts of pagan religious festivals were quite common in Caesarea.

Compared to Gischala, Caesarea was a much larger city. Gischala retained its Jewish morality and traditions; whereas Caesarea was tainted by the pagan beliefs and rituals. Ezri's world enlarged exponentially the moment he stepped inside the city gates.

"The handsome traveler would perhaps like a pan-flute?"

asked a middle-aged, attractive woman with a basket full of the multi-reed flutes made popular by the impish god of shepherds and flocks. "A good looking boy like you can capture the hearts of many of our local girls with a flute such as this," she said, thrusting one of her wares in his face.

"No, I'm not here to buy," Ezri snapped, speaking more harshly than he intended and feeling embarrassed that he had nothing with which to purchase anything.

"No money," she said perceptively. "Perhaps Sophia can find you some work if you have a wolf's heart, huh?"

"Really? Uh, what kind of work?" His stomach was now making enough noise that Sophia must have heard it. He was certainly interested—anything to quell his increasing hunger.

"For someone who is hungry and has no money, do you really care what kind of work it is?"

Looking around, Ezri said, "I suppose not. Where do I go?"

"Oh, I look like someone who does not have the means to employ a handsome young man?" Ezri shrugged helplessly, but before he could speak, Sophia continued. "I have the best work. You will not get tired doing my work, and you will make a lot of money for your effort. Are you a clever and daring boy?"

"I suppose. What do you mean exactly?"

Speaking more softly, she said, "Have you ever stolen?"

Not sure where this was going, but sure he had nothing to lose by telling the truth he said, "Yes."

"What did you steal?"

"Money, jewelry, two horses."

"Were you ever caught?"

"Once for stealing a widow-woman's horse."

"Oh, I see," she said laughing, "you are ruthless and gutsy. I can use you if you are also clever. You must remember that thieves must always be able to trust one another even if no one else can. Do you understand, boy?"

Ezri's sense of adventure was goaded though he was unsure he could trust this woman. He said nothing, only nodded his head.

Looking across the market, Sophia pointed to an old woman who was bent over with a burden of sticks used as kindling to start fires. "That woman's name is Irene. She is going to be our dupe. You must play this well to make it come off right. Over there," she pointed to a well dressed man several stalls down from where Irene was peddling her faggots. "He is the man I lifted this purse from earlier," she showed it to Ezri and quickly put the pouch back in the pocket of her skirt. "I am being more closely watched every day and must resort to more and more clever means to make my living."

"What do you want me to do? You've already made your theft. By the look of that purse, there must be a month's wages in there."

"Four," she corrected him, "but I want to erase any suspicion that it was me who stole the purse in the first place. I want you to walk up to Irene and act like you're pulling the purse away from her crying out at the same time that you saw her steal it. Can you do that young man."

"Easy, but how will you get anything from that?"

"Ah, that's the good part. Irene gets blamed for the theft, you take the money to the rich gentleman, he gives you a reward, and you and I will split the reward 30-70. Are you in?"

Beaming with anticipation, not to mention thoughts of a good meal, Ezri said, "Of course."

"One last thing," Sophia told him, "don't cross me. Remember what I said about thieves trusting each other?"

Ezri nodded.

"I have friends that would slit your throat if I told them that you left me standing here empty handed. On the other hand, you do well with this, and you just might have more jobs with much bigger pay-offs."

Ezri said, "Don't worry. I'll do good by you."

"Good, boy. I'll meet you afterwards at the mouth of Pan's cave. Do you know where that is?"

Ezri nodded.

"Don't let me down, boy."

CHAPTER SEVENTEEN

"You know, after our last conversation, I should have never allowed you in my house," Melchior said.

"I'm young. I'm supposed to struggle with life philosophies and to drive my elders to distraction," Gaspar said good-naturedly. "Besides I've apologized twice already. What more can I do?"

"Apologize one more time."

"You have it old friend. Will you forgive me?"

"What's to forgive? I never took you seriously anyway."

"Wha...?" Gaspar began, and then catching Melchior's humor burst into laughter.

"Enough foolishness. I want to read the scroll that Balthasar sent to us."

"But what about what you came to tell me at my house?"

"We'll get to that. I want to see the scroll."

"I won't show you the scroll until you explain what you inferred about Balthasar's ability to know things before they happen."

"That's not important. Let me look at his message."

"Melchior, I won't wait one more day to have my curiosity satisfied. What did you mean?"

Melchior rolled his eyes placed his big hands on the table. "Balthasar receives impressions of what will be. Some have said that he merely is extremely intuitive and reads people and situations well. The fact that he came out to meet us on our way to visit him was, for those of us who know him well, predictable."

"So, he does that frequently?"

"I don't know if I would say frequently, but I would say enough to make one wonder about how he does it."

Gaspar nodded his head in understanding and took the scroll from its pouch and rolled it out on Melchior's work table in his tower study. Both men read what Balthasar had found in the old scrolls of the Jews' holy book, his thoughts on the readings, and the questions that he had as a result of reading them.

"It sounds as though the Jews think that this person might be a world ruler and that his kingdom would be an everlasting one," Melchior said after reading Balthasar's notes.

"This note about the passage in Isaiah concerning the

Jews' god's servant being marred or disfigured doesn't make any sense to me as it didn't make any sense to Balthasar. He said he chose to include it anyway because he thought it might make sense later," said Gaspar, "but how could it be talking about the same person?"

"Let's leave that passage out and focus on the ones that do seem to be talking about this Jewish king." Taking up a piece of chalk, Melchior went over to a finely finished wall that was painted red, and wrote: *Of the increase of his government and peace there shall be no end, upon the throne of David, and upon his kingdom, to order it, and to establish it with judgment and with justice from henceforth even for ever. The zeal of the Lord of hosts will perform this.* Underneath it he placed a dash, and then asked, "What do we know this passage is telling us?"

Gaspar said, "The government will never end. That he will be a descendant of their great king David. That..."

"Slow down. I can't write that fast."

"Sorry, Melchior." He waited. "That he will establish a kingdom of judgement and justice that will be unending."

"That this king," said Melchior, "*will order* says to me that it will be a well run government."

"That's good. Is there anything else that we're missing?" asked Gaspar.

"Let's do the passage from the other text the same way to see what we can come up with," said Melchior. He wrote it down the same way as he did the passage from Isaiah. *I shall see him, but not now: I shall behold him, but not nigh: there shall come a star out of Jacob, and a scepter shall rise out of Israel, and shall smite the corners of Moab, and destroy all the children of Sheth.* "It sounds as if people won't recognize him, or, maybe, not recognize him for who he is. What do you think, Gaspar?"

"I think you're right. Write it down." Pausing again to give Melchior time to write, he added, "Maybe the star will herald his coming and a scepter will be his birthright? Am I reading too much into it?"

"I don't know. Let me write it down anyway." After he wrote Melchior said, "Smiting and destruction sounds like conquering. What do you think?"

"Yes, it's at least a good place to start."

For the next hour the two went on like this with each passage that Balthasar sent them. Gaspar began to write down their notes on parchment as Melchior ran out of room on the red wall. At the end of their brainstorming, Melchior came and stood beside his colleague and watched him write what they had written on the wall.

When Gaspar finished, Melchior said, "I want to tell you what I discovered the other night when I came to your house to talk to you. It is very peculiar what I came up with, and I want you to check my calculations after I tell you." He paused for a moment, went over to another table where a servant had left water and cups, poured two, and came back giving Gaspar one.

He sat across the table from Gaspar so he could look straight into the young priest's eyes. "I measured the distance of the star from here and found that it is only a few miles from the earth."

Gaspar stared at Melchior for a few seconds and broke into laughter. "Very funny. You've had your joke. Now tell me what it was that you were going to tell me." But when he looked at Melchior there was no mirth in his eyes or face. He was stone serious.

"That's why I want you to do the measurements too. I checked myself several times and I kept coming up with the same numbers. It seems impossible when you consider the distance of other stars, but my figures remained the same, 12 miles out from the earth."

Gaspar saw that his friend was not joking. This star didn't act like any of the other stars in the heavens, why should it not be different in this way too?

"I know this makes absolutely no sense, but we are left with the facts. If those are the facts, then what does that make the star, a celestial being of some kind sent to be God's personal herald? I don't know. The more we gain in knowledge of this star, the more questions we seem to accumulate."

Gaspar watched his friend talking and had no conclusions for him. Melchior was right. The more information they gathered, the less they seemed to know.

Gaspar agreed to stay at Melchior's that evening so they could keep their discussion going and Gaspar could check Melchior's calculations. With all they had to discuss, the king's sponsoring of the expedition seemed a trite matter in the scope of all that they were learning. Melchior was pleased that the king was absorbing all the expenses of the trip, but he immediately took the conversation back to the star and this Jewish king.

CHAPTER EIGHTEEN

Rachel and her mother, Nazli, left the temple compound immediately for the market place. Zand had designed a sedan chair where his wife and daughter could face one another while sitting on cushioned seats. The sedan had black wood twisted-rope poles that supported a white silk canopy. The sides of the chair were also of silk and could be rolled up and tied to allow a free flow of air.

The two women talked excitedly about the coming luncheon with the queen and what they hoped to find in the market by way of material. Nazli had already secured two of Seleucia's top seamstresses for the assembly of their outfits. Soon their conversation moved on to what all young women and mothers eventually discuss—future husbands for the daughters.

"So, do you have your eye on any of the young bachelors of the city," Nazli asked her daughter probingly.

"Not many. I find most arrogant and brash."

"Not many indicates that there might be some that interest you?"

"Not some, one."

Nazli had been leaning into her daughter, but now in true surprise she sat back on her cushion. "Only one? Who is this fortunate fellow who captures the heart of my daughter so utterly?"

"Mother, think for a moment. Who is the most sought after and most aloof of all of Seleucia's young men?"

"Gaspar."

At the sound of his name, Rachel's face blushed and she could no longer look her mother in the eyes. "He's mature, intelligent, good-looking, and a man worthy to be yours and father's son-in-law," she gushed.

"Not to mention that he's one of if not the richest man in Parthia. He is all that you say, but your father thinks that he has his position because of his wealth and his deceased father's influence with the king. Your father will take some work, but the real difficulty is how to get Gaspar's attention. He doesn't seem to have the same interests as other men his age. You are right. He is quite mature. Let me think on this for awhile. If my beautiful, intelligent daughter doesn't gain his attention, then maybe he truly is only a celibate priest, as many have conjectured."

At this comment Rachel's face became a reflection of concern.

"Don't worry, sweet girl, he is no match for your beauty nor my cunning."

A smile crept its way back to Rachel's face and both women laughed clasping each others' hands in anticipation of their conspiracy.

CHAPTER NINETEEN

Ezri loved the thrill and chance that he might be caught more than he enjoyed the result of his stealing. It was instinctual for Sophia to know so quickly what Ezri was capable of doing. He was born for this kind of life, and she sensed it.

Before he moved across the marketplace to frame Irene, the old seller of kindling, Ezri made sure that the gentleman whose purse Sophia had stolen was turned facing away busy haggling with one of the merchants. When the gentleman turned, Ezri moved quickly to Irene, placed the stolen purse in her hands, and then said in a loud voice, "How dare you steal that man's money! Give me that purse," pretending to pull the purse out of her hands. With the attention of everyone in the marketplace, Ezri strode over to the man to whom the purse belonged and handed it to him. The gentleman immediately checked for his purse to discover that it had been lifted from him without his knowing.

"Thank you, young man. It is reassuring to see that there are good and decent young people in the world. Who is it that stole my money?" Ezri gave a little bow and pointed to Irene, who had a look of horror and confusion. Unsheathing his sword, the man grabbed the old woman's right arm and and hit her sharply with the flat side of his sword breaking the bones in her wrist. Irene shrieked in pain falling down to the dirt. "That will be your punishment for stealing what doesn't belong to you," the man said, re-sheathing his blade.

Ezri did not realize that the Irene would be injured in the process of his ruse. His inclination was to help the old woman, but he kept up his subterfuge not wanting to be exposed for his deceit.

"Young man, please take this gold piece as a reward for your honesty," the man said crossing back to Ezri.

Taking the risk of losing his reward, but hoping for more, Ezri declined the man's generosity saying, "No sir, what I did was only right. Please keep your gold."

"You do my heart well. Here, take two gold pieces and share them with your family." As Ezri started to raise his hand to decline this second offer, the man said, "Please, I insist."

Ezri thanked the man, telling him, "You bless me in ways you cannot know. My family will put this kind gift to great use."

The man patted Ezri on the shoulder as the boy walked away toward the city gate. As he moved away from the scene Ezri could not help hearing and being affected by the sobs of Irene as she cradled her broken bones.

"Oh, my! I thought you lost everything when you told him to keep his reward," cackled Sophia at the predesignated meeting spot. "I'm giving you half because you got us twice what I expected. You may have a great future ahead of you, boy."

Ezri smiled and took his share of the scam. "Where can I go to break this coin down into a more usable form? I've never had so much wealth."

"You come with Sophia. I know just the man to help us. Before we do, we must get a meal in you." She took Ezri by the arm and led him down a path away from town.

CHAPTER TWENTY

"You want me to give my blessing to our daughter's pursuit of a relationship with Gaspar? Have you lost your mind, woman?" Zand exploded.

"In all respect, husband, you are not seeing the big picture," soothed Nazli.

"There is no big picture. Gaspar intrudes on my standing with the king and weakens my influence. You're asking me to bring the enemy into my household."

"Would it not be easier to deal with him if he was being influenced by the high priest's daughter?" she countered.

Zand sat stewing, but was no longer barking. Nazli knew she had her husband's attention.

"What better gift could we give our daughter and your line, but a rising star in Parthian government? Not only that, there is no wealthier man in all of Parthia. What a great marriage of opportunity and power it would be. Your daughter would only enhance his opportunities at court, and would be a wise counselor to him. Think beyond your own situation and to the legacy of our family." Nazli could see that she had her husband thinking and not reacting. She sat back and allowed him to ponder over what she had said.

Zand sat leaning forward, fingers interlaced with his fore fingers steepled, and his nose resting on his thumbs. Nazli could see his countenance transforming before her eyes. He looked up to watch his wife watching him. The smallest of smiles played across her lips.

"You are an enchantress, you know that," he said, teasing her.

"And you are a very fortunate man," she said as she moved over to sit on his lap kissing him lengthily. They held each other for a time lost in their own thoughts.

Zand broke the silence, pulling back and saying, "You know, I have great plans for Gaspar."

Nazli slapped him playfully on his chest, allowing him to pull her into another long, passionate kiss.

Rachel could hardly contain herself as she and her mother sat on her bed. They had excused the servants and had asked not to be disturbed.

63

"What did he say," Rachel asked.

"He is on board with our plan. Your father was the easy part . . ." Nazli began.

Interrupting her mother Rachel said, "But Gaspar is the hard part."

"Not hard, it will just take some time. He is leaving for Palestine in a few days. That can work much to our favor. We must be clever and make sure that the last image that he has before he leaves is you. That way, the whole length of his trip will be spent in contemplation of you and in the building of desire."

Rachel squeezed her mother's hands in anxious anticipation.

"A man like Gaspar is wise but unsuspecting of women's wiles," continued Nazli. "If we are too obvious, he will turn away from you. If we don't give him enough, he won't get it."

"Men are so difficult," said Rachel.

Nazli smiled and said, "You should hear what they say and think of us.

"Before he leaves, we need to present you to him in a way that appears you may not be his for the asking, but that you also might have interest in him."

"Oh, mother, how do we do all of that before he leaves? This is so complicated."

"Complicated, yes. Difficult, no," said Nazli reassuringly. Rachel looked at her mother with quizzical looks. Nazli pulled her daughter to her and said, "Don't worry. We women have been mastering this skill for centuries. If not for us, there would be no people on the earth."

"Now tell me. Who is that young man who has been showing interest in you."

"His name is Majid. But Mother, he's a great bore."

"Is he good-looking?"

"Yes, but. . ."

"Is he from a good family?"

"Yes, Mother, but. . ."

"Then he will be the perfect person to fan Gaspar's male impulses to win you for himself."

Rachel smiled at Nazli wagging her finger and said, "You are such a schemer. So how do we get them together so Gaspar can see me with Majid?"

"Simple. We have a dinner, invite lots of guests, and two of those guests are Gaspar and Majid."

CHAPTER TWENTY-ONE

When Phraataces' guard pulled up at Balthasar's home he had already packed all the personal items he wanted to bring on the trip. For the soldiers, it was merely an exercise of riding out to Nippur and turning around and coming back to Seleucia with the magus.

Two nights before their coming, Balthasar had had a dream about presenting the Jewish king with a gift. In his dream, he kept trying to see what was in the gift he was giving, but could never see it. No matter how he maneuvered in his dream, he was frustrated in his efforts to see the contents of his gift. That morning, Balthasar spent time asking God to tell him what gift he should bring. In his mind he heard clearly, "All that you have."

When the soldiers appeared at his doorstep late the next afternoon, Balthasar was gone trying to sell all that he owned. He had been very successful, but was having trouble finding someone to purchase his costly rugs. Finally, he had contacted a merchant friend who would come by later that day to pick them up. Balthasar had sold everything that he owned except for the Hebrew Bible scrolls he kept in his library and a small chest. He wanted to bring the scrolls to Seleucia to give to his old friend Melchior. Besides, no one in Nippur would have given him the amount that they were worth. The chest that he kept was to put the gold in from the sale of all of his possessions.

When Balthasar returned home, he was surprised to see the king's guard waiting for him there. The officer explained their presence to Balthasar's delight.

"Come in," Balthasar said in the hospitality of the east that was easily his way. "It is good that you came today because tomorrow there would be nothing on which to sit. I will have my servants prepare your meal, and you and your men will want to use the baths by the fortress so you can freshen up in a timely manner."

"We will take advantage of your advice of the baths now and come back for our meal, if that suits your reverence," said the officer.

"Splendid. That would be splendid."

"Over dinner, we can discuss the particulars of our departure."

CHAPTER TWENTY-TWO

Balzak had wanted to talk to Gaspar again about his conversation with Phraataces, and when his master had chosen not to come home that night, he was instantly angry. He felt as if he was losing command of everything. The more he tried to control circumstances, the more his control was slipping away. If he could just figure out a way to defuse the need for Gaspar to accompany the other two magi on this expedition, he could regain control, to some extent, of his master's career. Gaspar was not worried about it, so Balzak had to help him. His master would thank him in the years to come.

"Excuse me," Tala said, "but there is a messenger for you from the high priest."

"The high priest? What can he want of me?" Balzak said out loud. "Send him in."

Tala bowed and hurried out to the entry. "This might be just what I needed. Perhaps the high priest has concerns that could taper into our own benefit," he thought.

The messenger gave a nod at the door, proceeded to the table where Balzak was sitting, and said, "His reverence, the high priest, requests you to visit him in his chambers first thing tomorrow morning."

"You may tell his reverence that I will be there."

The messenger turned and exited. Balzak smiled and went to bed that night a contented man.

Melchior and Gaspar had stayed up late talking with too much wine to drink. Gaspar slept deeply in one of Melchior's spare bedrooms. Just before dawn, he dreamed that he was presenting the Jewish king with a gift. When the king's father opened the vessel, his astonishment was apparent at the costliness of the gift. Melchior stepped up in his dream to see what was in the container. Before he could see what was there, he awoke. He looked around his room feeling the frustration he experienced in his dream.

"What was in the vessel?" he questioned aloud.

He thought that it must not have been gold or silver because no one would put that in a jar made for frankincense or myrrh. He smiled at the thought process of his groggy brain. Maybe the good god is telling me to give the king a gift of frankincense or myrrh he mused. He then decided he would talk it over with Melchior at breakfast later that morning.

When Gaspar met Melchior in the dining room for breakfast the next morning, Melchior looked like he had been pushed over a steep slope.

"You look as bad as I feel," Gaspar quipped.

"Our owl's eggs should be here any minute. That will take the bite out of the goddess' drink."

Gaspar smiled weakly and said, "I want to talk to you about a dream I had early this morning."

"I too, have a dream to describe to you. Tell me yours first."

As Gaspar explained his dream, he could sense Melchior's growing excitement.

"Mine was almost exactly like yours," exclaimed Melchior, "except that in my dream I could smell the contents of my vessel—myrrh."

"Then I shall bring frankincense."

Melchior laughed and said, "I wonder what Balthasar dreamed?"

"On a priest's salary, I hope it was only flour."

Melchior laughed and then grew serious. "It is not coincidence that we had similar dreams last night. I get the feeling that we are being drawn further and further into something that is beyond anything we can imagine. It is uncommon that the god of the Jews would beckon to those who follow Ahura-Mazda. The gods keep to their own boundaries. Ahura-Mazda has either given his permission for this crossing over of borders, which is doubtful, or he is unable to prevent the Jewish God from doing so."

Gaspar looked at Melchior, grasping the impact of what he was saying but having nothing with which to respond.

"We are either most fortunate of men, or we are seeing the crumbling away of all that we have come to believe is true about the universe."

"Or both," said Gaspar

Neither had anything to add to Melchior's reflection and their conversation turned to less ethereal matters. Late in the morning, Gaspar headed back to his home inside the city.

CHAPTER TWENTY-THREE

The morning after receiving the message from Zand to meet with him, Balzak was a bundle of anticipation. He hoped that this would be the opportunity that would enable him to extricate Gaspar from responsibilities of this ridiculous expedition to Palestine.

He put on his best robes and set off for the temple. He did not like the fact that no matter what size animal or kind that he rode, he presented a comic figure. A standard size horse made his legs stick straight out on either side making him look ridiculous. His small pony invited children to run up to him and dance around him as he rode down the street. Camel's were meant for long desert travel, not for transporting little men a few city streets, so he chose merely to walk. His prowess at knife throwing made him feel as safe as any man walking the streets —especially those of this affluent district of Seleucia. His size made him an easy-looking target, but most of Seleucia's criminal element had heard at least one story of the little man with the deadly knives.

Cyrus offered to have the servants ready the sedan chair for him, but he felt that would make him look self-assuming. "No," he told Cyrus, "it is best that I walk."

"Would you like me to accompany you to the temple?" Cyrus proffered.

At first he thought to decline the young servant's offer. As he consider the idea another moment he realized that it gave him a certain amount of dignity to have a servant accompany him. "Thank you, Cyrus, I will accept your offer."

Cyrus genuinely relished the time he could spend with the little teacher. A lowly servant himself, he never had a chance to acquire formal training. Spending time with Balzak gave him an opportunity to learn beyond his station in life. Besides, he had a soft spot in his heart for the teacher, and Balzak honestly had affection for the witty, playful servant.

When they reached the temple, Cyrus said, "I will wait for you and accompany you back home if you wish."

"That won't be necessary. I don't want to keep you away from your duties. Thank you for your company this morning."

Balzak went around to the building that housed the offices of the priests. There was a courtyard spanning the distance between the offices and the temple. Zand was sitting at one of the benches awaiting Balzak's arrival.

Seeing the diminutive instructor, Zand rose to meet Balzak. "Thank you for coming to meet with me. What I have to talk to you about is of a personal nature so I thought that meeting out here in the cool morning air would be more to our liking than a stuffy building."

"I am honored to meet with your reverence wherever you might choose," said Balzak.

"You are kind. I need you to know that our topic this morning must be kept as a secret between you and myself whatever the outcome. May I request that confidentiality of you."

"Of, of course your reverence. I trust you with the topic of your concern. You are an honest man."

"Good. Now, broaching what I have to say is, shall we say—*awkward*. I will just be blunt. My daughter, Rachel, is very interested in your master, Gaspar. She and my wife want to have a dinner in two nights where Gaspar and several other noteworthy people will be our guests. I am concerned for my daughter's feelings, and don't want her to be unnecessarily hurt in her quest to interest your master. Has Gaspar ever shown any sign of interest in Rachel that you know of?"

Balzak thought that he was ready for anything, but this news took him completely by surprise. What a match of influence this would be for Gaspar. Except for one of the king's daughters, there was no more worthy match in all of Parthia for his master. She was influential and beautiful. Balzak couldn't believe how their fortunes continued to blossom.

"To be honest, I have never heard my master speak of any woman, but understand that this star business has him thoroughly preoccupied."

"Yes," Zand said with just a hint of irritation.

Detecting Zand's mood, Balzak changed his tack saying, "There is no more lovely and interesting woman in Parthia than your daughter. Would he not be intrigued by a woman such as she if given the opportunity?"

"I can only imagine that he would, but I am her father. You think that he may have interest if she intersected his orbit?" said Zand amused at his own wordplay.

"Your reverence is most witty. I think that he would. I will do all that I can to encourage this relationship. What is my part to be in all of this?"

"Only that you report to me if he has no interest at all. I don't want Rachel to make a fool of herself. My wife and my daughter have their feminine schemes to hatch. I am confidant in their prowess. May I trust you to keep our discussion a secret?"

"You may, your reverence. I see that there is nothing here that I am honor bound to tell my master."

"Good. I will trust you to let me know if my wife's schemes seem to be going awry."

When Balzak returned home he had just enough time to change into his day-to-day clothes before Gaspar got home. His whole perspective on Gaspar's trip to Palestine had now changed. With the high priest in Gaspar's court, he could be gone for ten years without it affecting his position with the king. Balzak's spirits could not have been higher when he asked Gaspar, "How was your time with his reverence Melchior?"

"It was very insightful. We both agree that the more we seem to learn about the star, the more questions we have. I am anxious to have Balthasar's input on all that we are learning. I am also interested to hear what he has to say about what Melchior and I think of the ideas he has sent to us."

"This expedition will be a great opportunity for you, Gaspar," Balzak said almost jubilantly.

"What has gotten into you? I thought you hated the idea of my going to Palestine? I haven't seen you this happy in months," Gaspar said quizzically.

Realizing he needed to control himself, Balzak brought his enthusiasm down a notch and said, "I just realized that I was being very selfish."

Gaspar smiled and went to change his clothes, wondering what was really behind Balzak's change in attitude.

CHAPTER TWENTY-FOUR

For several months Sophia and Ezri lived comfortably using the same kind of scam they perpetrated on poor Irene in many towns around the Paneas region. Ezri quickly found that he had been lucky when he initially refused the reward. The next two times he tried it, he only got a hearty slap on the back, a thank you, and no reward money at all. He also learned that he did not like accusing innocent people to cover his theft, so he modified the scam. Instead of placing the money in the hands of an unsuspecting passerby and then grabbing it away from him, he now came running from behind a corner of a nearby street yelling at the person whose purse had been lifted, "Sir, your purse was just taken by that man who disappeared down that street." He didn't mind stealing someone's money, but he didn't like causing innocents harm.

Sophia learned that she could trust Ezri and soon made him a full partner in her crimes, splitting everything with him down the middle. She was making more with him than she was before, so she wanted to make sure that she kept her source of steady income contented.

Ezri learned quickly. He was doing what he always wanted, feeling no remorse in taking from other people. It was a game to him, and people were always so thankful for the service he performed for them. Sophia taught him all that she knew, and she found in her young apprentice an empty cistern waiting to be filled with all of her years of nefarious experience.

Sophia had a confederate, Satanas, who she had been telling about Ezri and his natural abilities of deceit. Satanas led a circle of fellow thieves that did not participate in scams as much as outright theft. It was a loose association of villains with Satanas, brokering out criminal activity by calling on scoundrels who provided whatever personal talents he might need for a given job. He and Sophia had known each other for many years, and he used Sophia's talents from time to time when he needed a front to gain admittance for a heist he was planning.

Ezri had a smoothness and a gift of the theatrical to him when he was performing one of his cons. Because he loved the rush of excitement he experienced when pulling off a scam, this lifestyle was like a narcotic to him. The more deceit in which he was involved, the more he craved other opportunities. He never felt really alive unless he was part of a situation that put him in jeopardy. This gave him a coolness that was critical in his chosen occupation.

Sophia saw his talents and sought to cash in on her valuable find. She had never had more money than when she worked in tandem with Ezri. With a golden goose such as he, she knew she could make enough money to settle down someplace where her reputation was not so questionable, and she could lead a respectable life. When the time was right, she would introduce him to Satanas.

That day came sooner than she planned when Satanas came riding up to her door one bright spring morning. She saw him coming over a hill opposite her kitchen window. She walked out to meet him as he rode up to her small courtyard.

"I haven't had you as a visitor for some time. Do you have work for me to do?"

"For you, and for that boy who's been keeping you fed and happy."

"Not so loud. He doesn't need to know how good he is, or I'll lose him."

Satanas laughed. His laughter never had a mirthful ring —more like auditory contamination. "If he performs well in this job, his and your cut will keep you both living well for a year. How about it?"

"What do you have planned?"

CHAPTER TWENTY-FIVE

A messenger from the high priest dropped an invitation off at Gaspar's residence. Tala brought it to her master as he was working in his study.

"I have an invitation from the high priest, your reverence. Would you like to read it now?" she asked.

He thought that this was a thinly veiled attempt by the high priest to manipulate him before he left on his trip. "What makes this man so paranoid?" he thought, and then to Tala he said, "Give me the message. I better read it now. You may go." Tala bowed and left the room.

The message said, "His Reverence the High Priest requests your presence at a dinner to be held at his home in two nights."

The invitation gave Gaspar a sense of foreboding. What the high priest could possibly hope to accomplish in such a context defied his imagination. He sat mulling over the possibilities when there was a knock at his door.

"Enter," he said absentmindedly.

Balzak entered. He had told Tala to let him know as soon as the invitation came. Having gotten the information from her, he immediately went to Gaspar's rooms to observe his response.

"I have information from Cephas, your reverence," he said using the news to interrupt Gaspar at precisely this moment.

"Yes, what is it, Balzak?" Gaspar asked, still distracted by the invitation.

"Almost all of the goods he has transported to Seleucia have buyers. He is excited about the mark-up he has received on all of the items. This will end up being a lucrative venture for you."

"That is good news," Gaspar said without emotion.

"Your reverence seems to be distracted. Is there something with which I might help?" Balzak said probingly.

"Oh, Balzak, this fact finding expedition to seek the star's purpose continues to be a mixed bag. Just when it seems that everything about it is positive and exciting, something happens that alters the circumstances. I wish we could just leave tomorrow."

"What has transpired to cause you to be disparaged?"

"The other day in my audiencel with the king, I think that I caused the high priest concern over his standing with him. This expedition has heightened my visibility at court. I'm afraid it has made him think that I aspire to his position."

It took all of Balzak's control to maintain a serious, interested expression. "Why do you think that?"

"I just received an invitation to have dinner with him in two nights. I suspect that he will use the time to put me in my place and to challenge my thoughts concerning the importance of the star."

"Is it also possible that he may be inviting you to dinner to show that there is no animosity between the two of you. Maybe he only wants to mend any ruptures that he may have perceived as a result of your audience with the king? He may be realizing that being on your good side might bode well for him also."

Gaspar thought for a moment and then brightened, "You may be right. I am probably reading too much into the invitation. After all, the king did make it very plain that the high priest's prestige and position would not be affected at all by the findings of our expedition."

"I wouldn't give this matter another moment of concern. You are more a jewel in the high priest's ring than a thorn in his thumb," assured Balzak.

"I am wise to listen to your wisdom, faithful Balzak. Thank you for your words of encouragement."

Bowing his head, Balzak left Gaspar to his thoughts. "My master is being set up for great things," he thought. "Nothing stands in our way now."

Meanwhile at the high priest's home, two women sat across from each other at the dining table, planning where guests would sit, what conversations would be initiated, and how Rachel should act, talk, and look to attract Seleucia's most desirable bachelor.

CHAPTER TWENTY-SIX

Mid-afternoon of the day before Nazli and Rachel's dinner party Gaspar received a message that Balthasar had arrived and was at Melchior's home. Cephas had also indicated that he needed to see him that afternoon, so he rushed over to his warehouses to take care of business with him, which would leave the rest of the day for his two friends.

When he reached the warehouses, Cephas met him outside with a doleful face.

"We have a problem, Master," Cephas said showing Gaspar into the first of his warehouses.

Gaspar was taken back by the utter barrenness of the room. "How did thieves get in? Are both my warehouses empty?" he said with growing concern.

"Master I'm sorry I have let you down," Cephas said contritely. "Both your warehouses are empty."

Gaspar did not know how to respond. Nothing like this had ever happened before. He was wondering how thieves could have cleared out his warehouses so quickly and thoroughly. At that precise moment the guards he had hired walked into the rear of the building looking like dogs who had eaten their master's dinner.

Cephas continued. "I let you down. We had too many buyers and not enough merchandise. We were forced to sell everything at exorbitant prices. If I would have bought more, we would have made more," he said as a wide smile spread across his face. The men in back all broke into broad smiles as Gaspar gave an audible sigh of relief and hugged Cephas to him.

Once released from Gaspar's hug, Cephas said, "It was a scene of pandemonium. Buyers bickered between themselves over the price of the merchandise. Instead of selling our goods at conventional prices, we finally had to hold an auction. If we would not have done that, we would have been here for a year trying to mediate arguments. I've never seen anything like it.

"The guards we hired, Reverence, performed most admirably throughout the whole uproar. I have never seen hired guards perform so well as salesmen and diplomats. Had they not made the transition, we could have never pulled off the auction so successfully. Except for one or two disgruntled merchants, and you could probably guess who they were, everyone went away overjoyed at what they had purchased. It was amazing."

"I think the men's flexibility ought to be rewarded. Would a bonus of twice their wage be adequate?" Gaspar asked.

"You certainly have the resources to be that generous, Reverence," Cephas said.

The men came forward bowing and thanking Gaspar over and over again.

Raising his hand, Gaspar said, "You have done good work. I thank you. Whenever Cephas needs your talents in the future, know that each of you will be the first he contacts. Thank you for your hard work and loyalty." He pulled Cephas to the side and told him, "Pay the men immediately. Consider that first priority."

"It shall be as you have said."

"Are there any of these men we could employ full-time in other areas of our business, Cephas?"

"There are three that I have already sought out to be escorts for future buying trips. We can use them around here also for random errands between trips."

"Wherever we can create meaningful work, let's not cut corners."

"I understand. I will keep you apprised of areas where we can create both profit and work for men who want to do so."

The men were still whooping and hollering as Gaspar walked out of the warehouse. He knew that within a day Cephas would have a written report of all of their sales and expenses. He contemplated what he would do with all the wealth. He was already one of the richest men in the realm. "At what point is one's fortune big enough?" he wondered. He was glad of his financial success, but he felt that it was wrong just to use it for his own comforts. During his excursion he determined that he would give a lot of thought to how his money could best be used.

Balzak met him at the front door, "Has your reverence considered his attire for tomorrow night's dinner?" he asked.

"Balzak, Balthasar has arrived at Melchior's home. I want to go out and greet him there. You decide what I should wear. Nothing too ostentatious is my only caution to you. I don't want to wear anything that will eclipse the high priest's apparel."

"I was hoping you would leave the choice up to me. Have you heard from Cephas, yet?"

"I am just returning from the warehouses. I am most pleased."

"It seems Ahura-Mazda has smiled warmly on you these last few days."

"He has. I will give an extra thank offering to him

tomorrow during my duties."

Moshen opened the door for Gaspar and guided him to the stairs of Melchior's tower study.

"Moshen," Gaspar said, "I know the way to the study. Give your old legs a rest and let me climb the stairs by myself."

"My master does not have servants so that his guests should be rudely left to show themselves around his home."

"As you wish. I only thought. . ."

"But if you would not feel neglected," Moshen smiled weakly, "I would, this once, let you make the climb yourself."

Gaspar patted the old servant on his back, walked him to a bench in the entry, and made his way up alone the long flight of stairs to where his two friends were.

"Ahh, you are finally here. We can begin," Melchior said as he more pulled Gaspar into the room than greeted him.

"Wait, good Melchior. I wish to greet my young friend too," said Balthasar as he walked over to hug and welcome the new arrival.

"It is good to see you too, Balthasar. Your trip was without incident I hope."

"The squad of royal troops set a rapid pace. I don't think I have ever covered so much distance in so short of time. It was exhilarating and exhausting for an old man," Balthasar said using great facial animation that caused Gaspar and Melchior to laugh.

"Have we done with enough formality so that we can pursue the final preparations of our expedition?" Melchior asked good-naturedly. "I have been overseeing the preparations for the provisions of our trip, and I think that the only thing that was keeping us from leaving was Balthasar's presence. Now that he's here, except for any personal items, I think that we're ready for our trip."

"After tomorrow night, I can leave anytime," Gaspar said.

Melchior looked at Balthasar as if to ask if there was anything he needed to do before he left.

"I've been ready for the trip since I left Nippur," Balthasar said.

Directing his guests to chairs around the table, Melchior asked, "Balthasar, both Gaspar and I had dreams about what gift we should bring to the king. Have you reflected on what you might bring?"

"As a matter of fact I have. I too was convinced that I should bring something. It is among my personal affects. May I inquire about your dreams?"

Both magi looked at each other as to ask who should start. Gaspar laid out his hand to Melchior giving him first chance to speak. Melchior explained both of their similar dreams to Balthasar. At completion, he said, "Do you have anything to add, Gaspar?"

"That sums it up pretty well."

Balthasar laughed as he said, "How thorough is the one true God."

"What do you mean?" the other two said almost simultaneously.

"My dream was very much like yours, but I had to ask Him the next day what He wanted me to bring. The God of Israel is covering all of the details as He beckons us to this great event —even down to what gifts we should bring."

They sat looking at one another for a few moments when Melchior said, "What were you asked to bring?"

Balthasar brought two steepled fingers to his lips and said, "I think I shall leave that as a surprise. My gift required unusual sacrifice with particulars I am not willing to disclose right now. I know it is not fair for me to make such a statement, but trust me that it is best for me and for the two of you if I don't tell you at this time."

Gaspar was bursting to know, but didn't have the relationship with the wise magus to press him. Melchior, on the other hand, said, "What could there possibly be attached to the gift that you could not tell us? Are you going to have to die?"

Balthasar held up his hand and said, "When the time is right, I promise that I will tell all. Until then, help me keep my secret."

Melchior was visibly perturbed with Balthasar's answer, but before he could say anymore Gaspar said, "Have you gotten any other revelations concerning the star?"

"Oh, I nearly forgot!" said Balthasar as he jumped up and hurried out of the room leaving his two magi friends looking at one another questioningly.

After a while, Balthasar returned panting with three of Melchior's young servants who were each carrying a large clay vessel. After thanking the servants and dismissing them, Balthasar opened one of the jars and pulled out a scroll unrolling it on Melchior's document table. The other two hurried over to see what he had.

"This is one of the scrolls of the Hebrew Holy Book," said Balthasar as he carefully looked for a particular passage. After a moment he said, "Ah, here it is. This is their prophet Micah. He wrote, *But thou, Bethlehem Ephratah, though thou be little among the thousands of Judah, yet out of thee shall he come forth unto me that is to be ruler in Israel, whose goings forth have been from of old, from everlasting.* I have spent a lot of time contemplating the meaning of this text, and I think it is talking about the person they call the 'Anointed One', Messiah."

At this juncture in the conversation, Melchior was at his bright red wall with his piece of chalk, scribbling away. "What was the last section of what you read after *ruler in Israel*?" he asked. Balthasar repeated it for him as he finished the quote. "This word Ephratah. What does it mean, Balthasar?"

"I believe it is a southern district in Judah in which the town, Bethlehem, is located," answered Balthasar. "I have spoken with several Israelite acquaintances, and they tell me it is only a short distance south of Jerusalem."

"Do you think the one who is prophesied as the one coming out of Bethlehem is he who is heralded by our star?" asked Gaspar.

"I do. I believe our destination may be Bethlehem, in Judea, in Roman Palestine."

"What do you make of this last part which says, *to be ruler in Israel; whose goings forth have been from of old, from everlasting?* Is this some sort of god who has always been?" Melchior put forward.

"It seems to suggest an eternal being of some sort, yes," said Balthasar.

"So, are we looking for a child, a man, or a god?" inquired Gaspar.

The three men looked at one another. "I don't know," Balthasar said. "There is much that I do not know. I have searched the Hebrew Bible for other passages that could help us. There are other passages in the individual books of Genesis, Isaiah, Psalms, Jeremiah, and possibly many more, but what I've found—these are most helpful in locating the destination our star is pointing us toward.

"I believe we will understand more about the prophecies once we have witnessed their fulfillment and had a chance to live with them for awhile."

"That is not what I wanted to hear, but it does make sense," said Melchior.

"I am even more exhilarated about this excursion," said Gaspar. "I wish now I had not agreed to attend tomorrow night's dinner. I want to leave right now."

"We're holding up our expedition for a dinner party?" exclaimed Melchior.

"The high priest is having the dinner. I don't know how I can get out of it without damaging our relationship even more," Gaspar said regretfully.

"Zand is a good man, but insecure in his position. He can be both gracious and vengeful. It is well that you keep your appointment tomorrow night, Gaspar," said Balthasar.

"You know only too well," said Melchior. "It was your

questioning his policies that caused your banishment to Nippur."

"It is history now, my friend. All has worked for God's good since then," assured Balthasar.

"May I know what happened?" asked Gaspar unaware that he had moved forward in his seat.

"There's not much to tell, really. I thought we should use the excess temple offerings to help the poor in Seleucia, and Zand thought it wise to maintain a hedge against difficult times. In the end, I was sent to the temple in Nippur," reflected Balthasar.

"It was not quite so simple," boomed Melchior. "The holdings of the priesthood could run the entire Parthian government for a year. Your counsel was very sound and possible. The temple does not need to hoard the sum of money she possesses."

"I had no idea there was that much reserve in the temple coffers," Gaspar mulled.

"It is done, and nothing can be done about it now," reassured Balthasar. "We have much grander ideas to ponder than a past that cannot be changed."

Of course the old sage was right, but Gaspar determined that the temple funds were something that he would delve into once he returned from Palestine.

"Now," Balthasar said changing the subject, "what do we need to accomplish in the next thirty-six hours. . ."

CHAPTER TWENTY-SEVEN

When Abirami discovered that his son had run away with John's horse, Raven, he was almost inconsolable in his embarrassment and grief. In the next few months after Ezri's disappearance, he made sure that the boy's debt to the widow-woman was payed. He started paying off the debt for the theft of Raven, but Levi told him that he would not take money for a wrongful act perpetrated by the other man's son.

"When we catch your son, he will pay the price of his crime, not you," Levi told him.

"Let me do this to help purge my guilt. To do so would be a salve to my pain," Abirami pleaded.

"It is a useless reduction of your finances. I can afford to absorb the loss of the horse. I let you pay the penalty for the theft of the widow's horse because I knew she could use the money, and you needed the catharsis. I will not let you put yourself in needless debt because of a rebellious son."

Abirami hung his head and started to speak, but he could not formulate an argument against his employer. He merely said, "Thank you," and walked home.

When Miriam had died, it had just been Abirami and Ezri. As a boy, Ezri wanted to be wherever his father was. Ezri was an infusion of joy to his father's life that had been decimated when Miriam died. Up until the last few years, Abirami and Ezri were inseparable. Many a time, the people of Gischala were gladdened by the close relationship of the father and son. Ezri tagged along like a puppy, and Abirami's laughter at his son's amusing behavior was a common observation.

Without wife or son, life seemed to be an endless process of toil toward no apparent, worthwhile end. Each morning, sitting at his breakfast, he contemplated what death would be like. Each night as he walked home from work, he wondered if death wouldn't be better than the torture of living. Ezri had been, at one time, his closest friend. Levi had tried to console his employee, but Abirami had let himself detach from everyone. Abirami was as alone in the world as he could possibly imagine. He had put everything he had in his life into the relationship with his son. Ezri had taken precedence over everything in his life—even God. He had not prayed in years. Weeks would go by before he even had thoughts of God. On that night, he wondered what God would do if he ended his life. The reality was that he hoped he had good reason to commit the act. Instinctively he knew there was no good reason to kill himself.

His thoughts turned to Ezri once again. What if he quit his job and went to look for his son? Working that through, he realized that even if he found Ezri, there would be a very good chance that his son would not want to be found. Besides, he knew he had absolutely no idea where to look for the boy. He would simply have to wait for a time when Ezri would come home to him. Ezri chose to leave, and Ezri would have to choose to come home. His thoughts turned again to God.

"So, God," he said aloud, "what do I do now?"

He listened for God's voice. There was absolute quiet. His little house was as still as death.

Satanas had learned from his seemingly endless sources that there was going to be a shipment of gold from Jericho north to Capernaum, and then on up to Caesarea Philippi. A Roman guard had been commissioned by a rich merchant friend of Herod's, Matthias, to protect the shipment from Jericho to Capernaum, but it was the leg to Caesarea that had gotten Satanas' creative juices flowing. His source told him that most of the gold was to be kept by the priests of Pan, and a smaller portion was to be paid to a landowner in Caesarea. Satanas didn't know who the landowner was yet, but that was something he was definitely going to find out. It was not wise to rile the gods by stealing wealth that was entrusted to them. It was also foolhardy to attack a Roman guard of eighty men. But taking money from a man who was already too rich, and who was escorted by a contingent of armed country folk, that, was a different matter. Satanas could use the cool theatrics of a young man like Ezri in such a charade, and it would be worth it to pay him well.

Satanas laid the outline of his plan before Sophia. She watched his face as he drew in the dirt with a stick to describe the different locales of his plan. Her expression changed from cautious observation to jubilation. Before he was done explaining his plan to her, she was already imagining where she would retire from her life of crime.

CHAPTER TWENTY-EIGHT

The morning of the dinner party and the day before the magi's departure, Gaspar needed no one to wake him. He awoke fresh and in good spirits. When Balzak came in to wake his master, he found him already bathed, shaved, and dressed for the day.

"Balzak, I assume you have already picked out what I am to wear to tonight's party."

"Yes, would you like to see what I have chosen?"

"I would. I hope you did not choose anything too outlandish."

"I think you will find it suited to tonight's festivities," and with that he clapped his hands twice.

In trooped a grinning Cyrus and Amehlech. Cyrus held a black outer open robe, a simlah, that shimmered in the morning light. It was enhanced with two gold threads that ran down either side of the front lapels and around the cuffs of the sleeves. Draped over his left arm, Amehlech carried a white, silk robe, the kethoneth that was worn closest to the skin. The keffiyeh or headdress of desert peoples was of the same black material as the simlah, and was carried in his right hand. The cords that held the keffiyeh in place on his head were of braided gold.

"Excellent choice, Balzak. It is elegant, but not ostentatious. You have met my requirements exactly. Thank you. I can check that off my list."

Balzak was radiant in the warmth of his master's praise. It took all the discipline he could muster not to bring up the subject of Zand's beautiful daughter. He knew that Gaspar would guess their scheme if he tried to nonchalantly bring up Rachel in their conversation. The less said, he knew, the better. Still, the thought of the high priest's daughter and his master wed almost made him giddy. He found it much easier that day to hide his knowledge of the conspiracy than his own excitement.

"I need your help today to make sure all that I need is ready for the expedition," continued Gaspar. "The other magi and myself have decided we will leave tomorrow. We have much to do. Have Tala deal with my clothes. We will need Cyrus and Amehlech to help since they will be leaving with me."

Balzak felt his future coming together most favorably. Gaspar and the two young servants were blessed with the presence of a joyful Balzak. Not once did he lecture anyone. He even surprised them all at one point by making light of his nose getting in his way. Balzak's cheery disposition made it easy for Gaspar to be in heightened spirits when he arrived that evening at the home of the high priest.

CHAPTER TWENTY-NINE

Matthias and the centurion Laurentinus, the cavalry officer who would be leading the detail protecting the shipment of gold to Capernaum, had decided on a route several weeks before the actual transportation of the precious metal. There were two major routes that led north through Palestine. One, a western route, known as the International Coastal Highway, that paralleled the Mediterranean Sea until it bent east to Capernaum. The other was an eastern route, the King's Highway, that was well out of the way, and would mean several extra day's travel to reach the highway and then even more time to head back west to Capernaum. Taking either route would draw a lot of attention. Mathias preferred the most direct route along the ridge of the Jordan river valley to the southernmost edge of the Sea of Galilee, and then up her western shore to Capernaum. The road was not the quality of the other two, but the volume of traffic was much less.

At this time in history, the best place to store large sums of money was at a temple where people were superstitious about taking money from the gods. While the Temple of Pan was far from Jericho, the superstition surrounding it made it one of the best places in the region to store one's wealth. People's belief that it was an entrance to Hades kept them respectful of the site. The temple in Jerusalem had been a consideration, and would be safe enough in the present situation, but the innumerable uprisings of the Jews made it less desirable. The Romans saw the Jews' god as puny as they considered the Jews to be. If Rome ever attacked Jerusalem, all the precious items in the temple would be ransacked. No, he would take his money to a safer place. The temple of Pan was the best place to store this large sum of money because if trouble ever erupted, the Romans would be more likely to honor the temple of their own gods over the God of a foreign, inferior people.

Mathias did have a lingering concern that the quality of protection from Capernaum to Caesarea would not be enough to ward off those who might see his fortune as easy picking. His business associate in Caesarea, Yitzhak, assured him that he and his men would be more than enough for any bandit who might try to steal his gold. "These are quiet country people," Yitzhak assured him. "You worry too much. No one will even know about the transportation of the gold anyway."

Yitzhak was an honorable man, and he saw the world differently than Mathias. Mathias was wealthy because he had made his fortune through cruelty and a willingness to do almost anything to increase his wealth. The thought of an easy robbery, at his expense, did not sit well with him.

"Look, Laurentinus, Caesarea is only a little farther than Capernaum. What are a few more days to you? Aren't you and your men and the Roman state going to be paid handsomely for your work? What's a trip to Caesarea going hurt?" Mathias asked the centurion.

"Disobedience to my commander would mean death to me and my men. Your price is too high, Mathias. Friend of Herod's or no, I will not disobey or question my orders," the centurion said with cautionary tones.

"Would Herod appreciate knowing that one of his oldest friends was not being treated well?" Mathias threatened.

"Enough! I have my orders, and you do well not to question them."

Mathias knew he could not press the centurion anymore, or he could lose the guard he had. He would just have to trust that Yitzhak would be successful with his stretch of the transport. He was a good man, he reassured himself. Then a thought occurred to him, "What if I send along some insurance," he mused. "That's what I need—insurance."

For days Abirami had been sharpening the knife that he carried with him. Its edge had never been so fine. He felt that it needed to be kept in readiness for when he needed it. During that night of hopelessness, he realized why he had been consistently honing his knife. It was for a night such as this. He had asked God to answer him, and he had heard nothing. To a mind filled with despair, the way was clear to commit the coward's deed. Opening his tunic, Abirami raised the razor-edged knife to his chest, resting the tip over his heart, he placed his left hand over the pommel and his right hand over the other. He thought to himself that he would count to three and drive the blade between his ribs and into the soft muscle of his heart. A trickle of blood seeped out from under the point that would be his liberation from emotional pain. He was momentarily mesmerized as he watched the small red dot swell and become a small rivulet down his abdomen. It looked black in the pale light of the single lamp that flickered on the room's only table.

"Put down the knife!" a voice out of the darkness commanded.

Startled, Abirami dropped the knife, and looked around the room.

"Who is it? Who spoke?" Abirami said while still trying to focus his eyes to discover who might be hiding in the dark corners of the room. He picked up the lamp and looked carefully around the room. He checked the two other rooms to find no one but himself in the house. The blood that had run down his chest and belly was already congealing. He looked at it now realizing how close he had been to death. Had he really heard a voice, or was it just the cry of his own conscience warning him of eternal disaster? Whatever it was, he realized God had answered his prayer. If God wanted him alive, then there must still be purpose to his life. With the command to drop the knife had come the beginning of the first glimmer of hope that he had felt in weeks. He went over to the water jar, poured some of it into a basin, and used a cloth to wipe away the streak of blood.

"Thank you for saving me," he said looking up to the ceiling of his home. "It was Your voice who commanded me in my hour of peril to drop my knife. You have kept me alive for a purpose. In the days to come, show me, Adonai, what You would have me do with my life."

CHAPTER THIRTY

Gaspar arrived at the high priest's house riding his favorite mare, Yalda. She was a coal black beauty standing nearly fifteen hands high with a breeding line dating back nearly three centuries. Gaspar tried to ride her every day. Yalda would be sorely missed during the trip to Palestine. She and Gaspar had a special connection. Many was the day where Gaspar entered the stables to ride, the grooms would have Yalda ready, and she would be prancing like a yearling until Gaspar had stroked her nose and hugged her neck. Balzak had chosen Gaspar's robes to coordinate with his transportation as well as with the stunning black saddle trimmed with gold cords. Strands of gold had also been braided into Yalda's mane and tail giving the illusion that mount and master were one. The overall effect was just what Balzak had planned. Rachel watched from her balcony as most of the attendees arrived in sedan chairs. When Gaspar rode up, she found herself catching her breath. Gaspar swung out of his saddle looking like one of the heroes whose stories she had heard told to her as a young girl. Her knees felt weak and she steadied herself on one of the columns of her balcony.

Nazli had walked up behind Rachel only a few moments before and had observed her daughter's reaction to Gaspar's arrival. "He is a splendid specimen of a man, isn't he," she said.

Rachel could only gulp air and nod her head.

Majid, dressed in green and white silk robes, rode up on a bay stallion as mother and daughter saw the two men exchange pleasantries. "Majid looks very handsome tonight also," Nazli commented.

"He does," responded Rachel, but her eyes never left Gaspar.

"We must go down and welcome our guests. Remember that Gaspar should never get too much of your attention tonight. If anyone receives your focus, it must be Majid."

"I'm ready, Mother. You have coached me well. Please don't keep reminding me. It only makes me more nervous."

Nazli smiled as she looked her daughter over from head to toe. The only person who might draw more attention tonight than the young magus was the girl standing before her. "Your whole appearance is exquisite. Every eye will be on you.

Humility and graciousness will win the young man's heart tonight. Relax and be yourself."

"Mother! No more coaching or you will have to have one of the servants carry me down the stairs. My knees are already feeling weak and shaky."

Placing Rachel's arm through her own she walked her daughter down the hall and down the stairs as the guests applauded the arrival of their hostesses.

A stable boy took Yalda's reins after Gaspar had dismounted. Several of Seleucia's available young women made their way over to flirt with the dashing young priest. He was cordial to them all, but could hardly wait for the opportunity to escape their obvious intentions. It was not that he did not like women, it was that he did not like most women. Many times, he found them to be overly predictable and lacking social restraint. Women who came on too strong to him held no appeal whatsoever. His curse was that he was wealthy and good-looking and did not like being treated as such. There had been women in his life who he had friendships with and were intellectually stimulating, but he had never found one with whom he wanted to spend the rest of his life. When he stepped inside the door to Zand's home, Rachel and her mother were making their way down the stairs to the applause of their guests. Gaspar found himself taking a breath when he beheld Rachel for the first time.

The awed expression on Gaspar's face did not escape Nazli's notice. Unless she was hugely mistaken, his perception of Rachel was exactly what her's was of him. "This night is progressing perfectly," she thought. On cue, Zand welcomed Gaspar warmly into their home.

"Have you met my wife and daughter, Gaspar?" Zand continued as mother and daughter came up to join the high priest.

"I have not, but I would like to," Gaspar said, glancing at Rachel and feeling his face lightly flush.

"This is my wife, Nazli, and this, as you might guess, is our daughter Rachel." Zand noticed that his daughter's cheeks had also grown rosy during the introduction, and continued with, "This," grabbing Gaspar's arm, "is Gaspar, one of three of our priests who will be performing a fact-finding expedition to Palestine."

"Father has given mother and me a little background of your trip. It's frightening to think that you will be traveling in Roman controlled territories."

There was no forwardness in Rachel's manner. She merely talked to him as if he was as normal as anyone else in the room. Gaspar was enticed by Zand's daughter, realizing that his mouth had become uncommonly dry. Rasping, he said, "It's not so unnerving when one realizes that Rome needs open roads through our realm as much as we need roads through hers. We are only on a fact-finding quest and are not participating in any activity that would cause Rome to doubt our intents. We are, after all, priests. We should be very safe. Your kind concern is only matched by your stunning beauty." Neither Rachel nor Gaspar were prepared for this last remark. Gaspar wondered where it came from, wishing he could retract the statement. Rachel's cheeks reddened, framing her pretty smile. Demure eyelashes flashed to the floor as she found herself unable to reply.

"You will excuse us, Gaspar, we still have other guests to welcome," Nazli said giving Rachel a way out from responding to Gaspar's flattery.

Zand clapped Gaspar on the shoulder and said, "We are so glad you are here. Make yourself at home."

Try as she might, Rachel could not make eye contact with Gaspar again before she and her parents moved on to other guests. Her embarrassed reaction stole Gaspar's heart. Initially, he had felt foolish about commenting personally after having just met her, but now, long dark eyelashes sheltering deep, dark almond shaped eyes were all that occupied his mind. He determined at that moment that they must speak again before the evening was over.

The table was a large rectangle, filled with appetizers, carafes of wine, and jars of water. It was excellent for entertaining, but awkward for a man who wanted more personalized conversation with a beautiful young woman he had just met. Majid had been seated next to Rachel for the night's dinner—Gaspar directly across from them. Majid could make personal conversation with Rachel—Gaspar could only observe and participate in only the most general of topics.

Few in Seleucia did not know of the handsome, wealthy, young magus, Gaspar. The woman and her husband to his right were completely enamored with Gaspar's life and upcoming trip. The husband, Pesach, fancied himself an astronomer, and was fascinated with Gaspar's findings and theories concerning the new star. Pesha, his wife, found his expedition to Palestine to be one of the bravest adventures she had ever personally heard about. In any other situation Gaspar would have enjoyed their questions and insights, but tonight he could not keep his focus off the opposite side of the table. Gaspar was unimpressed with the flirtatious habits of many of the young girls of Seleucia. Rachel was not that way. She had a deportment that was graceful, intelligent, and warm. She exhibited no giddiness; no exhibitionism. In every way she was the epitome of Gaspar's idea of how a woman should present herself. The more he saw of her, the more he wanted to know this engaging woman.

Zand and Nazli observed Gaspar observing their daughter. Both were amused to see their scheme working so well. Majid had been the perfect foil for tonight's conspiracy. He was loud and boorish, giving Rachel the perfect partner to display her exquisite feminine characteristics. Gaspar's face read like a scroll. The more he saw, the more desperately he desired to acquaint himself with their daughter.

"You have done quite well for yourself even though you are still a young man," Rachel said to Majid.

"Not to brag, but my father's holdings have done quite nicely under my management," he responded too loudly for decorum, causing everyone around him to turn in his direction. "The Greeks have a story about a king whose very touch could change any object to gold. I believe that Ahura-Mazda has blessed me with such an ability," he continued.

Gaspar could hardly believe that anyone could be so pompous. He felt embarrassment for Majid's self-aggrandizement, and for Rachel who must be dying wondering how to respond.

Rachel's response was scarcely audible to Gaspar. Looking Majid square in the eye she said, "The good god is generous, but he also takes from those who do not deserve his favor."

"I have thought of that," Majid said, increasing once again the volume of the conversation. "I don't know of anyone in Seleucia who gives more to charities than myself."

At this, Gaspar could contain himself no longer. "Good Majid, the king is looking for a generous subject to fund our expedition to Palestine. Might I be bold enough to suggest that you contact him and offer to underwrite our travels. For one such as you, it would be a mere trifle. I beg your forgiveness for bringing this up now, but could it be that the good god brought us together tonight, the night before my departure, for such a serendipitous meeting as this?"

Gaspar had not spoken loudly, but every person in the room heard his proposal. Conversations decreased as everyone waited for Majid's reply. Gaspar felt Rachel's eyes upon him. He desired nothing more than to meet those sweet eyes with his own, but to do so would have betrayed his desire to put this braggart in his place.

Rachel's silky voice broke the silence. Placing her hand upon Majid's arm, she said with widened, concerned eyes, "Perhaps that is an unfair sum to request. Even to a wealthy man such as yourself, that is an enormous amount of money."

The hook was set. Rachel had played along with the ruse as if she had been an accomplice. Majid would have to comply after his blustering to her before, or suffer untold humiliation.

"No. . ., Rachel," Majid stammered forcing a smile to his face, "That. . . that is exactly the kind of investment I was talking about." Gathering momentum in his lie, he continued, "It is the very thing I wish all wealthy people would do with their riches. I had pondered this before tonight, and Gaspar's bringing it to my attention only confirms what I had already considered."

Rachel patted his arm, looked into his eyes, and nodded her head as if she bought everything that he was saying. In fact, she was so convincing that Gaspar became unsure whether she had played along with his setup, or had truly believed Majid's boasting. Could a woman like Rachel really be taken in by a person like Majid? He glanced across the table once more. Rachel's demeanor had not changed. She was respectfully listening to Majid drone on about the responsibilities of all wealthy people. Gaspar wondered if he had called the man's bluff or given him more fodder for boasting.

"Your enterprise has absolutely captured the imaginations of my wife and me," Pesach said interrupting his thoughts, "Do you have any other insights from the Hebrew Scriptures concerning this amazing star?"

The rest of the evening was filled with conversation about the star and his upcoming travels, but no topic drew him very far from his preoccupation of Rachel's own radiance. Not being able to sit and talk with her was making him miserable. "I'm leaving tomorrow for who knows how long," he thought. "I need more time to get to know this incredible woman."

The evening was drawing to a close, and Gaspar had not spoken with Rachel. His desperation at his circumstances made him decide to take drastic measures. Excusing himself from the conversation with Pesach and Pesha, he walked to the head of the table, leaned down to Zand's ear and said, "I will need to excuse myself soon, may I speak to you for a moment?"

Nazli's eyes rounded and a smile slipped across her face. Rachel had seen Gaspar excuse himself from the other guests around him and had watched his movement to the head of the table. It took all of her resolve to focus on her conversation with the woman on her other side who was an old friend of her family.

"Of course, let us move into the next room," Zand said giving a side glance to his wife who was now in a full smile.

Closing the door behind them, Zand said, "How may I help you, Gaspar?"

"Let me come straight to the point. I would like to talk

with Rachel before the night is over. If she agrees, may I have a few moments with her?"

"This is unusual, Gaspar. What could possibly be your purpose in such a meeting?"

Gaspar was squirming. He knew he sounded ridiculous with such a request, but he had to speak to Rachel to get a sense of her feelings for him. "Your reverence, Rachel is an extraordinary woman. You know that I leave tomorrow for who knows how long, and I want time to get to know her before I leave. I now it sounds outlandish, but I could not leave tonight without at least making an attempt to get to know her."

Zand thought back to the first time he saw Nazli. There was never a time he could remember when he himself was not smitten. He had known from the beginning of their relationship that there was no one else like Nazli.

"You will need a chaperone," Zand said snapping back to the moment. " At this hour it will have to be either my wife or me."

"If you would agree to that, I would be indebted to you," Gaspar said hastily.

Hardly able to wait to let Nazli know what had transpired, Zand said, "Have a seat. Give me a few minutes to see what I can arrange."

Gaspar sat down and tried to look casual, realizing he would be more at ease before the king than waiting for what would take place in the next few minutes.

Nazli was bursting with curiosity, and poor Rachel could do nothing but play the good hostess engaging in conversation with the guests around her. Zand's entering the room alone caused both women's eyebrows to raise. He sat down as if nothing had happened, leaned over to his wife, and whispered, "He wants to talk to Rachel before he leaves tonight. I have never seen a young man more love-struck than he."

"What did he say?" asked Nazli.

"Only that he could not leave on a trip this long and not have time to at least speak to Rachel. I told him that either you or I would need to chaperone if this was to happen tonight. It's proper that I bid farewell to our guests, are you comfortable acting as chaperone?" he smiled slyly.

Returning his smugness she said, "I would not miss it for the world. You can stay here with the other guests, and I will take Rachel to meet Gaspar in the other room by way of the kitchen." Zand gave her a questioning look and she replied, "She needs to be warned as to what she's headed for."

Zand nodded. After a few moments, Nazli casually walked over to her daughter and whispered in her ear.

In the adjoining room, Gaspar was up and pacing. "What have I done?" he chastised himself. "This is a ridiculous idea. But if I hadn't made my move, who knows whether someone like Majid wouldn't slip in and win Rachel's hand before I had a chance. Still, what right have I to even presume that I have a chance?" His self-talk went on like this until he heard the door on his left creek ever so slightly open to reveal Rachel. There, in the solitude of a room with no one else than she, Gaspar felt the weakness in his knees that Rachel had experienced only a few hours before. She was dazzling. The soft coloring of her cheeks only enhanced her irresistibility. They both looked upon each other unable to speak at first.

"She's in the other room," Rachel's voice broke the silence.

"What?"

"My mother said that she thinks it's fine if she stays in the other room," Rachel corrected, dropping those lovely lashed eyelids that Gaspar had already come to cherish.

"I see. Um, thank you for agreeing to see me."

"You're welcome."

"W- would you like to sit down?"

"Yes, yes I would. I feel a little weak in the knees," she said wishing she had stopped her mouth sooner.

"You too? I can hardly stand."

"He's as nervous as me," she thought, and then said, "Here, let's sit on this couch." They both laughed uncomfortably as they sat down.

"This was a marvelous party. Thank you for inviting me. I'm grateful that I had this opportunity to meet you."

"I have wanted to meet you," she said disclosing more than she meant to.

"I leave tomorrow on the expedition, and I didn't want to leave without having the opportunity to talk to you."

"Why?"

"I've never met anyone like you," now Gaspar was wishing that he had not divulged so much information.

"How so?"

He was feeling like she was pushing him to say things that should not be revealed this early in their relationship, but if the truth was told, he wanted her to continue on in this vein. "I never knew you before tonight, but I feel as if you and I have known each other forever."

Rachel gulped in air. She had hoped to hear him say things like this, never really thinking that he ever would. What he said, she felt.

Turning toward her on the couch, he said, "And you. Why did you agree to see me?"

Turning to him, she looked down at his hands. They were good strong hands, she thought. "I wanted to see you before you left," she said.

"Why"

"Oh, this isn't fair," she sputtered. "You'll make me tell all."

"Why, Rachel?" he prodded again, glad to be the one asking questions now.

She loved hearing him say her name. "Because I don't know anyone else who is like you." She wondered if she had said too much. Surely, everything that she and her mother had planned was now undone. Her eyelids dropped.

Taking her hands in his, Gaspar said, "And I have never seen or met any woman who makes me want to know her like I want to know you. I thought my heart would leap out of my chest when I saw you descend the stairs with your mother earlier this evening."

Gaspar lifted her chin. Tears pooled at the lower edges of her eyes. Tears trickled down her cheeks.

"So what do we do now?"

"I have to go soon. I want to come back to you and discuss certain matters."

"What might those be?"

"No, some things cannot be discussed tonight. When I come back, our time away will have either strengthened our feelings for one another, or made us realize our emotions got away from us. I can't imagine the latter, but I think it's prudent that we wait to talk about those other matters. You are worth waiting for, dear Rachel."

"Prudent?" she said teasingly. "Well, if it's prudent, I would like to say that I would like to see you again."

For a moment, they looked into each other's eyes. Rachel's eyes lit up as a smile creased her face.

"What? Why are you smiling at me like that?"

"I was thinking about how you played poor Majid—not that he didn't deserve it."

Laughing, Gaspar said, "And what about you?" Then mimicking Rachel, "Even to a wealthy merchant like yourself, that is an enormous amount of money!"

"Okay, I played along," she said. "I did love the way you put him in his place without disgracing him—even if he deserved that too."

"You were so kind to him when he didn't deserve your kindness. Your tact only made me want to know you more."

Rachel became sober. "I did what seemed to be right."

"You are a rare woman, Rachel." He drew her up to stand with him. Leaning in to kiss her Nazli interrupted his

95

intentions by walking into the room. "It looks to me like I should have stayed in the room."

Rachel ran to her mother. "Oh, mother. We have had the most amazing conversation."

"You were talking?" she said as her eyebrows rose.

Gaspar blushed.

Rachel chastised, "Mother!"

"They're all gone," said Zand walking into the room.

The four looked at one another as if to say, "Now what?"

"If I may," began Gaspar, "I would like to explain what Rachel and I talked about. We have discovered that we have similar feelings for each other, and I would like your permission," addressing himself to Rachel's parents, "to talk to you about matters that might affect both Rachel and me when I return from Palestine. Please trust me when I say tonight is not the time to discuss what I have to say. I do want you both to know that I hold Rachel in highest regard and thank you for this opportunity to meet with her."

The rest of the evening was spent in the warmest conversation Gaspar could ever remember having with the high priest. When he left, a tearful, happy Rachel walked him to the door.

"I can't help wishing we had met before this night," Rachel said.

"I can't help cherishing the fact that we met at all. You bring me great joy, Rachel. I shall miss you while rejoicing that I will return and be with you again."

They held each other's hands wishing that the night would stop in its unremitting march toward dawn. Gaspar pulled her hands to his lips and kissed them before he pulled away, leaving her to watch him ride off. At the gate he turned to see her still watching him until he went out of sight.

He said quietly, "I shall miss you, bright star."

CHAPTER THIRTY-ONE

The idea of entrusting a large sum of his gold and silver to a group of country peasants did not sit well with Mathias. He wanted to make sure that he did all that he could to protect his savings. That's why this meeting with a more worldly character was important to him. He needed someone who could protect his investment in case Yitzhak and his *bumpkins* failed in their task. True, Yitzhak had a reason to make sure that the gold reached Pan's temple safely because his payment for the livestock he had delivered to Mathias was included in this shipment. That was not enough insurance for Mathias. He had gotten where he was in life because he did not trust other people. He was not going to lose what he had worked so hard to acquire simply because he had all of a sudden changed his philosophy of life. Distrust had been a good mistress to him, and he wasn't ready to give her up for a lesser known lover.

Mathias had met Satanas a few years before and liked the fact that the man thought like him. He had sent his servant, Basil, to outline the details with Satanas. Basil was a giant of a man, easily seven feet tall. To say that he was unattractive would have been a generous compliment. He had a dull voice that, along with his great size and features, gave him the appearance of being slow witted, but he was anything but stupid. His keen mind and great strength had been an advantage to Mathias more than a few times.

Mathias had become innovative in how he used Basil's natural characteristics. Since people assumed the leviathan was dull-witted, he had taught Basil how to use that as an advantage over others. More than one unwary adversary was bested because he underestimated Basil's mental abilities. Basil and Mathias were a good match. Neither cared for the affections of humanity—they were bottom-line-men-of-business. Those areas of business where Matthias did not want to dirty his hands were Basil's specialty.

Satanas had gotten where he was as an agent of criminal activity because he had learned to be a reader of people's character. When Basil and Satanas met, it was truly a match of criminal professionals. The meeting took place along the western edge of a fertile plain, Gennesaret, that borders the northwest coast of the Sea of Galilee.

Exaggerating the slowness of his verbal delivery, as Mathias had taught him, Basil began the meeting saying, "My master – wanted me – to meet – with – you. Can – he trust – you?"

Satanas was just recovering from the enormous size of the man, and now hearing him speak made him wonder if he was dealing with the intellectual faculty of a small child. The first impression that Basil presented was what one would expect from a giant, ugly man. The image was too perfect. Satanas was immediately placed on his guard.

"I would never treat your master in a manner that would circumvent the admiration I have for him," Satanas responded.

"That's – good. I don't like people – who are – bad – to my master."

"I would venture that your Master's and my meeting was extremely serendipitous. I believe we will benefit from one another's ingenuity," Satanas assured him.

"You both – are smart – men."

Satanas had gained the knowledge that he was seeking. Basil was much more intelligent than what the big man let on. The giant did not flinch at the vocabulary Satanas had used with him. His guess was that he should be careful not to underestimate the giant's intellectual capabilities. He would need to proceed as if he was speaking to Mathias himself.

"What is it that Mathias says will be beneficial to us both?"

"He needs you – to – guard – his guard, Huh, huh, huh," the big man laughed as if both statement and laugh were well rehearsed and not made up on the spot.

"I don't understand," Satanas responded honestly.

Basil went on to explain the plans that Mathias had made with the Roman guard and with Yitzhak in Caesarea Philippi. "He wants you – and some of – your men to – follow the – Caesarean guard from – Capernaum to – Caesarea. If they – need help – help them. Master says – he will pay you good."

"So all I need to do is shadow this group that is guarding the treasure until it reaches Caesarea, and Mathias will pay me *good* for doing that?"

"Thaaat's it."

Satanas extended his hand and watched it disappear in the grasp of Basil's. Basil held Satanas' hand tightly, telling him, "If you - betray my master - in any way, you will have me - to deal with, and you don't want - to have me to - deal with."

Satanas withdrew his hand, rubbing it, as a few more details were discussed before the two men went their separate directions.

Up the road about a mile, Satanas met with Ezri.

"How did it go?"

"No news that my sources hadn't already told me. There is a new twist in our adventure, though," Satanas said looking smug.

"What is it?" Ezri asked, his curiosity peaking.

Satanas laughed out loud, "He wants to pay us to be a backup to his guard. And, get this: the guard is led by the man whose purse you returned in Caesarea."

"You're kidding!"

"I'm not. I'm finding it hard to understand why a provincial, who is as clean as they come, could get caught up with a person like Mathias. The man, from what I've heard, is totally unmerciful in business dealings. He is not the kind of man you would think Yitzhak would be involved with."

"Yitzhak. I must remember that name," Ezri said. "without him, I never would have met you."

"Perhaps. I have the feeling that destiny was going to have our paths cross no matter what the circumstances. The fact that Yitzhak knows you and trusts you—we can use that in my plan."

The two started riding north. "I'm hungry," Satanas said. "If we hurry, we can have supper in Capernaum." They kicked their horses into a canter.

Satanas had spotted in Ezri what Sophia had. He had natural abilities and had a disposition that fed on peril. The boy was someone for whom he had been looking for a long time. Ezri had potential. With the right mentor, he could make himself and his partner a lot of money. Sophia had done well in bringing the boy into her confidence. This job they were going to do for Mathias was going to make them rich, giving them the kind of start up capital they needed to do even grander crimes. Satanas was hungry, and it was hard to dream big when his stomach was empty.

CHAPTER THIRTY-TWO

Gaspar realized that he could have just as well spent the night talking to Rachel for all the sleep he got. When he did sleep, he kept seeing images of her dark, long lashed eyes, her scent, and the low smooth tone of her voice. He would then awaken and wonder if he and Rachel had truly confessed their attraction to one another. The idea that he had seriously contemplated a celibate lifestyle twelve hours before seemed foreign to him now. He could not help wondering if his world could be turned upside down so quickly by the beauty and presence of a single woman?

The night went no better for Rachel. Having the advantage of not leaving the next morning on a long trip, she did not try to sleep. She and Nazli had spent more than an hour rehashing what had taken place during her time with Gaspar.

"It sounds like we had a successful conspiracy," teased Nazli.

"I feel like we manipulated him, Mother. Would I have ever interested him if we hadn't set him up?"

"Listen to me, daughter. We gave him the opportunity to meet you. You did nothing false to lure him. You were only your wonderful self. The man that we hoped he is took over from there. Do not feel guilt. You have won for yourself a marvelous husband. Never doubt that when he returns, he will make you his wife."

Eventually, they were talked out, and Nazli kissed and hugged her daughter good-night. The remainder of Rachel's night was spent on her balcony watching the star and remembering looking into Gaspar's honest, compassionate eyes. She dreamed of what it would be like to be married to him. She thanked the good god over and over again that Gaspar had desired her as much as she did him. "Oh, how long these next few months are going to be," she thought to herself.

Well before Gaspar was ready to leave to meet Melchior and Balthasar, Balzak came into his room to find out how the dinner party went at the high priest's house. Gaspar was not sleeping well anyway, so Balzak's intrusion was a welcomed relief from tossing and turning.

"It went very well, but I know that you are going to

chastise me for what happened," Gaspar began.

"If it went well, for what reason could I chastise you?" Balzak said trying to remain calm.

"I met a woman," Gaspar said not knowing how to say all that needed to be explained.

"At a dinner party! Imagine, meeting a woman at a dinner party," Balzak mocked.

"Come on Balzak, this is hard enough without your making fun of me."

"I'm sorry, Master. Please go on."

"The high priest has a daughter whose name is Rachel. She is the most exquisite woman I have ever met. Her voice is like the pure tones of a harp. She's intelligent, and gracious, and her laughter makes me want to dance and run and. . ." noticing Balzak's face caused Gaspar to stop mid-sentence—the servant's mouth was agape in the most ridiculous expression. Gaspar's next comment was only, "What?"

"I-I-I've never seen you like this. She must be remarkable," Balzak said, honestly taken back by Gaspar's effusion.

"I sat across from her at the table. Majid, son of Sevent, was seated next to her. I have never seen a man so self-absorbed. She was the perfect hostess. Never once did she show any sign that he was rude or inappropriate. She engaged in conversation with him as much as any other around her. A woman of her quality could have easily ignored him and no one would have thought the worse of her, but she was absolutely heroic in her tolerance of the man.

"Before the night ended, I wanted to talk to her alone, but the evening was rushing by too quickly, and I knew I had to be well-rested for my trip. I excused myself from the other guests around me and went over to where Zand was sitting and asked to speak to him privately. We went into an adjoining room where I told him I wanted to speak to his daughter. He seemed a little surprised but acquiesced to my proposal." Gaspar then gave him a detailed blow by blow of what he and Rachel talked about and of his own promise to come back and speak to Zand and Nazli officially about their daughter.

"Well, no one can ever say that you work slowly," Balzak said smiling. Then as an afterthought said, "Did you kiss her?"

"Balzak, her lips are like those of a goddess. I was just about going to when her mother came into the room and interrupted the kiss." Balzak was giving that strange expression again. Gaspar stopped and said succinctly, "I kissed her hands."

Balzak took on a smile that lasted from that point until he waved good-bye later that morning to Gaspar, Cyrus, and Amehlech. "Don't worry about a thing. Cephas and I will ensure that everything is well taken care of in your absence. I will look in on Rachel from time to time also. Good luck, young master," Balzak shouted—his head shaking side to side as he did so causing his hair to do that funny thing it did catching first one side of his nose, and then the other. Seeing it, the three travelers laughed out loud in spite of themselves.

Rachel had bathed and readied herself early for the day. She begged her father to ride with her to the city gates to see Gaspar off.

"I don't know, Rachel, I'm not sure it would be seemly for you to do so. You've only just made the man's acquaintance," Zand said shaking his head.

"Father, he has almost said outright that he will come back and ask for my hand in marriage when he returns," Rachel said in exasperation.

"A young lady must not appear to be too forward," Nazli cautioned.

Rachel whined, "Mother! You're supposed to be on my side."

Zand and Nazli looked at one.

Shrugging in submission, Zand said, "No long good-byes, young lady. . ." was all he could get out before Rachel threw both arms around him and said, "We should leave soon. I'll tell the stable boy to get the horses ready."

Nazli stood back with her fists on her hips shaking her head at the two of them.

Surprise was written clearly all over Gaspar's face when his little entourage rode up to the city gates only to see Zand and Rachel waiting for him.

"Why are you here?" Gaspar said happily, dismounting, and running over to Rachel.

"And I thought you were a clever man," said Rachelle causing Zand to laugh out loud.

"I am honored to have you both here. Excuse me, but I was just so startled to see you. Seeing you one last time before I go is like a blessing directly from Ahura-Mazda himself," he said, taking Rachel's hand.

Seeing the two together, Zand realized that being here was good for both of them. The way Gaspar looked at his daughter, he knew that his wife had chosen well for Rachel.

Turning to Zand, Gaspar said, "Your reverence, I cannot convey to you how much it touches me that you have brought Rachel to see me off. Thank you. You are truly a priest of the good god."

Zand was taken back saying only, "Gaspar—any man

would do the same for his daughter." To himself he thought, this is a young man of humility. Maybe I have been too harsh in my perceptions.

Turning to Rachel, Gaspar said, "You have my heart. A moment will not pass that I won't be thinking of you and your sweetness. Good-bye."

Tears welled in her eyes, and she blinked them away. Emotion had taken her voice away. She could only reach out for his hands to hold them one more time. Gaspar grasped them both kissing each as if they were the most precious objects in the world. "Good-bye, my love."

Rachel put her hands to her face and could only squeak out a weak, "Bye."

Gaspar's camel hoisted to a standing position and Gaspar led his band of adventurers through the gates and out of sight.

CHAPTER THIRTY-THREE

The train of camels and horses stood in readiness for the expedition as Gaspar and his small contingent joined with them.

"I thought that you would have been here much sooner," Melchior interrogated.

"I had a terrible night's sleep, and I have news for you that I will tell you about when we are off," replied Gaspar. Riding up to Balthasar, he said, "Good morning. I apologize if I have delayed you so long."

"You are here right when you were supposed to be. Melchior has been as impatient as a woman getting ready to give birth. He'll be fine once we're on our way."

Before they left, Melchior had the king's guard, the Magi, and their personal servants, join in a circle, and said, "I believe we are all part of a great fact finding excursion that will reveal great truth about the nature of what we believe as the followers of the Ahura-Mazda. I know that most of you are here because of the wishes of your masters, or the decree of the king. I know that I speak for all three of us magi when I say we are honored to have you along for this important exploration. Commander Vahumisa, thank you ahead of time for the presence of you and your troops. We all feel safer knowing that you and your men are traveling with us."

Vahumisa grabbed the hilt of his sword and bowed his head in acknowledgement of Melchior's recognition.

"Join with me now," Melchior continued, "as we ask Ahura-Mazda to bless this expedition and that he would help us learn the truth however we may find it." Melchior then prayed a long and eloquent prayer over the expedition.

As everyone was mounting their animals, Gaspar spoke quietly with Melchior, "I thought you were struggling with belief in the good god. Why did you pray so fervently to him?"

"We have superstitious royal guards here to protect us. It is better they think that they are defending the priests of the god whom they honor than three agnostics who are not sure," he said, winking.

Gaspar shook his head smiling at his friend's pragmatism.

Vahumisa and his second in command took the lead of the caravan. The other eight dispersed themselves two-by-two

104

throughout the rest of the train, with two bringing up the rear. The three magi rode behind Vahumisa and his man.

"That was a kind pronouncement, Melchior, I would have expected nothing less from our astute and learned leader," Balthasar said.

"Yes," agreed Gaspar, "I don't think I have ever heard him deliver a more eloquent prayer."

"Be careful, my friends, Camels feet do better on dry ground than on slippery deposits. We would hate for one of our caravan to have an accident because of your fetid flattery," Melchior's response caused both magi to laugh.

"No one can pile it on like you, but we shall be careful." Balthasar said continuing to chortle.

The caravan moved along with only the padding of camel feet to be heard, and an occasional chuckle from behind them. Gaspar suspected it was because of the antics of Cyrus and Amehlech.

"This is going to be the adventure of my life," said Balthasar. "I can't tell you both how happy I am right now."

"You are easily made happy, my friend, but I share your sense of adventure and joy," Melchior agreed.

Gaspar rode along with a slight smile and distant look. His mind appeared to be somewhere else.

"And you, young one, do you share Balthasar's and my excitement," Melchior broke in.

"I do, and I agree that this is a marvelous enterprise. I am pleased to be here with you both today searching for the truth that is going to come to us. But something happened last night that has added to my happiness," Gaspar responded.

"You said you had something to tell us. Have at it, boy," boomed Melchior.

"Perhaps he still needs time to process his thoughts before he tells us, Melchior," suggested Balthasar.

"No, I don't need to process anymore. I only wish I could stop processing. I met the high priest's daughter, Rachel, last night." The two magi looked at each other with surprise. Continuing, Gaspar said, "I know it is strange, but I get the feeling that Zand wanted me to meet his daughter before I left on our excursion. I guess the truth is I don't care what his part was in last night's dinner, I can only say that I have met the woman who will be my wife. I can't get her off my mind."

There was a brief silence, and Balthasar said, "Tell us about the evening." Gaspar needed no coaxing. He told every detail that he observed and heard. Even impatient Melchior rode along seemingly hanging on every word, making the old Persian maxim true: *Even old men revel in the story of young men's love.*

Gaspar finished all that he had to say and looked at the two magi riding on his left side.

"Well," he said.

"I would say that you're in love," Balthasar responded, smiling. "I would say that Zand and his wife may have placed you where you could observe their daughter's outward and inward beauty. I would also say that you did a marvelous job of observing. That's what we magi do best, isn't it?"

"I suppose you're right," chuckled Gaspar.

"She is beautiful," piped in Melchior, "and I have never heard an ill word spoken of her. If she is the one you are to marry, apparently you have chosen well."

Sensing that it was time to talk about more pressing matters, Gaspar said, "I have drawn us off our purpose long enough. Tell me Melchior, what route are we to take to Palestine?"

For as long as people inhabited what the Greeks called Mesopotamia, the Euphrates had been the source of life for all who lived beside her shores. Along with its sister river, the Tigris, the two rivers had created the richest farming environment in the world. Both were natural waterways conveying trade and transportation for their populations. When they overflowed their banks, they left rich deposits that enhanced farmers' crop growing abilities. For two hundred miles, Gaspar and his friends followed the banks of the Euphrates to the fortress trading center of Dura-Europus. This border city had a strong military presence meant to dissuade any intentions Rome might have to use it as a staging point for military conquest of the region. Merchants of all lands were generally welcomed here because of the tax that was excised on all caravans entering her gates.

Their travel had been unremarkable except for the scenic variety they experienced along their way. There had been broad plains of wheat and barley. Orchards filled with pistachio trees, date palms, and citrus trees peppered their route. Vegetable farms displaying a broad array of crops were evidence of the richness of the Euphrates fed soil. Occasionally, domestic lands were interrupted with large tracks of wooded area and sporadic cliffs rose stunningly from the Euphrates shore. Fishing villages were all along the travelers' route. They could hear the fishermen's songs as they cleaned their nets by day. What historians would someday call the Fertile Crescent, Parthia had taken full advantage to advance the empire's wealth. At night, the mysterious star appeared to constantly move ahead of them, drawing them ever closer to Palestine. For eight days, the magi and their party enjoyed the beauty of the countryside before arriving mid-afternoon in Dura-Europus, a city that was truly part Roman and part Parthian.

The temple in Dura-Europus was a mammoth structure to Zeus, but included within it's walls were partitioned chapels to many of the gods of the Greek and Mesopotamian pantheon. As a regional temple, the three magi, known primarily as wisemen in Roman territories, were expected to sacrifice and worship there upon arrival. While the wisemen showed their respect to the temple and its gods, the rest of the caravan set up camp close by but outside the city's gates. Vahumisa paid both the city tax on caravans and a visit to the commander of the city. Phraataces had sent a message with him charging the commander to gather information on Roman troop movements in Syria and Cappadocia. Vahumisa was to collect intelligence as he traveled through Palestine, delivering information to the commander on his return trip. He was sure there were Roman spies in Dura-Europus, and he knew he must be careful to play the role of a non-military guard lest enemy eyes might be observing his movements. Careful though he was, he had been observed being saluted by one of his men in the manner of the Parthian army. From that point on he had been followed.

CHAPTER THIRTY-FOUR

"Master, after meeting with this man Satanas, I would not trust him as a backup cover for the gold shipment," Basil said. "I poked around some, and people suspect that he may be someone who is involved in a lot of the criminal activity around Galilee, Syria, and Paneas. Why don't you give me a few men who we can trust and let me be the added cover for the shipment."

"You've done your job well, Basil," Matthias reassured him. "I *will* be giving you trusted men to do just that. I need a man like Satanas to make sure that we know who we're dealing with. If it is anybody, I know that it will be Satanas who will try to steal my gold. By including him in my plans, we know who to watch. Having Satanas connected, all the other would-be thieves will stay away, not wanting to risk reprisals from him. I have effectively chosen who will be our concern."

A freakish smile spread across Basil's face. "I should have known not to worry. You are always one step ahead of the opposition."

Mathias allowed himself the satisfaction of an infrequent smile. "I would love to be there when Satanas is blindsided by his own plans," he thought. To Basil he said, "When this business is all over, perhaps we will take a trip to Rome."

Basil nodded his head in approval, knowing his master did not go anywhere without his trusted bodyguard.

Whether Sophia was involved in Satanas' plots or not, her home was a common meeting place for his criminal strategies. Satanas, Sophia, and Ezri sat in the cool morning shade of her courtyard working on the details of their felonious plans.

"Yitzhak is putting his band together for the protection of Mathias' shipment." Looking at Ezri, Satanas continued, "You must visit him today and ask him for work. It will be attractive to him to have a strong young man that he already knows he can trust to be part of his force. Make sure he sees an abundance of modesty and hard work once you are hired. You must appear beyond reproach in his eyes to protect our plans and yourself once this is all over."

"As soon as we are finished here, I will ride over to talk to him. I will be the picture of loyalty," Ezri beamed.

"Satanas, am I to have a part in this venture of yours?" asked Sophia.

"Yours is to be the most important of all. I have no mistaken understanding that Mathias' ugly, brute bodyguard will be watching our every move. You are to be his distraction. It will not be a pretty job, but it will be immensely important to the success of our scheme," Satanas explained. He had described Basil to Sophia before. She was no Aphrodite, but she did possess a matronly sort of beauty.

"For this prize, I would flirt with the Cyclopes himself," she said mirthfully.

"I'm not sure that Cyclopes wouldn't be the better looking of the two," Satanas laughed derisively.

"No matter. A man like that has never experienced the affections of a woman. It only makes my task the easier."

"I'm glad it's you and not me," said Ezri.

"And so is Basil," remarked Satanas. "Now listen, the two of you. Nothing can proceed until Ezri secures work and finds out the route that Yitzhak plans to take. Sophia, we need to put you in place to meet Basil. Time is of the essence. Do either of you have questions about what needs to be done?" Both co-conspirators nodded their heads. "Good. Ezri go and come back with good news."

Basil had returned with his men to the eastern shore of Galilee where the city of Hippos resided. His intention was to move into the area undetected so he and his men had freedom to move about. Unbeknownst to him, Satanas had had him followed. The day after he reached Hippos, Sophia was placed to spring her deception. Basil's men were camped outside of town, and he had stayed the night before in an inn near the marketplace so he could bring back provisions by mid-morning. Satanas had planted one of his men, Noam, at a vegetable stand where their drama was to take place. Sophia watched Basil move from stand to stand until he reached the vegetable stand where Noam waited. She moved in and started inspecting the produce. Basil picked up an onion sniffed it as his eyes met Sophia's. She smiled kindly at him and went on about her business.

Basil had two large baskets that could be attached to either side of his horse. He began filling them with onions, carrots, lentils, beans, beets, turnips and radishes.

"Oh, my goodness," remarked Sophia, "don't buy this produce. The vender across the square has much better vegetables to choose from." She placed her hand on Basil's, smiling into his eyes.

"Get out of here and let two men conduct their business," yelled Noam, the fake vender, slapping her with the back of his hand as he spoke.

"Hey, leave the lady alone. She was only trying to help," said Basil, grabbing Noam's arm in his powerful grasp, causing him to wince with pain.

Sophia fell to the ground biting down on the inside of her mouth, letting the blood drool out of the side of her mouth. She laid there unmoving waiting for Basil to help her to her feet. The big man was in unaccustomed territory. Never had he been a woman's protector before. He dropped the man's arm and knelt down to check on Sophia's condition.

"Are you all right?" he said.

Sophia placed her hand once again on his, pretending to have trouble getting up. Doing what was easiest for him to do, he gathered her in his arms and easily lifted her up. This action surprised Sophia enough that she almost broke character. Catching herself, she affected a swoon.

"I didn't know that you and the lady were together," stammered Noam. "You can have all the vegetables you want. I'm sorry I struck your wife."

"She's not my wife and we're not together," rejoined Basil. "I've only just met the woman."

Sophia, still feigning unconsciousness, moaned, put her arm around Basil's neck and nuzzled her face into his neck. Basil, very much outside his area of expertise, carried Sophia over to a tree and laid her in the shade. By now, several women had come over to see what the commotion was. One woman brought water and gently poured it over Sophia's forehead.

Blinking her eyes Sophia looked up at Basil and said, "Thank you for your kindness, I'm fine now." She stood to get up, but stumbled as she did so. Basil reached out a hand and caught her by the forearm.

"I feel so foolish. You have been so good to me. I wish there was something I could do to repay your kindness," she said, looking longingly into the giant's eyes.

"No, no, no. It was nothing. You were only trying to help me and that merchant was out of line doing what he did. I only did what seemed right at the time."

At this Sophia burst into tears. "It has been so long since someone treated me with so much respect," she said through sobs.

"Tell you what," Basil said grasping for something to say, "why don't you help me pick out the rest of the food I need for me and my men."

"Gladly," she said, wiping her eyes with her shawl. She grabbed his wrist and dragged him around the market picking out all that he would need. At one point, Basil asked why he should pay more for one pomegranate at one stand than at the one right next to it. She laughed, grabbed him by the arm, and hugged her head to his elbow saying, "Because the cheaper one is rotten inside." He didn't believe her and broke open the cheaper one. Sure enough, it was rotting. In spite of his distrust of almost everyone, Basil found himself liking this woman, not wanting to part with her presence. Never in his life had a woman shown any interest in him and it felt good to be friendly with her. Sophia's gaiety was infectious. She had done her part. Basil would be eating out of her hand by the end of the day.

Ezri rode up to Yitzhak's compound located just outside of Caesarea. Before Ezri had left Sophia's home, he and Satanas had rehearsed a response for every scenario they thought Ezri could encounter. Going over what he would say had added to the natural comfort he felt in these types of situations. A servant met him at the gate of the courtyard.

"I understand that your master is looking for men who are not afraid of work," Ezri said confidently looking the servant in the eye.

"May I tell my master who calls on him?" the servant queried.

"I am Ezri," he said plainly.

The servant told Ezri to wait at the gate until he returned. Shortly, he came back telling Ezri that his master was not hiring that day, and turned to return to the house.

"Wait," Ezri said, "I have news that your master must hear before he leaves to bring the shipment of gold from Caesarea."

The servant eyed him cautiously, saying, "Wait here."

This time when he returned Yitzhak was leading the way.

"Come with me," Yitzhak said, leading Ezri into a room in the house where two burley servants stood. He closed the door behind Ezri after they both entered the room. "Have a seat," he said, directing Ezri to a chair opposite his own. The two servants continued to stand, watching Ezri with obvious distrust.

"How did you come to know about our shipment?"

"Sir, a few days ago I made a delivery in Hippos for a business man in Bethsaida. I stopped at a local inn there to have dinner. While I was eating, I overheard a giant of a man discussing with a few other men how they were going to steal a shipment that you had undertaken to protect. I know you to be an honest man, and thought that I should warn you. You have been generous with me in the past, and I thought that I could return your kindness by helping you protect your shipment."

Yitzhak eyed the young man carefully. "You are that

young man who recovered my stolen purse in the market a few months back, aren't you?"

"Yes, sir, and you were extremely generous with me."

"I see," said Yitzhak continuing to study Ezri. "Remind me of your name."

"Ezri."

"Tell me, Ezri, what did this giant of a man look like."

"I have never seen a man so large. I would guess that I would come mid way up the man's abdomen. He had a ferocious voice and a terrifying face. His arms and legs and neck were thick as tree trunks. The plate from which he ate was dwarfed by the size of his hands. I have never in my life been so afraid of a man simply because of his looks," Ezri said in mock fear. The truth was that he had never seen Basil—trusting the description Satanas had supplied for him.

"You are describing the personal guard of Matthias of Jericho—the man whose gold I am to protect. The giant's name is Basil, and he is ruthless and frightening. I had always believed the man to be completely loyal. His involvement in any kind of subterfuge makes our task more difficult and dangerous. Did you hear any of the plan?"

"He said something about a Roman detail guarding the shipment until it reached Capernaum, and then stealing it once it had been turned over to you," lied Ezri.

Up to this point Yitzhak had been leaning forward carefully listening to everything that Ezri told him. Standing, he looked up at the ceiling, exhaled, and said, "This is very serious. We have no time to contact Matthias in Jericho. I will have to make adjustments from this end." Looking down at Ezri he continued, "Are you still wanting a job, young man?"

"I will help in whatever way I can," he said enthusiastically.

"You have already helped a great deal. Do you have a place to stay here in town?"

"No, sir."

Looking at one of his servants, Yitzhak said, "Show Ezri to a bed in the servants' quarters." To the other servant he said, "Bring me our best rider, I need him to dispatch a message to Laurentinus and advise him of the danger."

CHAPTER THIRTY-FIVE

Magi were known all over the civilized world for their ability to accurately read the stars. The curiosity of the priests of Zeus to hear the holy men's theory on the star they had seen made the magi's visit to the temple longer than what had been anticipated. The new star had caused as much commotion in the religious community of Dura-Europus as it had in Seleucia. The opportunity to question the eminent priests of Ahura-Mazda about the star was too much for them to pass up.

Balthasar had been feeling fatigued the last few days of the journey and the extended time at the temple took a toll on the old magi, causing him to collapse in the midst of the priests' questioning. Gaspar was with him when he fainted, catching him before he fell full force to the floor.

"Stand back," Gaspar shouted. "Let him have fresh air."

Melchior was a few paces away and commanded one of the priests to fetch water for his friend. Fortunately, Balthasar was only out for a few moments. He blinked his eyes as he came to, creating a sigh of relief in the other magi.

"How do you feel, old friend?" said Melchior as he knelt down beside him.

"I'll be okay. Let me just catch my breath here for a few moments and I'll be just fine," Balthasar reassured everyone.

The priest who had been sent for the water hurried in kneeling down with a tray filled with a pitcher of water, a bowl, and towel. "Would the great magus be benefitted by water?" he asked.

"Yes. A sip of water would be very refreshing," said Balthasar. Gaspar, who had the old wiseman's head in his lap, elevated him so he could drink more easily. Gaspar laid Balthasar's head back down after he took a drink and he looked up into the younger man's eyes. "Thank you for catching me," he said smiling weakly.

Gaspar smiled back and said, "You don't think I would just let you fall, do you?"

"I suppose not," Balthasar said closing his eyes once again.

"I will send one of the young novices to fetch Cyrus and Amehlech to bring a stretcher," said Melchior. "I don't think you should walk back to camp in your condition."

"I won't argue with you, my friend. I would like that," Balthasar said agreeably causing Gaspar and Melchior to flash each other looks of concern. Seeing their faces, he continued with, "I'm not going to die. This has happened before in Nippur. I just need rest and I'll be fine by tomorrow morning."

Melchior did not like Balthasar's pallor and the short, gasping breaths he was taking. Both he and Gaspar flanked his sides when Cyrus and Amehlech carried him back to the campsite. All four of the men took turns watching over the old priest that night. When he woke in the morning, the color had come back to his cheeks, but he was clearly not ready to travel. He spent most of the day worrying his friends with his frequent naps.

Rachel had seen Balzak before with Gaspar and had always thought him to be a comical looking little man. He had made good his promise to look in on Rachel for his master. The magi had been gone less than a week, and he had visited her twice. She learned that he definitely had comical mannerisms, but also found that he had an engaging intellect and an agreeable personality. After she had been visited by him a second time, she had one of her father's servants accompany her to Gaspar's home to repay his visits.

Tala answered the door and respectfully bowed when she saw it was the high priest's daughter. "You honor this house with your visit, my lady, please come in."

Rachel stepped into the entryway with her servant, Kahliq. Both servant and mistress were curious to see the inside of Gaspar's home, and the truth was that they both were a little disappointed at the commonness of it. They had expected a man as wealthy as Gaspar to have a home equal to the king, yet even Rachel's father's home was more elegant than this. Smiling to herself, she thought how different Gaspar was from Majid. Given Gaspar's riches, Majid would have displayed his wealth for all of Seleucia and Ctesiphon to see. The simplicity she saw in his home made him more easy to identify with and attractive to her.

"I have come to see Balzak if he is not too busy," said Rachel.

"He is out by the stables practicing his knife throwing. May I get you refreshments," said Tala as she gestured them toward seats in a sitting area just beyond the entry.

"Balzak's handling of knives is legendary. I would love to observe him," Rachel entreated.

Tala did not immediately answer, and then finally said, "My lady, Balzak does not like to be interrupted when he is practicing. He is very modest about his skill."

114

"I understand," reassured Rachel, "I will return if he commands me to do so."

Again Tala had to think before she spoke. "I suppose that would be fine. Only, my lady must know that he would never command you to do anything."

"I will take my cues from you. If you frown and become uncomfortable, I will apologize and take the responsibility for my actions telling him that I forced you to lead me to him," responded Rachel.

Smiling, Tala said, "My lady is most gracious. Please come this way."

Turning to Kahliq, Rachel was about to say that she would return soon, but seeing the anticipation on his face, she asked, "Kahliq, would you please come with us?"

"Yes, mistress," he rejoined happily.

Beyond the stables was a semicircular barricade with posts of different height stuck in the ground. Attached to the top of each was a circular piece of wood about 20 centimeters in diameter. There were two knives stuck in the barricade, one lay on the ground, and the others were stuck near the center of one of his scattered targets.

"My lady!" Balzak said in surprise, "I was not expecting your visit." Holding the knife he was about to throw behind his back like he had done something wrong, he moved over to the table where at least a dozen knives were laying, and set down the one he was holding.

"I am sorry interrupt your practice, but hearing that you were doing so I insisted that the servant bring us out to you. Please, Balzak, continue with your exercise," said Rachel.

"My lady, I would feel most uncomfortable with you here," began Balzak. "I would feel as if I was showing off. I was just getting ready to collect my knives and come in anyway."

"Please, Balzak. I have heard stories of your skill. Won't you just give me a little demonstration? Pretend that I am your pupil."

"I suppose you couldn't show any less attention than my master does," he said absently. "Each time you throw, you want every throw to be the same. I will teach you to throw correctly, and then every time you throw after that, you will throw that same, exact way. Do you understand?"

"Yes," said Rachel a little surprised at how quickly Balzak adopted the posture of teacher. "I will have to remember this aspect of his personality," she thought.

Rachel and Kahliq ended up spending more than an hour with Balzak, learning to throw. To both of their happy surprise Balzak said, "This session does little for you if you do not practice what I have taught you. I expect you both to come weekly to show me your improvement and to receive further refinements to your technique." He then handed them a dozen knives with which to practice.

Rachel found that she had enjoyed her time learning to throw knives more than she had anticipated. When she returned home, she planned to have her father's servants set up an area where she could practice.

As they were gathering the knives and preparing to put the rest away, Tala came running in with one of Rachel's father's servants. Bowing before she spoke, Tala said, "Excuse my interruption, but your servant, my lady, has important news for you."

Concern imprinted on her face, Rachel asked, "What is it, Hirmand?"

"Your father collapsed in the temple, and the priests have brought him home to rest in his bed. He and your mother desire your return.

CHAPTER THIRTY-SIX

Being with Sophia was like an elixir of joy for Basil. He was not one to laugh publicly, but he found that he could not stop smiling. Forgetting all about getting the food back to his men, he asked if Sophia would like to have lunch with him.

"What about your men. Won't they be wanting to eat soon?" she asked.

"I suppose you're right, but I'm hungry now. Will you eat with me or not?" he said more gruffly than he felt, realizing his feelings were on the verge of being hurt if she said no.

"I don't want to come between you and your men, but I am having a lovely time, and I don't want it to end," she said, realizing that she actually meant what she said.

One vender at the end of the market had roasted a goat and was selling portions to the market patrons. Sophia bought radishes, cucumbers, and barley flatbread to eat with the goat meat. She allowed Basil to lead her to a shady spot under a tree to eat their meal. While she performed the minor preparation, Basil went to the city well and brought them back fresh water to drink.

In all of her life, she could count on one hand the times she felt absolutely safe with someone. Sitting under that tree in Hippos, leaning her back against the arm of the giant Basil, she counted one more time that she experienced that sensation.

They sat quietly for several minutes enjoying their meal and being in each other's company when Basil asked, "Where are you staying?"

"There's a woman in the town who has been renting me a room," she lied.

"Is she expecting you to be there tonight?" he asked, afraid she would say yes.

"No. We're on a day-to-day agreement. Why do you ask?" she said, turning to look him in the eye.

"I thought if you didn't have any place to go, in particular, and you didn't have any place to stay, you could come with me," he said finding it important to look at his outstretched feet.

"I don't mean to hurt your feelings, but you know that I am not a woman for hire?" she said, hoping he was not expecting her to be.

"No, no! I did not mean to imply that," he stammered, realizing how he must have sounded. "I only meant that I would like to see you again, and if you had no where to go, you could come with me until I found you a place. I have no expectations that would smudge your character."

Sophia was now speechless. This whole situation was becoming more and more unpredictable for her. She found herself having strong feelings for this visual ogre of a man, wanting him to see her in the best possible light. Was she going to compromise the whole plan because she was becoming emotionally tangled with the person who was supposed to be the *dupe*?

"I like being with you too," she said, thinking how she would get information to Satanas if she were to go with him.

"You can come back with me to my camp tonight, and tomorrow we can come back to town to find you a nice place to stay," he offered.

"Basil, that is too much. Let me continue to stay here and you can come visit me whenever you wish," she countered, aware of how much she wanted to go with his plan. "Can you come see me tomorrow? I will meet you here at the marketplace."

"I will be here tomorrow at noon," he said.

They finished their meal together and said their good-byes leaving Sophia wondering how she was going to continue with her ruse feeling the way that she did.

Back at Sophia's house, Ezri was explaining to Satanas how well their scheme had worked on Yitzhak.

"I'm glad you briefed me as well as you did," remarked Ezri. "I would have really been stumped if you hadn't given me another plan to wheedle into his confidence."

"After a few more of these jobs, you will be finding that you will be able to think up tales of your own," assured Satanas. "I will teach you a lot in the years to come. If you remain loyal and teachable, there is no amount of wealth we cannot attain."

Ezri thought back to the dreams that he had of living well and having whatever he wanted. His father was willing to work himself to death for another man's prosperity. How foolish he realized his father was to settle for a life like that. He was grateful to be out from under his authority and to now be learning from Satanas. "I will work hard at this craft I have chosen for myself," he thought. "One day I shall return to prove how foolish my father really is."

"Remember," Satanas interrupted his thoughts, "you must be the picture of devotion. Try to anticipate Yitzhak's thoughts and do things before he asks you to. People like him see this as self-assuredness and signs of leadership. On the other hand, don't be afraid to ask him how you might do something that you're not sure about. You don't want to appear inept, but you also want to give him a few opportunities to feel that he is mentoring you. We want him to see you as a good worker and someone whom he can mold. Do you understand?"

"Yes," replied Ezri thinking that that was the very thing he was doing with Satanas. "There is not so much difference between law abiding men and thieves," he thought, "both have the need to shape lives and to be respected."

"There is no need for you to leave Yitzhak's unless it is extremely necessary," instructed Satanas. "I will get word to you if I need information or need to inform you of anything."

"How will you do that?"

"My very next words. There are columns in the wall surrounding Yitzhak's living areas. The second column south of the main entrance will have a flat rock, about the width of my hand, that I will place there. It is plain on one side and white on the other. Check it every evening. If you see the white side, I want to talk with you. So that you won't arouse any suspicion, go out every evening for a walk. Take your time, check the stone, and return. If someone wants to accompany you, let them. Once they tell you they're going inside, you simply tell them that you're not quite ready to go in yet. Always appear to be very casual in your deceptions," explained Satanas. "If we need to meet, I will meet you by the boulder at the fork in the road near Yitzhak's home."

"I know the place. Tonight after dinner, I will look for the stone. What should I do if I need to contact you?" queried Ezri.

"If you have information that is too important to wait for our signal, you will have to make up a reason to leave and come here. But only do so if it is absolutely crucial."

"Yes, sir."

"If the information is important enough that I should know about it, but time is not of the essence, place this red stone under the marker stone." He showed Ezri the red stone. "I will have someone check it every day. By the boulder is a large hollow tree. In it, I will place this message board and the red stone." Satanas showed Ezri a wooden board that had a recessed center filled with wax where he could write a message using a sharpened stick. "Use this to leave me information if you have a need, and I will use it to get information alerting you with the same red stone. Now, you must go. You should not be gone for too long or you may cause your new employer to wonder at your absence."

On his way back to Yitzhak's, Ezri could not help but anticipate what he would do with his share of the gold. There was no way to know how much gold his share would be, but Ezri could not keep his mind from jumping to all the things he could do with his split. Maybe he could set up his own base further into the hills. He determined that when this present job was finished, he would begin looking for a place where he could lay low for awhile if he ever had the need.

The life he was now living was everything that he had imagined. He loved the intrigue and the imminent danger associated with it. He once again compared this life to the one his father lived and thanked the stars that he was no longer trapped in that monotonous grind of daily repetition. Life was never better, as he saw it, and it was only going to get better.

CHAPTER THIRTY-SEVEN

Zand's ashen face and shortness of breath stopped Rachel short in her tracks as she rushed into her parents' bedroom. Nazli, who had been sitting in a chair next to her husband, got up to meet her daughter.

"What is wrong with Father?" Rachel asked, each woman holding on to the other's forearms.

"We think it is his heart," replied Nazli. "The other priests who were administering the sacrifices with him said they saw him first grab his arm and then his chest. He has been breathing shallowly since they brought him in, but he has not been conscious. I've been asking the good god to allow your father to open his eyes and let him speak to us."

Rachel hugged her mother to her, looking over her shoulder at her father's face. Zand's eyes fluttered and then he stopped breathing.

"Mother!" Rachel cried out.

Nazli turned to see that her husband had stopped breathing. Running to him, she knelt by the bed, sobbing, and reaching out in mid-air to her beloved husband, knowing that touching his now dead body would contaminate her and anyone she touched afterward. Rachel stood in the middle of the room with her hands to her face, tears running down her hands. Reaching back with her left hand, Nazli motioned for her daughter to join her by the bed. Both women wept together, bringing the other comfort in their grief.

It did not take long for the news to travel through the home of the high priest of Ahura-Mazda. Tala, who Balzak had sent to accompany Rachel and Kahliq to bring back news, ran back to tell Balzak what had taken place. Before the two grieving women had left death's chamber, Balzak had already arrived and was waiting to convey his condolences and assistance in any way he could.

Nazli gave him her hand, and Rachel hugged him and kissed his cheek. "You have rapidly become a valuable friend to me," Rachel said to Balzak. "Your quick response to our calamity shows your concern and is seen by my mother and me as a great kindness. Thank you, good Balzak for your friendship. You have performed honorably by your master."

Tears filled the eyes of the diminutive servant as he said,

"I value our relationship. I wish that I could allay your grief, but doing so would only reduce the honor your father deserves."

At this, both women bent to embrace Gaspar's servant weeping openly, allowing their tears to run unabated.

"My master would want me to make myself available to the two of you in any way that would bring you comfort and aid. Know also that doing so would honor me and cause blessing to fall on me if I could be of any assistance. I will leave you now to your preparations and to comfort one another. I will assign a servant to be at your gate to run to me at any time you may need my services."

The mourners thanked Balzak and promised that they would not hesitate to call on him if the need arose. As Balzak turned to leave, they saw Zand's body being removed to the Tower of Silence that was on one of the hills outside the city. Grief overcame mother and daughter as tears again began to fulfill their task of washing away the women's anguish.

Zand's body would be left in open exposure on the uppermost level of the tower until carrion birds stripped his body of its flesh in a day. A large hole in the center of the tower led to a depository below where his bones would lay, once the birds had finished their work and the sun had baked his bones for a year. Then his body would join others in the ossuary until nasellars, or pallbearers, removed the remains to be deposited in the Arabian Sea.

For a time, evil would have its victory over life through death, the followers of Ahura-Mazda believed, but the goodness of Zand's works would pave a celestial trail to the god in the heavens. Both women and Balzak knew that they could aid Zand on his way with good thoughts and works in the days to come.

Balzak walked down the path from the high priest's home angry at the thought of how Gaspar would want to be there to comfort the woman he loved. He also empathized with Rachel's pain. He felt vexed at his helplessness to report to his master, and outrage for the pain that his new friend had to endure. In fury, he brandished his two blades, sending them flying toward a small tree trunk thirty feet away sticking each only a few inches apart. Shaking his head, Balzak walked over and worked to unstick the knives that had sunk several inches into the tree. In his disheartened walk home, he felt very much like he did when Gaspar's parents had left this earth for the heavenly heights of Ahura-Mazda. He walked slowly, feeling weighted down, impotent, and old.

The priests came to Zand's home and performed the rites that were necessary to diminish the effects the evil spirits purportedly had on Rachel's father now that he was dead, to comfort the grieving of the living, and to protect them from the contamination caused by the dead man's decaying body.

For three days after a person's death, it was customary to fast from meat, eating only fruits, nuts, and vegetables in observance of the dead. Balzak made sure fresh portions were made up on a platter and sent to the high priest's home each day. For ten days no one was allowed in the room where Zand expired. A ritual lamp was kept burning in the room, until its fire, the purest form of the good god's presence, did the task of purification. The room was the place where Nazli and Zand had spent so much time together over the years that she could not think of sleeping there anyway. As priestly procedure would soon dictate, she would never enter that room again.

It was believed that people's souls were affected by the kind of lives they lived. The better the life and good thoughts they harbored, the better chance they had of reaching the abode of the good god. For them, the bridge spanning this life to Ahura-Mazda was a broad one that could be easily traversed. The amount of evil in an individual's life narrowed the bridge and his chances of a positive after-life experience. People who made war on the poor and helpless, cheated the aged, mistreated widows, lived lives of crime, and were murderers, their bridges were a razor's breadth and impossible to cross, causing them to plummet to a dark pit of anguish. No one ever knew, until death, whether their works and positive thoughts were enough to get them into Ahura-Mazda's presence. Rachel and Nazli could only hope that Zand's life as a priest and his loving acts would be his ticket to paradise.

The day after the allotted time of grieving and ritual cleansing had taken place, there was a messenger from the king and the new high priest wanting to speak with Nazli. He was escorted into the room where Zand had received those wanting to conduct official business.

"What news have you for me?" asked Nazli, wondering what could possibly be important enough to warrant a royal messenger.

"King Phraataces, king of kings, and ruler of the several realms, and the high priest, Daba, have sent me to remind you that this house is the home of the high priest. You have one fortnight to be out of this residence so that the affairs of state, as they relate to spiritual matters, may continue in a fluid fashion," pronounced the king's spokesman.

Nazli sat stunned. Now that Zand was deceased, was her place as his wife not respected? "Where am I to go?" she asked.

"That, my lady, has not been conveyed to me. I'm sorry

for your loss," he said sincerely.

"Daba has already been appointed high priest? He wasted little time in replacing my husband," she said feeling betrayed by her husband's friend and associate.

"It appears so," the messenger said not sure how to respond.

"Th-thank you," Nazli said. "You may go if you have nothing further to report."

The king's messenger bowed and left the room. Nazli sat at her chair numbed by the information she had received. She had no idea what she was to do. She sat there for several moments unable to think or work out a plan for herself and Rachel.

Falling to her knees, Nazli prayed, "Oh, Mazda, hear the prayer of your daughter who loves you. What am I to do? My husband, your faithful servant, and I have always sought what we thought best in order to serve you and to bring about a productive world where you are praised. Show me what to do, and protect me from thoughts that allow Angra Mainyu, the evil spirit, to gain a greater foothold in this world."

She spread out prostrate on the floor and wept. There was no sensation of divine presence—no solace to be found where despair prevailed.

"My dearest friends, I promise you that I am ready to continue with our excursion. I do not need to return to Nippur. And even if I should, I would not. How could I live with myself if I backed out now?" Balthasar assured the other two magi.

In typical direct manner, Melchior said, "What concerns me is whether or not you will live. I do not want to play with your wellbeing. Your life is more important than what information we may discover on this trip."

"I do not agree. Even if my health was an issue, I would be more than willing to chance it in order to live out this experience, as long as I could, with the two of you," Balthasar responded with passion that halted Melchior from responding.

"Good Balthasar," pleaded Gaspar, "how could Melchior and I live with ourselves if something happened to you while you were with us on this trip."

"Listen," Balthasar said placing one of his hands on each man's arm, "I promise you I will not die as a result of the exertion of this journey." Smiling, he continued, "Besides, what else does an old man have to look forward to?"

"I still don't like it," Melchior said breathing hard. "You make sure you let us know if you need to rest."

"I will."

Shaking his head as he got up, Gaspar patted the old

magi on his back as he made his way to the camels.

  Cassius, the Roman spy who who had observed Vahumisa receiving a Parthian salute, had kept himself close but out of sight of the expedition's members while they were camped by Dura-Europus. Vahumisa had tried to be careful that neither he nor his men treated each other as military personnel, and the blunder of the salute had gone unnoticed by both he and his subordinate in that it was a very normal part of their daily routine.

  Seeing now that the caravan was mounting up, Cassius hurried to his camel inside the city gates so he could follow the movements of what he thought might be Parthian spies sent into the empire to acquire Roman military information. He himself was just returning from a similar mission to Ctesiphon where he had been gathering information for Rome. The Parthians had dealt Rome crushing defeats in the past and Caesar was anxious to set those humiliations to right. If Cassius could come away from this accidental windfall with useful intelligence, who knows what the empire might be willing to pay for it. He would have to be careful and look for the right opportunity to cultivate a useful relationship. All he could do for now is wait and watch.

CHAPTER THIRTY-EIGHT

Basil returned to his men in the early afternoon with the food he was to have brought them much earlier in the day. The men were grouchy about his returning so late, but no one had the cheek to complain. All of them had been through skirmishes together, and each of them knew he did not want Basil as an adversary. If angered, he could whip the whole lot of them. More than one of his men noticed that Basil was in better spirits than was typical for the huge man.

A meal was hastily prepared, and after they had eaten a good bit, one of the men made a comment to Basil.

"Basil, you seem in a good mood, did you eat somebody on the way back to camp?" This statement brought a big laugh from the others.

"No, but the thought of breaking both your arms has me feeling pretty good, though," Basil responded, enjoying the banter, bringing on an even a bigger roar from the group.

Someone else piped up with, "Break both his arms and legs, Basil, and he'll be twice as useful as he is now."

Basil, acting like this was a good idea, began chasing the man, whose arms he had promised to break, around and through the group as everyone else catcalled.

"Don't let him catch you, we'll never hear the end of his bragging," said one.

"I think Basil bought himself some additional speed when he was it town," said another.

Basil finally stopped, out of breath, and resting his hands on his knees said, "I'd have caught you if you would have run straight," causing another uproar from the group.

The men were catching their breath when one of them said, "I think Basil met a woman in town." As quickly as it was said, the band detected an immediate transformation in the giant.

"What are you saying?" Basil said with murder in his tone.

Realizing he had misspoken and his life was now in real danger, the man said, "Basil, I meant nothing by it. I was only teasing."

"You think a woman couldn't want me?" he said with growing intensity.

"Look, Basil, I spoke without thinking. I-I'm sorry. Of course a woman could want you. It-it's just that because a woman would make any of us happy, I just meant. . ."

Before he could finish his appeal, Basil said, "Just stuff it!!" and walked over to a tree away from the others and sat down.

He fumed under the shade of the tree while his men sat quietly, hardly speaking and then only in hushed tones. "Maybe they're right," he thought. "Why would any woman want a great beast like me?" He realized for the first time that Sophia may have had ulterior motives in encouraging his affections. The more he thought about it, the more he believed that could be the only reason she showed any interest in him—she had a purpose other than affection. "Why was I so foolish. I should have known better," he chastised himself. He had visions of grabbing her by the throat and demanding the reason for her enticements. When he got the truth from her, he would snap her neck. He sat there brooding for a long time feeling idiotic and used.

The chance of being caught and the excitement of playing out his deception gave Ezri the thrill he had missed in working for Levi, his father's employer. Ingratiating himself with Yitzhak was a game that made the hard farm work tolerable for him. Within a few days of employment, Ezri could already see evidence of Yitzhak's growing trust in him. He had always observed people, what they did, and how they did it. Over the years he had learned to do a lot of things just from watching what others did. More than he realized, he was able to put some of the things that he observed into operation. Having a fertile mind and a penchant for bluffing, whenever he was asked to do something he was not sure how to do, he found that he could usually figure it out and pull off the deception of having done the activity before.

Within the first week of working for Yitzhak, the rider that was sent out to make contact with the Roman detail returned just after the men had finished their noontime meal. Yitzhak met the man as he road into the compound.

"Were you able to make contact with the centurion?" Yitzhak queried. "Did you have any problems? What news does he send?"

"Yes, I was able to find him. No, I didn't have any problems, and he thanks you for the word that you sent to him through me," replied the servant.

"Thank goodness you made contact with him. What does he say about Basil's treachery?"

The servant answered, "The centurion said he had met the giant before and was glad to have news of his deceit before they had to meet him in a skirmish. He told me that they already were using forward scouting parties, but he would add another one. He also had assigned a party to the rear of the detail in case they were being followed. The centurion doubted that anyone would try to follow them from their rear. He believes that a force would most likely attack from hidden placements after having kept track of their movements from an advanced position of the military unit."

"Did he mention any changes to their route?"

"He did. Instead of continuing north up the west side of the Sea of Galilee from Philoteria, he will take the eastern road through Hippos and then on up to Capernaum."

"Is there anything else that you need to tell me before I send you to the kitchen for something to eat," asked Yitzhak studying his servant's face.

"Only that the centurion seemed unconcerned by the information that I brought him. It was apparent that he thought he could deal with the situation without much trouble."

Yitzhak was relieved by the servant's statement, and he also realized that Basil may not be planning to attack the the Roman guard, but would wait until the shipment was transferred to the civilians. He was beginning to wish that he had never volunteered to lead the group that would be protecting the treasure from Capernaum to Caesarea. He wished he could come up with a plan that would scare off any would be bandits. As with anything a person thinks is simple when he's never done it before, this enterprise was turning out to be much more complicated than what he originally thought.

During the master-servant dialog, Ezri watched from the servant's quarters to see if he could extract any information that he could pass along to Satanas. It did not escape his notice that Yitzhak appeared more troubled at the end of the two men's conversation than when it began.

Momentarily, Yitzhak went over to the servant's quarters to delegate the afternoon duties. As the rest of the men went off to their appointed jobs, Ezri took the opportunity to approach Yitzhak to pump him for information.

"Sir, may I speak with you a moment?" Ezri asked.

"What is it?" Yitzhak said absently.

"I could not help but notice that you were upset after receiving news from the centurion. Is there anything I can do?" he said appearing to be concerned.

"No I wish there was," Yitzhak responded. "Go on and attend to your chores. Thank you for asking."

Ezri wanted to get more information from him, but deciding to wait for a better time, he said merely, "Yes, sir," and went to join the rest of the men in their work.

Noam and Sophia had met just north and west of Hippos on the beach of the Sea of Galilee after she left Basil. She was troubled by the feelings that she experienced with the big man, and wanted to talk to someone about them. Noam was no one with whom she could confide, nor would she want it to get back to Satanas. If he ever found out, her life would be worth nothing.

"He seemed to be quite taken with you, Sophy," sneered Noam. "You was leading him around like a pet goat or something."

"My name is Sophia, Noam," she chided. "Call me by my right name or don't use any at all."

"I was just using it endearing-like. Don't be angry with me, old girl," he said apologetically.

Sophia thought his choice of names only went from bad to worse. "If a man like Basil thinks too long about our afternoon together, he may become leery and crush my skull the next time he sees me. I'm not out of the woods with him yet. We'll see what happens tomorrow," she said ignoring his attempts to apologize.

"Oh, say, you could be in real danger, Sophy-a," he said remembering to use her correct name at the last second. "What ya going to do if he decides to hurt ya?"

"You'll just have to use that long stabbing knife of yours to puncture his heart. Discretion will be important in order to get close enough to sneak up behind him and stick him. Try not to hit a rib or we'll both be dead," she said in warning.

"I hope it don't come to that, Sophy-a," he said shaking his head. "A man like that don't come down easy."

"You let me deal with the giant," she reassured him. "I've dealt with mean men before. I know how to get my way. Still, you be close when I meet with him tomorrow."

Sophia arrived at the marketplace in Hippos early the next morning so she would not miss Basil if he decided to come early himself. She could not help shaking her head at herself for her interest in this man. As a younger woman she had attracted many men and scammed many more who were much better looking and not as dangerous as Basil. "After all these years," she thought, "I can't believe he is the one who makes my heart flutter." She had run different scenarios through her head the night before trying to anticipate and respond to any mood Basil might show up with the next day. "I'll be fine, as long as I deal as innocently with him as I can," she reminded herself.

It was several hours before Basil showed up. Sophia had already worked out in her head reasons why he would not return early as opposed to later. The first, and she thought most

129

unlikely, was that he discovered he wasn't interested in her. In that case he may not show up at all. Another reason was that he couldn't believe a woman like her would fall for him, and he would feel awkward about seeing her. The most likely reason he might show up later is because he thought she might be trying to pull something over on him, and in this situation, her life would be in great danger if she failed at her task of convincing him that her affections were true. She had faced this circumstance before, but never with so powerful of an adversary. She saw him as he first entered the marketplace. The expression on his face alerted her that she must be wary and calm. "Come on, Sophia," she assured herself, "trust your experience and your knowledge of men." She nodded her head toward Noam, who was behind one of the stands, letting him know she expected the worst and to be ready.

Walking out into street where Basil would better notice her, she approached in a brisk walk, smiling. "Where have you been?" she said putting a false pout on her face. "I was afraid you were not going to show."

"I'm not sure that I should have come. I almost turned around a few seconds ago to go back to camp," he said showing more candor than he wanted.

"Have you changed your feelings towards me?" she said aware of the truthfulness of her concern. "I thought we had such a good time yesterday."

Basil looked around uncomfortably and said, "Can we go somewhere else to talk?"

"Certainly." She stood off, not flirting with him or grabbing his arm as she did the day before.

Basil led her to a place outside the city walls, turned to her, and said, "Why have you been so nice to me?"

Sophia had been watching his eyes, and now let hers drop to look at the ground. "I didn't want to hurt you." She looked back up into his face seeing the pain the statement had caused him. "You had been so kind to me. I didn't want to just run off after that. I admit that your size scared me at first, but I realized after awhile that you were worth getting to know. The more time we spent together, the more I realized I wanted to be with you." Now she had to be very careful. "What made you ask that question?"

He had been studying her face while she had been talking, but now his eyes looked past her weighing what he would say next. "I couldn't believe that someone like you could be interested in a big ugly man like me."

She grabbed his hand, her eyes brimming with tears. Blinking sent rivulets down both cheeks. Bending down to her level, Basil reached out with his massive thumbs and wiped away her tears.

"I'm sorry for fearing you in the beginning because of your great size," she wept, "but I soon got to the point where I wanted only to be with you. Would you forgive me?"

"There is nothing to forgive. You gave me one of the best days of my life. It is me who should ask for your forgiveness for doubting your intentions," he said shaking his massive head.

With all thought of guile dissolved, Sophia asked, "Would you hold me like you did yesterday when you rescued me from that disagreeable merchant?"

Basil leaned down and lifted her up as easily as one would a babe. Putting her arms around his neck, she kissed him long and gently. Basil returned her tribute, thanking Aphrodite for her favor.

CHAPTER THIRTY-NINE

During the next few days of the magi's travel from Dura-Europus to Damascus, Cassius was able to steal up close enough to listen to some of the evening conversations around the campfires. He noticed that the men who were obviously brought along as guards usually ate together at one fire, while the servants and the men who were, or he thought might be masquerading as magi, ate at another fire. One night, he was able to sneak into one of the guard's tents and look through his effects. He was watchful for the weaponry of the Parthian warrior. No evidence of longer broader swords could he find, nor the longer recurved bows of the Parthian horse soldier. Hearing a rustling outside the opening flap, Cassius slipped out under the back wall of the tent. He stopped his breathing and listened for any sound signaling the entry into the fabric dwelling. Sensing no movement, he slunk back out into the dark and its cover. He walked to the place where he had tethered his camel, slipping behind a hill where he would spend the night.

"There is something that is not right about this caravan," he said to his camel as he made his own camp. "I want to observe them more closely. Tomorrow, I will see if they will let another traveler into their camp." After he had fed his camel a mash of dates and oats, he sat himself next to his dromedary and ate his meal of dried meat, flat bread, and water before drifting off to sleep.

Next morning as the camp was waking, a lone rider came up to the caravan. Vahumisa and another of his men met the man as he came up to within a hundred yards of the encampment.

"What is your business, traveler?" said Vahumisa, he and his subordinate with hands on the hilt of their swords.

"I've been traveling by myself for a few days," Cassius responded. "The temple priests in Dura-Europus told me of your group and that I might be able to join up with you. You are headed to Palestine, are you not?"

"Where we are headed is of no concern to you," Vahumisa said assertively. "It is unwise for you to be out in these lands by yourself, and you should have taken that into account before you left."

"I won't be any trouble to you. Just let me join you until you reach Damascus. From there, I will join another caravan that is headed for Antioch. I just want the safety of your numbers."

Before Vahumisa could send Cassius away, Gaspar joined them and asked, "What seems to be the trouble, Vahumisa?"

"This man wants to join our caravan under the auspices of our numbers adding to his protection." Then back to Cassius he asked, "What do you have that is so valuable that you need our protection?"

"I am simply a traveler, and am seeking the safety of your numbers." Cassius then took out his purse and poured its contents into his other hand. "You see. I have no great wealth. Only the assets of a traveler that a band of cutthroats would not mind murdering me to get at."

"I don't see any harm in his joining us for the few days we have until we reach Damascus. Couldn't he sleep around your campfire?" asked Gaspar.

"All right, but be warned that I will accept no shenanigans. Any trouble and we'll be leaving you to be a feast for the vultures," warned Vahumisa.

"Thank you, thank you. You will have no trouble with me. I promise that I will be of as much help as I'm allowed."

Gaspar went on to introduce Vahumisa and himself to their new companion. "Come with me, Cassius, and I'll let you meet the rest of the men in our party."

The day went without incident, and when the time came to set up camp for the evening, Cassius was true to his word. He helped with the feeding of the animals and the building of each of the campfires. When all the men had finished their meal and had settled into campfire conversation, Balthasar asked Cassius, "You have a Roman name which is familiar to many in Parthia. Cassius, as you may know, was a general that suffered great defeat at the hands of the Parthian army."

"I am from Macedonia. My father bought his citizenship and wanted me, as his first son, to have a Roman name. Cassius was extremely wealthy. I think my father hoped that carrying that name would make me wealthy also. To me, it's just a name."

"We inherited a lot from your ancestors, Cassius. At one time, the Macedonians were the rulers of our land. There is still much in Parthia that is reminiscent of the Hellenist culture," said Balthasar.

"I suppose that is true," mused Cassius, "and now Rome rules Macedonia and Parthia rules the eastern part of what was Alexander's vast empire. I wonder who will someday rule Rome and Parthia?

"Enough about me. What brings three magi out into this

wilderness?"

Melchior glanced at Vahumisa, and he nodded as if to say, 'tell him.' "You see that star up there, young man?"

"Yes."

"Have you noticed anything different about it?" Melchior continued.

Cassius shook his head.

"It doesn't behave like any other star in the heavens. It moves from west to east, stops mid-sky, and then doesn't move for the rest of the night. It appeared only a few months ago. The three of us believe that it heralds the coming of a new world leader. We have come to seek him out and discover if our theory is true."

Cassius sat looking up into the sky. During the time that Melchior spoke, the star appeared to have moved some distance toward the east.

"Where will it stop its easterly course?" asked Cassius.

"About right there," pointed Balthasar. "About center of the night sky."

"We measured the distance of the star from the earth," said Gaspar. "Instead of millions of miles from here, it is but a few miles above our heads."

Cassius was now intrigued himself. "What does it mean?"

"We don't know," said Balthasar. "That's why we have come to find out why it's there, if we can. The Jewish prophets had something to say about the star and why it has come. Our task is to find out the truth."

"What if you find out that it signals the coming of a great conquering Caesar," asked Cassius.

"Then we find out that there is a great conquering Caesar coming," smiled Melchior.

"We don't believe that that will be the case," said Balthasar. "More likely, this ruler will be a Jew."

"Why do you say that?" asked Cassius.

"Because the Jewish scriptures speak of the star, all of the information that we have concerning the star seems to be directing us toward Palestine, and Jews have long awaited another deliverer, much like their great prophet and leader, Moses," Balthasar continued.

"Do you have any speculations as to what this means for the two great Roman and Parthian Empires?" Cassius said voicing true questions.

"I suppose it means that they will end," Gaspar responded. "Maybe this new ruler will be the leader of the empire that replaces both of them."

Vahumisa had sat in on the magi's campfire to feel out

their new companion's motives. At one point the other soldiers had moved over to the magi's group to listen in on the conversation that had everyone fascinated. Each man was lost in the gravity of what Gaspar told them. For the first time, every person in the group grasped the import of their adventure. This would be something their children would tell their children.

"How will you find this personage?" Cassius now asked with more personal than political interest.

"The star seems to be sent to direct us, or, possibly, anyone who seeks after him," reflected Gaspar. "The god who sent the star wants us to know who the star designates. I have no doubt that we will find who that is. The Heavens know that we are searching for the answer to this harbinger. Whether the god who sent it is Jupiter, Ahura-Mazda, or Yahweh—the Jews' god—the divinity who has placed the star above our heads is aware of this expedition."

"Well said," enjoined a smiling Balthasar. "This is a great time for humanity. I can feel it. We are standing on the threshold of a great event. We are truly blessed to be involved in an occasion of such momentous impact. Cassius, it is no accident that you are here tonight. Whatever god has arranged these circumstances wanted you here to be a part of this trip."

Cassius chuckled uncomfortably. He had no intention before tonight of going to Palestine, but there under the star, around a campfire, out in the wilderness, he realized he wanted to see this spectacle to its end.

"You would let me go with you?"

"What harm could it bring?" assured Balthasar. "This is God's sign to all mankind, or He would not have made so obvious a sign to announce His intentions. Even if your intentions were evil, you could not thwart the plans of God."

Cassius felt himself become uncomfortable in the light of Balthasar's last statement. He was now convinced that the expedition was not one that was overtly harmful to the Roman empire, but the answer to whom was the star heralding would have great ramifications for Rome. He had no doubt that the Parthian king knew of the expedition, and was possibly even funding it. For the same reason the king of Parthia would want to know the person to whom the star was announcing, Caesar would also like to know, as well. He decided there and then that he would stay as long as no one became suspicious of the 'why' of his presence.

"My business is not of a nature that I must hurry. If you would allow it, I would like to see this exploration to its end," requested Cassius.

Gaspar, who was sitting next to him by the fire, shook his hand and said, "That is good news. It will add more input to our evening conversations to have you with us."

The other magi heartily agreed with Gaspar, but Vahumisa eyed Cassius warily. "I will need to keep a watch on this one," he thought. He would make sure that the rest of his men would also keep a sharp surveillance on the newcomer.

One of the temple acolytes whom Balzak had befriended and taught to throw knives appeared at Gaspar's home with news concerning Nazli's expulsion almost simultaneously with the time that the envoy showed up at the high priest's home to give Nazli her notice of eviction. Wasting no time, he immediately had all the servants readying rooms for Rachel and her mother to move into. The guest house located across the back lawn and garden from the stables was immediately filled with the personal affects of Gaspar's servants. Their rooms were vacated to make room for Nazli and Rachel's servants. Nazli would be given Gaspar's mother and father's room, and Rachel would be offered the guest room that had a balcony overlooking the garden. While all the preparations were being made, Tala was sent to the high priest's home to invite Rachel and Nazli to dinner that night.

Tala was announced about the time that Nazli had completed her prayers to Ahura-Mazda. Rachel received Tala and agreed to dinner before her mother had a chance to tell her of their parlous circumstances. Nazli entered the reception area as Tala was leaving.

"Wasn't that one of Gaspar's servants?" queried Nazli.

"Yes, it was," Rachel responded. "She brought us an invitation to have dinner with Balzak tonight. I agreed to her request because I want to get away from the house."

Nazli's eyes dropped to the floor as Rachel's word choice broached the cause for her fragile emotions.

"Is there something wrong, Mother. Should I not have agreed to go?"

Nazli looked up into her daughter's eyes with tears glistening in her own. "I just received more un-welcomed news and your phrasing reminded me of it afresh. I suppose it will do us both good to go out this evening."

"Mother, tell me the news."

"I don't want to upset you more. Let's just go, have dinner, and forget our grief for the night."

"I have to know. Your not telling me has to be worse than knowing."

She realized that her daughter was right, of course, and that she must tell her now. Rachel steeled herself for what her mother had to say. To her credit, she took the information very well.

At the completion of her mother's explanation, Rachel said, "What will we do?"

"We will go to dinner tonight and try to act as if all of our problems do not exist."

CHAPTER FORTY

A thick blanket of snow covered the tents and the animals of the magi's caravan. Wind beat the sides of the tents causing the heavy snow deposited on their roofs to loosen and slide to the ground. The night had the appearance of mid-day caused by the light that was emanating from a single bright star in the sky. The camels and pack animals had frozen during the night looking like live statues of themselves. Gaspar plodded over to one of the camels and began prodding the ice away with a stick. As the ice fell away, he discovered not a camel but a strange looking animal with tree-like antlers. Once the the ice was broken away from the head, the curious looking animal was able to break the rest of itself free from his frozen imprisonment. Gaspar went around and freed the other frozen animals. As each animal was released, it in turn helped in releasing the others. Before too long, all the previously frozen animal statues revealed identical creatures as the one Gaspar had originally freed.

Going around to each tent to wake up his companions, he was surprised to find in each tent great stacks of gold. Walking back to his own tent he heard a voice saying, "If you sleep any longer, we may as well spend another night here." The young magi opened his eyes to see the smiling face of Melchior.

"I had the strangest dream," he said squinting into the morning light.

"I hope she was pretty," teased Melchior.

"It wasn't that kind of dream," corrected Gaspar. "It was a dream about cold, snow, and this camp."

Melchior becoming more serious said, "Tell me what you dreamt."

Gaspar told his friend what he saw in his dream. When he had almost finished his explanation, Balthasar walked in and inquired what it was that Gaspar was describing. He then repeated it all for the old magi's benefit too.

"What do you think your dream means?" asked Balthasar.

"I don't know. I don't know what to think. One thing is for sure. The large amount of snow, those strange looking deer-like creatures, and the great amount of gold doesn't seem to go together," Gaspar replied. "The star lit up the whole countryside."

"You either have an active imagination, or this is a portent that you should not take lightly," Melchior said with Balthasar nodding his head in agreement.

"We can discuss this more today when we travel," said Balthasar. "Right now we have our own star that appears to be beckoning us to follow."

Nazli and Rachel arrived at Gaspar's home to a jubilant and excited Balzak. Both women looked at the other with questioning expressions as the little servant greeted them with incongruous enthusiasm.

"My dear friends, I am thrilled that you have agreed to come tonight. We have much to discuss, and the other servants have prepared a scrumptious meal. Please, come in, come in."

Tala stood off to the side and was smiling in anticipation of the night's events. In fact, the whole staff seemed to be bursting with anticipation for what neither woman could guess. The servants' joyful countenance became infectious, and Nazli and Rachel soon were able to put aside their unresolved future.

Once the meal was completed, Rachel, not able to hold back her curiosity any longer asked, "Balzak, you mentioned that you wanted to discuss something. Would you like to let my mother and me in on what the topic of our discussion will be?" Nazli looked at her daughter with raised eyebrows, causing Balzak to laugh outright and to wave his hand excusing Rachel's forthright question.

"Please, my lady, your daughter's question is not out of line. It is a perfect segue into what tonight's affair is all about."

Tala, standing nearby, placed her hands over her mouth to stifle a squeal of delight. Rachel looked first at Tala, and then to her mother. Both women looked at the other as if to say, "What is going on?"

"The other staff and myself have been busy all day in preparation, my ladies," began Balzak. "This house has not been used to its potential or capacity since the days that the master's parents ran it. The rest of the staff and I would like the two of you to consider moving into the main house with your personal servants. We have moved all of our things into the guest house. You, my lady," indicating Nazli, "will stay in Gaspar's mother and father's room. You," nodding to Rachel, " will stay in the favored guest room down the hall, and your servants can stay in the wing for the servants . What do you think? My master would be greatly put out with me if I did not make this offer to you. Won't you say that you will at least think about it?"

Nazli and Rachel could not help but see the expressions

of hope cast on Balzak's and Tala's faces.

Nazli began with, "Your offer is most generous, but. . ."

Before her mother could finish, Rachel said, "We will need to think about it. May we see where we would be staying?"

"Rachel!" Nazli said chidingly.

Balzak laughed, and Tala jumped up and down clapping her hands in unrestrained excitement.

"Your daughter's request is appropriate, my lady," Balzak said warmly. "Of course we would not want you to make so momentous a decision without first inspecting your quarters. Please, come and see what we have prepared for you."

Standing in the hallway after seeing their rooms Nazli said, "If I were to concede to your offer, I would insist on a lesser room than Gaspar's parent's old room."

"If the master was here, he would insist on your staying there," countered Balzak.

"If your master was here, I would still insist on one of the other guest rooms," said Nazli without deviation.

"If I promised you could have one of the other rooms, would you come?"

"Mother, this is impossible. We have no where else to go. Why are you acting this way?"

Nazli's face broke from unyielding to relenting. "All right. Thank you for your gracious offer, good Balzak. Of course we will accept your hospitality."

Down the hall the trio could hear Tala's squeal of delight causing them to break into laughter.

"My master will be so pleased," said Balzak bowing to Nazli. "Tala, prepare the wine so we can discuss particulars of our guests' stay."

"At once," they heard Tala say as they moved their conversation down to the sitting room.

"I have been thinking about your dream," said Melchior as the three magi rode abreast of one another with Balthasar in his place in the middle.

"And what have you thought?" asked Gaspar.

"The dream you had last night seems heavy with symbolism as opposed to actual windows to your future. Such dreams are often impossible to fully understand until they are coming to pass or have done so already. Did you have a sense in your dreams of a divine presence even though there was none visible?"

"I don't think so, but let me think about that for a while."

"Are there parts of the dream that seem to have more of a realistic nature as opposed to a symbolic one?" inquired Balthasar.

"In all of my dreams, the only thing that is constant in that regard is the star. Somehow, this star we are following is the same star in my dreams, and it seems to hold the key to my future."

"In your dream," Melchior continued with his investigation, "did you explore all the tents, and were they all filled with gold?"

"I did explore them all, and they were all filled, every inch, with gold. Why do you ask that question?"

"Gold always has ties to obvious wealth of some kind, whether its physical or maybe spiritual," said Melchior stroking his beard. "Gold is the more obvious of your dream's symbols. The animals that you have described with branched antlers are unlike anything you have ever seen. Is that right?"

"Yes. They have long, stocky bodies with relatively short legs. They are similar to our fallow deer, but beefier and grander racks of antlers.

"Very interesting, my boy," said Balthasar. "As you have more dreams and more details appear, make sure that you keep us updated. I am convinced that your dreams are not the product of an active mind, but are messages given to you by a deity. A day is coming when all of these dreams will come together and make sense to you. I suggest that you start keeping a journal of your dreams, being very specific as to their content."

"Excellent advice Balthasar. Who knows how long Gaspar's dreams may occur. If they take place over a long span of time, he could easily forget important details," Melchior offered.

"Your advice is sound, my friends. In Tadmor, I will purchase writing materials."

They moved along for some time without saying anything important. None of the magi noticed that Cassius was riding behind them listening to everything that was said. Their candid discussion made him more convinced than ever that this was no spying expedition, but was, in fact what they had told him. "Could a star really be a sign of a coming world leader?" he wondered. "No one I have ever been with has had discussions like these three, that's for sure."

CHAPTER FORTY-ONE

Noam watched as Basil carried Sophia over the nearest hill stopping from time to time to kiss her. "The old girl's got him under her spell," he said aloud. Shaking his head and smiling, he walked back through the city gates to get himself some of the lamb that the vender was cooking at the far end of the marketplace.

Satanas had used Noam before as a man on the inside to collect information for him. This was the first time he had ever had Noam and Sophia work together. The two had met a few times, but, truly, they were little more than acquaintances. When he saw Sophia walk back into the city through the gates, he didn't have to know her well to know instantly that something had happened between Sophia and Basil. There was a liveliness to her step, and her face was radiating with happiness.

He eyed her closely and said, "It appears you have the beast-man right where we want him."

Noam displaying his special ability to annoy Sophia, caused her to respond curtly, "I don't think he'll give us any problems."

"You was very convincing in your actions when I saw you being carried over the hill."

Sophia could feel herself becoming defensive, wondering how much the fool had observed. "You don't have to worry about me carrying out my role in our enterprise. I've done this before."

"You have?" he said implying more than what was stated.

"Have at it," she challenged him. "What are you getting at."

"I'm just wondering if more than kissing took place on the other side of that hill. If so, I wonders if you is for us, or for him."

"You're disgusting. I won't discuss this with you," she said as she made to move away from him.

Grabbing her arm and pulling her around to face him, he said, "Maybe Satanas would like to have an answer to the same question I'm wondering."

"Satanas would never doubt my loyalty. Let go of my arm."

Noam stared her in the eyes for a moment, and then let go of her arm. He watched her as she walked through the marketplace and out the city gates. He knew that she and Satanas were long-time friends. If he was wrong about Sophia's intentions, and let out what he thought, his life would be in peril. If he was right and kept his mouth shut, all he would be out is a relationship with a woman he barely knew. Not being a courageous man, he decided to go with the latter scenario.

The ride back to his camp was most pleasant for Basil. He never imagined that a woman would give herself so entirely and passionately as Sophia had done with him. The world seemed to him a joyous place to live. If he had known any love songs, he would have sung one. Nearing camp, he checked himself to make sure that his men did not find reason to tease him. He tried not to think about meeting Sophia again the day after next, knowing that the thought would put an unintentional smile on his face that he did not want to try to explain to the others in camp.

The first thing that he saw when he rode into camp was one of the scouts, who had been sent to keep track of the Romans, talking with the rest of his men.

Seeing their leader, one of the men said, "Basil, come hear this. The Romans have changed their route."

"What?" Basil bellowed. "They better not be planning treachery."

The scout said, "I don't know what they're planning, but instead of turning west and moving up the coast to Philoteria, the Romans went east and look like they're going to camp on the southeastern tip of the Sea of Galilee."

"I don't like this," said Basil. "Let's break camp, leave two men to watch our things, and the rest of us will find out what the Romans are up to. They may be planning to meet someone between here and Capernaum to unload some of the gold." His concern, up until now, was what Satanas might do. He felt foolish for not considering that the Romans could also be tempted to deceit with such a large sum of gold in their possession. If the Romans decided to be duplicitous, Basil knew that he and his fifteen men could do little to hinder them. A century of trained, battle hardened troops would wade through he and his men with nary a casualty.

While Basil and his men broke camp, two Roman scouts observed their movements from behind an outcropping of rocks at the top of a hill to the south. When they felt that they had seen enough, one stayed to continue observations while the other rode back to inform Laurentinus of Basil's whereabouts.

Yitzhak had kept to himself the last day making it difficult for Ezri to get any information from him. The young man had stayed alert hoping he could get some useful details that he could report to Satanas. Unfortunately for Ezri, work around the farm continued in a predictable manner.

That evening on his walk, Ezri went to the flat stone and saw that its white side was facing up. He knelt down, lifted the rock, and recovered the red stone left for him by Satanas. Slipping down the road to the fork, he passed into the trees to where the hollow tree held Satanas' message. Removing the board filled with wax, Ezri found a clearing where he could read by moonlight. He read the note from Satanas: *Basil and his men have left their camp near Hippos to keep an eye on the Roman troop movement. Basil's camp is being watched by Roman scouts. Keep your ears and eyes open.*

Ezri shook his head. "How does Satanas come up with that kind of information?" he wondered. After he smoothed out the wax and replaced it in the hollow tree, he stole back into the servants' quarters and found no problem in falling fast asleep.

CHAPTER FORTY-TWO

On the third day out from Dura-Europus the expedition was faced with a cold wind that forced them to wear layers and wrap up in their robes. The cold made the camels irritable and the wind made conversation almost impossible. Each man rode along occupied in his own thoughts. Gaspar used times like these to let his mind wander aimlessly on the subject of Rachel. Always impressed on his imagination was the memory of her large almond shaped eyes looking back at him through long innocent eyelashes. He wondered what life together would be like with her. At times he would close his eyes trying to recall the feeling of her soft, feminine shaped hands in his own. Daydreams like these both gave him pleasure and increased his longing for her, leaving him wondering if their time together was only just another daydream.

Every morning Vahumisa sent a patrol out comprised of two of his men to scout ahead. This morning they were late in returning. The expedition was still about a day out from the oasis city of Tadmor. Once reaching the oasis, his concern over being raided by bandits would be greatly diminished. Desert cutthroats were always an issue, and he hoped his scouts had not run into these wandering marauders. He tried to reassure himself that his men were good soldiers and would have taken proper precautions not to be found, but he also knew that desert bandits were exceptionally good at stealth. He turned his camel back into the wind, which the animal deemed most disagreeable, to warn the other soldiers to be on their guard.

Vahumisa was making his way back to the lead position of the caravan as they began to crest a hill. The two men that he had sent out earlier that morning came riding on their camels toward them with their hands bound behind them and gagged. Cresting the hill behind them were at least a dozen desert people. While they were making their appearance, several score of desert riders emerged from gulleys and hills on either side of the caravan. Vahumisa realizing the magi were at the head of the procession, sped his camel to take the lead once again. As he neared the front, one of bandits rode forward of the two restrained scouts putting up his hand indicating that Vahumisa and the whole caravan should halt. Vahumisa, pulling up even with the three magi, could not speak quietly in the wind so he only motioned with his hand for them to stay put while he advanced toward the bandit. The man who was holding up his hand yelled for him to stop as his men behind him drew bows directing them at Vahumisa.

"Why have you tied up our companions and threatened us with your weapons?" Vahumisa said trying to speak over the wind.

"You are in no position to ask the questions. You will not speak until I have told you to do so. I suggest that you do nothing until given permission, unless you want to become target practice for my men. Do you understand?"

Gritting his teeth, Vahumisa nodded his head.

"Good. What are you transporting through our territory and how can you relieve my friends and their families of their daily hardship of surviving in a hostile land?" the leader said in mock concern.

Balthasar raised his hand to the head bandit and said, "May I speak for us?"

"I suppose you will do as well as any."

"My friends and I would like for nothing more than to help relieve any suffering that you and your people are experiencing," Balthasar began bringing laughter from the bandits who were close enough to hear what he was saying. "My two magi companions and I will do whatever we can for you, but know that we are on an expedition for what we believe the good god, Ahura-Mazda, has called us to undertake."

During Balthasar's last few words, the bandit leader's whole demeanor dissolved. "You are magi?" he said in genuine interest.

"Yes the three of us are, and the rest have agreed to help transport us on our mission."

"Put down your bows, you fools," the leader spoke angrily to his companions. "Do you want to invite disaster upon us?" And then speaking to Balthasar he said, "We would be honored to escort you and your friends to Tadmor." Motioning to his men who were closest to the two bound scouts he said, "untie them and let them go back to their friends." Back to Balthasar he said, "My name is Farshid. May I ride along side your eminence and inquire about your trip?"

Vahumisa looked at Gaspar with a look of befuddlement, receiving only raised eyebrows and shoulders in return.

"Farshid, my name is Balthasar, this is Melchior, and this is the youngest of our sect, Gaspar. I would like nothing more than to talk to you about our expedition."

On first notion, Vahumisa did not like the idea of Balthasar telling a band of cutthroats their business, but then, upon further thought, he realized that maybe the safest course in this situation was to be completely open about their journey.

Soon Farshid and the magi had a whole group of bandits riding around them wanting to hear all about the star and its import, asking question after question. The wind continued to be a hinderance to conversation, so much of what was said by the magi was relayed to others who were farther away. Melchior and Balthasar had not found this much interest even among the young magi acolytes. The rest of the day sped by for the three religious men as they got to pontificate to their heart's delight. The soldiers realized that they would probably never be more safe than they were that day and could not help but relax.

When they reached sight of Tadmor, Farshid told Balthasar that it was time for him and his band to leave the caravan.

"Why don't you stay with us and share a meal with us tonight?" suggested Gaspar.

Farshid and the men around him laughed at the offer. "You are most generous, eminence, but the elders and the military of Tadmor would not welcome our presence so near their city. Thank you. Know that you are always welcome in our lands. We will watch for your return. May the good god keep you safe and bless you."

"May his countenance bring you peace and security, my friends," said Balthasar.

As the bandits rode away the three magi and Vahumisa looked at one another and broke into laughter.

CHAPTER FORTY-THREE

The roman cohort had already set up their camp for the night at the time that Basil and two of his men climbed to the top of a nearby hill to spy on Laurentinus and his men.

"There doesn't seem to be anything amiss down there," whispered one of Basil's men.

"Yah, they don't look like they're planning anything wrong," said the other.

Basil looked at the two, barely keeping his rage contained. "And how would they look differently if they were?"

The two looked at one another hoping the other had a good answer to Basil's question.

Motioning to the two men to follow him, Basil began to make his way down the backside of the hill opposite the Roman encampment. As they made their way to their tethered horses, Basil began second guessing his beliefs concerning the Romans' deceit. They may have simply made a decision to go up the east coast instead of the west coast of the Sea of Galilee. They had no way of knowing that Basil was only moving into place to protect the group that would be guarding his master's treasure once the Romans released it to Yitzhak. Basil had come this way to Caesarea so as not to interfere with the Romans' work. "Maybe," he thought, "I've been completely wrong in my judgment."

At that point in his thought process, Basil and his two companions heard a swooshing like arrows being fired. Before any of them could react, all three lay sprawled out on their faces, arrows sticking out of their backs.

"Yep, that's the big one and the leader that the centurion told us about," said one of the cavalrymen. "I sure wouldn't like tangling with him."

"I'm glad he said to shoot first if you see him, and ask questions later," said the other. "He's more than I would want to contend with."

"Grab their horses. We'll go back now and let the commander know that the giant has been eliminated."

The soldiers grabbed the horses and led them back over the hill to the encampment.

The next day, Laurentinus brought a detachment over to cut off the heads of Basil and his followers, buried the bodies in shallow graves, and put their heads on stakes using them as grave markers.

Basil had promised that he would meet Sophia early the next morning in the marketplace. Sophia was giddy with anticipation. The hours ticked away and still there was no sign of the big man. Sophia was not the most honest of people, but she did know human nature and was good at reading people. She knew that by the time the sun was halfway in its trek across the sky that something must have happened to Basil to keep him from coming. The man's feelings for her were real, and he was as smitten with her as she was with him. The only reason he was not there that day was because something very important came up that kept him from being there.

There were melons at the market that earlier had caught Sophia's eye. While she waited for Basil, she decided to buy one and have it for her lunch. Noam was covered with dust as he rode in through Hippos' gates. Sophia saw him and started moving to another part of the marketplace hoping that he would not see her. It was too late. He had already fixed his eyes on her and was riding in her direction.

"I don't want to speak to you right now. Please leave," she said.

"This is important, old girl. We need to go some place where people won't hear us."

"It better be important or I'll have have my big friend finish your lesson on how to treat a woman."

"I don't think that will be happening," Noam said with real sentiment.

"What do you mean?" she said looking at him suspiciously.

"Just come on outside the walls for a bit."

Sophia followed him out the gates and sat with exasperation on a large stone inside the trees that bordered the road.

"So what's so important?"

"Sophia, I'm no good at telling things like this, but I went out early this morning to see what your big friend was up to. I found where they had made camp, but there was only a couple of his men there. On my way down the shoreline, I ran into that Roman regiment. I didn't want to raise their suspicions, so I just kept moving south like I was traveling that way."

Sophia was beginning to get vexed with his story and said, "Is there a point and an end to this?"

"I'm sorry, Sophie, er-ah Sophia. I'm telling it as fast as I can."

Her eyes were now boring holes in his skull and her arms folded in annoyance.

"I came up on three graves, Sophi-a. The Romans had cut off the men's heads and stuck them on poles to use as grave markers." Noam hesitated.

"Yes?"

"I'm sorry, Sophia," he was speaking slowly and deliberately, "one of the heads was your giant's."

Sophia's hands dropped to her lap, unconsciously she made circular motions with her hands on her abdomen. After a few moments, she stood up and walked deeper into the trees. Noam watched her walk away, and then realizing that there was nothing for him to do, he went back into the city to find something to eat.

Yitzhak had continued to keep to himself until one morning he caught Ezri by the arm and said, "This evening, after you finish your chores, I want you to join the rest of the men and me in the main house to discuss the route we will be taking with the gold shipment and what our individual responsibilities will be. The Romans will be here in a few days, and I want to be ready to move out as soon as we can."

"Yes, sir," he said as he turned to catch up with the others who were going off into the fields.

"Ezri, I'm glad you're part of the group that's doing this," Yitzhak said. "It's comforting for me to know that you are honest and loyal."

Ezri stuck out his hand to shake Yitzhak's and said, "You can count on me."

Yitzhak smiled, patted the boy on his back, and said, "I know I can."

Walking back to the fields, Ezri was surprised how much it meant to him that Yitzhak felt that way about him. For the first time since joining Satanas in his scheme, Ezri felt conflicted. "Why should I care what he thinks of me?" he tried to convince himself. "I've never cared before." Then a voice inside him said, "Maybe it's because you never gave anyone a reason to before." He hurried his steps to catch up with the others who were almost to the fields.

"Hey, wait for me," he called, hoping that interaction with the other workers would erase the thoughts he was thinking. "This is no time to grow a conscience," he told himself.

The day progressed as it was planned, and Ezri soon was able to shake the scrupulous thoughts he had had earlier in the day. By the time his work was completed he was back to his old self. A few of Yitzhak's other most trusted workers joined Ezri as he walked to the main house.

"What do you think the boss wants to talk to us about?" asked one of the other hands.

"I don't know," Ezri lied. "I suppose we're going to find out soon enough, though."

"I wonder how much extra pay we're going to get for this?" asked another one.

Ezri shrugged his shoulders, and thought, "Whatever it is, it wouldn't be enough for me."

The men walked to the front door and told Yitzhak's servant that they were there for the meeting. As they entered the atrium, Ezri noticed Yitzhak and his wife, Menucha, on the other side of the entryway

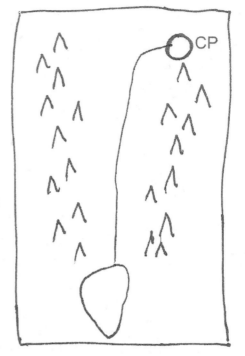

obviously engaged in a heated discussion. When Menucha said, "I don't know why you had to be so foolish as to agree to lead this excursion!" all the men's attention turned towards the contending couple. Seeing they had drawn unwanted notice, Yitzhak and Menucha moved through the doorway into an adjacent room. Ezri and his fellow workers looked at one another with raised eyebrows as the house servant showed them into a large room where several men were already waiting. On the wall was a large thin piece of wood with a very rough drawing of the Sea of Galilee at the bottom and two rows of upside-down V's—Ezri assumed were mountains—on either side that extended from the northern end of the Sea to the top of the wooden map. In the upper right hand corner of the veneer was a circle with CP written next to it standing for Caesarea Philippi . Up the middle was a line that represented the Jordan River connecting the sea with the circle. Yitzhak came in and motioned everyone to a tray of water where cups had been prepared with slices of cucumber. Taking a cup, one of the boys saw the cucumbers and nodded his head in approval of the refreshment. Ezri took a cup and extracted one of the cucumbers from the water and munched on it as he sipped the refreshing liquid.

Benches had been brought in for the meeting and Yitzhak asked everyone to find a place to sit or stand behind.

"Some of you know why you're here— others know only that I've asked you to consider a dangerous endeavor for a sizable sum of silver. If after I have explained what our little adventure will entail and you want out, no one will think the less of you."

There was a murmuring among the men. Holding up his hands for them to get quiet, he went on to explain the nature of their trip and why it must remain a secret whether they chose to be a part of it or not.

After his brief explanation, Yitzhak told them, "Now you know why I have asked you to be here this afternoon. Are there any who would like to bow out at this time?" He paused, looking around the room. One of the young men with whom Ezri worked looked sheepish and did not meet Yitzhak's gaze. "Jessie, are you with us in this task?"

"Sir, I don't want to let you down, but I really don't want to be involved in any of this. I'm sorry," he said, glancing around.

"No, this is why I have not given any specifics about our mission, so anyone who wants out can get out without worrying about keeping his mouth shut about the particulars. Thank you, Jessie. You may leave," Yitzhak said smiling. "Is there anyone else who does not want to be involved?" Seeing that the rest of the men met his eyes with their's, he continued with the details of his plan.

"On the wall, I have drawn this map of the area from the upper Galilee to Caesarea."

One of the men who was a close friend of Yitzhak's said, "You've captured that part of the country beautifully." The comment produced a good laugh for the others in the meeting.

"Okay, okay," Yitzhak said, motioning the men with his hands to calm down, "we've had our fun, now please pay close attention.

"It will be our responsibility to move a shipment of gold, that a Roman cavalry unit will deliver to Capernaum, and make sure it arrives safely to the temple of Hermes near Caesarea Philippi." He dragged his finger from the northern shore of the Sea of Galilee to the circle he had placed on the map. "Since we will be transporting the gold by way of donkeys, and because the safest route will be along these hills to the west of the Jordan River, we will be using horses instead of camels. Riding along the crest of the hills will give us a panoramic view of any trouble that might come our way. The distance is twenty-six miles. I plan to make that distance in a day and a half. The round trip will take four days, and each of you will receive four weeks wages for your participation." Looking around the room he asked, "Are there any questions."

"What will be each of our responsibilities?" Ezri asked.

"Most of you will be riding with me, as a show of force that will, hopefully, dissuade anyone who has plans of stealing our shipment. Ezri, I want you to ride with Podarces as one of the lead scouts." Podarces was the the young man who Yitzhak had sent to deliver information to Laurentinus, the cavalry commander. "I will rotate the rest of you in twos to tail the main force making sure that we are not surprised from behind. There are fifty of us in all. Our numbers should prove formidable to any gang of thieves who would want to interfere with our delivery."

Many of the men nodded their heads in agreement. Although none of those present had ever undertaken an adventure like this before, each felt relatively secure and brave with the number of men with whom they would be riding.

One of the other men present asked, "When will we be leaving?"

"The Romans should be in Capernaum in the next few days. We will leave the day before they arrive at Capernaum. Unless you have any more questions, you're free to leave."

Those on benches got up to leave and the men in back began filing out the door. As they were doing so, Yitzhak asked Ezri and Podarces to stay behind for a few minutes.

"I want to talk to you both. There's none of the young men that I trust more than you two. If either of you chooses to let me down, our chances of success fall greatly. If there's any reason to not put my full faith in you, please let me know now."

Yitzhak looked first at one boy in the eyes and then the other. Podarces spoke first, "I am completely loyal to you sir. You may trust me."

Ezri was surprised by how much he wanted to tell Yitzhak at this point of Satanas' plans and how he was involved. "Focus on the prize, you idiot," he told himself. "I'm your man," he told Yitzhak meeting his eyes.

"Good. I knew that you were good boys. I want one of you always out in front of us at least two miles scouting. Each of you will take turns reporting back to me while the other rides point. If you see anything that looks out of sorts—even if it's just a hunch—I want to know about it. Do you understand?"

Both boys nodded their heads.

"What if we can't find the other scout after we've reported to you?" asked Podarces.

"Then you will race back to me, and I will send you out with more riders to find the other boy and to look for any trouble that may have arisen." Yitzhak looked at both of the young men and said confidentially, "You boys have the most dangerous responsibility, and I will pay you an extra two month's wages for your peril."

The boys thanked him for his generosity. Ezri was aware of his growing respect for his employer. Yitzhak was honest and forthright. He could see why a man like Matthias would use Yitzhak to transport his wealth. He found himself wishing that Yitzhak had not gotten involved in this business. Stealing from a less honorable man would be much easier.

"We will talk more right before we leave. Do you boys have any other questions?"

They shook their heads, shook hands with Yitzhak, and walked out together.

"I have been so busy, I haven't gotten a chance to get to know you," commented Podarces.

"That's true. How long have you worked here?" inquired Ezri.

"All my life. My father and mother died when I was young, and Yitzhak took me in and has always made sure that I've had a roof over my head and food to eat. He is an extremely good man, Ezri."

"That is obvious. He is an easy man to follow." Levi came to Ezri's mind immediately, and like Levi, working for him was better than working for most other men, but in both instances, one was still just working for another man. As he saw it, there was no future in working for another man.

"A few of the other workers told me that you like to go for walks at night. Would you like some company tonight?" asked Podarces.

"I would like that. It would be nice to talk to someone other than the trees," Ezri said chuckling.

"I have a few things that need my attention before dinner. I'll see you after."

Podarces walked towards the stables and Ezri walked outside the compound and headed directly for the flat stone he and Satanas had agreed would be the place where they sent messages to one another. When he got to it, the white side was facing up indicating Satanas was waiting for him or had a message for him. He lifted the stone to find a red one under it, and then headed off into the woods where he could read the message Satanas must have left for him in the tree.

CHAPTER FORTY-FOUR

Gaspar's servants were overjoyed during the time that Rachel and Nazli moved into the big house. Rarely do servants have the opportunity to feel like they contribute in a major way to another's well-being. True, the house, everything in it, and all the food technically belonged to their master, Gaspar, but they felt that they were part of the household of Gaspar, and each considered that he or she had given something to the whole effort of making a new home for these women who meant so much to their master. Singing could be heard in all areas of the house displaying happy men and woman who reveled in making their home hospitable to two women who were without one.

"Are the servants always so happy in their chores?" Rachel asked .

"To be a servant in the house of Gaspar is to be well treated and respected," Balzak said earnestly. "But, no, the staff are all happy because you and your mother are here."

Rachel blushed. "I can never express how much you have lightened my mother's and my burdens. Having a place like this to come to not only is comforting to us, but it also saves us from the humiliation of having to live as peasants."

Balzak had to reconcile the fact that he very much liked Rachel, but she no longer held the position in the empire that would help to elevate his master's fortunes. He knew Gaspar would be angry if he and the other servants did not come to Nazli and Rachel's aid during this time of deprivation. He could only hope that Rachel's upbringing would be useful to his master even after the present downward turn in the girl's fate. Besides, this kind of charity would go far to help Ahura-Mazda in his battle with the evil god, not to mention his own quest to reach paradise in the next life.

"That would never do for the woman who has captured my master's heart," Balzak responded, bowing as he did so.

Most of the servants in the high priest's home stayed with the residence. The only servants who moved in with Nazli and Rachel were Kahliq and Ara. Zand had acquire Kahliq when the servant was but a child. Ara had been a personal servant to Nazli and Rachel since Rachel was a toddler even though she was but three years older than her mistress. Balzak had made room for a dozen servants thus causing most of the servants who had moved into the guest house to move back into the servant wing of the main house. Everyone's spirits were so elevated that they really did not mind the inconvenience of moving twice.

Nazli's conduct during the day of moving had not been impolite, but Balzak, as did Rachel, noticed that she was not herself—she was withdrawn. Both attributed her mood to all the transitions she was having to make in her life and gave her space to work through them. Balzak remembered how Gaspar's mother had taken the death of her husband, and he, more than Rachel, feared for Nazli. It was for reasons similar to this that Ara caught Balzak in one of the upstairs hallways and asked if she could have a moment with him alone. He led her out to the garden between the house and the stables where they could be out of sight and out of earshot.

After they were both seated on a marble bench, Balzak asked, "What can I do for you, child."

Ara smiled at Balzak's endearing epithet and said, "I think that you should be apprized of my lady's mood, sir."

"I am a servant just like you. Please call me Balzak. You refer, I presume, that your lady, is the elder?" Balzak asked.

"Yes, um. . . Balzak. It is understandable with all that has transpired the last few days that my lady's appetite and sleep should be affected, but I have never seen her like this before. I don't want to alarm the daughter, but I do want to have other people watching her lest she should come to harm through her own neglect."

"I do not know her as well as you, but I have noticed that she walks in a fog of depression, as one would expect. I will help you keep an eye on her, and hope that she is able to overcome her grief and depression by means of time and the nurture of those who love her."

"I hoped you would be compassionate. Thank you for hearing me out. I think that we should get back to the others before we are missed."

Balzak stood and motioned her with his hand down the path toward the big house. Nazli had watched the pair from her bedroom window. She could not hear their conversation nor read their lips, but she knew that the topic of their conversation was her. She turned moodily back into the room, closed the hallway door, and collapsed on the bed and wept.

Those on the expedition were still in good spirits when they reached the outskirts of Tadmor. The city was on the ancient trade route that linked the Roman empire with the orient. Tadmor was an inviting city with columns on either side of the road leading up to its gates. In talking with one of the merchants in another caravan, Melchior found out that the Romans referred to the trade route as the Silk Road because of the Latin lust for the expensive fabric.

"The Romans cannot get enough of the rare cloth," said the merchant. "As a result, Chinese coffers brim full with Roman gold. No one has been able to conquer Rome, but the Chinese silk merchants own more of Rome's gold than do the Romans," he said laughing.

Balthasar was not concerned with the commerce that maintained the beauty of this old city that dated back to the Jewish king, Solomon, he wanted to speak with the rabbis who spent their time teaching in their synagogues.

"I want to compare what the rabbis of this city have to say about their Messiah with what I was told by Jews in Nippur, and how He relates to this star that we are following," he told Gaspar.

"I will tell Vahumisa of our plan to visit the synagogue, and ask him where he plans to camp tonight. Would you not profit from rest before we meet with the rabbis?'

"Gaspar, I'll be fine. You talk to Vahumisa, and I will find out where we need to go. And, oh, yes. Bring Melchior back with you."

Gaspar gave Balthasar a look of concern prompting the old wiseman to say, "Go on. I'll be fine. Get Melchior and hurry back."

Returning with Melchior, Gaspar saw that Balthasar was talking with a man who was at least as old as him. It turned out that the old man was one of the rabbis, and when they walked up they heard him say, "Unless you were to convert to the Jewish faith, you would not be welcome in the synagogue."

"Although I have great interest in your God, I cannot say that I am ready to convert. Is there a place where we could meet and talk?"

The old rabbi stroked his beard as if he had to think through the ramifications of meeting with this man, and then said, "Near the east side of the marketplace are benches under the shade of the trees where we can sit and talk. I could meet you there when the marketplace opens in the morning."

Noticing that Gaspar and Melchior had walked up behind him, Balthasar said, "Pardon my manners. These are my friends and fellow magi. May I bring them along with me?"

The rabbi bowed with his hand to his heart to the magi, and said, "Of course. I will see you all in the morning," and walked away.

The magi made their way back to the caravan and Melchior asked, "Who is that, and why are we not welcome in their temple?"

Balthasar raised his hand to calm Melchior before he got himself worked up. "That is the rabbi, and his name is Yacob. The Jews are a strange people. They believe that they are the sole chosen people of their God. They have rules for interacting with those races that are not Jewish and are outside the faith. Those who are not Jews are called Gentiles. In their holy scriptures they have rules for worshipping in the Temple that is located in Jerusalem. The closer one gets to the room in the Temple they call the Holy of Holies, the more restrictions there are on those who may enter. The Jews believe that their god is God. To associate with those who have allegiance to other deities, is to run the risk of defilement."

Melchior and Gaspar looked at each with surprised expressions, and Gaspar asked, "Then why did the old man agree to meet with us at all?"

"I said he runs the risk of defilement by meeting with us. A Jew can become unclean by touching a dead person, by touching another person who has touched the dead, by worshipping with an unbeliever, or by touching a woman who is menstruating."

"I see," Melchior said. "Not so different from the followers of Ahura-Mazda."

"Indeed. You should also know that the Jews have but only one Temple that is in Jerusalem. They have educational worship centers in many cities that they call synagogues. It is the synagogue that he cautions us about visiting, I would guess, until he could verify that we had not done anything to defile ourselves."

Closer to the caravan the magi's attention was diverted by loud laughter. When they got closer, they saw Cyrus and Amehlech in the middle of a crowd of other caravans. They had been telling the story of how Balthasar had defeated the desert bandits single-handedly.

When Balthasar came into sight, Amehlech pointed to him and said, "Behold, our champion," which brought about cheering and more laughter.

"Soon, my old friend," Melchior said to Balthasar, "the story will get told so many times that people will have you breathing fire and flying on a magic carpet."

"I suppose so," mused Balthasar.

Cassius moved out of the crowd and approached Balthasar. "May I have a word with your eminences?"

Balthasar nodded as did Gaspar and Melchior.

"I noticed that you were talking to the old rabbi. If you will be meeting with him, I would like to join the conversation unless you will be speaking of matters that are none of my business."

"Of course you may join us," Balthasar said as he looked

at the others for approval. Getting it, he continued, "We will be meeting him in the morning to the east of the marketplace. After breakfast, we can walk there together."

"Thank you, I appreciate your indulging me."

"Think nothing of it."

Around the campfire that night, Amehlech and Cyrus sought to outdo each other with the retelling of the day's events, as group after group came by to hear the fantastic story. By the time the story had gone through its sixth retelling, and was becoming more preposterous each time, Balthasar said, "I am going to bed before our young companions deify me."

CHAPTER FORTY-FIVE

There is nothing more intoxicating than new love. To have it dashed away before it ever has a chance to blossom is compounded grief. Sophia sat by the Sea of Galilee, down from the hilltop city of Hippos, with her feet in the water watching the waves lap onto her legs. "I felt safe and loved for the first time in my life," she kept saying to herself. "Why is love possible for everyone else but me?" she said weeping into her hands. She heard a rustling of bush and sand behind her. The first thought in her head was that someone wanted to rob and kill her. "Let them," she thought. "Death will be easy."

What she next heard was the unwelcome voice of Noam. "Sophia, I know you would prefer not to talk to me, but we should be getting back to Caesarea. Satanas would like to know what has happened. If we leave right now, we could be in Capernaum just after dark."

Sophia said nothing, staring with red eyes out into the sea.

"Sophia, If you want to stay here for awhile, I could come back for you in a couple of days."

She knew if she didn't go back with Noam now, she would have a hard time explaining herself to Satanas. She was already unsure what the man would do to her once he found out about her feelings for Basil. "I'll go with you now," she said resignedly. Then realizing she wanted to know what Noam was going to do with the information he had, she asked, "Listen, is there any reason to tell Satanas about what went on between me and Basil?"

"I can't tell that it did any harm to any of our plans. I don't know why he should know."

Getting up and brushing the sand from her clothes she said, "I appreciate that, Noam, I do. I haven't been very patient with you during our time here in Hippos. Well, what I'm trying to say is. . . I'm sorry."

"Thank you, Sophia. We should get going." Noam helped Sophia up the slope to the horse and pony he had tethered to a branch. He helped Sophia onto her pony, and then bounded onto his own. For once, Noam kept from talking. For once, Sophia didn't mind his company.

The note that Satanas had left for Ezri told him that the Romans would be in Capernaum in two days. Ezri used the time to write back to Satanas on the wax tablet about Yitzhak's meeting, an overview of the information he had told them, and the responsibilities he had assigned to Ezri and Podarces. With the knowledge he now had of the Roman's arrival, he knew Yitzhak would have his team leaving for Capernaum sometime the next day. Satanas and Ezri needed to meet before that happened. The last bit of information that he wrote on the message board was that he would meet Satanas that night after everyone in the compound had gone to sleep. After he composed his message on the wax surface of the hollowed out board, he placed it in the tree, and took the red stone so Satanas would be alerted later that night.

Ezri discovered that Podarces had an engaging, witty personality. They had eaten their meal together that night, and Ezri was looking forward to their walk. He did hope that Podarces would not be as talkative during the walk as he had been during supper—he had an appointment to keep with Satanas.

The eating area for the compound was a large open-air room with a roof supported by four thick poles with benches and tables for meals. Yitzhak came in when the men were almost finished with their supper and said, "The Romans will be in Capernaum in two days. Those of you who are going with me, be ready to leave tomorrow, mid-morning." He looked around the room as if he had something else to say, thought better of it, turned on his heel, and walked out.

"Do you still want to go on our walk?" Podarces asked.

"Of course. I'll probably be getting up early anyway. Anything I have left to get done, I'll do then."

During their walk, Ezri made sure that they stayed away from the side of the compound where Satanas, or one of his men would be retrieving Ezri's notice. Most of what Ezri told Podarces that night were lies, given the fact that their conversation revolved around what each remembered of his family. Ezri made his past sound very similar to Podarces' making the other boy feel that the two had a shared past. There was some regret to telling all the lies, but Ezri realized he would not be able to be truthful with the other boy given their circumstances and the nearness of their mission. Besides, Podarces had bought everything he said about why he left home. A person like Podarces would never understand the reasons why Ezri had to get away from his father, Levi, and Gischala.

The loyalty and responsibility that he felt toward Yitzhak made Podarces less talkative during their walk than he had been at dinner, feeling the need to be well rested for the week ahead. After less than thirty minutes, he excused himself and went back into the servants' quarters. Ezri stayed out, walking casually out to the road when he heard a man calling him from the direction of the compound.

"Ezri! Ezri!" It was Yitzhak.

Ezri ran back towards his employer and said, "Yes, sir."

"Ezri, why are still out? Shouldn't you be getting your rest? We have a grueling few days ahead of us. You should make sure that you are fully rested."

"You're right, but my mind won't stop running. I'll just lay in bed and toss and turn. Walking calms me, and then I'll be able to come in and sleep."

Yitzhak patted Ezri's shoulder. "You're a good boy. Don't be out too late."

"I won't. Thank you." Ezri watched the man turn and walk back toward the house, and then he turned and walked a way down the road. Looking back to make sure no one was watching him, Ezri snuck into the woods to wait for Satanas at the boulder.

The night was clear, the moon was full, and the air's coolness refreshing. The stars, unobstructed by clouds, shone with all their glory. Ezri's thoughts drifted to what he would do when he had his share of the gold. The idea of having a place, that only he knew about, continued to intrigue him. He had been thinking about different areas where he had been in the surrounding mountains north of Caesarea. None of the landscapes that he envisioned were exactly what he visualized for his hideout. "When this business is through, finding a place for me to retreat is going to be the first thing that I do," he thought. So lost in his ruminations was he that Satanas' coming up behind him caught him completely off guard.

"Satanas!" he said much louder than what he wanted.

"You should be more careful. Never be in a position where someone can sneak up on you."

Ezri nodded, feeling foolish for letting his mind wanderings put him in a compromised position.

Squinting under the moon's light at Ezri's note to him, Satanas said, "So Yitzhak has you as a scout, huh? We can use that. Did he mention how he would use you?"

"We're going to be riding atop the western ridge of mountains that hem in the Jordan valley. Podarces and I will be on a rotation scouting out in front of the main group so that the other can feed Yitzhak with regular reports of any activity."

"Your note says that there will be a total of fifty men guarding the gold. I have sixty. That should be more than enough to accomplish what I want to do. There will be two times that we will attack the caravan. The first time, while you're scouting and the other boy is reporting to Yitzhak, we'll draw as many of the main guard out as we can so we can ambush them and reduce their numbers. We'll do this right before you make camp on the first day. They will want to be fresh when they turn east with the Jordan to make the last leg of the trip. That will be the most advantageous part of the trip for us—it's heavily wooded and hilly with more valleys. The trees that cover the mountains in that stretch of the trip will force Yitzhak to move down to the river valley. We have several men designated as archers. Once the caravan moves into this portion of the trip, we'll start picking them off one at a time from the last man forward. When you are within a few miles of Caesarea, we'll carry out an attack that surrounds them with our full contingent. We will leave no one alive, and take the gold. To make sure that we leave no one who can tell the story, we will launch a final assault when you are on your last rotation as scout, making it possible to pick up the other scout in our raid." Satanas then smiled his unsettling smile. "I'm sorry you will miss all of the fun."

Ezri did not know what to say, so he said nothing, smiling weakly.

"Don't worry. Your time will come. We will keep in advance of you and the other boy. I'll be taking the main body of men out early tomorrow morning to camp to the east where the Jordan also bends east toward Caesarea. I will be keeping you informed when the other scout is reporting to Yitzhak." Satanas paused, and then looked at his apprentice. "We're going to have a lot of money, boy, but we have to maintain our focus all the time for next few days. No daydreaming."

"Yes, sir." Ezri could feel his face redden as he thought about Satanas sneaking up behind him earlier.

"I'll keep in contact. Any questions?"

"No, sir."

"Then I'll see you on the road." Satanas moved back through the trees and disappeared in the darkness.

Ezri walked back into the courtyard and made his way to the servants' quarters. He laid on his cot for a long while that night. Thoughts of the gold that he would own in a few days would not let him sleep. In the last few hours of the morning, sleep finally encompassed him.

CHAPTER FORTY-SIX

Early the next morning, Satanas and his thirteen archers went down to where the Jordan curved to the south and rode the ridge of mountains, in the opposite direction that Yitzhak and his men would be taking when they brought the gold back to Caesarea. The rest of his men, which made up a much larger contingent, rode along the Jordan west to where they would set up camp for the evening. It was near mid-day when Satanas' group came to a significant dip in the ridge where one could follow a shallow, gradual spillway down from the ridge into a wadi below. The wadi curved back parallel with the ridge about halfway down the mountain. It would mean an earlier attack in the day than he had planned, but he could not ask for better geological conditions for an ambush. They spent time in reconnaissance of the area to make sure they had a clear escape route through which to run after leading Yitzhak's men into their trap. The wadi widened significantly after the curve. This would be where Satanas would hide his ambushing archers. The three that would play the role of bait would ride through the other ten archers, once beyond them, the three would then provide protection from any of Yitzhak's men who might try to pursue the ambushers when they made their retreat. The archers had spent the last two weeks practicing shooting their bows from the back of their horses. Although they all were accomplished archers, none of them had ever had the need to be able to fire from the back of a horse in full motion.

The archers followed Satanas back up to the top of the ridge. "The more of their men we can eliminate from the big assault at the end," Satanas explained, "the more likely we will all live to enjoy our share of the loot."

The men laughed applauding his ingenuity.

"If we can wipe out ten to fifteen here, and then another ten later that day, we should be in a very good position to kill off the rest the following day."

The group moved along easily, feeling confidant in what they had to accomplish. Many of the men joked and conversed in the high spirit of anticipated wealth. Satanas' eyes never stopped scrutinizing the landscape. He too, was sensing the inevitability of triumph. He smiled his unsettling smile, turned his horse north, and said, "I've seen enough. Let's go meet the others at camp."

Ezri was surprised to be wakened by his new friend. "I thought that you would be up early," teased Podarces. "Are you going to be ready to leave when Yitzhak calls us?"

Rubbing his eyes sleepily, Ezri responded, "I only have a few things to pack and I'll be ready to go. Should we see if Yitzhak needs help with anything before we go to breakfast?"

The boys found Yitzhak and six other men loading provisions on three donkeys. Six other donkeys were being readied so they could carry the gold back to the temple of Hermes. Ezri felt a surge of excitement course through him when he realized the four pack animals purpose. He could not help but wonder what all of that gold would look like.

"Can you use two more sets of hands, sir?" asked Podarces.

"We're almost done here," said Yitzhak looking over his shoulder, "but in the second storeroom, at the end of the stables, are weapons that I have borrowed that need to be laid out so that the men can come by and arm themselves."

Ezri and Podarces looked at each other and then raced to the door of the storeroom, leaving Yitzhak and the other men smiling and shaking their heads.

Podarces unlatched the doors pulling them open. Ezri rushed into the large room where he saw swords, shields, javelins, two bows, two quivers of arrows, and three other large bundles of arrows tied with jute laid out on a long table. To Ezri, this represented an immense quantity of weaponry. He wondered if Satanas had taken this into account. On the opposite side of the room was another table of equal length bearing but a few miscellaneous farm items. The boys removed the objects from that table and placed it outside perpendicular to the building with one its short sides against the wall. They had just begun to move the weapons from the one table to the one they had placed outside, when Yitzhak and the other men came to lend a hand. With nine of them, it took no time to arrange the swords in one stack, the shields next to the the swords, and then the bows and arrows next to them. The javelins were already tied together in three groups with rope, and they were balanced in the corner created by the table and the outside wall of the storage house.

When they finished with that chore, Yitzhak said, "I'm hungry. Let's go eat and we can finish what few things we have left after breakfast."

That morning they had fresh warm roti—a flat bread—melon, and dried meat. Many of the other workers were coming in from early morning chores as Ezri and his group came into the covered eating area. When the men had seated themselves, Yitzhak stood on one of the benches to the side of the pavilion, and motioned for their attention.

"I will be absent for a few days. As always, when I am not here, Omet will be in charge." Yitzhak paused collecting his thoughts. "The errand that the other men and myself will be undertaking is very dangerous. For several days I have wished that I had not so readily volunteered for this task. But the dye has been cast and I must complete what I may have foolishly adopted. Pray for me and the rest who will be with me, asking God for protection over us. Now, before I use up all of your attention spans, let's eat."

Menucha looked on, standing by one of the posts that supported the roof of the eating pavilion. Putting her hand to her mouth, she hurried away to the big house. Ezri and several other of Yitzhak's men saw her hastening into the house. The workers felt compassion for her; Ezri wondered how she would run the estate without her husband. He stopped his contemplation, understanding that such thoughts could only hinder the success of their plan. "There were always going to be casualties," he told himself. "I better get used to it."

Noam and Sophia reached Capernaum well after the sun went down. Sophia was almost asleep on her pony when they stopped. She dragged herself around helping Noam collect wood for a fire. While Noam built the fire, Sophia got out bread, a fig cake, and raw almonds that Noam had packed for their trip back up north.

Sitting on a rock he had rolled over by the fire, Noam said, "Tomorrow we have to make contact with Ethan so he can get information to Satanas about what has happened the last few days." He was careful of his word choice so as not to upset Sophia.

Sophia sat looking at the fire through a fog of grief and exhaustion. "Noam, I'm going to bed," she announced. She walked over and grabbed out a blanket that was stuffed into one of the two bags she had draped over either side of her pony, stumbled over by the edge of the fire, curled up in her blanket, and took only a few moments to cascade into a deep sleep.

Noam watched her go through her motions. After a few moments, he got up and brought the bags that were hung over the withers of both their animals closer to the fire. Nestling in his blanket he looked up into the sky and watched a star for a few moments that appeared to be moving easterly in the sky. He did not think much of it as he turned over and closed his eyes until morning.

The sun had not climbed over the horizon the next morning and the sky was still a deep blue. "Noam. Noam. Noam," he heard Sophia whisper as she shook him to a conscious state.

"What is it, old girl?" Noam asked not really caring, and wanting desperately to be left alone.

"I hear someone in the bushes, Noam," she hissed in his ear. "You have to wake up and go see who or what it is."

"All right, all right!" he said in exasperation. Picking up the knife he kept under his head when he slept at night, Noam crouched down, and moved stealthily into the bushes where Sophia was excitedly pointing. He had gotten no more than six feet into bushes when a man jumped up from behind him putting a knife to his throat.

"Put down your knife," the man said with a raspy voice. Sophia began looking frantically for her knife. "You better stay still, or this guy won't live to see the sun come up."

Sophia's movements ceased.

"Ethan?" Noam said with growing awareness.

"Yah. Why?"

Noam turned and punched his attacker with the butt of his hand against the man's shoulder knocking him backward. "What do you think you're doing scaring me like that?"

Laughing, Ethan said, "You was sleeping so soundly I didn't want to wake you up."

Sophia stood looking at the two men with incredulous indignation.

The two men hugged each other and came walking back to the campsite each with an arm draped over the other's shoulder.

"If you aren't a pair. Satanas must be awfully upset with me to have me working with idiots like you," Sophia said half whimsically and half in earnest.

The two men continued laughing not paying any attention to what Sophia had said.

"How long you been skulking around back there, Ethan?"

"I just got here not long ago. I couldn't help taking advantage of a good situation."

"Well, you sure scared me."

The two men laughed again.

Over a simple breakfast of hard bread and figs, Noam told Ethan what had happened to Basil and the two men that were with him while Sophia walked down to the sea to freshen up.

"They cut off their heads and used'em for headstones?" Ethan asked when Noam had finished his report.

"I think they did that to scare others from trying to pull

anything."

"I'm glad we're going to be dealing with a bunch of country folk and not the Roman army."

"You're right there." At this point Noam laid his hand on Ethan's arm and said, "Hey, listen. This whole business with the heads really upset Sophia. I'd appreciate it if you didn't talk about it while she's around."

"Sure, Noam. She doesn't seem to be the kind of woman who'd be bothered by something like that."

"I think, normally, she isn't, but I think she's nervous about her head being used for the same purpose."

"Oh, yah."

Noam had been good to his word, and had not let out any of the details about Sophia and Basil's affair. He could not help wondering if this might come back to bite him later on. He and Ethan talked awhile longer about how much each of their splits were going to be, and how they would spend their share. Before Sophia returned from the water, Ethan had taken off to tell Satanas the news he had been given.

"Where's your friend?" Sophia asked walking back into camp.

"He needed to get the news back to Satanas. You know, er, ah, having the big guy out of the picture changes things a lot."

"Thank you, Noam. I know there's going to be times where we have to talk about the circumstances surrounding Basil's death. It's okay to talk about it, but I appreciate your not wanting to hurt my feelings."

Noam smiled, nodding his head, and then both of them were quiet.

"Um, Sophia?"

"Yah, Noam."

"Could you be pregnant?"

Sophia winced. "I could be." She stared into the ashes from the fire the night before. "I hope not."

Noam nodded his head and joined her staring into the ashes.

CHAPTER FORTY-SEVEN

"I've been thinking, Balzak," Rachel said after she and her mother had been at Gaspar's house for a few days. She had joined him each day to practice her knife throwing. The expectation of having to ever use the skill to ward off an enemy never crossed her mind, she simply enjoyed the sport of it. Balzak was like any man, having the company of a pretty, good-natured woman certainly did not make his daily work-out any less enjoyable. "With our sudden decline in social status, might it be possible that Gaspar could desire someone else?"

Balzak gaped at her momentarily and then said, "My master is no such man. If he has professed his love for you, it is because he loves *you* and not your station in life or your wealth. I will hear no more talk of this. The master would be deeply saddened to hear you speak thus. Please don't ever mention this to him, unless you find that you no longer love him as you thought you had."

"I don't think that I could ever not love Gaspar. I am honored that a man of his character would feel as he does towards me. But I have wondered if he would have noticed me if I hadn't been the high priest's daughter."

"All my master needed to do was to meet you. Be assured, dear girl, that he would have loved you the moment he saw you no matter what the circumstances." Balzak went over to her, took her hand, kissed it, and put a throwing knife in it. "Let's not talk about things that aren't true."

At the mention of Gaspar loving her, Rachel looked at Balzak with a silly expression that caught him off. "You think Gaspar loves me?" she said dreamily.

"Oh, my young woman. That is not for you to hear from me, but from my master. Now, let me see your stance."

Since mother and daughter had come to stay at Gaspar's estate, Nazli had been in bed day and night, preferring to take her meals there—which she rarely ate, and then only little.

"I have brought you fresh, warm fig cakes, nuts, and melon, my lady," said Tala opening up Nazli's door just enough to peep in her head.

"I am not hungry," Nazli said. "Maybe I'll have something to eat later in the day. I'll let you know."

"Begging your pardon, ma'am, but you've hardly eaten

anything the whole time you've been here. What would my master think of me if he came home and found you ill-fed?"

"Thank you for your concern. I'll eat later," Nazli said rolling over and covering her head with her blankets.

Tala moved farther into the doorway and was going to protest more, but thought better of it and walked down with the breakfast tray to the kitchen. She had just set the tray on one of the tables when she heard Rachel laughing and Balzak's voice outside. Rushing to the door, she stepped out and intercepted the two coming back from their practice.

"May I have a word with you two?" she asked bowing her head to the two of them.

"Of course, Tala. You look concerned. Is something wrong?" Rachel inquired.

"It's your mother, my lady. I'm concerned about her habits since coming here to live," Tala rejoined.

Balzak's face clouded over with a look of concern. "I assume you refer to her isolating herself in her room. She has just lost her husband and her home. Isn't her behavior to be expected?"

"I would expect it, yes," began Tala, "but she still must eat. When she does eat, she hardly has anything at all. Ara says the same thing when she takes food up to my lady. A bite here, and nibble there. I'm concerned that she will make herself sick if we don't get her out of bed and get some food into her."

"I should not have gone out this morning," Rachel said. "I should have stayed with Mother and tried to sooth her emotions."

"This is not your fault, Rachel," said a fatherly Balzak, and then correcting himself, "my lady."

"I don't mind that you call me Rachel, Balzak."

"Thank you, but there is a time and a place for decorum," he nodded to Tala and himself, "and a time for familiarity. As I said, this is not your fault. Don't take that on yourself. If you want to be by your mother's side and encourage her, do so. Taking on the responsibility for her condition is foolhardy."

Smiling, Rachel placed her hand on Balzak's arm and said, "I know what you're trying to tell me, and I will work at keeping a proper perspective, but Tala has made me aware that for the first time in my life, my mother needs me." Looking at Tala she said, "Thank you, Tala. I will go and clean up and then be sitting with my mother." Rachel hurried into the house leaving Tala and Balzak looking at each other.

"I think our houseguest will find her way out of this. She has much to live for," comforted Balzak.

"I hope she realizes that before it is too late. No matter what happens, I did want you two to be aware of my concern for my lady. I feel better knowing that you both know what my fears are."

As she walked back into the kitchen, Balzak reflected on what both she and Ara had told him. Balzak had spoken encouraging words to all three women, but now he felt his own concern rising.

Melchior woke to Cyrus and Amehlech's laughter. They were still recounting the past day's events with greater and greater fabrication as they made the morning fire and unpacked the food for breakfast. Melchior shook his head, amused at their imaginative abilities. He stepped out of his tent and stretched in the chilly morning air. Seeing that it was quite chilly, he stepped back in and wrapped a blanket around himself. When he came out again the two comedians had ceased their chatter.

"We're sorry, your eminence, if we woke you," said Amehlech.

"I was awake anyway. Your wit and laughter makes me happy. Don't think of apologizing for it."

"Just the same, we should have been more considerate."

There was a comment that Melchior wanted to make to Balthasar concerning their discussion the day before they were visited by the bandits, and he made his way into the old magi's tent. When he entered, he saw Balthasar laying on his back staring blankly at the tent's ceiling.

He yelled, "Balthasar," and ran over to his friend and pressed his ear to his chest. Balthasar did not move or blink, but Melchior could hear the man's heart beating. Reaching an arm around the old man''s shoulders, Melchior sat him upright and slapped him sharply on the chest. Balthasar took a deep breath as his eyes fluttered to consciousness.

"What are you doing?" Balthasar said looking stupefied at his colleague.

"You were unconscious. I thought at first that you might be dead."

"Ridiculous," snarled Balthasar. "Is Gaspar up yet? We should probably get going so we can meet with the rabbi."

"How do you feel?" queried Melchior.

"I am fine. How should I be? Go on. Go make sure Gaspar is up. I want to leave within the hour."

Melchior watched his friend for a moment and then left saying, "I'll be right back."

Balthasar went over to his water basin, poured water into it, and rinsed off his face and hands. "They pamper me like I'm a doting old man," he said, drying his hands and face on a towel.

Gaspar was sound asleep when Melchior went into his tent. "Gaspar, wake up. I want to talk to you."

"Melchior, I was sleeping so soundly," Gaspar whined, rubbing his eyes. "You do sound concerned—what is it?"

Plopping down on a folding stool, Melchior told Gaspar what he had experienced in Balthasar's tent moments before.

"He was just staring up and unaware of your presence?" restated Gaspar.

"There was no acknowledgment of my being there until I rapped him on the chest with the flat of my hand."

"And he was breathing?"

"Yes. I am concerned that we may lose our friend on this trip, Gaspar," Melchior said, sadness dripping with each word.

"What can we do? You and I both know that he will not listen to returning to Nippur until our journey is ended. I know he would feel better if he rested for a few days, but he refuses to let us stay in any place long enough to let him do that. Since we left Dura-Europus, he has been exhausted at the end of every day. He refuses to slow down."

From the other side of Gaspar's tent flap came Balthasar's voice, "And I won't slow down until we meet the Messiah." Balthasar stepped into the tent and placed his fists on his hips and said, "Now you two listen to me. I'm an old man. I should have been dead years ago, but I'm not. I'm not because God wanted me to be a part of this trip. I want you two to stop trying to ruin the last days of my life. I don't want to be any other place than here with the two of you on this trip. Stop worrying about my death, and start helping me live what life I have left." He looked at them with stern resolve. His face then softened into his benevolent smile. "Rejoice with me these days I have left. No one lives forever, and I have outlived most. This task that we are endeavoring is a suitable end to my life. I am happy. Won't you be happy with me?"

"I will do as you wish," relented Gaspar.

Melchior had been studying a spot on the ground as Balthasar spoke. He lifted his eyes that were misted with tears and said, "As always, your wisdom is irrefutable. As you have said, so it will be."

"Good. Now get ready for the day. We have an appointment to keep."

Rachel had been sitting with her mother all morning and it was well past lunch. Nazli had not moved off her left side. A few times, Rachel had gotten up from her seat and checked to see that her mother was still breathing.

Ara poked her head in the room and motioned for Rachel to come out into the hallway. On a table, Ara had set the two meals she had prepared for her mistresses. "Do you want to try to get your mother to eat?" she asked. "Either way, you should have something, my lady."

"Thank you Ara. I will have something and then see if I can waken Mother and get her to eat."

"Yes, my lady."

Rachel watched Ara walk down the hall.

Later, after trying and failing to get her mother to eat, Rachel sat down again. "If nothing else," she thought, "at least she's on her right side now."

Tala peeped her head through the door and motioned her out to the hallway as Ara had done. "There's a gentleman downstairs who said he would like to see you. His name is Majid."

Rachel groaned. "Just when I thought the day could not get any worse. I don't want to see him alone, Ara. Would you please fetch Balzak and ask him to attend me while the gentleman is here?"

Tala hurried away, and Rachel thought to herself as she walked down the hall, "This way I don't have to keep putting him off. I'll be direct and be done with him." A shadow of guilt crept into her thoughts. "I did use him to get Gaspar's attention. I must remember to treat him well."

CHAPTER FORTY-EIGHT

About mid-day Ethan saw Podarces acting as scout along the ridge of mountains to the west of the Jordan valley. Shortly thereafter, he saw the rest of Yitzhak and his men about two miles behind. Ethan was in a hurry to get to Satanas before nightfall, but he slowed his progress so as not to draw attention to himself. When he was out of sight of Yitzhak's band, he again quickened his pace, pulling into camp just before the rest of the outlaws had settled down for supper. Satanas smiled his eerie smile, which even discomforted his men, beckoning Ethan to join him.

"Did you see Noam and Sophia?"

"I did, Satanas," Ethan said getting off his horse. "They told me that the Romans killed the giant and two of his men. They said they cut off their heads, stuck'em on sticks, and used'em for grave markers."

"Lousy Romans. Well, I didn't want to have to tangle with Basil anyway. By the time the rest of his men get word from Mathias as to how to proceed, our business will all be done. Everything has been greatly simplified. Instead of dealing with two separate groups, we just have Yitzhak and his men." Satanas inhaled deeply. "I can smell that gold already." The men standing around him roared their approval.

Yitzhak and his men made good time the first day, so they stopped well before sundown and made fires to roast the two goats they brought along for the first night's meal.

After that first day, Yitzhak had told them that there would be no camp fires. The biscuits, fig cakes, and nuts that they brought would have to suffice until their transfer of the gold was completed. That night the men told stories, laughed at one another's jokes, enjoyed the roasted goat, and fresh cucumbers and onions they would not get to eat again until the end of their commitment of guarding the gold.

Yitzhak stood up in front of his men, who were all now crowded around the fire. "Tomorrow we will meet up with the Roman guard. We will camp tomorrow night near the Roman encampment, and then we will transfer the gold to the asses the next morning to start the most dangerous part of our responsibilities. Sleep well tonight. Don't drink. You will want to be at your most sober tomorrow and the next few days. Remember, it is not just you. We all are depending on each man." He looked straight at Ezri when he made this last statement. Ezri's initial thought was that Yitzhak suspected his treachery. He realized this was a ridiculous thought or Yitzhak would have never allowed him to be part of the guard. The men soon dispersed, took out their blankets and made beds for themselves around several of the fires.

The next morning Satanas sent Ethan back to Capernaum to keep track of Yitzhak, so he could let him know when the group was traveling north again. Yitzhak had his men up bright and early so they could reach Capernaum before the Roman guard got there. The men wrapped themselves in their blankets to block the the cold chill of the early morning hours as they progressed south.

Ezri had been riding next to Yitzhak for a few minutes after delivering his report about the road ahead. Yitzhak had insisted on Ezri and Podarces practicing this procedure on the trip south to Capernaum so that the process would be familiar to them. No one would attack them now without anything to steal.

"Do you think anyone would attempt to attack a group as large as ours?" asked Ezri.

"I don't know, honestly. I hope that no one knows about the shipment, but that is probably naïve to think that."

Ezri thought, "Yes it is."

"Still," Yitzhak continued, "we might get lucky, and if any marauders do see our numbers, they may decide the risk of being killed is too great, and steer clear of us. I would like to think that would be the greatest possibility. I think we've done a good job of keeping it secretive, but secrets do get out. That's why Podarces' and your job is so critical to our success and safety. If we can know that we're going to be attacked and where, we stand a greater chance of bringing everyone and the gold home.

"I hope you're right, sir," said Ezri. "I want to thank you again for giving me this opportunity. I'll do right by you."

"I know you will, son. I'm not worried about you or Podarces fulfilling your roles in this adventure."

Ezri smiled and said, "I better get back to Podarces before he starts wondering where I am. Thanks for the talk." He heeled Raven in order to catch up with Podarces.

Riding away, he heard Yitzhak say, "I like our talks."

Ezri could not help thinking that his employer sounded a lot like his own father and Levi. He shook his head not as sure as he once was that men like them were foolish.

CHAPTER FORTY-NINE

It had never occurred to Rachel that she would have to face Majid again after the dinner party. His good looks and popularity with the young women of Seleucia and Ctesiphon had caused her and her mother to assume he would merely move on to another of the many girls who sought his attention. Her conscience was smarting with the knowledge that she had purposely used the young man to gain Gaspar's attention. She was hoping that Majid was not there now to challenge her intentions. She took a deep breath before she descended the stairs that emptied into the foyer below where Majid was waiting. Some of the grand houses of the sister cities had large curving staircases that led down into massive receiving rooms, allowing their owners to make impressive entrances. She was glad that Gaspar's home was more modest, and that she would not be making a spectacle. The stairway was at a right angle to the foyer, so Majid did not even see that Rachel was in the same room as he until she had taken a few steps away from the base of the stairs. She glanced down the hall leading to the servant's quarters and was pleased to see that Balzak was already making his way towards her. A smile came to her face as she watched his comical movements—his short legs taking two strides to anyone else's one, and his ever-present knives, one on each hip. When he reached her, he gave her a reassuring look and then held out his hand directing her into the foyer ahead of him.

Majid's good looks and well built frame were only superseded by his boundless ego. As he had boasted at the dinner party, he was an excellent man of business. Through his self-aggrandizement, he had been trapped into footing the cost of the magi's expedition.

Majid stood when Rachel entered the room and showed only the faintest look of disappointment when he saw Balzak following.

"Beautiful Rachel, it is good to see you again. Thank you for agreeing to meet with me unannounced," he said bowing his head.

Rachel dropped her eyes, bowed her head, and dipped slightly at the knees as was custom.

"Thank you, Majid. How are your father and mother?"

"They are well. I am sorry to hear about the death of your

father. That is part of the reason why I have come."

"It is most kind of you to do so," she said without fabrication. "But please, I have forgotten my manners. Let us sit, and I shall have refreshment brought in." She motioned to one of the male house servants who had positioned himself where he was in Rachel's sight line. He came over to the trio, bowed, and Rachel said, "Please bring sekanjabin for our guest and Balzak and me."

They moved over to couches that had been arranged to enable easy conversation. Rachel sat on one couch and Balzak stood off to her side. Eyeing the diminutive servant and glancing at his knives, Majid sat across from her.

"I was hoping to speak with you alone," Majid said nodding toward Balzak.

"Balzak has become like a father to me in the absence of my own. Besides, he has been instructed to personally look out for my safety by his master," Rachel smiled unassumingly.

"But you surely do not feel that you need to be kept safe from me."

"If you want to talk to me, Balzak stays," she said as Balzak nonchalantly placed his right hand upon his knife.

"I see," he said, his eyes squinting. "Then I shall come straight to the point. Not only I, but several who were also in attendance at your party, feel that you used me to gain the attention of Gaspar, the master of this house. How do you answer that accusation?" Majid said with conspicuous emotion.

"Be careful where you tread, sir," warned Balzak. "You are a guest in this house, and the lady to which you speak has the same command here as does the master."

Placing her hand on Balzak's arm she said, "Thank you, Balzak, but I need to answer these accusations. Majid should know the truth." Turning to the young merchant, she said, "What you say is absolutely true. My mother and I schemed to gain the attention of Gaspar and did use you because of your bearing and reputation in the city. To many of the eligible young women of the city, you are very desirable. We thought that you would most likely forget about me as soon as the party was over because you are attractive to so many of the women in the sister cities."

Majid observed Rachel for a moment allowing his eyes to roam to Balzak's hand on his dagger. He momentarily looked Balzak in the eye, and then looked back to Rachel. "You spin a good tale."

"If I have hurt your feelings in any way, I ask for your forgiveness," said Rachel.

"I was made to look foolish in front of many of the most prestigious people of Ctesiphon and Seleucia. Everyone is talking about it," he said.

"I think most people didn't think any more of the evening than that you and I were sharing dinner conversation because of our close proximity at the table."

"You and Gaspar used me to pay for his expedition."

Balzak stepped in at that point and said, "You go too far, sir. My master has no need of your wealth. He, as you know, is a man of formidable means. Do not go so far as to make baseless accusations."

"Because Gaspar hides behind his priestly robes and the king's favor, he has become untouchable. When he returns I will have words with him. I'll see myself out." Standing, he walked briskly to the door, letting himself out before a servant could open it for him.

The servant who was bringing the drinks returned as the front door slammed. "Would my lady and Balzak care to have their drinks?"

"Yes. Please," said Rachel. "Balzak, come sit and let's talk about what just happened."

Balzak moved to the couch that was closest to Rachel and sat down. Rachel thanked the servant for their sekanjabin.

"I could not lie outright to Majid. What I told him was the truth." Then smiling she said, " "Well, I suppose I embellished his standing with the young women of Seleucia a little bit."

Balzak rolled his eyes and said, "You were right to tell him the truth. I think it was kind of you to embellish what you did. I'm not sure he bought it all considering his reaction. He's a proud boy from a proud father. The saying that the fig does not fall far from the tree is appropriately used here."

"What do you think the fallout will be from all of this?"

"Oooh, I don't know. I don't think that you should go out alone for a while until he has time to cool down. At least until Gaspar returns, Rachel."

She smiled and pressed his arm. "Now is a time for familiarity?" she said playfully.

"Yes, it is," he smiled, patting her hand. "A man like Majid holds on to slights for a long time. He will be less likely to act once Gaspar returns. Until the master returns, we must be careful, and you may want to start carrying a knife. You probably won't need it, but I'd rather be overly cautious than have you harmed."

"He would have never even come to my father's house," she said with rising ire.

Speaking calmly, Balzak told her, "But your father isn't here, and Gaspar isn't here, so we must be careful. I'm sorry, child."

Rachel picked up her sekanjabin and sipped its bitter

sweetness. "Thank you for bringing my mother and me under your roof Balzak. I don't know what I would have done if it were just Mother and me."

"You don't need to thank me. You have brought joy to this house." Looking around as if someone might come in and ask them to do some work, Balzak said, "We have some time before supper. Would you like to go out and throw knives with me?"

Rachel giggled, grabbed his hand, and pulled him out to the knife throwing range.

The three wisemen and Cassius were at the agreed upon benches to the east of the marketplace, waiting when the old rabbi came walking up to them. All of them stood to greet him.

"Thank you for meeting us, eminence," said Gaspar.

The old man waved his hand and said, "Just rabbi, call me Rabbi."

"I am Gaspar, this is one of our traveling companions, Cassius, another magus, Melchior, and you have met Balthasar."

"We did not exchange names, young magus. My name is Reuben Ben Hillel. It is customary to call me Rabbi." Reuben paused for a moment and the others could tell that he was formulating what he would say next. "Magi are also called wisemen, if I am not mistaken."

"That is true," said Balthasar looking out the corner of his eye to his friends.

"Some believe that you practice magic. Is that also true?"

"There are some of our cult who have chosen to study the magic arts, but none of the three of us focus on that aspect of our training," said Melchior, "although Balthasar sees things that will happen, and our young friend has what appear to be prophetic dreams."

"I see," said the rabbi stroking his long beard.

"Is there a problem?" asked Balthasar.

"I can only answer your questions about my faith. I do not want to get into a discussion or debate over our two faiths. May we agree to that?"

"Of course," Balthasar stated nodding his head as he motioned for them all to sit down.

Sitting with his hands in his lap, the rabbi said, "How may I help you, then?"

"There is a new star in the night sky that does not behave like other stars. Do your scriptures speak of such a star?"

"Not to my knowledge. I know of no such star mentioned

that is a portent to any great event. There are references to stars in general, and as a comparison to celestial beings both good and evil. To my knowledge, there is no reference to a new star in the heavens," Reuben said directly.

The magi looked at one another questioningly if not with disappointment.

"In your holy book," said Balthasar, "it says, *There shall come a Star out of Jacob, and a Scepter shall rise out of Israel and shall smite the corners of Moab, and destroy all the children of Sheth.* In our own prophetic writings it says, *when the heavens are illumined by the brilliance of a new star that rises out of the west, men will follow it to find he who is the true ruler all.*"

"I can't speak to your prophecies, but the one from the Torah, the first five books of the Bible, speaks of an individual not a literal star. The personage mentioned here, as in other parts of the Bible, is the political figure we know as Messiah who will deliver Israel from her oppressors and reestablish the ten commandments."

Cassius could not help thinking of all the 'messiahs' that had sprung up all over Palestine claiming they could bring order to the land and liberate the Jews from their Roman overlords. He wondered if such a child were to be born, whether Rome would allow him to live.

Reuben continued, "In the east, stars refer to kings, I am told, and here, it is the same. It is not so much a portent of a coming ruler, but the star *is* that ruler. I'm sorry you have come so far to be frustrated in your journey, but such are human attempts to know the plans of God."

Melchior and Gaspar both began to speak, but Balthasar placed his hands on both of their arms and said, "Thank you for meeting with us, Rabbi. Would that we could have had your insight before we left on our journey."

"It is all right. I hope you are not too disappointed."

"We are, but such is often the path for those who seek truth," said Balthasar.

The men stood and watched as the rabbi walked back toward the synagogue.

When he was out of range of their voices, Melchior said, "I had more questions that I wanted to ask him. Why did you not let me speak?"

"He obviously, long ago, formed his opinions, and he was not open to looking at his suppositions in a new light," said Balthasar. "We know what we observe. The star moves as no other star, and it appears to be moving with us and directing us toward Jerusalem. To ask him more would have only annoyed him."

"I suppose you are right. I was hoping to get more information."

"As was I," sighed Gaspar.

"So, will we continue on until we see this thing through?" asked Cassius.

"Of course," said Balthasar. "I'm more convinced than ever that we are on the right track."

"How so?" asked Gaspar as the other two men gave each other questioning glances.

"For some reason, the Jewish God wants us to see His king of the Jews. He wants us to obey Him. We have all the information we need," he said as he started back to camp.

The other three shook their heads and followed after the magus.

When they reached camp Balthasar was relieved to see that Vahumisa had already packed everything and was moments away from being ready to leave.

"Vahumisa, you are a good man. We need to leave as soon as you deem us ready," said Balthasar as he crawled onto his kneeling camel.

CHAPTER FIFTY

Late in the afternoon of the second day out from Caesarea, Yitzhak and his men reached Capernaum and camped west of the town by the tiny sea. The Romans showed up not long after and set up their own encampment not more than a quarter of a mile from Yitzhak's. He had met the centurion only one time before, but it had not been that long ago, and Yitzhak easily recognized the man.

"Hail, citizen," said Laurentinus as he rode up with his four lieutenants to Yitzhak.

"Hail, commander," said Yitzhak not quite comfortable with the language of the Roman military. "It is good to see you again."

"And you. I invite you to have dinner tonight. I would speak to you about your mission and the man for whom you perform it."

"There is a disquieting tone to your invitation. Is there something wrong, Commander?"

"I must see to our encampment, but I shall speak freely at dinner. When it is fully dark, come to our sentry and tell him that Laurentinus has sent for you. He will let you inside our enclosure, come straight down between the tents to the large tent, and we shall talk then." Turning their horses, the Romans trotted back to the detachment of cavalry soldiers.

Since they were so close to the Roman military, and they did not have possession of the gold yet, Yitzhak let his men make fires and roast a lamb for their evening meal. Well before the lamb was roasted, Yitzhak made his way over to the Roman camp.

One of the sentries called out to him, "Halt, identify yourself and state your business."

"I am Yitzhak, and Laurentinus has sent for me."

The sentry pointed down the center row of tents and said, "Leave your horse here, and follow this path to the big tent in the middle of the camp." Another sentry came up and secured the horse near the entrance.

Walking between the rows of tents, Yitzhak could hear the conversations of the cavalrymen. Most were laughing at the stories they were telling. At one tent he overheard the sad tale that has been familiar to all armies in all times of a soldier whose betrothed had left him because she no longer wanted to wait for him to finish his military commitment.

When Yitzhak reached the big tent, Laurentinus was standing at the opening.

"You are a punctual man. That is good."

Yitzhak smiled disarmingly, "Who in his right mind would keep a Roman officer waiting?" He wished he would have said something else as soon as he said it.

Laurentinus produced a good-natured laugh, to Yitzhak's relief, slapped him on the back, stretched out his hand and said, "That is very funny. Tonight may not be as dull as I anticipated."

When the meal was brought into the tent, Yitzhak immediately wished he could have eaten before he came. He was served military fare: salted beef, hard biscuit, honey, and water. Although the meal was meager, he was pleasantly surprised by how much he enjoyed the commander's conversation. The military leader had come from a farming family and the two of them warmed up to the other by swapping stories from their childhoods. As they were finishing their meal, one of the cavalrymen brought in wine and a small bowl of figs. Laurentinus poured their wine and settled back into his chair. Yitzhak had had only a few encounters with the Roman soldiers and had found them to be brash and elitist. This Roman was neither, Yitzhak found him to be a man he could call a friend.

"Yitzhak, thank you for your company tonight. If I might be straightforward," Yitzhak nodded assent, "most Jews don't have much time for Romans. You have encouraged me to be more," he paused searching for the right word, "hopeful."

Yitzhak laughed and said, "Since you brought it up, I was thinking similarly of you."

Laurentinus steepled his fingers in front of his mouth and grew serious. "I can now call you friend. The reason I asked you here is because I have heard that you are a good man. Now that I have spent time with you, I know that to be true. And since you are a good man, there is all the more reason to warn you of any entangling relationship you may have or could have with Matthias in the future. How well do you know this man?"

"Not well, really. We have had a few innocent business dealings over the years. What do you know of him."

"Only that he is merciless with those who cannot pay on time, and he has friends in high places that he uses to eliminate those who get in his way. Be very careful that you don't ever get in a position where you need his mercy because he has none. If I would have known the kind of man you are, I would have taken the time to get permission to take this shipment of gold all the way to Caesarea Philippi, but I hated being manipulated by this scoundrel, Matthias. I'm afraid I have put you in a very dangerous position."

"You and your men can't join us?"

"No. Tomorrow I must leave for Caesarea Maritima. If my business wasn't so pressing, I would ride with you to Caesarea Philippi. You must be careful. I would not put it past Matthias to rob you, blame you, and then take your estate to cover his loss. Do you trust the men who are with you?"

Yitzhak's reservations about his being capable of completing this operation successfully had him worried before—now Laurentinus had him on the verge of panic.

"Yes, all of my men have been handpicked by me. I trust them all explicitly."

"That is good. You have scouts?"

Yitzhak nodded his head and then explained how he was deploying them.

"I wish I could give you a half dozen of my best men, but I need them in my duties. There's a chance that no one knows of the shipment, but I doubt it. Expect everything, and think through how you're going to meet each problem. The most important advice that I can give you is don't let your men get separated. A simple ploy would be to try to fragment your forces and then pick you off little by little."

"I am now terrified, Laurentinus. I see now that I should have never have volunteered for this. I was foolish to think I could handle it. When I initially spoke with Matthias, it sounded like an adventure. I am such a fool."

Laurentinus looked into the farmer's eyes and said, "You can do this, my friend. Don't let your men bunch up together. Have them ride two by two at least two horse lengths apart. Station a few more men around the gold and express to them the necessity of constant vigilance. If you are to be attacked it will come at a time when you are relaxed and not paying attention. Remind them to stay alert."

"Your expertise has already given me some comfort. I will utilize the information you have given me. Thank you."

"If you would like, I can come over to your camp tomorrow morning and give some simple instruction to your men that will help."

"I would like that very much," Yitzhak said. "It is getting late, and we need to get an early start."

Laurentinus walked his friend to the entrance to his tent. "I will come to your camp first thing in the morning. Have your men ready."

The two men grabbed each other's right forearms in a Roman handshake and Yitzhak made his way down the row of military tents to the sentries.

The peaceful lapping of the sea on the shore and the gentle breeze did nothing to ease Yitzhak's concern as he walked his horse back to camp. "You're going to get yourself killed, you fool," he said as he kicked a rock into the water.

The picture of Basil's head on a stake marking his grave came vividly to Ethan's mind as he neared the two encampments down by the seashore. He knew the Romans would have scouts set out about their camp, and he did not want to look suspicious to them in any way. He kept his distance and tried to appear to be nothing more than a common traveler. Sometimes, he knew, the best cover was to be completely in the open. The camp that he set up was a distance from Yitzhak and his men, but close enough that he could see when they broke camp the next morning. The little fire he started provided ample heat to roast the sizable tilapia he caught in the Galilee. He was just wiping his hands from eating half the fish he caught when a Roman cavalryman rode up to him and asked why he was camped there.

"I just finished work in Scythopolis, and I'm on my way home," he lied.

"Why did you choose this spot and not a place in town," asked the Roman.

"I'm not a rich man. I thought I could catch my supper and be safer near all you Romans, than by myself. Do you want me to move?"

"No, you're all right where you are. Just don't do anything foolish."

"I'll be quiet as a lamb."

The soldier glared at Ethan and then turned his horse and rode towards the Roman camp.

Ethan watched him for a few moments, shrugged his shoulders, and went over and threw a few more branches on to his fire.

Later that night Ethan heard a man's voice calling his name. He knew that Noam and Sophia had traveled to Capernaum when he had gone to fill Satanas in on what had happened with Basil and his two men.

"Noam, I'm over here. Follow my voice," Ethan said in a heavy whisper. Clouds had obstructed the moon and movement on the rocky shore was made difficult in the absence of the lunar glow.

"Aahhg!" voiced Noam. "I thought I'd never find you. Did you reach Satanas?"

"I did."

"What'd he say?"

"Um, he was glad that Basil was out of the way. He thought that'd make our plans run smoother."

The moon began to peek out from behind the clouds and

Ethan could see that Noam's hair was a mess and that he had several scrapes and bruises on his arms and face.

"You want to go clean the blood off blood your face and arms. The rocks and branches had their way with you it looks like to me."

"I suppose so. Come talk with me while I clean off." They both walked down closer to the water where Noam found a rock to sit on while he rinsed the blood from his face and arms.

There was a gash in his shin that started to ooze blood once he finished cleaning it. Ethan jumped up, ran to an olive tree a distance up the hill and returned with leaves Noam could use to press against the injury to quell the bleeding. Noam looked up, and said, "I suppose I'll have to take Sophia back to Caesarea myself."

"Yep. I got to travel fast once the gold leaves. Her pony won't be able to keep up."

"Is there anything more I need do before we start back?"

"I can't think of nothing. Just keep yourself out a trouble 'til the job's done. It shouldn't be more'n a couple to three days."

"All right, Ethan, Sophia and me'll leave tomorrow. We'll meet up with you in a few months or so to divvy up the fortune."

Ethan watched Noam pass beyond the light of the fire into the darkness. Shortly thereafter, he heard him groan after knocking his shin on another rock.

"Sophia'll be cleaning more of his cuts when he gets back to their lodgings," Ethan chuckled as he poked the fire with a stick.

CHAPTER FIFTY-ONE

Each day Rachel went to her mother's room and each day Nazli refused to remove herself from her bed. Though she was inactive, she continued to lose weight due to her lack of eating. If she ate anything it was only a few mouthfuls, and she only had a few sips of water each day. In a very short time she took on the appearance of one who was already dead. Ara, Tala, and Rachel could not entice her out of her bed, nor could their most desperate coaxing induce her to eat but a few bites of food a day. Her body and her hair had not been cleaned in days, giving the room a fetid odor that met any who came into her room. One day, Rachel had had enough.

"Mother," Rachel said looking down on her mother's upturned face, "I know that you miss Father, but I need for you to get better. I can't believe the woman I have known all my life is the one who is lying here allowing herself to die. I cannot believe how much weight you have lost, and this room reeks from your unwashed body. Mother, please! Come back to me."

Nazli's eyes remained closed. She did not move. Rachel moved nearer to see if her mother was breathing. Nazli's eyes flashed open, causing her daughter to jump.

"You cannot know what I feel. I have lost the man I love, my station in life, and my home. My life will never be the same," she said, her eyes aflame.

"You have not lost me. I'm here. I love you. Gaspar will give you a greater station in life than you had before. Father cannot be replaced, but life must go on," Rachel entreated.

Nazli's glare softened. "I am tired. Let me sleep. When I awake, I will summon Ara to help me bathe." She turned over pulling the covers over her head.

Rachel knelt down and kissed her mother's head through the covers. "I love you."

Nazli's steady, heavy breathing was the only reply she received.

The room lightened perceptibly when Ara poked her head into the room and motioned to Rachel to join her in the hallway.

"I am sorry to disturb you, my lady, but I couldn't help but overhear your conversation with your mother. What are we going to do?" Ara asked, her eyes filled with concern.

"I don't know. We have pleaded with her, coaxed her, and now I have been very direct with her. We can't make her want to live." Rachel's eyes filled with tears as she said, "It's as if she's never really cared for me at all. How could she willingly leave me?" She dropped to her knees and sobbed into her hands. Ara bent down pressing her mistress against her legs.

"She loves you, my lady." Ara said smoothing Rachel's hair. "She just can't see it through her grief. Don't you remember how close the two of you were? Never doubt that she loves you."

"I know, Ara, but I just can't stand to see her like this. I have lost my father. I do not want to lose my mother, too. I want to believe that Gaspar loves me and will come back to me, but what if this time away makes him realize that he really does not love me?" Speaking through fresh sobs she said, "What if I lose all three?"

Dropping down to the level of her mistress, Ara said, "From what the servants of this house say, you have no fear of that. Their master is an honorable man. Don't add false fears to your already burdened heart, my lady."

Rachel looked up and smiled through her tears. "You have spoken wisely. If I let myself go down that road, I'll be lying next to my mother in no time. Thank you, Ara."

Her servant was just about to suggest that they walk in the garden when Tala appeared at the end of the hallway. Seeing the two other women on their knees, and one crying, she rushed towards them. "Are you all right, my lady?"

"Yes, yes, Tala. Thank you. I was concerned about my mother and Ara was comforting me. Do you need us for something?"

"No. I came up to see about your mother, and from what I am seeing here, I suspect there's no change. I'm sorry."

"Me too," said Rachel.

At that instant, the small table-side gong rang in Nazli's room. The three women rushed into the bedroom.

"Ara, please prepare my bath," said Nazli.

"Right away, my lady," Ara said smiling at Rachel as she left. Tala bowed as she exited the room. Rachel smiled and went over and kissed her mother.

Pulling the covers back, she said, "Come, I'll help you get ready for your bath, Mother."

The trip from Tadmor to Damascus was at least a four day trip if the caravan encountered no obstacles. Balthasar was in high spirits. Whatever malady had caused his friends to be concerned for his health before seemed to have disappeared completely. The weather, for the time, was cooperating and they

188

experienced no more chilly winds. Mornings usually necessitated a blanket around the shoulders, but by mid-morning everyone was riding comfortably in their robes. Amehlech and Cyrus kept everyone upbeat with their antics and stories. At one point, when Cyrus was riding backwards in his saddle, supposedly mimicking Amehlech, Vahumisa became so tickled that he nearly fell off his camel. His men dared not laugh, but the three magi found themselves having to hold on lest they meet his same fate.

Gaspar's thoughts returned again and again to the woman in Seleucia with the beautiful, dark eyes. He wondered if she thought as often of him as he did of her. How fortunate was Balzak getting to visit her every few days, he thought. Balzak surely had entreated her to learn to throw knives, and Gaspar wondered if she had indulged him.

Most frequently the magi's conversation revolved around the star and the person to whom it was pointing. They began to notice that at the beginning of their travels, the star seemed to be merely in front of them, but the farther west they progressed, the more the star appeared to be leading them. While it was still moving easterly every night, it was farther down in the southern sky. Balthasar expanded their possibilities the second day out when he suggested that the star may not be leading them to the birth of the King of the Jews, but merely to the person who may already be born.

"He could be a man by now," suggested Balthasar, which led them into a discussion that lasted that whole afternoon.

When Ara finished Nazli's bath, she and Rachel expected to see her get dressed and join everyone downstairs. She asked for her sleeping clothes instead and went back to bed.

"Maybe we expect too much, Ara," Rachel said.

"How so?"

"She did get up today and take a bath. Tomorrow she may ask for breakfast."

"I hope you're right, my lady."

The women were standing at the top of the stairs when they heard a, "Psst!"

Down at the bottom they saw a smiling Balzak motioning with his head toward the knife throwing range.

"Let me change," said Rachel. "I'll meet you there in a few minutes."

CHAPTER FIFTY-TWO

Laurentinus was true to his word. The next morning as Yitzhak's men finished with their breakfast, the Roman commander rode up with two of his officers to the disarrayed civilian camp that had a haphazard grouping of the tents. There was none of the perfect rows of displayed in the Roman camp.

Seeing his new friend, Yitzhak strode over to where the Romans had reigned in their horses. The horsemen dismounted and one of the officers held the reins to Laurentinus' mount.

"Good morning, Laurentinus," said Yitzhak. "It is good to have you here. Thank you for coming."

"You are most welcome, and good morning to you. How soon may I speak to your men?"

"Right now." Yitzhak turned to his men sitting around in groups and yelled, "Come. Sit around the Commander. He has agreed to give us instruction that may save your lives."

The men gathered around the Roman and listened as he went over those things he had mentioned the night before to Yitzhak. When he had finished his crash course on military strategy and defense he said, "No matter what. Don't let anyone draw one part of your group away from the other. Maintain your solidarity as a group. If you become separated, you will be more easily defeated. My last point I want to leave you with is the same as the one I started with. I can't overemphasize how important it is for you to stay alert the whole time. As soon as you become lethargic, is when you are in the most danger from attack." He looked around from man to man, and then continued, "You have chosen a difficult, and possibly deadly task, but you can be successful if you remember what I have instructed you this morning." Turning to Yitzhak he said, "May your God protect you and your men."

The men dispersed, getting themselves ready for the return trip to Caesarea. Yitzhak shook Laurentinus' hand and said, "Thanks, again, my friend. I will not forget your kindness."

"I will be in your region of the empire in about six weeks. I will look in on you then. I hope to find you doing well."

"As do I," Yitzhak said with a sardonic smile.

"When your men are ready, come to our encampment and we will transfer over the gold," Laurentinus said as he walked over to his horse, leaping into the saddle.

While the Romans galloped back to their camp, Yitzhak yelled to his men, "I want to leave in half an hour."

As they rode away, one of the officers asked the Roman commander, "Do you think they will come out of this alive?'

"I'm not sure my little training with them will be of much advantage. In the heat of the battle, they will revert to what comes naturally to them. They have not been drilled to react as disciplined soldiers." A look of concern came over Laurentinus' face. "If they encounter an opponent who has laid out his plans well, they will be lucky to come out alive..I wish now I would not have been so belligerent with that son of a dog, Matthias. I hope my desire to teach him a lesson does not spell death for this good man and his friends."

"Since we do not leave until tomorrow, could we not spare eight of our own men to take them a part of the way?" suggested the other officer.

"Yes, that is very possible. Choose seven of your best men to escort them with you until noon."

"It will be as you command."

Ethan lay in his blanket watching the activity of the two camps farther down the beach. He had a few figs and a hard biscuit that he chewed on wanting to time his departure slightly ahead of Yitzhak's group. When he saw the civilian camp move en masse to the Roman camp, he knew it was time to ride north and alert Satanas that Yitzhak's group was on the march.

While Ethan was riding with haste to connect with Satanas, Laurentinus and Yitzhak were saying good bye to one another. The commander explained to his friend that the Romans would not be leaving until the next morning, so he would be sending eight of his men to ride four in advance and four in the rear of Yitzhak's men until they were well north of Capernaum.

Yitzhak welcomed the transition afforded by having the Roman detachment ride with he and his men until mid-day. The full emotional and psychological weight of transporting the gold did not fall on Yitzhak until he watched the eight Roman soldiers ride south to meet back up with their unit.

"Podarces! Ezri!," Yitzhak shouted. The two boys came riding up from just a few places back.

"I want you to ride ahead a couple of miles and then begin our rotation of reporting back to me. Be careful. If something doesn't look right, don't be courageous, ride back to me with your report."

The two boys nodded their heads and raced off.

Farther north, beyond the ambush point, Satanas was

staggering the rest of his men along the trail to ambush the men who would be bringing up the rear of Yitzhak's guard. The device that was used was simple. A pliable branch was secured at one end to a tree. The other end had all of its branches sharpened to a sharp point. Added to the sharpened branches were larger sticks that were also sharpened and then fastened to the branch. Four men then bent the branch back into the trees and was blocked with a stake. The branch was set so that it would swing in behind a rider and impale him through the back. Small, light- weight branches were place in front of the device to hide them from sight. Three of these contraptions were created along the road where Yitzhak's group would be riding.

These traps were meant not only to kill and maim but to cause fear and panic in the guard with the hopes of causing some of them to abandon their mission.

After the archers staged the initial ambush, they were to ride ahead to hide in predesignated places in the trees to also snipe at the riders. Between desertion, death, and serious injury, Satanas hoped to diminish the guard to only a few men that could easily be overwhelmed with his larger numbers.

Satanas had little regard for human life, but he did understand his need to maintain superior numbers. As he made sure that all of his plans would be precisely executed, he repeated endlessly, "Preform your task with as little risk to your own life as possible. The success of this undertaking is based on our ability to have greater numbers when we ultimately face them in open battle."

Satanas had everything in place the way he wanted it. He thought, "Now, the only thing to do is to wait for Yitzhak and his country bumpkins."

Yitzhak's guard was told before they left to pack their water, dried meat, and hard biscuits where they could get to it easily. Supplemental water for the horses was carried on donkeys, but each rider was to include a skin of water for his own mount. About an hour after the Roman detachment had left them, Yitzhak signaled that they should stop for lunch and water the horses. He had divided the men into groups of ten, and each group took turns eating and watering their horses while the rest stood guard. During the third rotation of eating, Podarces rode in from scouting.

"Sir, we've seen nothing so far. As you have probably observed yourself, the main road along the Jordan isn't even traveled much today. It looks like you've chosen an excellent day to make the transport," Podarces observed.

"Keep bringing me back information like this, son," Yitzhak said smiling. "As far as I can tell, we're a little more than a third of the way there. I suspect the most dangerous and obvious place for an attack will be in the wooded area where the Jordan turns northeasterly towards Caesarea Philippi. From here on out is where I think an attack will most likely come. Stay alert."

"Yes, sir." Podarces had great affection for his employer, but he was tiring of hearing him say to be alert.

"Rest and water your horse before you return to relieve Ezri. Keep up the good work."

Yitzhak's attention was redirected to several of the men who were laughing and joking. He left Podarces to make sure they were not distracted from their purpose. Podarces watered his horse, took out his meal, and ate it as he rode ahead to replace Ezri.

It had just occurred to Ezri that Satanas may not be the only thief who might be trying to steal Matthias' gold. The concept unnerved him a bit. He thought that he probably should not be quite so lackadaisical about his assignment. He had nothing to fear from Satanas' men, but what about somebody else's? Just then he heard someone down a gully say his name. He was startled for a second, and then realized he did not have to worry about a person in hiding who called his name. He turned Raven to follow the gully down to a level spot on the side of the mountain. There he saw the host of archers waiting in ambush for Yitzhak's men.

"Hey, boy," one of the archers said. "Satanas told us to make sure we let you know that this was going to be the first place we hit the shipment. He went on to explain how the ambush would work. "Has anything changed on your side?"

"No they'll be coming right along the ridge up there," Ezri pointed to the mountain he had just descended. "I think they probably have stopped for lunch and to water the horses. The other scout is reporting back to them right now. The main body will be along probably within the hour, I suspect."

"All right, boy. You watch yourself."

"And you do the same."

Ezri rode back up the gully and topped it just in time to see Podarces riding back towards him.

Waiting for the other boy to catch up to him, Ezri said, "Have they stopped to eat."

"Yah. They shouldn't be long, though. Did you see something down there?" Podarces pointed down the gully.

"No. It just looked suspicious, so I gave it a look. Just mountain and trees," he said nonchalantly.

The two boys rode together for about half of a mile and then Ezri turned back to give his report to Yitzhak. He wanted to make sure that he was not with the main body of riders when they reached the ambush point. Shortly after leaving Podarces, he heeled Raven to a trot.

When the archers saw Ezri ride by heading south, the man who had spoken with Ezri got the two archers in place who were to be the decoy.

When Ezri met up with Yitzhak he was surprised to see how much progress they had made.

"Everything is still clear," Ezri said, conscious that he had even less time than he had hoped to get back to a safe point beyond the ambush.

"I like that kind of report. We may get through this after all," he said pulling his tunic up in back to wipe the back of his neck. It was a mild spring day, but his anxiety had made him sweat more than he normally would have. "You haven't seen anything that even made you suspicious?"

"I did hear some birds that I thought might be someone giving a signal," he laughed, "but when I checked it out it was birds."

"All right," Yitzhak chuckled, "it makes me feel safer knowing that you're checking out even those kinds of hunches."

"I should get back to Podarces."

"Stay alert," he said as Ezri rode away.

The archers saw Ezri ride up to the gully, slow his pace, give his head a nod behind him, and take off again.

"They're not far away now. Everyone look sharp," the archer Satanas had left in charge said. He rode down to join the main contingent, leaving the two decoys hiding in recesses of the mountain.

Having had a break and just eaten, Yitzhak and his men were feeling a little lazy and confident that no one would attack them from a vantage point where they could see trouble coming from all directions. It was at this time that they passed the gully where Satanas had placed his men for the first ambush. Yitzhak, in the lead, passed first. The men had gotten complacent about keeping their distance from one another and had bunched up. Several men passed by the gully when the two archers stepped out from hiding and loosed four deadly arrows into four of the guard before they knew what hit them. The two assassins made as much noise as they could running and sliding down the gully. Above, Yitzhak's enraged men came cascading down the dry waterway lessening the distance, every second, between them and their antagonists.

Yitzhak was screaming, "Stay in your formation! Stay in your formation!" but the expectation of catching and punishing their comrades' killers made the men's resolve stronger than their judgement. Eighteen men raced down to the level area and turned to their right thinking they would now easily apprehend the cowards who had attacked them. The horsemen in front did not register their peril until swift arrows penetrated their chests and heads. Horses screamed as arrows lodged in their throats and chests. Riders in the rear slammed into those who had either already died or were trying frantically to turn their horses and run away. Panic reigned. The archers sat astride their mounts and easily snuffed the life out of seventeen of the pursuers. The last remaining rider was trapped under his felled horse shrieking for mercy. One of the archers rode over to the man, dismounted, took out his knife, slit the man's throat, and wiped his blade on the man's tunic. The men who had played decoys had mounted their horses by now and were leading the rest of the archers along the base of the mountain until they reached a path that led them to the road through the forest. Of Yitzhak's fifty men, only twenty-eight remained.

Up on the ridge, Yitzhak and his men could hear the mayhem taking place below.

"What do we do?" one of the men screamed at Yitzhak.

The truth be known, the gentleman farmer did not know what to do. If this was a lion attacking his herd, he would know what to do. Who could know how to respond in this kind of mayhem?

"Hold your position," Yitzhak said sounding much more in charge than he felt.

Soon the sounds of carnage stopped and Yitzhak with two other of his guards made their way cautiously down to where all of the men lay who had been duped by Satanas' trap. Two of the horses were dying. Yitzhak unsheathed his sword and put the animals out of their misery. The ten horses that were either unhurt or had minor scrapes, Yitzhak said to bring them along with them.

"What should we do about the men?"

Yitzhak looked around at the faces of the dead men he had just shared a meal with and said sighing, "I'll come back with some men in a few days to bury them. We can't stop now. We'd be easy targets here."

One man made like he was going to object, but then realized that was all that they could do.

Once they reached the top of the ridge with the horses, Yitzhak became conscious of the fact that the riderless animals would be just one more thing for them to worry about.

"Let them go. We can't be worrying about horses and gold." Motioning with both his hands for the men to gather around him, he continued with, "This has been a grievous attack on our friends. I will come back with servants, and anyone who wants to, to bury those who were just killed. I can't help but think if those men would have followed the commander's instruction, we would have only lost four men and not over twenty. Listen to me. We can no longer do as we have done. Maintain your distances, and remember to stay together." He turned to take his position at the head of the entourage, and then whirled around in his saddle. "I'm sorry for the loss of our friends. Let's do our best to make sure that we don't lose more needlessly. You will want to grieve, but in doing so you will put yourself and the rest of us in danger. Please. Stay alert."

Down almost half their number, the procession no longer had the numbers to ward off a direct assault, and not one of them was unaware of that fact. Several were speculating how they could get out of this debacle before they too suffered the same fate as their comrades. Yitzhak himself wondered if he would ever get to hear his wife say, "I told you so." The high spirit that had once prevailed was now replaced with dread and foreboding. Each man said a silent prayer hoping that God would protect him until they reached Caesarea.

Ezri caught up once again with Podarces and was wondering how many men were lost in the ambush. He was glad that he had not made close ties with either Yitzhak's men nor with Satanas'. One could only guess as to how many on both sides lost their lives. Before he had his hands on his share of the gold, he hoped he would not have to be one who had to kill another to get it.

"What's wrong, Ezri?" said Podarces noticing the distress in Ezri's face.

"Nothing. I guess I was just wishing we were back at the servants' quarters with all of this behind us."

"Yah, I know what you mean. The closer we get to the wooded portion of our trip, the more nervous I become. Do you honestly think anyone knows what we're doing?"

"I don't see how. Everyone Yitzhak has chosen to be on this mission is a close, trusted friend of his. Still, information like this seems to leak out no matter how careful a person is," Ezri said, wishing his friend would stop talking about this and head back to give his report. He could not stop wondering if he had done anything to raise Yitzhak's suspicion of the part that he had played in the day's events.

"Large sums of gold and careless talk seem to go hand in hand don't they? I'll head back to Yitzhak and be back before you know it."

With Podarces gone, the nagging feeling that he was being watched intensified. "What had he to be afraid of?" he asked himself. But he could not shake the feeling that there were eyes that were watching him.

Ezri turned around to see if the other scout was still in sight. He wasn't. When he turned around again, coming up out of a ravine was a small, slender man with a smile on his face. Relief washed over him when he realized it was Ethan whom he had met once.

"I been watching you and the other boy, waiting for him to leave."

"You scared the life out of me, Ethan," Ezri said.

"I want to warn you that the first booby-trap is several hundred yards beyond where you'll enter the woods. Don't be in the back of the pack then. That first one will come from the right side, and the second two, farther in, will come from the left."

"Thanks for the warning. Do you know how many people were killed in the ambush?"

"Those fellas just passed me not long ago down by the road near the valley. None of them were killed, but about twenty of the farmers were."

Ezri blew out air. "I don't think Satanas thought the ambush was going to be that successful."

"I don't think so either. That farmer was a fool to get involved in this. I almost—I said, I almost feel sorry for him," Ethan said laughing.

"Yah, me too," Ezri said not enjoying the other man's humor.

"I got to go. See you, boy."

Ezri waved at the crude man, relieved that he was at last gone.

When Podarces reached Yitzhak and the others he was shocked to see how few men there were riding with his boss.

"Where is everyone?"

"They were foolish and paid the ultimate price for it," Yitzhak said gloomily.

"So they're dead?"

"We were ambushed by two archers. They killed four of our men and ran down a path on the other side of the mountain. Eighteen of our men rode after them, and all of them were killed. I think there was a large number of archers waiting for our men when they reached the bottom. They didn't have a chance."

"What are we going to do?"

Yitzhak took a deep breath. "We're going to deliver the gold to Pan's temple. Have you seen anything up ahead?"

"No, but now I don't know if our scouting is doing much good. They obviously know we're out ahead of the group, and are hiding from me and Ezri."

"Because of that, I'm tempted to bring you both in with us. I don't want to place you boys in any more danger."

"It sounds like wherever we are is going to be dangerous. Why don't you let us broaden our search, and see if we can do a more effective job."

Yitzhak stared into the young man's eyes for a moment, and then said, "All right, but be careful. Don't take any chances you don't need to. I don't want to find any more of my friends dead."

"We will be careful. Since we'll be expanding our exploration, we'll not be reporting back as frequently."

Yitzhak nodded his head and reluctantly sent the boy on ahead.

CHAPTER FIFTY-THREE

Gaspar had gotten writing materials in Tadmor, complying with the advice Balthasar had given to him. At first he thought he could catch up on recording his dreams while he rode, but between all the conversation with the other magi and the swaying of his camel, which made him nauseous when he wrote, he decided to leave that chore for nighttime. Besides, trying to juggle all the writing materials on a camel's back was a skill beyond his abilities. When he sat in his tent at night and tried to log his dreams, those dreams often turned to his dreams of he and Rachel. He was not typically a man who was easily moved to passion, but Rachel fired his heart like no other woman he had ever met. Progress was made in his recording, but his thoughts of Rachel impeded it.

The act of recording his dreams helped him focus on them and to put them in perspective. The dream with him standing on a hilltop outside an unknown city with the star coming closer and closer to him still did not seem to make anymore sense now than after he had first dreamt it. The dreams he had had more recently about the strange looking animals and the frozen camp had a distant future feel to him, and therefore, were not as haunting. He felt frustration in his understanding of the dreams in that they only elicited feelings — nothing precise or tangible. The magi had lots of discussions about the dreams, but nothing of note came out of them.

Balthasar became more and more animated and excited each passing day of the trip. Soon, his incidents at Dura-Europus and the Oasis at Tadmor were almost forgotten. Damascus was a welcomed sight for the travelers. Situated by the Abana River near Mount Qasyun, surrounded by the lush and fertile plain of Ghutah, Damascus was truly the "pearl of the middle east." Much to Balthasar's chagrin, the caravan stopped for two nights in Damascus to enjoy the beauty of the city and partake of the city's excellent melons and grapes. After traveling many days in the desert, it was comforting to spend a few days in a climate and surrounding that was very much like their own Mesopotamia.

"Our quest is to find where the star will lead us," said Balthasar. "We can dawdle in Damascus on our return trip."

"The men are tired, and frankly so am I," reasoned

Melchior. "Let us enjoy a day of resting our back sides from the monotony of all day travel."

"I suppose you are right my friend. I will try to curb my anticipation."

Instead of continuing south from Damascus on the King's Highway, the caravan took the southwest route, the Coastal Highway, toward Hazor. Once a powerful city of centuries past, Hazor was now little more than a village. Mount Hermon's snow-tipped peak offered a breathtaking backdrop to this beautiful plain that each of the travelers, even Balthasar, was loathe to leave.

CHAPTER FIFTY-FOUR

Ezri was not surprised to see Podarces' horse in a lather when he returned. Playing the role, to which he was becoming more adept, he said, "Whatever is wrong? Has something happened?"

Raising his hand, signaling to let him catch his breath, Podarces said, after a few more gulps of air, "They've been ambushed. Twenty-two are dead."

For an appropriate reaction, Ezri did not need to pretend; the episode horrified him. He wondered if such things would ever stop bothering him. One day, he hoped, it would all just run off his back.

"How did it happen?"

Podarces told him all that he knew. Ezri thought how ridiculous those men were to chase after Satanas' decoys. He had determined that heroics were for losers. Never would he allow himself to be placed in danger in order to save another's life.

Shaking his head, Ezri said, "How foolish they were."

"And after the Roman commander had just warned us against that this morning," Podarces said thinking he continued Ezri's thought.

"Yah. Well what now?"

"Yitzhak was thinking that he wanted me and you to come back to be with the larger group for protection, but I talked him out of it" (To which Ezri gave an inward sigh of relief). "I told him that we would expand our scouting boundaries so we could hopefully spot another attack before it comes."

"I agree with you," Ezri said realizing how much Satanas' schemes would be jeopardized if he were riding with the main body. He hoped that he would be able to get word to the others not to kill Podarces or Yitzhak would insist on discontinuing his scouting duties. "Tell you what. I'll take the right side of the road and explore out to a few hundred feet, and you do the same on the other side."

"That sounds good to me. Yell if you see or hear anything at all."

It wasn't long before the barren mountains gave way to wooded hills. It was here that Ethan had warned him that the first booby-trap was hidden. He had to look hard to find it, but eventually he discovered it well camouflaged with branches from surrounding trees and bushes. Not far from it he almost ran over the man who was placed there to set it off, causing his horse to shy. The noise caught Podarces' attention who was not far on the opposite side of the road.

"You okay?" Podarces yelled.

"Yah, just kicked up a rodent of some kind and startled Raven. You see anything?"

"No. I hope I don't."

Ezri dismounted, walked over by the bush, and knelt down to Whisper to Satanas' man. "Listen. If any of you kill the other scout, Yitzhak will insist that I join the large group. Can you get word to the rest?"

"Yes, as soon as I set off this trap."

"I have an idea. I'm going to say that I discovered the next trap and report it to Yitzhak, or he's going to start thinking that our scouting isn't doing any good. I hope Satanas agrees."

"You'll have to face him, boy."

"How far is the next trap?"

"Not more than a mile."

Ezri said nothing else and quickly remounted. Waiting until after this booby-trap was triggered was the best time to go back and give Yitzhak the next report, he decided.

What had started as an exciting adventure that morning was now a heavy cloak of apprehension. Each man's thoughts were occupied with the thought of how does one fight an enemy who will not reveal himself. It was one thing to be gallant against a foe who came at you in the open. It was another to sit and be easy prey for a cowardly assailant who skulked in hiding places, waiting to kill and run. These were not timorous men, but the gold held them capture. They could not leave the treasure unprotected to hunt ensconced cowards. The gold held them prisoner to the road—and gullible to ambush.

Yitzhak was thinking the same thoughts as the other men. He didn't want any more of his men, most he called friends, to die. He pondered how he could transport the treasure differently so he could increase the chance of success, and save the lives of the men around him. He thought of dividing the gold up between the men and having them take multiple routes back to the temple of Pan. If some got captured, Matthias would be short that much gold. From what he had learned from Laurentinus about Matthias, he realized the powerful man would most likely take the loss out of Yitzhak's estate. It was useless to wish he had never gotten himself tied up in this business, but he could not help thinking the thought. He was not a man of action —he was a pragmatic farmer. His preferred method of making decisions was to mull over an idea for days—sometimes weeks, before he made his choice. Unfortunately, in this situation, his set of skills were not a good fit. When faced with adversity, everyone reverts back to a comfortable mode of operation. Yitzhak mulled when he needed to act as he and his men rode despondently along entering the wooded area of the upper Jordan Valley.

Blood chilling screams from the rear brought Yitzhak out of his gloom. "Everyone move to cover," he shouted. Dismounting, he ran to the rear of the procession to find two of his men dangling in mid air with pointed stakes of wood protruding from their chests. One was dead, and the other was moments away from the same fate.

"Bring me a horse. A few more of you help me get Aaron down," commanded Yitzhak.

By the time the men were in position to get the dying man down, he had expired. They worked for some time getting their comrades off the stakes. Finally, one of the men had the idea of loosening the ties that held the large crosspiece of the booby-trap in place, and they were able to pull the stakes from the men rather than pull the men off the stakes.

"What should we do with them?"

Yitzhak stared at the two men—himself covered in their blood. "Help me move them into the woods, and we'll come back and bury them when we come back for the others."

Twenty-four men were now dead. "How many more are going to die?" he wondered.

The twenty-six remaining men stood just off the road looking at their fallen companions.

One of them looked up at Yitzhak and said, "I don't know if I can finish this, Yitzhak. I have a wife and family. I want to see them again."

The farmer heard other men voice the same concern. He could not object to their thoughts—they were voicing his.

"What do you suggest we do?" he whined. "We can't just leave hundreds of pounds of gold to a bunch of murderers and thieves."

"Why not?" asked one of the younger men.

"It sticks in my throat. Evil men gaining a prize like this one, and having to do nothing for it but hide like cowards and kill off fifty good, decent men. I hate the idea!" Yitzhak was gaining courage as he spoke. "I won't just give it to them. I have learned from the Roman commander that Matthias, whose gold most of this is, is a treacherous man himself. It's not for him that I will guard this gold, but for principle. I won't give the gold over without a fight."

"Do you call this fighting?" said one man. "I don't call riding along and getting picked off at our enemy's leisure, fighting. It's foolhardy."

At that point, they heard the sound of horses running up the road. One of the men nearest the road yelled, "It's the two scouts."

Yitzhak made his way back to the road as Ezri and Podarces reigned in their horses.

"Did you see something?" asked Yitzhak.

"Ezri discovered a booby-trap of some kind up ahead about a mile. It looks like some kind of contraption that was designed to impale a rider in the back," said Podarces.

Ezri looked around and asked, "Why are you all dismounted?"

"The device you just described killed two of our riders," answered Yitzhak. "We moved them off the road until we could come back to bury them.

"What your information tells me is that we are in store for a lot more traps if we stay on this road. Somehow, whoever is behind these assaults has learned about our mission. We need to change our strategy. We're going to move down and take the road next to the river. We'll push the horses and hopefully give ourselves enough distance before whoever is after our gold has realized we're no longer on our present path."

One of the men said, "I like this idea, Yitzhak. This might work."

"That's not all. There are twenty-six of us left. We'll send the two scouts out ahead of us, but we will no longer have them rotate. They will both go out together and come in together. I'll ride lead in front of the gold. Six of you will surround the donkeys carrying the gold while one will bring up the rear. Two of the six with the gold will be our archers—one on either side. Keep your bows strung with arrows ready. The rest of you will spread out on either side of the river about one hundred feet abreast. Hopefully, this will give us enough warning if our 'friends' decide to attack us again. Keep in sight of one another, and if you hear or see anything out of the ordinary, let out a whoop."

The men nodded their heads in agreement with the plan. With the new strategy, despondency was replaced with hope. Ezri was now put on the spot to figure out how he was going to let Satanas know of the change in plans. If he would have known that the cutthroat who sprang the trap was hiding in nearby bushes listening to everything that was said, he would not have had to worry.

As soon as the men had mounted and left, Satanas' man ran back down the road and deep into the trees where his horse was tethered to a tree. He raced up the road Yitzhak and his group had abandoned to inform Satanas of the change in plans.

"I was foolish to think that even a farmer would stay on the same road and let me just murder his men one by one," said an angry Satanas to the man who had been with Ezri.

"I'm sorry, Satanas. What do you want us to do now?"

"Help me round up the men. We'll have to hurry to stay ahead of the shipment. Meet me with all the men at our campsite west of the road."

Satanas hurriedly discharged two of his men to scout out Yitzhak and get back to him by dark with Yitzhak's position. He hoped that they would not try to keep moving through the night, or he would never be able to catch up to the gold.

The whole disposition of the group had changed since Yitzhak had diverted them to the river road. Each man felt as if he was now on the offensive rather than merely waiting to be butchered—they were now the hunters and not the hunted.

As the sun began to draw down in the sky, Yitzhak could feel the stress of the day taking its toll on him. Slowing his horse so he could talk with the men surrounding the gold, he asked, "Do we rest for the night, or do you think we should press on?"

"We're all exhausted, Yitzhak," said the man who had known him since they were both small boys. "I wouldn't mind if we stopped and rested for a few hours. I'm almost asleep in my saddle."

The other men agreed that that assessment was true of them also. Yitzhak told the closest out-riders that as soon as the two lead scouts returned, they would be stopping for a few hours rest, and to pass on the word.

Satanas' two scouts had little difficulty finding Yitzhak's group. One of them stayed and kept an eye on the gold, and the other set off to tell Satanas where their approximate location was.

When Satanas heard their location, he realized that Yitzhak would be coming dangerously close to his camp. "We'll need to move camp and maneuver outside their patrol," he told his men. "When they've settled down, we can have our archers rain a few volleys of arrows into their camp. I'm sure they'll set up watchmen. We may be able to further reduce their numbers by taking them out. Changing their route made us scramble a little, but I think we're going to come out of this as well as I originally planned," he said, his malignant smile creasing his face. "We took out more of them than I thought we would by this time, so I'll settle for a minor change in our scheme." Switching topics altogether, he said, "Don't just stand there, let's get this camp broken down. We've got gold to steal."

The exact whereabouts of the thieves' camp was not precise in Ezri's mind, but he knew he could get close enough to it to find it if he could just get away from Podarces for awhile. His opportunity came when the sun was getting close to setting.

"Ezri, we should get back to the others to report before it gets darker."

"I would like to go on a little farther before I turn back. I've got a feeling I'll be sorry if I don't."

"Then I'll go with you, and we'll still go back together."

"No, we should give Yitzhak the information that we think it's clear up ahead. You go back, and I'll be right behind you."

Podarces scratched his head. "I don't know Ezri. Yitzhak was pretty clear about staying together."

"I'll take responsibility for my actions. You go on back. I promise, I'll be right behind."

Podarces did not like the idea of Ezri going on alone, but it was clear to him that he was not going to convince Ezri to go back with him. "You be careful out there, Ezri. Those killers could have caught up to us by now. I know Yitzhak is not going to like this at all."

Ezri smiled and waved the other boy on. As soon as they were a good distance from one another, Ezri kicked Raven into a gallop. He had traveled maybe two miles when he heard someone say his name from off to his right in the trees. He pulled up and made his way toward the voice. Out from the trees walked Damon, a big, thick chested man with a well-cropped beard.

"Where you running to?" he said.

"To find you. I need to let Satanas know that Yitzhak has changed his route."

"He already knows that. They broke camp not more than an hour ago. He's already moving in to surround Yitzhak's men. He left me here to warn you, if you came this way, not to be in camp tonight. Come on. You and I can catch up with him together."

Yitzhak was not pleased with Podarces' news, "You let him go on alone? I thought that I was very clear that you two were not to leave each other's side."

"He was insistent that he go up ahead to scout around, and that I should get back to you with our report. He said he would be right behind me."

"There's nothing to be done now but wait for him. I don't want to risk anyone out there alone tonight. With any luck, he'll be back and my concerns will be for nothing."

The rest of the men were notified to come in. Yitzhak set up watches that consisted of eight to ten men in each watch.

The others ate a hasty meal and tried to get as much sleep as they could. Feeling safe being off the other road, most of the men had little trouble getting rest.

Podarces was the only one who could not sleep. He felt responsible for Ezri's absence. As soon as he heard the heavy breathing of the other men, he slipped into the night, past the watch, and down the road to see if he could assist Ezri.

Ezri and Damon moved quickly through the woods toward Satanas' position. They came to an abrupt stop when nine big men, who had hidden behind trees, surrounded them.

Looking at Ezri, the one who appeared to be their leader said, "You're one of the scouts with the bunch that are guarding the gold, aren't you?"

Ezri was unsure what to answer, so he said nothing.

"Come on, we're hired by Matthias to watch over your group. My name's Ravid. Looks from your numbers, we should have gotten here sooner. This guy," Ravid pointed to Damon, "one of Satanas' thugs or is he with you?"

Realizing the position he was in, he lied saying, "He's with me. We were trying to get a closer look at where these men were who have been killing members of our party."

"I wouldn't go any closer. They're beyond this rise a little bit. That's a rough bunch. You'd be better off to head back the way you came and alert Yitzhak as to their whereabouts. My guess is that they're going to attack your group well before the sun comes up. If I was you, I'd get that bunch moving before Satanas' boys kill off the rest of you. Tell Yitzhak there are nine more of us who Satanas doesn't know about. We'll be keeping out of sight of Satanas so we'll have the element of surprise on our side when they decide to attack you."

Ezri knew Satanas had expected Basil's men to go back to Matthias before making any other plans. This information was crucial for Satanas to know, but he could not think how he could do so without jeopardizing his life with these men who he knew were no people to toy with. Damon looked at Ezri and jerked his head back to the way they had come.

"Thank you for your help. We'll make sure Yitzhak knows about your help and that he needs to get moving," said Damon

"You should hurry. This bunch looks like they're getting ready to move out again real soon."

Ezri and Damon walked back in the direction they had come. When they had gotten out of range of being heard, Damon said, "I need to circle around and approach Satanas from the other side. He'll have sentries out, and we can tell one of them what we know. You should go back to the other camp and let Yitzhak believe there's no problem. With you gone, his ears will be perked up for trouble. Once he's seen you, you can then slip away when it's convenient.

"By the way, thanks for covering for me back there. I thought I was headed for the River Styx for sure."

Ezri shrugged and continued on his way to the road. The other man moved quickly to the far side of Satanas' encampment making sure that he kept out of sight of Ravid's group. Ezri had gone only a hundred yards when someone stepped out from a tree and grabbed Raven's halter startling both horse and rider. After his initial start, he saw it was Podarces.

"What are you doing out here," Ezri said in anger. "You scared the devil right out of me and Raven." He said with annoyance, and then to himself wondered, "How many more people are going to step out from behind trees tonight?"

"It looks like you've been playing with the devil. What were you doing with that man?"

Ezri was completely caught off guard. Thinking fast, he said, "That was a man who Matthias had sent out to back us up if we ran into trouble."

"Why's he headed toward that group of men who are planning to ambush our group?"

"He's just moving in to see if he can hear their plans. You and I need to get back to Yitzhak and let him know what's going to happen."

"Oh, we're going to let him know a lot of things. I'm sure he'll want to know about what I've seen in the last few minutes."

Ezri dismounted Raven as Podarces started to walk back to his own horse that was tied to a tree farther back toward the road. He made sure his sword was loose in its scabbard as he said, "I don't understand what you're getting at, Podarces."

Podarces did not turn around, continuing to advance toward his mount. Ezri let go of Raven's reins, made a quick movement toward Podarces, slipped out his sword, and stabbed the young man though the back. Podarces wheeled around and voiced a hacking sound as he dropped to his knees and then fell face forward to the ground. Ezri looked in horror at what he had done. He stared at the dead body before him, and then at his sword that was smeared with the young man's blood. Nausea swelled in his gut making his head feel light and woozy. He turned, emptying everything in his stomach on the ground. Wiping his mouth, he knelt down and cleaned his sword on the young man's tunic. He continued to look at the corpse before him who in life had thought Ezri to be his friend. Hearing Raven rustling in the grass behind him, he moved over to grab the horse's reins and climbed into his saddle.

It galled Ezri that circumstances like this were bothering

him. He wondered if Satanas knew how much killing upset him, would he still trust him with so much responsibility.
Determination filled him to be less sensitive in future dealings. He made the resolution, but deep in his heart he knew he would always feel the shame and horror of his actions this night.

As Ezri neared the camp, he was stopped by one of the sentries. "Ezri, is that you?" Seeing that it was, he said, "You are a welcomed sight. Yitzhak and Podarces will be glad to see you."

There was no campfire to guide Ezri, so the man pointed him in the right direction. Loud breathing and snoring of tired men sleeping greeted him as he neared the camp, leading Raven by his reins.

"Ezri," someone whispered. The person approached him and grabbed him by the shoulders and said, "I am so glad to see you. Did you have any trouble?"

Ezri now recognized the silhouette in the darkness—it was Yitzhak.

"No trouble. I just wanted to follow my hunch. I knew you would be mad, but I didn't want to see any more men die if I could help it."

"You're a decent young man. If you were my son I would have whipped you after I hugged you," Yitzhak said as he hugged the boy. "Podarces will be glad to know you got back safely. He's sleeping over by the horses." Yitzhak's words stung him as he recounted the reality of his crime. Still holding him by the shoulders, he reiterated, "I'm so glad to see you."

Ezri gave his employer an awkward smile and headed in the direction of the horses. Raven had had a long day. Before Ezri snuck off again, he made sure that his horse was watered and given one of the special fig and oat cakes they had brought along for the horses. Raven was tied to the same rope the other horses were tied to that was stretched between two trees.

He needed to see where the sentries were stationed if he was going to have any hope of sneaking off with a horse in tow. He definitely did not want to be in camp when the arrows started raining down. If he had to, he would leave Raven and walk out.

CHAPTER FIFTY-FIVE

"I want you five archers one mile ahead of the gold, hiding in the trees, where you can either cut off their escape or pick them off while they're in route to Caesarea. Go now," Satanas commanded. The archers nodded that they understood his directions and left to take up their stations.

"The rest of the archers I want to position yourselves in sniper locations in the trees encircling their camp. Make sure you're outside their sentries, but close enough to hail down arrows when you're given the cue." Those men also hurried off to ready themselves for the assault.

Damon came running into camp at that point. "Satanas. You need to take into account Basil's men. They did not return to get new plans from Matthias. They're observing us from a distance ready to lend aid to Yitzhak's group when the time is right."

Satanas' eyes grew wide as his usually calm demeanor transformed into rage. He grabbed the bigger man by the shoulders and asked, "How many of them are there?"

Damon pulled back from Satanas' grasp and said simply, "Nine."

"How well are they armed?"

"I don't know. The one that I talked to carried a sword and a knife in a calf sheath. They are a rough bunch—nothing like that group of farmers we've been following."

"And they're observing us right now?"

"Yep."

"Are they close enough that they could have heard our conversation just now?" Satanas said calming down to his cold, calculating self.

"No. They're quite a distance from our sentries."

"Are they surrounding us, or in a group?"

"When they surprised Ezri and me, they were in a group over there about three hundred yards," Damon said motioning with his head in the direction of Ravid's group.

"Good. I would rather eliminate them now than later." Waving one of the younger men to himself, he told him, "Nereus, go now and bring back the five archers I sent ahead." Pointing out twelve men, he directed, "Go out of camp towards the gold, and when you're out of sight circle around behind Matthias' men.

210

Once you're in place wait about fifteen minutes and quietly kill any guard they have set around their camp." Satanas motioned for them to go and they took off.

Ezri quickly discerned that there was no order in the sentries' movement; there were often big gaps in their system of watch. Untying Raven, he led the horse easily beyond the perimeter guard and stole back to Satanas' camp.

"Ezri," someone whispered from above him. "Is that you?"

"Yes," Ezri said looking up into the trees. "Are you setting up for another ambush?"

"Yah, all of us archers are in place. If you're headed back to Satanas, you should get there just about the time that he'll be leaving to come here."

"Thanks," Ezri whispered, urging Raven in the direction of the cutthroats' camp.

Before long, Nereus returned with the five archers. Satanas gave them quick orders to encircle Ravid's camp. "when you see us rushing their camp, try to take out as many of them as you can. They will either run to face our charge or try to escape into the waiting swords of the dozen men I sent to block their retreat. Be careful not to shoot any of our men. When we get too close for you to take safe shots, stop shooting and join the battle. Any questions?" Receiving none, he sent them out the same direction he had sent the previous twelve.

"Remember," Satanas said turning to his remaining number of men, "when we attack Matthias' men we need all of you for the assault on the gold caravan. Don't be overly heroic, and cover the men around you. We'll need every man we can spare to pull off this robbery."

The men continued to mull around acting casual as they began to arm themselves. When everyone was ready for the charge on Matthias' nine men, Satanas yelled, "Get them," and his thirty-plus men ran in the direction Damon had told them to charge.

Thinking they had the element of surprise on their side, Ravid and his men were relaxed, though they had been observing the movements of Satanas' group. When they saw Satanas and his overwhelming numbers racing toward them, there were a few seconds where they were paralyzed in place. It was during that time that the archers began shooting into the group. Satanas' men sent to block Ravid's retreat had successfully and quietly killed the two men set as perimeter guards. The archers were not as effective. One arrow gashed the shoulder of one of Ravid's men and one arrow killed a man piercing his neck, but the remaining five men were unharmed. When they turned to run from the frontal assault, they were met by Satanas' twelve men. Seeing no chance of saving their lives, the five remaining men formed a small circle, back-to-back, to take on Satanas' men, hacking ten of them to death before the fight was over.

As the last of Ravid's men fell to the sword, Satanas' men sent up a cheer.

Satanas immediately quieted them with livid fury. "Stop this! Your voices will carry through the woods, you fools!" He backhanded the man closest to him and pushed two others to the ground. The cheering died as suddenly as it erupted. After they had loosed their last arrows, the archers had run in from their positions to join the melee, arriving just as Satanas was demanding their silence. His wrath was in search of a victim. His eye caught sight of the archers.

"Archers! Stand before me," he commanded.

Each of them hurried to do his bidding. Satanas was not calming down. If anything his rage was only fed by their obedience. He walked up to each man and punched him in the stomach. Most of the men dropped to their knees at the force of his blows.

"You are not archers. You are pranksters playing out your stunts while others die. We should have had to fight but one or two of them. You will do better when we attack the gold caravan, or you will face the same fate as those you failed to protect. I hired you to kill men with your arrows. If you can't do that, you will die." He ended his last three words in a crescendo that left him panting for air. Taking a few breaths, he said, "Do you catch my meaning?"

The archers nodded their heads, but did not meet Satanas' glare. Before walking back to the camp, he backhanded the last man sending him sprawling.

By the time Satanas reached the camp, he had calmed down once again. He was unaccustomed to losing his temper, and it made him dislike those he felt made him lose it. Ezri was sitting on Raven when he walked into the camp's main area.

"I see you attacked what was left of Basil's men. Did we lose any?" Ezri asked.

"Too many, but not so many that we can't finish what we need to accomplish." Not wanting to relive the debacle, he said, "I'm changing our plans. These archers can't hit a house if they're standing inside it. They will join us when we surround Yitzhak's camp. I'll let the ones we've already positioned do the dirty work. I want you with us on the perimeter to help kill any who would try to escape the volleys of arrows."

Ezri nodded his understanding. "I will not let myself be

traumatized with killing this time," he vowed to himself.

The clash between Satanas and Mathias' men gave Yitzhak a little more time to process his situation. Because he and his men would be reaching the temple of Pan, left unmolested, by noon the next day, he knew that whoever it was who wanted the gold would have to make his move soon. The best time for them to ambush the caravan would be that night. A plan dawned on him. He began collecting his men around him to announce a change in strategy.

Ravid and all of his men perished at the hands of Satanas, but they bought Yitzhak just the amount of time he needed to put his plan into action. The last of Yitzhak's men were in place when Satanas arrived with his main contingent.

Satanas, who saw himself as an excellent judge of human ability, would find himself lacking before the night was through. The "farmers," as he liked to refer to Yitzhak's men, were going to prove their mettle this night. Lifetimes of hunting and stealth would serve the "farmers" well as events unfolded. Satanas had brutal men on his side who were of poor character, able to kill without batting an eyelash. Yitzhak's men were family men who valued honor and loyalty, and had lived lives that fostered in them skills that were going to be useful in evening out the odds by night's end.

Satanas' men made a human circle around the camp. From their positions, they saw a man in the camp get up, walk over by the fire, warm himself and then go back to where he was sleeping. Other men could be seen sleeping, scattered around the various camp fires.

Unknown to each of the cutthroats who were slowly closing their circle around the camp was that Yitzhak's men had secretly hidden themselves in couples around the perimeter. When they had gone to take up new positions, they came upon some of Satanas' men and put an end to their villainous lives. The rest of Satanas' men were now moving slowly into the 'farmers' two-man ambushes. So quiet and stealthy were Yitzhak's men in their work that they were quickly bringing the odds into their favor.

Many of the farmers had hunted together for years. They had developed a simple, but effective, form of hand gestures which were used to great benefit in this type of battle. Satanas' men thought that they were the hunters. Many found out too late that they were the hunted.

When Satanas' men, unbeknownst to him, had been pruned down to less than thirty, he gave the signal to begin the rain of arrows on Yitzhak's camp. After fifteen volleys of arrows from the the ten archers, there was no stirring in the camp. Not one of the huddles under the blankets moved. Each of them had at least two arrows protruding from their lifeless forms. The archers came down from their perches in the trees and joined the other men as they slowly constricted their human circle that was closing in on the camp. One of the cutthroats used his sword to nudge one of the bodies. It didn't move. Now that he was close enough to inspect the body more closely, it didn't look quite right to him. He pulled back the blanket. There lay a pot of flour on its side, and an assortment of rocks to form what was to look like legs. The other men began pulling blankets away from the oddly shaped human forms just as Yitzhak and his men sprang upon them.

Satanas died early in the battle. One of Yitzhak's archers sent an arrow right through the villain's heart. Yitzhak was in a life and death struggle when another of the cutthroats stepped back from his kill to see that he merely had to stick his long knife into the good man's back. Yitzhak stood straight upright for a moment and then toppled forward, lifeless. That man, in turn, was then killed by one of Yitzhak's men who stabbed him from behind.

Ezri stood in the distance watching in horror the carnage being played out before him. The battle was incredibly brief and bloody. Both sides were killing the other until there was only a lone man standing. He had received several wounds to his abdomen. His blood streaked face made him hard to recognize. The truth was that Ezri could not remember if the man was one of Satanas' or Yitzhak's. Ezri moved in closer to the camp.

"Ezri," the man said weakly. "Help me."

Walking over to the man, Ezri watched him fall to one knee while holding his hand over one of his abdominal punctures. Looking down, he pressed his other hand over one of the other wounds, and then he rolled to his back.

The man looked up at Ezri and said only one croaking word, "Help." His hands then slacked to his sides and his eyes stared blankly into the sky. Ezri turned away and vomited into the bushes.

CHAPTER FIFTY-SIX

The sun rose and found Ezri sitting on a rock, traumatized by what he had seen the night before—his eyes riveted on a lifeless Satanas. The man was supposed to teach him everything he needed to know to make his way in the world. Now he was dead. His eyes drifted over to the corpse that was in life, Yitzhak. For the first time in many years the fog passed from Ezri's mind. He realized that Satanas died because he was a treacherous man. Yitzhak died in the same battle, but he was a man of honor and wholesome ideals. Ezri did not know what to think of his thoughts right then, but his heart was beginning to change.

In the distance, a donkey brayed. The sound brought him to his senses. As if slapped in the face, he thought, "There's enough gold on those donkeys to more than seed any future enterprises I might conceive." His mind began to start clicking again. He needed to get off this path and hide the gold before someone came along and began asking questions. He was not sure what he was going to do with the fortune at this point, but he also did not want another bandit to steal it from him. He remembered a series of caves farther north where he could hide his trove until he could safely come back to fetch it.

The pack animals were tethered to a rope tied between two trees. Next to them were the packs of gold laying on the ground. Ezri could not help himself. He wanted to see the treasure that had serendipitously fallen into his hands. Opening one of the packs, his breath was taken away by the sheer amount on just one of the individual pouches. Each pack held over fifty bags of gold with each bag containing what looked to be several hundred gold pieces. The reality of the gold caused a cold chill of fear to run through him. He quickly closed up the pouch and began loading the donkeys with the treasure. Next, he tied the donkeys—train fashion—to one another so he could lead them to the caves he had in mind. Wisely keeping off the main road made him less likely to run into anyone else, but his progress was slowed in the process. Urgency and greed obliterated any sense of hunger or thirst. A few hours after noon he arrived at the caves he had been considering. There was one in particular that he had in mind. To enter it, one had to press between a huge boulder and the cave's mouth.

Standing, looking at the mouth of the cave, Ezri's hard exterior began to soften as he thought back to the carnage he had witnessed just hours before. Up until last night, he had only stolen possessions that could be replaced. Podarces' life could never be replaced. All those men who had literally given their lives for the dream of unimaginable wealth now lie on the cold ground with nothing to show for their lives. They had not only lost their own lives, but they had taken the lives of others whose families would grieve their deaths. When he had stolen before, it was a game to him. This night had been no game. What he had done to Podarces had been no game. He would never be able to wash the memory of his friend's murder from his thoughts. Dropping to his knees, he sobbed into his hands in remorse for what he had done.

Looking through tear blurred eyes he raised his eyes to the sky wishing that there was some way to make right what he had participated in a few hours before. He thought, "I could hide the gold and then tell Matthias where it was." What he knew of Matthias, his life would not mean much if that man knew he was alive. Matthias was no better than Satanas. He might as well kill himself right here and now. No, he would hide the gold and sit on it until he was given clear direction as to what to do with it.

After starting a small fire, Ezri took a branch, wrapped some cloth he had taken from one of the dead men back at the battle, and made a kind of torch to use in the cave. There were no animals inside, only solid rock sides and ceiling, and cold dirt floor. Sticking the torch in the moist ground of the cave, he used his hands to dig into the ground—clawing with his fingers. It soon became apparent to him that to continue this way would only leave him with bloody stubs for fingers. Taking out his knife, he dug furiously at the dirt. His digging stopped when he heard the animals' movement outside. Looking out the cave's entrance, he saw no one. His paranoia persuaded him that he should unload the gold and take it with him inside the cave while he worked. Once the gold was safely inside the cave, he removed all the gear on each pack animal, slapped them on the rump, and chased them off. Still needing Raven, he tied him to a branch a short distance from the mouth of the cave. As he walked back to finish his work in the cave, he saw a stout stick and a slab of bark he could use in his efforts. His new tools increased his output, and he soon had buried all six packs of gold along the side one of the cave walls, but not before he filled his purse with an ample number of gold coins for later use. He was careful to spread the dirt with his hands so as to hide his work should anyone happen to use the cave for shelter.

Contented with his work, Ezri went outside to see about

hiding the entrance to his cave. There was only one side of the large stone that shielded the entrance to the cavern that one could enter. Ezri began looking for a shrub he could transplant to obscure the entrance even more. Spying a bush that was about his height, he set about digging the hole in which to plant it. When he completed the hole, his stomach would no longer let him work without attention. Getting out his water skin, a hard biscuit, and dried meat he had in the pouch hanging off his saddle, he sat down with his meager meal to eat. Hunger had a knack for making even the most simple of fares taste like a banquet, and this was no exception. He felt the need to finish his work and get out of the area before anyone spotted him, so he ate the meal quickly.

Nourished and feeling somewhat strengthened, Ezri began his work of digging around the bush he wanted to transplant. This effort took him much longer than he expected, but he eventually had the bush and its roots out of the ground, planted by the boulder, and watered with the remainder of his water. Gathering dead branches from the surrounding area, he stuffed them down between the boulder and the mountain to obfuscate the entrance even more. Looking over his work, he decided that the only thing left to do was to get more water for the transplanted bush. Once he had that done, he would need some place to go until the predictable uproar over the gold shipment had settled. He thought if he went to Hazor, he could meet up with a caravan, and maybe travel with them until the time was right for him to return and do whatever he planned to do with the gold. He wished he could use the gold in some way to erase the malignity he felt festering in his soul. There was a part of him that just wanted to take the gold and run, but he knew that search parties would be out combing the hills trying to locate it, and in the end, he would still have to deal with the feelings that were torturing him. The best thing he could do was leave the treasure there, and come back for it at a later time.

Sophia and Noam had waited a day, and then started back toward Caesarea. Noam still gave her plenty of emotional space. It was obvious to him that she was still mourning over Basil. Secretly he wondered what Sophia saw in the giant. She was no beauty and her best days had come and gone, but he thought she still had enough looks to attract a more agreeable mate than Basil. He left her to her thoughts and the two rode along in silence.

Their second day out, late in the afternoon, they came upon the foul odor of death. Moving in the direction of the stench, they came upon the slaughter that had happened the night before. Left in the sun, the bodies had already begun to take on the repugnant odor of death. Sophia had to walk away from the scene, feeling herself becoming light headed and nauseous. Noam moved in among the bodies to identify who had died.

Walking over to Sophia he said, "Looks to me as if everyone was killed. I can't find Ezri's body, though. He may have been killed earlier, or he hasn't returned from scouting."

"Is the gold still here?"

"I don't see it," said Noam as he was going through the pockets and purses of the dead men collecting coins and valuables. "The donkeys that carried the cargo aren't anywhere to be found."

"Do you see any tracks?" Sophia's voice was taking on a tone of panic.

"There's no way to pick up any trail. There's too many prints of animals as well as humans around here."

Sophia's voice raised in volume and pitch now. "Someone has the gold and we don't know who that might be or where he may have it right now. We've done all this planning and are going to come away with nothing!"

"Calm down, old girl. At least we. . ."

Sophia interrupted him saying, "I'm not an old girl and I want my share of the gold."

"As I was going to say, at least we're not in the same condition as Satanas. Things could be worse. We also don't know if whoever has the gold isn't hiding it right now to return to it when this all settles down. I would like to know where we stand as well as you do, but all we can do is wait a month or two and see what happens. Sorry," he began to say 'old girl,' but quickly changed it to, "Sophia."

She didn't like what he had to say, but she knew he was right. There was nothing to do now but wait and see if whoever had the gold would be contacting them to give them their share.

"Let's go, Noam. There's nothing we can do here. We might as well get home so we can start the hard task of waiting."

Noam nodded his head and brought Sophia's pony over to her holding it while she mounted.

Taking a bag from his saddle to store his findings, he said, "We'll split this up when we get back to your house."

Watching him replace the bag on his saddle, Sophia turned her pony to the road and coaxed it around a few rock outcroppings to get back on to the main road.

CHAPTER FIFTY-SEVEN

As soon as he could do so, Ezri reluctantly traded Raven for a camel in Hazor. Gischala was so close to Hazor that he was afraid of being spotted by someone who might recognize him or Raven. The horse and he had been through a lot together, and it was difficult letting the him go, but there was no way to predict who might see him or the horse and maybe recognize one of them. His facial hair was growing in thicker now than when he was living in Gischala, and wearing a Keffiyeh, a middle eastern headdress, would hopefully mask him from anyone who would be able to identify him.

Riding east out of Hazor about a mile, the first caravan that he came upon was the one with the three magi. Vahumisa was in the lead with one of his lieutenants; Gaspar, Balthasar, and Melchior were riding abreast behind them talking away.

"I see you are heading south," said Ezri, turning his camel to ride alongside Vahumisa. "I am a lone traveler seeking the protection of numbers in my travels. Would you consider adding another member to your group? I will pay my way."

Before Vahumisa could respond, Balthasar said, "Come talk to me, young man. I would like to ask you a few questions."

Slowing his camel to allow the magi to catch up to him, he asked, "What would you like to ask me?"

"Have you been to Jerusalem before?"

"I have not. I hope to go there this trip," he said being able to answer truthfully on both counts.

With a contrite look, Gaspar said, "Forgive my inhospitality. My name is Gaspar, and these are my dearest friends and traveling companions, Balthasar and Melchior."

"There is nothing to forgive," Ezri responded.

"Then tell us what you are doing out on this road alone. Are you a merchant?" Balthasar inquired.

Laughing, Ezri said, "No, no. I am just a traveler seeking ideas of how and where I might live out my life. I will not always have this freedom to journey where I wish. I want to do so while I am still young."

"You are young, that cannot be argued. And what of your parents?" Melchior quizzed him.

"Alas, my mother died giving birth to me. My father died two years ago. Before he died he bade me to take part of my inheritance to travel and seek my future because he knew that that was something I've always wanted to do."

Gaspar looked for approval from his two companions as he said, "Please, continue with us until your heart beckons you in another direction." The other magi nodded in agreement.

Up front, Vahumisa leaned into the lieutenant and said, "I wonder if his majesty would have chosen to fund this expedition if he knew how many strays we'd be collecting on the way."

The lieutenant laughed and agreed with him.

Nazli had not eaten since her bath three days before and no amount of coaxing from Rachel could get her out of bed or get her to eat.

"Your mother has slipped into a deep depression, my lady," Balzak told Rachel one morning at breakfast. "Gaspar's mother went into a similar depression when his father was killed. We have to find something to make her want to live."

"I have tried everything I can think of to boost her spirits, but nothing seems to brighten her. Balzak, I can't believe this is my mother. She's always been so strong. Father used to lean on her for everything. In many ways, she was as much the high priest as he was. They discussed everything. I think her being so unceremoniously evicted from our home made her situation feel more desperate than it is."

"That could be true. It sounds like she felt needed when your father was alive, but now she has lost that purpose. What if we change our approach?"

"How do you mean?" Rachel's big eyes flashed to attention.

"Well, we've all been entreating her to eat, and to get out of bed. What if we started bringing concerns to her, asking for her advice and help?"

"You're brilliant!" Rachel said clapping her hands.

"We'll have a feast introducing you and her to some of Gaspar's friends. He doesn't have many—most of them are on the expedition with him, but that doesn't matter. We'll accost her with all kinds of details." As Balzak spoke he became more and more animated causing his hair to catch on one side of his nose and then on the other, occasionally, brushing the hair from his face altogether.

His enthusiasm and humorous antics made Rachel jump out of her seat, run over, and kiss Balzak on his head.

"Balzak, you are wonderful. When can we start with the plans?"

"As soon as I finish eating this melon."

Balzak called a meeting of the whole house staff. Ara was as thrilled with Balzak's idea as Rachel had been. She,

Tala, and Rachel were put in charge of all the preparations for the meal, and Balzak said he would see that invitations would be sent to the appropriate people when the time came.

Watching the three women chatter gaily about their plans for the dinner, Balzak was secretly concerned for how long Nazli would survive. He knew she could go days without food, but her unwillingness to consume more than a sip of water each day could be deadly. If they were not able to change her pattern very soon, he knew she would die within the week.

Vahumisa decided to spend the night just to the south of Hazor, which caused Ezri no little concern. He would have preferred that the caravan would have made more distance that day, but he did not want to raise questions as to why it should matter to him. For the next few days he would just have to be more cautious about exposing himself to other travelers.

Cassius and he quickly discovered that they enjoyed an affinity for the other. Each was careful not to disclose much about his personal background little knowing how much in common their occupational choices had in common. The caravan snaked along the western side of Palestine that next day, enjoyed the company in which each found himself, and laughed at the ever-present antics of Amehlech and Cyrus. The caravan had very early settled into a natural order with Vahumisa and one of his men always leading out, they were followed by the wisemen, who in turn were followed by Cassius and Ezri. Behind the two additions were four more of Vahumisa's men who were trailed by Amehlech, Cyrus, and the pack animals. Another four soldiers brought up the rear.

After Rachel, Ara, and Tala had made their preliminary plans for the dinner, Ara went up to Nazli's bedroom to attempt to engage her in the plans. Rachel and Balzak went out to the knife throwing range to hone their skills. Rachel had advanced to a point where Balzak wanted her to start training in defensive and tactical knife fighting. For that morning's training, he handed her a pair of trousers that she was to wear from then on. She came down from changing beaming with anticipation.

"You have learned to stick a knife from a variety of distances," began Balzak. "Now I want you to do so while moving. We will practice this half of our time, and on defensive fighting the other half."

Rachel did not have to say anything in reply to reveal how excited she was for this next phase of her training. She bounced on her toes unaware that she was doing so, making Balzak smile at his student's unmistakable zeal.

"First, we will have you stand with your back to the

target. You will turn and throw two knives in succession," he said while moving Rachel into position.

The first time she tried, she bounced the butt end of the first knife off the target, and stuck the second.

"What we're teaching you here is two things," Balzak said as he picked up the knives and brought them to her. "If you ever have to use your knives, you won't be readying yourself and throwing—you'll be moving while you're judging the distance to your target. Let's try it again."

The whole first half of their lesson that day involved Rachel facing away from her target, while Balzak varied the distance of the moveable targets he had. Kahliq enjoyed joining Balzak's sessions whenever his work allowed him time to practice, and Balzak needed someone that day with his stature for the second half of Rachel's training.

"Kahliq will join us the next few days for at least the second half of our time together," Balzak instructed. "We need, how shall I say, someone who is closer to average height than myself to assist you in this part of your training.

"Kahliq, I want you to walk up behind me grab me around my body pinning my arms to my side."

Kahliq nodded his understanding.

"Then grab me, and Rachel observe closely."

Running up from behind Balzak, Kahliq grabbed him around his arms. Balzak immediately stamped down on Kahliq's instep, which loosened the big man's grasp of him, which allowed Balzak to spin and thrust the heel of his hand within an inch of his assistant's nose.

Kahliq's eyes rounded when he saw Balzak's hand coming at his face, and then broke into a smile when he saw he was not going to be hit. "Thank you for not breaking my nose and my foot," he said limping slightly as he moved away.

"Did you see what I did?" Balzak asked Rachel turning to her.

She nodded her head.

Bending down he pointed to the place on her foot where she would stomp on her attacker. Standing up, he said, "When you punch up at your assailant, you will not hold back as you will today. Once you have struck him, you will duck out of his grasp, and roll away from him as you arm yourself with your knives. Do you understand?"

Again, she nodded that she did.

They walked through the whole maneuver once. Then they went over the move multiple times giving her lots of practice, and Kahliq a sore instep.

"Hopefully, you will never have to use this maneuver, but if you do, it will buy you time to use the skills we will be working on from here on out." Smiling at his engrossed pupil, he said, "You have made much progress today," and then speaking to Kahliq, "Thank you for your service today, my friend."

Kahliq smiled sheepishly and said, "You're welcome?"

CHAPTER FIFTY-EIGHT

On the second day of Ezri's joining the caravan, they spent the night on the northwest shore of the Sea of Galilee. Being ten miles from Gischala made him feel like he had breathing room. The last time he was there was with Satanas. Disquieted is how he would express spending any amount of time with Satanas. On the other hand, the short time he was with the magi, he experienced a quieting of his spirit. The gold didn't seem to matter as much to him as having the peace of mind that these men seemed to possess. He had always thought that having great wealth would answer all of his problems, and now that he had more than he knew what to do with, he almost wished he could remove himself from it.

Everyone helped with setting up his area of the camp while Amehlech and Cyrus prepared the meal. That night they would be eating the lamb they purchased along the road that day from a sheepherder they met. Amehlech always did the butchering that needed to be done, and Cyrus was a master of seasoning and roasting. Supper would be delayed in preparation that night. No one complained, looking forward to what they knew would be a meal worth the wait.

Talk around the fire that night led, as it almost always did, to the star that was guiding them now and not just pointing them in a general direction.

"The star is definitely directing us in a southerly route as opposed to a westerly one?" commented Gaspar.

"It does," said Melchior. "Which seems to go along with my calculations as to its distance from us."

"How so?" asked Vahumisa.

"My measurements indicated that this star is but a few miles distance from earth. The typical star is many millions of miles more distant than that. If the God of Israel has sent this star to guide us, and it looks now that He has, the star would have to be in close proximity to the earth to be able to direct us so exactly. A distant star could not be so precise without streaking millions of miles to do so."

Ezri could not help being brought into the conversation. He did not know yet what the star was supposedly leading them to, but Melchior had produced all kinds of questions in him.

"If the stars are millions of miles away, wouldn't they

224

have to be absolutely enormous in order for us to see them?" Ezri asked.

"Yes I've thought about that," Melchior said rubbing his forehead. "This star, if my calculations are correct, must be much smaller. Maybe it's a bright messenger of God. Balthasar has informed me that the Jews believe these messengers are called angels—great winged creatures who resemble men. This star, as the others have heard us say before, is like no other star in the sky."

Ezri continued to ask questions well into their dinner. By the time the travelers were licking their fingers, he had heard enough to want to see this affair to its end.

"I hope that I am not intruding on your business, but would you mind if I were to come along with you on your quest?" Ezri inquired.

Balthasar laughed out loud and slapped his knees with both of his hands. "Of course you may join us. You are not the first to ask to do so," he said looking at Cassius.

Ezri looked at the man sitting beside him, "You are not an original member of the group?"

"No, I too was completely absorbed in their odyssey, and asked if I could come along. Even with my untrained eye, I can see what the magi mean by the star's deviant behavior. It does not move across the sky, it's leading us. I hope the Jews' God is a benevolent one."

"How do you mean?"

"If this star isn't leading us to the Jewish God's anointed one, it could be leading us to our death. The Jews are his people; we are not. We could be intruding on a sign he has set up just for them."

"That is a very perceptive thesis, Cassius," remarked Balthasar. "From what I have read of Yahweh, their God, He believes that He is all mankind's God. The Jews are to be his messengers. While your idea is an intriguing one, I don't think we need to worry about His not wanting us to search out where the star leads."

Chuckling, Cassius said, "I'm relieved to hear you say that. Your perception of this god is a much more agreeable one than mine. I would rather that he is leading us to himself for good rather than for evil."

Everyone around the campfire agreed with him in open amusement, but Cassius had introduced an idea that none of them had considered before. To soldiers who tended to be superstitious anyway, Cassius' interjection was not one they would easily shrug off.

Weakness and an inability to speak coherently were now

some of Nazli's symptoms. Balzak's idea of bringing Rachel's mother in on the plans for the dinner had failed. A doctor had been called in and he told them what they already knew—if Nazli would not drink water, she would die.

Rachel's pleading had no affect on her mother. The doctor explained how to take a cloth, dip it in water, and gently squeeze drips of water into Nazli's mouth. This appeared to work for a while until Nazli spewed the contents of her mouth out onto the floor. Again Rachel's thoughts returned to how she could not believe that this woman wasting away in front of her could be the woman she had known all of her life.

Her daily exercises with Balzak gave her opportunity to work out her frustration in a productive way. In just a few days, she had improved markedly in movement and throwing accurately. At first, as she ran laterally by the targets, she had a tendency to try to throw her knives across her body which made her throw weak and inaccurate. Balzak taught her to run, take a step with her left foot toward her target, throwing with deadly accuracy.

When Rachel was outside the enclosure of the range, she did not wear trousers, but long dresses which were hardly appropriate for a lady to wear when training for knife fighting. Balzak had a local leatherworker design two calf straps, each having a single knife sheath attached to it. This way, Rachel could still appear the proper lady and always have her weapons within easy reach. Her trousers protected her in practice from any accidental indecent displays. If she did get herself in a situation when not practicing, she could make up her mind between a possible indecent display and her life.

When Balzak gave her the gift of her calf sheaths at the end of one of their practices one day, she couldn't have been more excited if he had given her a turquoise necklace. She hurriedly attached them to the outside of her trousered calf, begging him to show her how to use them.

"Tomorrow, my lady, tomorrow. I have other work I must do today. You are making excellent progress. Soon, I will have nothing left to teach you."

The teacher in Balzak loved the fact that he had such willing pupils in Rachel and Kahliq. Surprisingly, Rachel possessed a natural ability for knife throwing that was equal to his own. The only aspect he held over her was experience and years of practice. If Rachel would have known that her lithe, knife throwing teacher was well into his fifties, she would have been even more impressed with his prowess. Though he looked a mere ten years her senior, he saw her as the daughter he would most likely never have. He was proud of her work and the relationship they were cultivating. If Nazli were to die, which he believed was now inevitable, he would care for Rachel like his own daughter until his master returned to take her as his wife. To have the two people he loved the most soon be united under the same roof made him feel a most fortunate man. Leaving the practice field that day in good spirits, he looked forward to the day when Gaspar would return and bring his joy to its zenith.

There was a Roman fort near the ancient fortification on Mount Megiddo which was where the caravan would spend the next night before they turned off the main route by the sea and followed the road that went due south toward Jerusalem. The fort was simply called Legio after the Sixth Roman Legion that was stationed there. Since Damascus, the caravan had been traveling southwest. With the anticipation of the direct route to Jerusalem and a mere three day's journey ahead, everyone could sense the general excitement in the group to be so close to their destination.

The next day's travel through the Jezreel Valley exhibited field after field of crop-laden land. Workers stopped in their labors to observe the magi's small caravan. Caravan's were not rare to the locals, but people of all times have been drawn to a parade no matter how accustomed to them they may have become.

Ezri's mind, when not in conversation, constantly returned to the image of Podarces laying dead on the ground. Balthasar had noticed the pained look the young man had when he was left to himself and had determined to talk to him about it when the time was right.

The excitement of meeting a great person sent from the Jew's deity preoccupied Ezri's mind, as it did everyone else in the band, so there was some emotional relief when his attention was on that.

What to do with the gold played on his mind frequently, and he knew the longer he stayed away from recovering it, the better chance he had of not being discovered. Sophia and Noam knew nothing about his surviving the botched robbery, and he wished he could get a message to them about his being alive. He also knew that the longer they waited to get their share, the better chance they had of not be implicated in the robbery. At least the way it was, he reasoned, they would not have to live with the ever-present reality of the gold and wanting to get their hands on it. When he finally could contact them, they would be able to rejoice in their fortuity all the more. As much as he could figure, it was best that he continue with his present course. His being the only one who knew about the gold and where it was hidden was the safest strategy he could take at this point. Besides, Matthias would be unmerciful to anyone he caught being associated with the theft.

Both the newcomers felt the need to keep certain aspects of their lives to themselves. The intelligence that Cassius would be bringing to Caesar would garner him a profitable reward. This detour had cost him some time, but because of the generosity of the magi, it had not cost him anything financially to join the quest. Within a week, he would be headed to Joppa to take a boat to Rome where he would give the emperor the information concerning this new king. He had never been to Jerusalem, and he wondered what circumstances would await him and the rest of the group there. Surely, he thought, this king would be born to one of the great men of the Jews' holy city.

CHAPTER FIFTY-NINE

John and Levi were out working with a few of their servants among their olive trees, near Gischala, when a hired man came riding up in a hurry.

"John, I think I have found your horse, Raven," he said before he could dismount.

"Where?" father and son said simultaneously.

"A man who deals in horses and camels near Hazor has him stabled there. He said he wasn't going to sell him, but if the owner had him stolen away, then he would sell him to you for the same price he had paid for him."

John looked at his father. "What do you think, Father?"

"You miss that horse. I think it's worth looking into. You'd recognize that rascal if you saw him?"

"That I would," John said with a smile. "Maybe the horse trader can give me a clue which way Ezri went."

"You have no way of knowing whether it was Ezri who sold him your horse. Ezri may have sold him to someone else who sold it to the horse trader." cautioned his father.

The hired man interjected at this point, saying, "I described Ezri to him, and he said that I had given an accurate description of the man who sold him Raven."

Father and son looked at each other, and Levi said, "You better take a few men with you, son." To the hired man he said, "Did you find out how many days it's been since Ezri made his purchase?"

"The trader said it was just yesterday."

"Be careful, John," his father warned him, "you don't know how many men he's riding with."

"I would love to catch up to him and take some of what he's cost us out of his hide," John said through clenched teeth.

"If you catch him, you bring him back here, John—that's all. Don't make a bad situation worse by taking matters into your own hands. Let the Gischala elders and me deal with him from a legal standpoint."

John did not like what his father had to say, but he said, "Yes, Father," and thought, "it won't hurt if I rough him up a little."

"Listen," Levi continued, "don't spend days looking for him. Ezri's smart in the ways of deceit. If you don't find him in a few days, you're not going to. I want you back by noon no later than two days from now. If you do find a hot trail, send one of the men back to let me know where you're headed. After that, if you haven't caught up to him, I want you to head home by week's end. You understand?"

"Yes, Father."

"And don't forget to tell your mother where you're headed. She won't worry as much if she hears it from you."

John nodded his head, the hired man handed his horse's reins to him, and took the horse to fetch the five other men he would be taking with him.

Laurentinus had finished his business in Caesarea Maritima and was heading back with his men to Caesarea Philippi to check on his friend Yitzhak. He had a foreboding that all had not gone well, and he hoped that his instincts were false. His first night out from the lavish Mediterranean city, he planned to lodge he and his men at the garrison at Megiddo. That happened to be the same night that Gaspar's caravan camped nearby. It was common for caravans to overnight near Megiddo because there was no safer place to stay than within the earshot of a Roman fortress. This made the Parthian guard who accompanied the magi uncomfortable, but they saw the wisdom in it. There was no reason for the Romans to suspect them, and chances were that they would never see a Roman soldier that night so common were trade caravans in the area.

That night there were two other caravans camped near the Roman outpost. As was Vahumisa's custom, he avoided joining with other caravans much to the magi's dismay. He reasoned that if they were not with other groups, there would be no chance of a loose tongue getting them in trouble with foreign powers. This particular night, Vahumisa's advice was discarded. Laurentinus and three of his officers rode up on horseback after the men had settled into storytelling mode. Cyrus had just finished telling Ezri the story about their meeting the desert bandits. The rest of the men had heard him tell it at least a dozen times, but they all laughed again and were still doing so when the four cavalrymen rode into camp. Vahumisa had set a guard, as always, and one of them escorted the Romans to his location. The laughter died down abruptly when the camp's eyes caught sight of the newcomers. Conversations became hushed as Vahumisa, Melchior, and Gaspar got up to meet the soldiers.

"Welcome," said Gaspar extending his hand to Laurentinus.

"Thank you," said the commander. "I do not want to disturb your evening, but I am anxious to know if you came through Caesarea Philippi in your recent travels?"

"We did not," said Gaspar. "We came down on the Coastal Highway from Damascus. We did not go west of Mount Hermon." Gaspar looked at the Roman as if waiting for more information.

"Does anyone in your group know a man—Yitzhak of Caesarea?" asked Laurentinus.

Ezri could feel himself squirm at the Roman's question. How did this man know Yitzhak, he wondered. Then he searched his mind to remember if he had ever met the commander. He was sure that he had not, but did this mean that the Romans might be in the area where he hid the gold for a long time to come? He decided there and then that he would let the gold rest in hiding for a considerable duration before he went to dig it up. It did occur to him that this Roman might be the same one who brought the gold up to Capernaum. If so, he may have even more reason to continue to ask questions and try to find the cache.

Melchior turned to the rest of the men in the caravan and asked, "Do any of you know this man of whom he speaks, Yitzhak?"

The men shook their heads. Ezri's mind raced to think through whether it would be expedient to make up a lie about how he would have known Yitzhak. He could think of no advantage, so remained silent.

"Thank you," said Laurentinus. "We'll leave you now. We will be in the garrison until tomorrow. If you think of anything, please come and ask for me. My name is Laurentinus. Again, I am sorry to disturb your conversation." As he turned to leave, Gaspar made a movement toward him like he was going to ask him to stay. Vahumisa put up a hand to stop him, and then he merely saw the centurion back to his men.

The Romans rode away toward the garrison as Vahumisa watched them leave. Gaspar walked over and said, "I was just going to ask them to join us, commander."

"And that is why I stopped you."

"We are here on the most innocent of motives. We have nothing to hide."

"The Romans are our nation's enemies. If they ever learned that we are Parthians sent on a royal fact-finding expedition, they would lock us up and question us until we were all as old as Balthasar."

"You are right. I need to be more careful about whom I invite to join us."

"I am very glad to hear you say that, your eminence." Hearing the men laugh, he said, "Amehlech is on a roll. Come. Join me by the fire."

Gaspar followed the commander with the realization that if he was not careful, he could end up in a Roman prison never able to see Rachel again.

231

Judith, John's mother, was the first person he sought to help him in his quest to bring back Raven and to apprehend Ezri. Quickly telling her the circumstances, he employed her to make ready the provisions that they might need. He rounded up three of his father's men to aid in the search, stopped back by the big house to pick up his provisions, kissed his mother, and headed for the next nearest estate. Uri was a close friend of his whose father owned the land next to his father's. Relaying the information about Raven and Ezri to him, John did not have to wait long for Uri to get himself ready. The land next to Uri's was owned by a man who had a son, Gil, who was two years older than Ezri and Uri. Gil was often mistaken for being older than his years because of his common sense and patient manner. He took even less time than Uri to inform his family where he was going and what their mission was.

The three had known each other since childhood, and had developed a trust and close friendship. When Raven was initially stolen, John and his friends combed the hillside in search of the stolen animal. Their friendship would have been enough to recruit them for this task, but the fact that they had recent information on Ezri's whereabouts gave them more than enough incentive to ride with John.

The six men arrived in Hazor about the time the animal trader was closing up his business.

"You made good time getting here," said the trader. "I just spoke with your hired man this morning. He must have ridden like the devil was after him."

"We did hurry to get here," began John, "and we're still in a hurry. When I come back I'll pay for my horse and the expense of boarding him. Right now, I'd like to make sure it's Raven, and while you're at it, you can tell me about the man who sold him to you and which way he left."

The trader showed John his black stallion—it was Raven. Hugging the animal's neck, John smiled at Raven's obvious pleasure.

While John stroked the neck of his horse, the trader said, "The man who sold me your horse, or rather traded me for a camel, was in here just yesterday. I thought he seemed like he had a lot on his mind, and that it was strange that he wanted to trade this fine horse for one of my camels, but I see all kinds in my business."

"Did he say anything about where he was headed?" asked Gil.

"He muttered something about finding a caravan to travel with, and headed east out of town on the road to Damascus."

John ran to the horse he had been riding and vaulted

onto the saddle. Riding over to the trader he said, "Will you hold Raven for me until I return?"

"I will hold him for a few weeks, if you've not shown up, I cannot guarantee that he will not be sold if I'm offered a good price."

"That is fair. I'll be back well before then."

The six men rode furiously out of Hazor toward Damascus and away from Ezri.

CHAPTER SIXTY

The House of Gaspar was violently awakened one morning by Ara screaming, "She's dead! My lady's dead!"

Rachel rushed from her room to her mother's to see Ara rocking back and forth on her knees, sobbing by Nazli's bed. Kahliq and Balzak reached the room just after Rachel. They watched the young women's ululations. Seeing the two women he loved most in the world in emotional torment wracked Kahliq. He and Ara had been bought when just children to be slaves in the high priest's home. They had always looked after each other as both looked after the women of Zand's house.

Balzak walked over to Rachel and put his arm around her waist to give her support. The tender gesture unleashed even more of her grief. She slumped to the floor, as Balzak, on his knees, cradled her to himself, letting her vent all her sorrow.

Kahliq knelt down beside Ara, and she leaned into him allowing him to comfort her broken heart.

Tala stood at the door weeping for Rachel's loss. Balzak looked over his shoulder at the young servant girl and waved her to his side.

Speaking quietly he said, "We must remove the body before contamination is allowed to spread. Send one of the servants to the tower of silence to bring back the pallbearers to collect Nazli's body."

Tala nodded and hurried away.

Rachel looked up into the eyes of the small man who had come to mean so much to her. "You're all I have left, dear Balzak. Please don't leave me."

Balzak gulped, pushing down his emotion, "I never will."

After departing from the trader in Hazor, John and company rode hard until the sun set. The horses had worked hard that day and needed resting, so it took little consideration to stop for the night. The next day they planned to rise early, push the horses until noon, and if they found no sign of Ezri, they would head back to Hazor to pick up Raven.

In some ways, John wished he had picked up Raven and just returned home. Ezri had always been slippery, and hunting him down had only made him more annoyed that the thief was able to elude him once again. That night he had recurring dreams of Ezri being within his grasp only to lose him. In one dream, he reached out to grab Ezri as the ground gave way below him and Ezri was able to escape. Another time, he saw Ezri across a crowded village square and was unable, because of the mass of people, to reach him before he left through the gate to the village. The next morning he woke up frustrated and surly.

The sun was high in the sky when John slowed his horse to a trot and then to a walk. Looking clear to the horizon, he searched for any sign of a caravan in the distance. There was not even a hint of a dust cloud. He pulled his mount to a stop.

"What is it, John. Do you see something up ahead?" asked Uri.

"No. I don't see anything, and I don't want to spend any more time on this thief. He's a waste of my time. There was a stream not far back. We can give the horses a good watering, eat, and head home."

"I know it's hard to say that, John," said Gil, "but I think you're making the right decision."

Shrugging, John turned his horse toward Hazor and let the animal choose its own pace to the river.

Rachel had never given up hope that her mother would regain her will to live. Nazli's surrender to her depression was incomprehensible to her daughter. Feelings of being unloved and unwanted saturated her emotions. The joy of being married to Gaspar that she had wanted to share with her mother and father would never happen now. Her thoughts returned again and again to that happy morning when she begged her father and mother to let her see Gaspar off. She remembered Gaspar taking her hands and kissing them and calling her his love, before saying good-bye. That day, not so long ago, seemed now like a lifetime past.

Sitting in her room, gazing out into the garden, she said, "O, dearest Gaspar, do not leave me alone in this world. Come back to me." Emotion welled up in her and she gave herself to her emotions.

Outside her bedroom door Balzak heard her words and now her deep heaving sobs. He whispered, "Gaspar, come home soon."

The next few days were uneventful for Gaspar and his entourage. Vahumisa had gotten them up early and had them ride a little longer than normal the next two days so they would arrive in Jerusalem in early afternoon of the third day. Gaspar rode most of the time alongside his magi friends. From time to time, he would drift back to converse with Cassius and Ezri, or drop back farther to enjoy the comedic antics of Cyrus and

Amehlech.

At night, the mysterious star continued to move southward in the sky as if it were appointed to point them, solely, to the Anointed One. Ezri found himself drawn in by the drama the star presented. He became no different than the others in this way. Their questions were now his questions. Why was the star directing them? Was it truly sent from God? Would they be able to locate the person to whom they believed this star pointed? How would the star make it clear what building, field, or mountain to discover the Messiah? Ezri was caught up in the riddle as much as everyone else. His heart had always pined for adventure, and these wisemen from the east were his tour guides.

There were aspects to the Parthians' surroundings, once they left the wooded hills of Galilee, that reminded them of their homeland. Sometimes, beyond the hills of the western Jordan valley, they could see endless fields of wheat and vineyards in large number. This fertile land was similar to Mesopotamia. Olive groves were a constant, cascading down the shallow soiled hills to the plain below. Varieties of citrus and apricot groves, peppering the valley, were a result of trade with the far east. Separate landowners' fields could be identified by the familiar towers where he or a hired hand could keep watch over the crop during harvest season.

Meandering along was peaceful, and it was much to be desired over an arduous trip. With them always was the excitement of finally reaching Jerusalem and hopefully finding answers to their nescience.

Jerusalem came into view late in the morning of the third day. Built on two hills, the city was like a beacon to the surrounding countryside. Few in the ancient world had not heard of the spectacular temple to the Hebrew God. The engineering of the earthen platform for the temple was a marvel in itself. Tons of dirt had to be moved from the northwest hill of the temple mount to fill in and level the valley to the west creating the platform that would support the whole structure. Huge stone walls kept the dirt and rubble in place, and also formed the foundation for the walls that encircled the temple, its accompanying buildings, and courtyards. Each side of the temple complex was six hundred feet long. The temple to Yahweh stood on the flattened mountain Moriah where Abraham went to offer his son Isaac, and God provided a lamb in his stead. The city itself extended onto the adjoining mountain, Zion.

At the sight of Jerusalem's walls and the temple rising above, Vahumisa signaled to have one of his men come forward to join the other escort at the front of the column. When the soldier arrived, Vahumisa dropped back to ride with the magi.

"What is it, Vahumisa?" inquired Melchior.

"I would like to discuss with you the next few days that we will be in the city. What will you be requiring of my men and me?"

Balthasar had the most experience in these kinds of situations, so the other two magi looked to him to speak. "We will need someone to announce our arrival to Herod or whomever he has left in charge of the city if he is absent. Surely the leaders and religious officials of the city are aware of the birth of the king of the Jews and where we can find him. It is customary for magi to visit great personages, so Herod, or his official, will not see our coming as out of the ordinary. Would you be willing to act as our herald to Herod?"

"I would consider it a privilege. I have had experience in this before. I will begin thinking through what I will say to his majesty and have it ready for your approval by supper tonight."

Melchior's eyes grew wide and he slapped the commander on the back, "Hah! What will take you so long?"

Vahumisa began to say that he could do it before then, but when he saw the smiles on the three magi, he understood Melchior's jest. Shaking his head, he heeled his horse back to its lead position. As he did so, Balthasar said, "At supper will be fine."

Their custom had become to eat their noonday meal en route so not to lose time. Today was no different. Their enthusiasm to reach the Jews' holy city was such that they would have all gone without any meal that day. Nearing the city, Vahumisa began to ask questions of others on the road of the best places to camp and where he should go to pay the caravan tax. His intelligence told him that the hillside to the west of the city was the best place to set up for the night, and that he could pay his tax at the Fortress Antonia on the north side of the city. He also learned that Herod was in the city at this time and that his residence was located on the same side of the city as they would be camping. Once he had helped find a place for the campsite, he planned to make an appointment to see Herod and pay the caravan tax.

There was something about this Jewish city that looked familiar to Gaspar. At one point, he asked Vahumisa if they could pull to the side for a moment. Balthasar and Melchior looked at their young associate as if he would explain himself to them.

Surveying the countryside around them, Gaspar said, "This is the city. This is the city of my dream. Now that I see it, I know that this is where we are supposed to be. We are very close to fulfilling our destinies."

Balthasar clapped his hands together in excitement, and

Melchior only looked on in wonder at the ancient city.

Ezri leaned over to Cassius and said, "I wanted adventure. It looks like I'm going to get it."

Cassius nodded his head and said nothing.

"I can't wait to see the city tonight in the moonlight. Then it will look exactly like it did in my dream," Gaspar reported. "Come, let's get camp set up. We have a great ruler to meet."

Supper had already been prepared and everyone was eating when Vahumisa returned from his errands. Amehlech brought him a plate with goat cooked in a sauce of garlic, onions, bay leaves, milk, and flour with lentils and flat bread on the side. When he had seated himself, Cyrus brought him a cup of wine.

"Did you have a successful venture into the city?" asked Melchior.

"I did," Vahumisa said simply scooping up a large portion of the sauce with his bread. He chewed for awhile and then filled his mouth anew with a mouthful of lentils.

Finishing his second bite, he went to eat a portion of the goat when Melchior grabbed his hand and said, "Not another bite until you expound on what you've said."

Vahumisa could no longer keep a straight face and broke into laughter. His men, seeing him in a rare moment of jocularity, spewed whatever food or drink they had in their mouths. Soon, the whole camp was laughing with the commander. Melchior looked around as if to say, "What was so funny?" which reduced everyone again into fits of laughter.

Once the laughter began to die down, Melchior said, "Now can you tell me what happened?" Again, the campsite was in an uproar.

Balthasar, wiping the tears from his eyes, said, "Don't say another word, my friend, if you want to hear about Vahumisa's day."

Melchior looked at the old magi and only shook his head.

"The first thing that I did was to go to the palace to see about getting an audience with Herod," said Vahumisa composing himself. "They told me that it would be several days before we could see him but that they would send a messenger to our camp the morning of an afternoon meeting or the afternoon before the next morning's meeting."

"So they wouldn't give you an exact time?" asked Gaspar.

"Evidently, there are so many trying to gain an audience that he has had to go to this system so people are not made to wait at the palace for days at a time."

"Well, I for one would love to visit the temple of Yahweh and try to get answers from some of their priests about the star and the person who it heralds," said Balthasar.

"While you are all sightseeing, my men and I will take two shifts to keep watch over the camp, and to wait for any news from Herod," Vahumisa stated. "I also went to the fort to pay the tax, and the Roman guard there seemed to be quite tense. I don't know what has them keyed up, but I would suggest that we keep as low profile as possible while we're here in Jerusalem. Rather than touring in large groups, I would suggest that you keep yourselves to smaller groups of four or five at the most, so as not to arouse suspicion."

"The Jews are always looking for one they call the Messiah to come and lead them in an ouster of the Roman occupation. There is always someone claiming to be this Messiah," said Cassius.

"There you have it," began Vahumisa. "Don't give the Romans any reason to suspect your activities. We're just visitors here. Let's not give them any reason to think otherwise."

Everyone nodded their heads and soon were caught up in their own conversations. Talk came to a halt when Melchior said in his booming voice, "Look at the star tonight! It's moving down in the sky just south of the city."

The deviant star that had until that night moved imperceptibly slowly, though on it's own course, was now moving noticeably lower in the southern sky and then it came to a stop. Everyone by now was standing and staring.

"What does that mean?" Asked Ezri.

Maintaining his watch on the star, Balthasar said, "I suppose it means we're getting closer to our destination. Hopefully, we will get to see the king of the Jews sooner rather than later."

CHAPTER SIXTY-ONE

"I'm sorry, Balzak, my mind is elsewhere this morning," said Rachel as her third knife throw in a row sailed way wide of the target. "Maybe we should try this tomorrow."

Balzak had hoped to get Rachel's mind off of her mother's death by bringing her down to the knife throwing range, but it had not been a successful diversion. Nazli's funeral had been two days before, and Rachel's doldrums had not slackened.

"As you wish, my lady," said Balzak.

Looking at her teacher with only the scarcest of smiles she said, "So formal."

"The situation seemed to dictate formality."

"Balzak, I know that you are concerned for me. Do not fear that I will go down the path that my mother did. I have too much to live for. I am sad that my dreams of sharing the life of my husband and children with my parents will never be a reality. I won't let the loss of that dream ruin my future, but I must have time to grieve." Seeing the concern in his eyes, she walked over to the little man holding out her hands for his, and said, "Please don't fret."

"As you wish, dear Rachel."

Tears came to her eyes as she squeezed his hands. She turned before the tears fell down her cheeks as she walked back to the house to change into the clothes she would wear for the day.

Standing in her room staring out the window, she decided that a trip to the market might be the very thing she needed. Knife throwing took concentration. She needed something that she could do without thought. Wheeling around to the servant gong, she clanged it with the striker to hail Ara.

"Yes, my lady," Ara said entering her mistress' room, seeing her remove her trousers.

"I wish to go to the market today. Please let Kahliq know and that he should ready my father's sedan chair for you and me to ride."

"How soon?"

"I wish to have lunch at the marketplace."

"I'll see to it. Would you like me to lay something out for you?"

"After you talk to Kahliq, you may ready my bath, and

240

choose something appropriate for me to wear."

Ara left, and Rachel reclined back on her bed. Her thoughts drifted back to the night of the dinner party and of how rakish Gaspar had looked when he rode up on Yalda, his black mare.

"How simple would my grieving be if you were only here to hold me in your arms," she said, tears returning to her eyes.

The morning after arriving in Jerusalem, Vahumisa and four of his men took the first guard of the camp while the rest of the members of the caravan took off in small groups to see the sites of the city.

Ezri, a trained thief, wrapped his purse several times around the belt of his trousers and wore a tunic over them. Most of his gold he left in another purse buried two steps inside the northwest pole of the tent he shared with Cassius.

Vahumisa sent two of his soldiers with the three wisemen, and asked that they send a report back if they should leave the temple before noon. "I want to be able to get word to you if Herod should contact me this morning to meet with him this afternoon."

"I understand," said Gaspar. "I can't believe we'll move on from the temple before noon, but if we do, I'll be sure to send one of your men to let you know where we will be headed."

"Thank you, your eminence. If you encounter any trouble, I will be here."

Gaspar smiled his approval and clapped the commander on his back.

As far as big cities of the ancient world went, Jerusalem was of modest size. It could not compare with the likes of Ctesiphon, Athens, or Rome, although it did have most of the amenities one would expect in a major metropolitan area. Public baths, a theatre, a hippodrome for sporting events, and two areas designated for markets were all a part of the city's makeup. The old city bustled like any major population center throughout history. One could not say Jerusalem was spectacular, but he could say that it was pleasant.

There was one aspect of the Jews' holy city that did stand out, and that was the temple area. The enormity of the temple's platform amazed the magi. Living in Mesopotamia, they had seen great structures and ziggurats that seemed to stretch to the sky, but the skill and effort involved in excavating so much earth was astounding even to them.

Melchior could not help himself. He soon found a man who seemed to know a lot about the temple and the platform's expansion during Herod's reign. A good hour was spent listening to the man talk and probing him with questions as they

241

investigated the support walls of the platform that were the foundation for the temple and all that was associated with it. Their tour guide finally had to excuse himself because he realized he was running late for a meeting with a local merchant.

"I have never seen anything that matches the size or skill necessary to create this kind of engineering marvel," gushed Melchior. "I can't wait to see what's on it."

Gaspar and Balthasar were as dazzled as Melchior with the achievement, and they too found themselves hurrying to see the structures atop the platform. When they got to the base of the stairs that led up to the temple area, Balthasar motioned to the other two that he needed to rest before climbing the stairs.

"Should we return to camp, Balthasar. We can see the temple at another time," said Gaspar.

"No, no, I am fine. I just need to catch my breath."

Balthasar sat on the first step leading up to the temple for several minutes with his eyes closed. Melchior and Gaspar looked on with concern.

"I am fine, you two old women," Balthasar said without opening his eyes. "I'll be ready to go shortly." In a moment he looked up, the color had returned to his face, and he walked up the flight of thirty steps without assistance from either the magi or the soldiers.

When they reached the landing at the top, Melchior put his hand on the old wiseman's shoulder and said, "You know, I'm going to stop worrying about you."

"I'm glad you're finally using your head," he said stepping through the Golden Gate into the Court of the Gentiles.

Expecting to see an unimpeded view of the temple, Balthasar was taken back to see only another wall in front of him. The others stepped in behind him finding that they were as nonplussed as Balthasar.

"How many barriers to their God do these Jews have?" Gaspar vocalizing his thought.

"There appears to be a sign by the entrance to the wall," Melchior noted. Reading it out loud, he said, "My Greek is a little rusty. Let me see. It says, "Beware. Gentiles may not pass beyond this point on penalty of death.""

The five Parthians stood at the base of the stairs leading into the temple proper. There were fourteen steps from where they stood, which they would learn later was the Court of the Gentiles, up to the Beautiful Gate. Across the expanse before them, through another opening and another expanse, they saw the front of the temple of Yahweh.

A priest came up to them and said, "If you are not Jews, you must not enter into the next area."

"We are travelers to your land," said Balthasar. "Do you

have a moment to explain the cultic significance of the partitions?"

"Yes, I have just finished my duties. I have time. The walls around the temple are here to protect people from unintentionally defiling Adoni."

"Adoni?" queried Gaspar

"We do not say the name of Adoni because we believe His name is too holy to speak. Because He is holy, we have set up these boundaries to protect people from committing sacrilege.

"This large outer area is the Court of the Gentiles. It is open to the whole world, and that is why it is so much larger than the other areas.

"The area beyond this sign you have just read is the Court of Women. All Israelites are welcome to enter here through what we call the Beautiful Gate. The court is a perfect square with each side measuring two hundred feet.

"Beyond is Nicanor's Gate. There are fifteen semicircular steps leading up to that gate that leads into the Court of the Israelites. It is only seventeen feet in depth and two-hundred feet wide.

"Next is the Court of the priests, where, if you look closely through Nicanor's Gate to the left, is the altar where sacrifices are performed. The large building at the back is obviously the temple itself which houses the Holy Place and the Holy of Holies. Do you have anymore questions?" he said with a warm smile.

"We have many," Melchior boomed.

Motioning with his hand to the west end of the Court of the Gentiles, the priest directed them to a portico saying, "Please, let's sit over here in the shade."

So caught up were the wisemen with what they were learning of the Jews' faith and rituals, they never inquired about the star. Before one of them had a chance to remember to ask about it, one of Vahumisa's soldiers came running up to them out of breath.

"Vahumisa has sent me to inform you that King Herod will meet with the three of you at supper tonight."

Strapping her knives onto her calves for the first time to go out in public made Rachel feel adventurous. She spun to face the door while lifting her skirt, grabbed the knife from her right leg sheath, and stuck it in the door within an inch of where she had aimed. Seconds later came a knock and a tentative voice that said, "My lady?"

"I'll be out in a moment," Rachel said rushing over to pull the knife out of the door to re-sheath it on her calf. She opened the door to see Tala waiting, big eyed.

"Is everything all right, my lady?"

"Yes. Why?"

"Well," said Tala looking down at Rachel's right leg, "it appears the hem of your skirt is caught on the hilt of your knife."

Rachel looked down to see that what Tala said was indeed true. Looking back at Tala as she lifted the hem over the knife, she saw her stifle a giggle.

"Your teacher would be proud of you, my lady." Tala said in fun. "Ara and Kahliq are waiting with the sedan chair in front."

"Thank you," Rachel said, her cheeks coloring.

Rachel had not been away from Gaspar's estate, other than for the funeral, in days. It felt good to be out in public again. The noise and hurry of the city energized her—making her feel alive. From time to time, she could not help running her hand over the knives beneath her clothes. It felt foolish thinking it, but she almost hoped she would have an opportunity to use them.

The sedan bearers slowed when they neared the marketplace. "Would you like us to take you in, or would you rather go in on foot," said one of them.

"We will take Kahliq with us and go on foot. Thank you," Rachel said as the bearers lowered the sedan for her and Ara to exit. As soon as she stood up, she saw Majid and Sevent, Majid's father, on horseback not twenty paces away. She froze.

"What is it, my lady?" asked Ara.

Rachel said nothing, only made the faintest of nods toward the two men.

Majid was laughing, and as his head turned in Rachel's direction, he saw her immediately. His smile became a smirk as he maneuvered his horse to pull up alongside the sedan chair.

"I heard about the death of your mother," he said never losing the smirk. "I am sorry to hear it"

"Thank you," Rachel said never looking up into his eyes.

"I see your grief has not lessened your arrogance," he said. His face turning hateful.

By now Sevent had pulled next to his son. "Come along. She has fallen beneath our social rank. You should not be seen talking to another man's concubine."

At this, Kahliq stepped between the sedan and Majid, his hand moving to the hilt of his sword.

Rachel pulled the curtains back and placed her hand on the shoulder of her servant. "Enough," she said, "if these two honorable men have nothing better to do than verbally attack a mourning daughter, then leave them alone. They are the ones to be pitied."

"I do not need your pity. You add insult to insult. You will live to see the day when I shall have my revenge on you," Majid said as he heeled his horse forward almost knocking a beggar woman over.

"I am sorry, my lady," said Ara. "Would you like me to have the servants bear you home?"

"No, I will not let Majid take away the joy of a beautiful day. Come Kahliq. I'm hungry."

CHAPTER SIXTY-TWO

John and the others with him arrived in Hazor late in the afternoon the day after they had decided to turn back from their pursuit of Ezri. The trader came briskly out of one of the stock pens walking up the road to meet them with what looked to be some urgency.

John, tired and downcast, slowed to a stop as the horse and camel handler approached them. "You look in a hurry. What's lit a fire under you?"

"I talked with a man this morning who said he saw that young fellow, who sold me your horse, meet up with a caravan north of town and head back south with them toward Jerusalem. There were three holy men with the caravan who he says were headed for Jerusalem."

John looked at the other men who were with him. "What do you think?"

Uri said, "I think we should check it out."

John looked to Gil. "Gil, is this going to be a waste of time?"

"I think if we have a chance to bring this thief to justice, it's worth the trip. Let's go get him."

Speaking to his father's hired men, he said, "You two ride back to my father and let him know that we're going to hunt for Ezri in Jerusalem. Tell him we'll be back in no more than a fortnight. Thank you for coming with me. I'm going to send this horse I'm riding home with you. Raven's fresh and I'm anxious to ride him again."

John paid the the trader Raven's cost, boarding, plus a small bonus before the three friends took off down the road to Jerusalem.

Matthias was in a rage when he heard what had happened to his gold shipment.

"If everyone is dead, where did my gold go to?" he screamed at the man who brought him the news.

"Sir, what I have told you is all that I know. Your giant and two of his men were killed by the Roman guard because they thought Basil was a bandit scouting them out to rob the gold. The rest of your men went up north to give aid to Yitzhak, but they were found out by the thieves and murdered before the big battle. Clearly, they fought well. There were more of the bandits' men killed than them. As far as the gold is concerned, it has just disappeared."

Matthias knew the messenger could not help the message that he was conveying to him, but it took all of his control not to kill the man where he stood. "Get out," he yelled, sending the harbinger of ill news scuttling out the door. "I should have known not to put my gold in the care of that north Galilean rube," he muttered aloud. "I have to figure out how to recover it."

The day after the confrontation in the marketplace, Rachel was again training with Balzak.

"I had you bring that old dress with you today so you can wear it over your trousers. I want to teach you how to roll away from your attacker, come up to your feet armed with knives ready for throwing. Kahliq, I want you to play the attacker, and I'll be Rachel. Rachel you watch my movements so you can imitate them when it's your turn."

Kahliq grabbed Balzak from behind. Balzak stamped down beside Kahliq's foot, dropped through the big servant's arms, somersaulted forward as he armed himself with his knives, turned, and threw the two knives successively at two targets on either side of Kahliq.

"Kahliq, that was perfect, except when Rachel does it, don't forget to fall to the ground to avoid her throws."

"I will," smiled the servant, "and, thank you for not stepping on my arch. I'm just recently walking without a limp."

"Now, Rachel, don't get discouraged when you try this move. You're wearing a dress—I am not. You're a coordinated girl. You'll get it."

The remainder of the morning Rachel practiced the move Balzak had shown her. By the end of the day's practice session she was doing much better. In a day or two it was clear that she would have the move mastered.

"You have done well today, my lady," said Balzak.

"Soon," chimed in Kahliq as he was leaving to do his chores, "I will be calling you to protect me when I go to the market."

"Thank you, Kahliq. I will always need and treasure your protection."

Balzak watched Rachel's servant leave. "He has been good to you these many years, hasn't he?"

"He has. I have always felt safe when he was with me."

"That reminds me. If you ever find yourself in a situation where Kahliq cannot help you, remember that once you have thrown your knives, you are unarmed. Always keep one of your knives in case you have to do the close-in fighting I have been teaching you." He then smiled slyly. "You are not only the most beautiful woman in all of Parthia, you have become, quite possibly, the most deadly."

"Ooh, Balzak. You do know how to charm a woman, don't you?"

The news of that night's audience with Herod changed all the plans for the day. The wisemen took advantage of the Roman public baths while the same soldier who brought them the news returned to camp to have Amehlech and Cyrus lay out their finest robes for the evening's supper.

It had been days since the magi had taken the time to scrub off the dirt of their travel. When Amehlech and Cyrus arrived, all three were found in warm baths soaking after their cleansing baths.

Each of the magi had colors that were his own representative colors used in his official robes worn on special occasions such as this one with Herod. Balthasar's robes, cape, and turban were yellow silk trimmed in silver. Melchior's were imposing colors of deepest purple and black silk woven into wide bands for his robes. Deep purple silk were also the material of his turban and cape. Both were trimmed in a similar silver fashion as were Balthasar's. Gaspar's silks were scarlet trimmed in broad gold brocade at the cuffs, lapels, and bottom hem of his robes. The cape had a thinner brocade of the same pattern around its perimeter, and the turban was all red except for a magnificent gold pin of his father's that was worn front center.

Amehlech and Cyrus had taken the trouble to ready the wisemen's camels to ride to the palace. Both servants had changed into clothes that were more suitable for the attendants of great magi.

Riding to the palace, Balthasar could not help reflecting on an earlier time in his life. "I remember as a young magi loving occasions when I could don these robes. Now, I am almost embarrassed to wear them."

"I have never liked them," Melchior said. "They cost too much for as often as they're worn. That's the problem with silk. If one could wear it every day, it would be wonderful. But it is so expensive—though it wears like a mail shirt, one finds himself saving it for only rare occasions."

They rode along in silence until Melchior interrupted it asking, "What about you, Gaspar?".

Shrugging, he said sheepishly, "I still like wearing them."

Sensing his discomfort, Balthasar said smiling, "An unpopular idea voiced truthfully, is better than an approved one told to flatter."

When the five travelers reached Herod's palace,

Amehlech and Cyrus helped the two older magi dismount their camels. Not waiting for his servants to help him nor for his camel to kneel, Gaspar threw his right leg over to the left side of the camel, and slid off the beast's side.

"I will stay with the camels," said Amehlech to Cyrus, "if you will see to their eminences announcement to the king."

Cyrus walked up to the guards in front of the palace and gave the names of the three wisemen who would be suppering with Herod that night. While Cyrus waited for the guard to return, another man walked up with his servant to the magi.

The man nodded his head in respect and said, "My name is Annas, I am the high priest of the most high God, you must be the wisemen with whom Herod requested that I have supper."

"We are magi from the East," said Melchior. "This is Gaspar and Balthasar, and I am Melchior." All three men bowed their heads out of respect to the high priest.

"We have questions we would like to ask of you, but no doubt, his majesty, too, would like to hear your answers," said Balthasar.

Annas closed his eyes, lifted his head to the sky, and said, "All questions will be answered tonight." Looking to his servant he said, "Go, have me announced to his majesty."

Watching the young man hurry off, Gaspar said, "We had a chance to visit the temple today, and one of your priests was most hospitable to us. He sat for a long time with my friends and me answering our questions with great patience."

The high priest smiled ever so slightly, and nodded his head once again.

Balthasar said, "It is kind of you to take time to meet with us tonight. We thought that we would only have an audience with the king. Your being here also is a great honor."

Annas smiled another slight smile and said, "We should move up to the gate. His majesty will be sending for us any moment." So saying, the high priest moved ahead of the magi towards the palace's entrance. Gaspar and Melchior looked at each other with raised eyebrows. Balthasar said and did nothing but fell in behind Annas.

Herod's palace was nothing like the palace of King Phraataces at Ctesiphon—it was more along the line of the lesser kings of the Parthian empire. The rooms were more impressive for their size than in their splendor. The four priests were admitted into a large hall used by Herod as both a dining hall and a place to entertain guests for parties. Each magus was announced separately as he came into the room. The high priest was announced last and with the most pomp.

Each dinner guest was escorted to his place at the table. Herod was seated at the head, Melchior and Balthasar on his left, Gaspar to his right, and Annas at the far end. Servants encircled the table, standing far enough back so they could not overhear the private conversations of the guests.

"Welcome, magi," said Herod. "I am honored that you have accepted my invitation to dinner. I thought that this would be much less formal and more conducive to conversation than an audience."

"This venue is a most hospitable one indeed," said Balthasar. "Your forethought honors us."

"I was glad that the high priest was able to join us on such short notice," said Herod. Looking at the priest, he said, "Your willingness to join us tonight is appreciated."

Annas smiled thinly and nodded.

As the men had been talking, the servants poured wine and brought in toasted bread, cut into small two-inch squares, topped with quail baked in garlic and goat cheese.

Herod proved an accomplished conversationalist, keeping everyone at ease, asking pertinent questions, and engaging everyone in whatever topic was being discussed at the time. During their pre-dinner intercourse, pomegranates and nuts were also brought in as part of the appetizer to the meal. Everyone was caught up in conversation, except for Annas. Though he did not sulk or act unbecomingly, he watched, listened, and wondered why Herod had invited him to a dinner with idol worshippers.

The main course of lamb that had been cooked with minced garlic, rosemary, mustard, honey, and cashews was brought in as the conversation was just beginning to flag. The meat was garnished with sliced carrots, cucumbers, and radishes. Baskets of bread were placed in easy reach of each guest, and more wine was poured into each man's goblet. Melchior rubbed his hands in open anticipation of the meal that was brought before them.

"It is our custom," remarked Herod, "to thank our God for the food that we eat. High priest, would you honor us with your prayer?"

Annas stood. All three wisemen looked to see if Herod did the same. He sat, so they sat.

"Lord of heaven and earth. You have made all that there is, and are the bestower of all good gifts. We thank you tonight for the provision of good food to your people and to those who come before you unaware of your great glory. May your peace rest upon us, and may you find us faithful."

Annas sat down.

Waiting for the king to take a bite before they did, the magi enjoyed the first savory morsel of the lamb that had been cooked to perfection. When each person finished eating, a bowl of lemon water and a towel was brought to each dinner guest to rinse his fingers and dry his hands.

"Come," said Herod, "let us adjourn to the couches and speak of your purpose in Palestine."

Directing his guests into an adjacent room, the magi looked at one another, wondering if there was more meant to Herod's seemingly innocuous pronouncement. The couches were well cushioned and soft. Melchior reminded himself that he would be a rude guest if he were to fall asleep when their host was talking.

"So, now, what brings you to Jerusalem, and why have you asked for this audience?" asked Herod.

Although Gaspar felt as if he should acquiesce to the other two magi in this case, they motioned to him to speak for them all.

"My friends and I have observed in the heavens a new star that does not act as other stars, and we believe it heralds the birth of a great king. The star has literally led us to Jerusalem. We wanted to ask you, since you are a king in the land of Israel, where is He who is born king of the Jews?"

Herod's face went from that of interested attention to astonishment. Annas' face also became even graver than it had been before.

"Annas, have you heard anything said about a newborn king of the Jews?" Herod said, forgetting to refer to him as high priest.

" I have read nothing, to my knowledge, of such a star."

Turning to the wisemen he said, "Do you have any other signs that have led you to our land?"

"We don't, your majesty," said Gaspar. "Our purpose in coming was to worship at this king's feet. In our own histories, we have a single prophecy concerning a star that will introduce to the world a great ruler.

"May I hear the prophecy?" asked Herod.

""When the heavens are illumined by the brilliance of a new star that rises out of the west, men will follow it to find he who is the true ruler all." We believe this king to be a king sent from God."

Gaspar had hoped to be helpful by giving Herod more information, but it seemed to have an opposite affect. The affable host seemed to transform in just a few moments into an introspective introvert. The wisemen sat in tense silence for a moment wondering if Gaspar had said too much or if they should have held their questions for someone else.

Turning to Annas, the king said, "Do the Scriptures say anything about king and a star?"

"I will need to confer with the other religious leaders and

get back to you, your highness. We know of the one who will be God's anointed who will return Israel to its glory, but such a person will be evident in the way that he manifests the power of God. If you will excuse me, I will go now to call the Sanhedrin all together."

"Yes, yes, go now," said Herod.

It was at this point that Balthasar intervened. "Would your majesty like for us to call on you at a later time after the high priest has had time to collect his data?"

"Wha...? Yes, that would be propitious to be sure. I hope your eminences understand?"

"Of course we do," said Gaspar, looking at Melchior as if to say "What's going on?"

Herod clapped his hands for one of the servants to attend him. "Please show the magi out," and then to the wisemen said, "I'll contact you as soon as the high priest gets back to me with more information."

The magi stood on the steps to the palace not sure what had just taken place. One of the king's servants had informed Amehlech and Cyrus that the audience was over, so that by the time the magi had descended the stairs, their camels were waiting for them.

Back in the chamber where the wisemen had spoken with Herod, he was riddling the high priest with questions.

"How could these idol worshippers from Parthia know more than you about this star and its importance?"

"Your majesty, as you know, the Jews have long expected a deliverer to come who would resemble King David. Less than two-hundred years ago people were heralding the Maccabees as messiahs. Our people have always looked forward to the coming of the Messiah."

"Never has an outside entity come to our borders looking for the messiah. I wonder if there is truth to what these wisemen say? What if this person is such a king? What will happen to me?"

"You are the present king of Palestine. This person the wisemen seek is completely unknown."

"What are you getting at, Priest?"

"Do you not hold the present advantage, sire?"

Herod's face brightened. "Yes, yes I do."

CHAPTER SIXTY-THREE

Matthias paced the floor of his luxurious home in Jericho. He ran through his mind the events leading up to his missing gold shipment. Basil had been killed with two of his men by the Roman guard. If he would have told Laurentinus before hand about his men, he might have saved Basil's life. People were important to Matthias because of what they could do for him—he felt no emotional attachments to anyone. Basil would be hard to replace. His loyalty, strength, and intelligence would be hard qualities to find in a new servant.

Walking over to his desk to a wax tablet where he was keeping track of his ideas, he wrote, "Send a servant to Caesarea Maritima to verify that Laurentinus and his detachment had in fact been there during the time of the theft." Matthias thought that the only way that everyone could have been killed was if a third party had seen to it. If Laurentinus was involved, he reasoned, all it would take would be for his men to kill whoever was left alive, hide the gold, and then come back to it once he had retired from the military. He wrote himself another note, "Keep track of Laurentinus for the next few years." Matthias knew the commander well enough to know that he was a soldier for life. If the life-long soldier retired in the next few years, he could have him followed to make sure he was not involved in the gold theft.

The merchant ran through the events again. Something did not add up. The process was like grasping at a phantom. Every time he felt as if he almost had an answer, it would slip through his fingers. The more he pondered, the more he realized he would just have to set someone up in the Caesarea Phillipi area to nose around for the next few months. "If only I had Basil," he said out loud. Walking over to his tablet, he wrote, "Find someone trustworthy to spy in Caesarea."

Turning back to his pacing, he said, "But who can I trust?"

Breakfast the next morning at the campsite of the magi came and went without any word from Herod. When the wisemen had returned from their supper the night before, everyone in the camp was waiting to hear what they might have learned. Melchior explained to them how the king and the high priest reacted to Gaspar's question and how the magi had quickly been ushered out with a promise that they would be sent for once Herod heard from his high priest. The discussion had continued well into the evening, and was picked up again at breakfast the next morning.

"You told us," began Cassius, "that the whole tenor of the evening changed after Gaspar told them that he believed the star was leading you to the king of the Jews."

"That's right," said Melchior, "both the king and the high priest's faces dropped."

"Here's my question to you. Why did it affect them in that way do you think?"

I've thought about that," Melchior said rubbing his chin. "Herod is a king in Israel because Rome wishes him to be so. Anytime the emperor Augustus wants to remove him, he's gone. As long as he is useful to Rome's interests, he remains where he is. If someone else comes along who can do Herod's job better or is better suited to the position, Herod is out of a job.

"Likewise, if a new ruler comes into power, the high priest could be replaced by a man who represents the desires and policies of the new king.

"There is also the reality that this new king could try to upset the whole Roman power structure, because of a direct confrontation with Rome, and cause problems for anyone who is now in a position of authority."

Ezri could not help being pulled into the drama of the discussion. "There are those all over Israel who have been waiting for the one they call the Messiah to run the Romans out of Israel and reestablish Israel as a major power in the world. Many people in the upper Galilee area believe that his coming will be soon."

"We have discussed this one you call the Messiah," said Balthasar. "We magi believe that this king of the Jews may very well be this man."

Cassius jumped back into the conversation warning the magi saying, "There have been quite a few who have claimed to be the Messiah already. The Jewish leadership and the Roman authorities are on the lookout for anyone making such claims. I caution you about using the word Messiah when talking to Herod or the high priest."

Balthasar nodded his head and said, "Thank you, Cassius. I will remember what you have said."

"I'm getting antsy here in Jerusalem after last night's audience with Herod," said Gaspar. "The star last night appeared to be moving on south. As soon as we hear from Herod, I think we should move south with the star."

Since Jerusalem was the major city in Palestine, everyone had anticipated that it was the destination for the caravan. But Gaspar was correct in that the star did look to be continuing to move in a southerly direction. Talk continued throughout the morning with soldiers and servants popping into the discussion as their responsibilities were completed.

"I think it will be wise for us not to say any more than what Gaspar has already told them" said Melchior. "Any of the ideas conveyed here, should stay here. Some of the notions that we've expressed, according to what Cassius has warned us, could cause the authorities here to suspect our intentions. So, if anyone asks you why we have traveled all this way, we will say truthfully, 'We are following the star to see the king of the Jews.' We don't need to tell them about any of our speculations."

The group nodded their heads in agreement.

"Master, your appointment is here to see you," Matthias' old servant Ira announced.

"Tell him that I will see him momentarily."

"Yes, sir." Ira paused at the door, and then said, "Master, may I speak with you briefly?"

"Of course, Ira. If you keep it brief."

"As I walked up to your room, I could not help but overhearing you say something about wishing you had Basil back, and wanting someone you could trust. I don't want to be impertinent, but is there something I can do that would help you?"

Matthias eyed him for a few moments. Ira had always been faithful as a servant. He had even confided in the old man at different times and had received wise counsel. Lifting his head and squinting at his servant, he said, "Maybe you can help me. When I have finished with this meeting, we will talk."

"Yes, master," bowed Ira, "I'll send in your appointment."

Cyrus and Amehlech were just getting up from the discussion about the star and the king of the Jews to begin preparations for lunch when a soldier rode into camp, jumped off his mount, and hurried up to the circle of men sitting on stones around a cold campfire.

"I have a message for the three magi from the king. Come as you are. His majesty wants to see you immediately."

CHAPTER SIXTY-FOUR

For the next few days, Balzak was going to be helping Cephas on one of his short buying trips to a few of the smaller tradesmen around the Seleucia/Ctesiphon area. While Gaspar profited from this effort, it was done more to help the economy in the immediate area, and to give tradesmen another outlet for their wares. Kahliq was put in charge of the servants in Balzak's absence, a chore that came easily to the former head of Zand's household. If the position was one that Kahliq sought, Balzak decided that it was an area he would not mind relinquishing so he could be free to work more closely with both Cephas and Gaspar when he returned. The idea was one that he would put away on a memory shelf until his master came home and could make a determination on the matter.

Several of the male house servants, along with Cephas' servants who helped him, would be taken on the trip. The only male servants left in the house with Kahliq were the two who also carried the sedan chair in case Rachel wanted to go into market or visit a friend.

Rachel's life had been in such a turmoil the last few weeks that she had had little time to connect with her friends. There was really only one that she had missed seeing and that was Parandis. The day that Balzak left, Rachel sent a note, by way of one of the chair bearers, to her friend asking if they might see each other soon. Parandis, herself, had missed Rachel and had thought that Rachel had had enough time grieving and should start receiving friends again. When Rachel's servant showed up with her note, Parandis made the servant wait so she could respond immediately.

Parandis' father, Saiar, was an official in the city government of Seleucia. The two families had been longtime friends. Parandis' mother had died two years before, her father believed, of disease found in contaminated water. She had taken but a few weeks to die, her body unable to hold down food or retain water. Rachel had been the first person to contact her after her mother's death. The two girls relationship burgeoned through Parandis' mother's death, and Rachel had shown herself to be a present and compassionate friend.

When the servant showed up with a note announcing that Parandis would be visiting that afternoon, Rachel was overjoyed. Ara and Tala helped her make preparations for the welcomed guest.

"Rachel, I have been so excited to see you. It's been weeks since we've seen each other," Parandis said as she hugged her friend. "To lose both of your parents in such a short span of time. It must be an ordeal. How are you holding up?"

"I am actually doing quite well. Gaspar's servants have treated me magnificently. That has helped a great deal. I miss my father and mother, but I am not in despair. Balzak, Gaspar's closest servant, has treated me like a doting uncle."

"That is so good to hear," Parandis said as Rachel showed her friend into the sitting room. "The whole city is talking about you and your mother moving into Gaspar's home. Tell me about that."

"I will. Would you like some cool sekanjabin to drink while I fill you in on everything?"

Taking the drink that Rachel poured her, Parandis sat back and spent the next hour hearing all that had happened since the two friends had seen each other last. It was good for Rachel to talk to Parandis. Being with someone who knew and loved her parents meant a great deal to her. The depth of history and shared experiences allowed Rachel to confer deeply and emotionally with Parandis. The two women wept when Rachel spoke of her father's death, and wept again when she told of her mother's emotional and physical decline. They laughed and hugged when Rachel explained she and her mother's scheming to attract Gaspar. Parandis squealed in girlish delight hearing of when Gaspar left Seleucia and kissed Rachel's hands. Rachel's friend's face darkened when she heard of how Majid was used in the mother/daughter plot to snare Gaspar.

"Majid is a proud, haughty man, Rachel. His ego will never let him put this affront behind him. You must be careful. Majid is vengeful." Parandis looked into her friend's eyes. "Rachel, what made you and your mother choose him out of all the eligible men in Seleucia and Ctesiphon?"

"He just seemed like the most desirable and the one least to be affected by a romantic trick. Many young women see him as appealing. I just thought he would go on to another woman."

Parandis sat with her face in her hands, peering over her fingertips. "Until your handsome champion comes home, you should not go out alone."

"Balzak has made that very clear. I won't," she said crossing her legs inadvertently showing a portion of her calf sheath.

Reaching down and lifting the hem of her friend's skirt, Parandis said, "What is this?" seeing the knife she said, "and why are you wearing knives on your legs?"

Pulling her skirt down and out of the grip of her friend, Rachel said, "Shh, Parandis. I will tell you, but you must keep this all a secret."

A smile crept along Parandis' lips, "Oh, much has changed since we last talked."

Rachel took the other woman's hand and pulled her out to Balzak's knife throwing range.

Hoisting up her skirt, Rachel grabbed the knives from either calf, threw the first at a target twenty feet away, sticking it dead center. She took the knife in her left hand, put it in her right, and threw it at a target thirty feet from where the two women stood driving it in low of center.

Parandis' eyes opened in surprise, "Much has changed since we last talked."

"No one must know about this, Parandis. Promise me you won't tell."

"Balzak's knife throwing skills are almost a legend around the sister cities. Has he been teaching you?"

"He has. You haven't answered my question."

"Of course you can trust me to keep this secret. How much has he taught you?"

A smile came to Rachel's pretty mouth, and she said, "Much has changed since we last talked."

Taking her friend's arm, Parandis said, "My childhood friend has certainly become a woman of mystery. What other secrets do you have that you haven't told me?"

"There's no mystery. Balzak teaches me because I enjoy throwing knives." She looked off thinking for the right phrase, "It relaxes me."

"You can call it relaxing, I will call it mysterious. What do you think Gaspar will say when he returns to find that his genteel beauty is a trained assassin?"

"Oh, Parandis, you are so dramatic. Why would Gaspar care whether or not I can throw a knife? That's ridiculous."

"Is it? Men like to think that they can protect their women. What happens when your sweetheart steps up to protect you from a would-be attacker, and before he can do anything, a knife goes whizzing by his ear and embeds itself in the attacker's head?"

"I think he'll be glad we're both safe. Please don't make this bigger than it is, Parandis. I'm grieving my parents, and the man I love and hope to marry is not here to console me."

The woman who moments before was confidently throwing knives at wooden targets was once again her friend of fifteen years needing her friend's succor.

"I will not make your life more difficult to bear. Forgive me for speaking out of my own fears. Gaspar obviously loves you very much and that is what I will help you focus on until he returns to you."

Rachel hugged her friend to her and then did what only one can do in the presence of a true friend—she wept without restraint. Parandis stroked her friend's hair and let her weep until there were no more tears to cry.

Ira had been summoned to his master's study, and when he arrived was asked to wait out in the hallway. Time passed, making Ira more and more conscious of the household chores he still had to accomplish. Finally, after waiting for almost an hour, Ira was called into Matthias' study.

"Master," Ira said, bowing as he entered the room.

"I'm taking you up on your offer, Ira. You will travel to Caesarea Philippi and pose as a retired merchant. I will send men with you to make sure you get there and get settled. I will send merchants from time to time to add legitimacy to your cover, and to bring back any information that you think I need to know. Live a normal looking life to anyone who might observe you, but I want you to be nosy and find out anything you can about the whereabouts of my gold shipment."

"What about expenses?"

"When the men I send come to visit you, I will also give them your living expenses and information on any leads I may acquire from my end. Someone will come to you every six to eight weeks. You will need to make sure that you make your allowance last between those visits. Don't live too frugally. Remember you are a retired merchant. I've given explicit instructions to the man I'm sending with you to set you up in a residence befitting your position. I'm sending one of the younger servants, Even, with you to take care of your needs, but that is all he is to do. You are being sent to gather information and make sure that I am the only one who hears it."

"Yes, Master."

Matthias pulled out two small identical lock boxes. "These will be used by us to insure that our correspondence to one another is kept secret. We will place our messages to one another in these boxes, and the men I send will act as curriers. Any written information should be placed immediately in your lock box and hidden away in a spot that only you know about. No one must ever know the content of the information that you and I send to each other."

"Yes, Master."

"Tomorrow, you will go to town with one of my servant women who see to my wardrobe to buy you clothes befitting your new position in life."

"You are too kind, Master."

"This expense will be well worth it if you make it possible for me to find my lost fortune."

"You may trust me to work hard to find you the answers you seek."

"I know you will. One last thing. I am not paying you to be daring. Remember I know that you are an old man, and I don't expect you to do the things I would have expected from Basil. The information that you acquire is the most important thing you will do for me. If you get killed before you can get what you know to me, you will have failed me. Do you understand?"

"Yes, Master."

"Good. You'll leave in three days. Your duties are suspended until then. Get yourself ready to be my spy in Paneas."

Gaspar, Melchior, and Balthasar were ushered immediately into the king's presence. There was a stir of Jerusalem's citizenry that increased the closer one got to the royal palace. Herod's guards had to push a path for the magi when they approached the palace on their camels. The whole city was agitated by the notion of a star proclaiming the coming king of Israel. Like any city, the speed by which information traveled had been almost as remarkable as the star and the king of the Jews.

Inside the palace, standing on and around the royal dais were Herod—on the throne— the high priest, and most of the religious and civic leadership known as the Sanhedrin. All of them had been in a feverish discussion up to the point when the magi were shown into the throne room. Entering into the suddenly hushed room, all three bowed as they approached Herod's throne.

"Your majesty, we came as soon as you beckoned us. Please excuse our clothing. We were told to come as you see us," said Gaspar.

"My guard did as he was instructed. Your appearance is not in anyway unbefitting. Please, tell the members of the Sanhedrin what you told me about the star," Herod said watching the magus closely.

Gaspar glanced to his left where the other magi stood. "Several months ago, we observed a star in the sky that moved in a westerly course, that never continued past the midpoint of the heavens. The other magi with me consulted our charts and found no star like it ever recorded. It was a new star. We started following it from it's source in the western sky, but once we reached a certain point in our travels, the star led us south to Jerusalem. In our journey, the star seemed to move ahead of us

260

—directing us as we traveled."

"Why do you think that it heralds a new king of the Jews?" asked the chief priest.

"When we were in our home city of Seleucia the star rose in the west and appeared to stop right above our city every night. We guessed that it rose from the west to point us in that direction, so we started following it to its source. It has led us to Jerusalem. We surmised it was a portent signaling the birth of a great king of the Jews. Do your scriptures tell of where this great king is to be born?"

Herod looked to the high priest who said, "The prophet Micah says, *But thou, Bethlehem Ephratah, though thou be little among the thousands of Judah, yet out of thee shall he come forth unto me that is to be ruler in Israel; whose goings forth have been from of old, from everlasting.*"

"This Bethlehem," said Melchior, "does it still exist today?"

"Of course, it is but a few miles to the south of Jerusalem," responded the high priest.

At this point, Herod clapped his hands and said, "I wish to be left alone with the magi. I want you all to wait outside."

The high priest continued to stand beside the king as everyone else filed quickly out of the room. "I'm sorry, but I want you to leave too," said Herod.

The high priest began to protest, but thinking better of it, bowed his head and curtly left with the others.

When the throne room was empty, the magi looked at one another as Herod began to speak. "This information that you have brought us has strong political ramifications tied to it, as you can imagine."

The magi nodded in unison.

"It is my desire to see that this is handled in a manner that is befitting a king of Israel. Do you remember when the star first appeared?"

"We do. The three of us noticed it almost simultaneously. It was three months, one week, and a few days ago," said Balthasar.

"So if the child were born about the time that the star appeared, he would be a little over three months old."

"That's if the star appeared at the child's birth," began Gaspar, but before he could go on, Melchior tugged at the back of his robe notifying him that he should not continue.

"I see," Herod said smoothing his beard to a point. "I want you to go to Bethlehem and the surrounding area, if you have to, find this child, and bring me news of him. If there is such a person, I would like to pay homage to him."

"Your majesty," Balthasar said happily, "we would be

honored to bring you back news of this great event."

Herod smiled, and stood up, "I am glad that you followed correct protocol and sought me out before going farther in my kingdom. There are those who would work against you in this endeavor. I encourage you to speak to no others about the star, the child, or what has been said between us today."

"Yes, your majesty," the magi said together.

"Good. Find this child, and bring me back news of him."

The wisemen bowed and left from their audience with the king of the Jews.

Once the three magi were on their camels heading back to their camp, Gaspar asked, "Tell me your impression of our time with King Herod?"

"I'm not sure," Melchior said speaking just loud enough for the other two to hear him. "The response by the chief priest, that ruling council they called the Sanhedrin, and the king does not seem to be one of great joy."

"That is most perceptive, my friend," said Balthasar. "We need to be careful while we are here in this land. There are forces at work that I don't think we fully understand. We need to be careful what we say to everyone except to the three of us. We may have been much too free with our ideas up until now."

"Can we trust the king?" asked Gaspar.

"I say we don't trust anyone until we get back on Parthian soil," cautioned Melchior. "I think the people that began the trip with us are trustworthy, and we should have no trouble with them. We might want to be a little more cautious with our two additions."

"What do you suspect, Melchior?" queried Balthasar.

"Nothing really. Now that we're alerted, though, I think we should be careful around those we don't know as well as the rest."

"That is good counsel, Melchior, although, we can't completely shut ourselves off either or they will think something's amiss," cautioned Gaspar. "I think we should keep any further epiphanies to ourselves, and let our discussion with the others be no more than what we've already revealed."

When the wisemen returned to the camp, the rest of the caravan listened without comment the news from the wisemen's second audience with the king. The oldest and the youngest of the magi acquiesced to Melchior's wisdom and experience to give the others the information they had been anticipating to hear concerning their audience with Herod. Melchior chose to tell them exactly what was said without revealing that Herod had excused the Sanhedrin at one point, and that he had caused the magi to question his sincerity.

When he finished his brief update of the audience with the king, Melchior announced to the group, "We can reach Bethlehem by nightfall if we all kick in and help. Let's see how precise the star will be in directing us to the king of the Jews."

After Ira reached Caesarea, he saw why Matthias had wanted Benjamin, the man he had sent to protect Ira along the way, to pick out a place for the old servant to live. Matthias knew his faithful servant: he would live as humbly as possible to save his master a few denarii. Ira would not have chosen a home that would have convinced people that he was a one time successful vendor. Ira complained to Benjamin that the home cost too much and was too big, but Matthias had been quite clear as to the particulars of the home. He had made sure that Benjamin bought a home befitting Ira's purported station. Reluctantly, Ira moved in with his servant to a roomy residence on the outskirts of Caesarea Philippi. In the next few days, Benjamin saw to it that the house had all the amenities of a successful merchant's home. No amount of protesting from Ira could dissuade Matthias' agent. Whenever Ira's protestations became too much, Benjamin would say, "Would you rather I follow your orders or the master's?" This always stopped the old man's argument but did little to erase the disapproval visible on his face.

When Benjamin finally left to return to Jericho, Ira and Even looked the part they were to portray. The old servant wasted little time in planning how he could make money for his master while maintaining his cover and accumulating the information for which he had been sent to collect. As he sat on the roof of his new home that first evening after Benjamin left, Ira enjoyed watching the sun go down as he sipped his cup of fresh squeezed lime juice and honey.

John, Gil, and Uri rode into into Jerusalem as the wisemen's caravan left for Bethlehem. If Ezri had known that the three Gischala friends were so close, he would not have ridden as relaxed as he was. In fact, he would have come up with a reason why he needed to take a different route than the caravan's. That night he felt, for the first time in his life, that he was part of something much greater than himself and his own selfish pursuits. His execution of Podarces still weighed heavily on him, and he determined that the cost of his murderously acquired wealth was not worth his anguish. The life that he had allowed himself to be drawn into was becoming more and more repugnant to him. The torment he felt, as a result of Podarces' murder, was a punishment with which he would have to live.

The star appeared in the sky just as the last rays of the

sun dropped over the western horizon. It moved quickly from its western origin dropping to almost the tops of the hills in front of Gaspar and his companions.

"What do you make of that?" Gaspar asked watching the relative rapid rate of the star.

"I believe we are very close to our journey's end," said Balthasar cryptically.

Leaning forward in his saddle, Melchior said to Vahumisa, "Let's pick up the rate. We have but a short way to go now. The animals won't mind the brief increased pace, and I'm growing impatient."

"As am I," said Balthasar which brought a guffaw from Melchior and Gaspar.

The night sky had gone from a deep blue when the star first appeared to what was now an ebony canvas covered by a splash of infinite celestial clusters.

Vahumisa raised his hand and slowed his camel to a stop when they came to the first outlying hovel of the village of Bethlehem. "Should we make camp near here or progress on into the town?"

Melchior looked to his right to Balthasar, and Balthasar looked to Gaspar. "We have followed the star up to this point. It looks like it is resting just above the rooftops of the houses on the other side of the village. Let's go over there. If we're not sure where to go once we've done that—we can make camp on the far side of the town," Gaspar said looking to the other magi for approval.

"Sounds good to me," Balthasar nodded.

"To me too," said Melchior.

The caravan curved its way through the main street of the little village. With each step that the animals took, nearing the southern edge of the tiny community, the star intensified in brightness. When Vahumisa's camel came to the gate of a house at the end of the street, the star lowered in the sky until it was directly over the building.

Vahumisa looked back to the wisemen who were now following him in single file due to the narrowness of the street. "Is there some mistake?"

"I don't think so," said Balthasar. "This is our destination."

The wisemen had changed their dress in anticipation of meeting the Messiah, and were in their rich, silk robes. Without a word, the camels knelt to allow their riders to descend. Balthasar motioned to Cyrus saying, "Bring the gifts."

Hearing the movements of the travelers outside, a young man came to the door to observe the wisemen.

A woman's voice from within was heard saying, "Joseph, what is it?"

"It is a caravan that has halted in front of our house."

Gaspar led the other wisemen down the short, earth beaten path to the house. Reaching the the man, Gaspar asked, "Are you the one of whom the Jewish prophets have spoken?"

"I am not," Joseph's eyes shown as he spoke. "Please come into our humble home and meet Him. I am the child's father, Joseph."

The wisemen stepped through the small courtyard into the house where a single lamp dimly lit the visages of mother and Child.

"I am Mary," the woman said, "and this is the child you seek. His name is Jesus."

Gaspar, Melchior, and Balthasar fell to their knees and slid forward so that their bodies were flat to the packed earthen floor.

"Praise be to God," said Melchior.

"Praise Him above all things in heaven and in the earth," worshipped Gaspar.

"This is the Son of the most high God," prophesied Balthasar. "Blessed are you Mary for you are blessed above all women. May the God of glory receive honor and praise and glory forever."

The boy, Jesus, had been sitting on his mother's lap, and when Balthasar had finished his pronouncement, He toddled over to the old magi and hugged his head. Balthasar looked up into the Child's eyes as his own misted over and he recognized He whom his heart had searched for all his life. Jesus pushed Himself up from Balthasar's head and laughed a toddler's joyful laugh. Mary came over, knelt down, and pulled her Son onto her lap once again.

The wisemen continued worshipping while Mary held Jesus. Joseph, standing inside the door, joined them in their worship of God. There was no awkwardness. Praise in that setting seemed as natural as discussing the weather.

Gaspar raised his head and came to his knees waiting for his friends to finish their exaltation before the King of Israel. Balthasar was last to rise, looking into Mary's eyes.

"You have come a long way to be here this night," she said.

"We have, your highness," said Gaspar.

"You must not speak to me so," said Mary. "I am only a maid who God visited to tell me that I would bear His Son. I am of low birth, and only by the glorious grace of God am I here before you tonight."

"You have heard God speak?" asked Melchior.

"He told me of Jesus' coming birth before Joseph and I were wed."

"His angel appeared to me," expanded Joseph, "before I could end our betrothal. He said that I should not be afraid to take Mary as my bride because the baby in her womb was conceived by the Holy Spirit, and that he should be called Jesus. His name means rescuer or deliverer."

"This is marvelous to hear," said Balthasar. "I look forward to all that he will achieve in His life."

"We have all thought what the wise Balthasar has stated, and we have brought gifts for the Child Messiah," said Gaspar. He turned and motioned for Cyrus standing outside the door to come forward with a small chest and two stone jars exquisitely carved.

Melchior took his jar of myrrh, walked over to Mary and Jesus, bowed his head and gave his gift to her saying, "May he always carry the sweet aroma of the Most High God."

"Thank you," she said smiling.

Gaspar brought forth his gift, knelt down, and said, "Frankincense. May His life be an aroma of praise before God most high."

"Bless you," Mary said.

Balthasar had trouble getting to his feet. Melchior and Gaspar rushed to help their fellow magus. Cyrus brought the chest to him and held it out. Balthasar opened the lid and revealed that it was full to the brim with gold coins. Motioning for the young servant to hand it to Mary, Cyrus bent down on both knees, lowered his head, and held out the treasure to Jesus' mother.

Balthasar invoked, "May the riches of heaven adorn Jesus' life."

"And to you peace," Mary said placing her hand on the old man's. "Your presence and your praise brings honor to our Son—God's Son."

"May goodness and mercy follow you all the days of your lives," said Joseph.

"I would like to ask one more favor of you, and then we shall leave you in peace," said Gaspar.

"Of course," said Joseph, "anything within our means."

"The others in our caravan have a great desire to see the Child also. May they see him?"

"That," said Joseph joyfully, "is something we can do very easily. Come, wife, and bring the Child. But before you do, please tell us of how you knew to come here and about your journey."

Balthasar smiled and said, "May we go out to your courtyard to sit? Our story is a long one."

After the magi recounted all of their stories, Joseph and Mary invited the members of the caravan to see the Child. As

266

each came to see the Child, they bowed before Him. When Ezri's turn came, he became strangely conflicted. He wanted to see the Child, but something pulled inside him, telling him he was not worthy. At the last moment, he pushed the feeling aside and followed the example of everyone who had gone before him.

The last to bow before young Jesus was Amehlech. As he knelt before the child, who was standing by Mary, he was overcome with emotion. Tears cascaded down his face and fell to the toddler's feet.

"Pardon me, my lady," said Amehlech as he became so flustered that he used his own hair to wipe the Child's feet.

Mary placed her hand on the young man's head saying, "Your tears are the greatest gift that has been given our Son. Do not apologize for a grateful offering."

Amehlech stepped back and joined the rest of his traveling companions' gaze on the holy family. Gaspar's eye's ascended to where the star had been shining before. It was nowhere to be seen. It had vanished.

"We have reached our destination," he whispered.

As everyone headed back to their mounts, the wisemen came up once again to Mary and Joseph.

"Thank you again for letting us meet your Son," said Melchior.

"It was no trouble," smiled Joseph. "Jesus came for the world to see and to know. It is our place to make sure that all who want to see Him, do. Peace be with you."

"And to you," the magi said in unison.

CHAPTER SIXTY-FIVE

Gaspar and the rest of the caravan set up a makeshift camp down the road from Bethlehem less than a quarter of a mile away. Their plans were to return to Parthia the next day over the same route as they had come. There had been discussion about going home another way, but other paths took them miles out of the way, and now that their mission was accomplished, the desire to return home burned vigorously within them.

Early the next morning as they slept, Gaspar, Balthasar, and Melchior had identical visions. In their dreams they each saw the star that had led them on their journey. The star's brightness increased in its intensity until they had to shield their eyes from its brilliance. Slowly the star faded, became smaller, and descended to a level just feet above the ground in front of them revealing that it was in reality an angel. They bowed in deference to the heavenly presence as he spoke.

"You must not return to your home by way of King Herod. You must take an alternate route."

After he spoke, he faded until there was only night around them.

Melchior woke first and stiffly found his way to Gaspar's tent. "Gaspar. Wake up."

"What is it, Melchior. It's still night."

"I had a dream."

The statement brought Gaspar to a sitting position. "I had a dream too. Tell me what you dreamt."

Melchior related his dream to Gaspar.

"I had the same exact dream. We should wake Balthasar."

As soon as the words were out of the younger magus' mouth, he heard Balthasar say from outside the tent, "I had the same dream as the two of you. We should go now."

The three went around the camp waking everyone and telling them to get ready to leave. The first person they woke was Vahumisa. As soon as Gaspar told him about the thrice dreamed dream, he agreed with the magi's decision. Once everyone was wakened and stowing their gear away, the wisemen met with Vahumisa.

"All the shorter routes," said the commander drawing a map in the dirt, "take us through Jerusalem. If we take the

268

southern route through Hebron, Herod would expect us to take the faster rode by way of Arad. I suggest we turn east at Hebron to En-gedi and follow the rode south along the shore of the Salt Sea."

The wisemen looked at each other, nodded their approval to one another, and Gaspar said, "Let's do it."

Cassius had been looking over Vahumisa's shoulder as he drew in the dirt and said, "I will need to leave the caravan at Hebron. I have business that must be seen to. I will take the west road to Gaza when we reach Hebron."

"You have to do what you must do, my son," said Balthasar. "I have enjoyed your company these many days."

The other three began to shake his hand and wish him well, but he stopped them.

"Wait. I am not leaving yet. Let's hold off on our good-byes so I don't have to suffer leaving you twice."

His comment was met with much patting on the back and hugging despite his protestation.

Before the sun rose that morning, the caravan was again moving south and farther away from Parthia.

Sophia had been home nearly a week and realized that it could be months before whoever had the gold contacted her about her share. It was also quite possible that whoever had it may want all of it for himself. Satanas had always been the one to make sure everyone got his fair share, and he was now dead. She realized that should she get a chance to get her hands on the gold, her cut would be enormous. Her traditional way of making a living bore great risk to her now. To get caught doing petty filching would be foolish if she were to come into a large sum of money. As much as she hated the thought, she began to see that the safest, smartest thing for her to do was to land a legitimate job that would get her by until the gold became available to her. She decided that the next day she would go into town and see what kind of work she could find.

Benjamin had left the day before, leaving behind what looked to Ira like a ridiculously large amount of money for him to live on the next two months. The old servant woke up early with the sun, excited with the possibilities of what he could do with that kind of money to seed a new business venture. He sat at the table thinking through exactly what his plans were going to be.

Even woke moments after his new master had eaten a quick breakfast and was heading out the door for town. "Will you be home for a noontime meal, sir?"

"Don't worry about any meal for me until supper," Ira said

happily as he stood at the door, "but don't start anything until I return." He closed the door and hurried off for a day of errands.

Walking over to the window, Even watched the old man walking briskly down the lane. "Working for this master is going to be very different from Matthias," he said smiling.

The marketplace in Caesarea was already bustling with the activity of merchants getting their wares set up for a day of selling. The first stall that Ira approached had a merchant who dealt in pottery.

"I am just now setting up, and have more items on my cart. Is there something in particular that you are looking for?"

"Not really, but I do have a proposition for you that may increase your overall sales. Are you interested?"

"Of course, but if your deal involves buying from me on consignment, I am not interested."

"My business proposition has nothing to do with anything like that. I will accept all the financial risk. I ask only that you will work with me. Interested?" the old man said closing one eye and looking at the merchant with a single eye.

"I'll listen to what you have to say."

"Good." He described which house was his and continued with, "Come there at the end of the work day, and I will have supper prepared for you. I will tell you and the others of my plan."

The man scratched his head and looked at the honest faced man. "I'll be there."

For the next few hours, Ira spoke to everyone in the market about his plan. Around mid-morning, Ira was giving his pitch to a trader of leather goods, and a woman stood by listening to what he was saying. As he walked away from the booth the woman approached him.

"Do you have a cook for this crowd that you're attracting?" she asked.

"My servant and myself."

"I will make you a deal."

Ira smiled. "I thought that I would be the only one offering deals today."

"I will fix the meal for you for free. If you like what I fix, you can hire me to cook for you."

"And if I don't?"

"I won't bother you again."

Rubbing the sides of his mouth Ira said, "Meet me at the far end of the marketplace in one hour, and we will see how well you cook."

The woman turned and started to walk away when she heard the old man call to her.

"I forgot to ask. What is your name?"

"Sophia. You may call me Sophia."

The morning after John and his buddies arrived in Jerusalem, they immediately began asking questions about the magi and their caravan. There was no need to inquire very far before they learned that the wisemen had caused quite a stir in the city. Finding that they were less than a day behind their quarry, the young men set off in earnest to catch up with the caravan and the horse thief.

CHAPTER SIXTY-SIX

The few days that they had gotten to ride together and talk had been enjoyable for Ezri and Cassius. Since both men were in vocations that demanded secrets and falsehoods, neither knew the other as well as he thought he did. Their psychological makeup drew them to the lives they had chosen for themselves, and that similarity probably had as much to do in drawing them together as anything else. The thirteen miles from Bethlehem to Hebron gave the men an opportunity to converse as honestly as they were willing to during their time together.

"We seem to have much in common, Ezri. I will miss our talks," said elder man of eight years.

"Yes, I have felt that too. I'm a little concerned how I will spend the days of travel when you leave."

They rode along in silence for a moment, and then Cassius asked, "You could come with me. Have you ever been to Rome?"

"I have not, and I have always wanted to see it."

"Why not come with me, and I will show you the wonders of the empire's capitol city."

A smile spread across Ezri's face as he contemplated Cassius' offer. If he did accept the spy's offer, he would be gone for months, which would give plenty of time for the uproar surrounding the gold shipment to settle down. Still, the star, which disappeared once they reached their destination, and the mysterious magi who had followed it from distant Parthia, held his imagination captive. He wanted to see this adventure to its end, though he knew not why it attracted him the way that it did. He was convinced that the magi had been chosen to see the child, and such a miraculous occurrence would have to have further repercussions in their lives. More than anything, he wanted to see why they were the ones who were led by the star to Bethlehem.

"As much as your offer fascinates me, I have to say no. The wisemen are on a once in a lifetime journey, and I want to see where it leads them."

"I can't blame you. If I didn't have such pressing matters, I would join you. If you are ever in Rome, try to find me. I want to settle there, and I will make sure that you are well taken care of during your stay."

Ezri reached his hand over to Cassius and the two shook

hands. "I will come to Rome one day, and I will look for you."

Conversation made the time pass without notice and before either man knew it, they were ascending the hill to the city of Hebron. As much as Vahumisa would have liked to have spent the night in the shelter of a city with a Roman outpost, their situation had changed dramatically, and that was now a liability and not an asset.

With all the drama of the last few weeks of Ezri's life, saying good-bye to his new friend affected him emotionally and unexpectedly. He found himself almost in tears watching Cassius ride away toward another life.

The caravan made its turn to the east toward En-gedi and for a few miles, at least, Gaspar felt like they were headed toward home and to the woman he loved.

Plans had been made the day before for Rachel and Parandis to spend the afternoon at the marketplace. Rachel thought that having the two sedan bearers would be sufficient, but Kahliq would hear nothing of it. He insisted on being there personally to protect her and Parandis if the need arose.

"Kahliq, Parandis' father is an important city official. Majid would never intrude on us with her there. His wealth would not protect him from accosting a city official's daughter," Rachel argued.

"Ah, but you are not that city official's daughter. There is no reason to take risks. Besides, what would your future husband and my future master think of me if I let something happen to you?"

"All right, Kahliq. You may have it your way, but I think you're taking on too much of Balzak's paternal protection."

"Thank you, my lady. I value your comparison."

Rachel rolled her eyes saying, "It was not meant to be a compliment."

Parandis arrived with one of her female servants, Farah, excited that she and her close friend were on their first outing together after having been out of touch these many weeks.

The girls chattered the whole way to the market. Reconnecting with Parandis had been an effective antidote to her grieving the loss of her parents and her longing for Gaspar. Kahliq noticed how Rachel perked up when she was with her longtime friend, and he made a mental note to encourage their seeing each other in the future.

"Rachel," said Parandis as the sedan stopped at the entrance to the marketplace, "we simply have to visit that dressmaker I told you about. I want you to see her work. It is positively amazing what she can do. She can make you an outfit that will make your magus' eyes pop out of his head."

"I'd prefer them in his head, but I don't mind if he finds me attractive."

"I don't remember you being so droll," Parandis said giving her friend a sideways look.

Getting out of the sedan, the girls hurried into the crowd, much to the consternation of their servants.

Farah and Kahliq chased after the women, catching up to them only after no little jostling of other market patrons in the process.

"My lady," spoke Kahliq, "that was most unwise of you to hurry off as you did. Please let Farah and myself know when you are going to be affected with another burst of exuberance."

"I'm sorry, Kahliq. I forgot myself."

Shopping with Parandis made Rachel feel as if nothing had happened to change the course of her life. For a brief period she returned to a time when both Zand and Nazli were alive and life was much simpler.

For Kahliq, the only good thing about being at the market with three women was the joy he saw in his mistress' face. He had always been amazed at how many times a woman could turn over the same piece of cloth and inspect it before she bought it. Before long, he began to daydream, and it was at that instant he realized Rachel was gone.

Over thirty men showed up to eat supper at Ira's home. Sophia had been a blessing sent from God as far as the old man was concerned. If the meal would have been up to he and Even, it would have never taken place. Both Ira and Even had waited and served all their lives, and had done a moderate amount of cooking for a few people, but the ability needed to pull off what Ira had planned took another set of skills that neither man possessed. Ira and Even watched her in open amazement. Sophia had singlehandedly saved the day, or, in this case, the meal.

As everyone was finishing his dinner, Ira stood on a bench and said, "Gentlemen, may I have your attention." He waited for the courtyard to still.

"I have been a merchant for most of my life, and I have enjoyed the time I have spent helping people find the items they need. I have always wanted to retire to this region, and I don't want to completely shut down my life's work. I also don't want to work as hard as I once did," he paused to let the laughter subside. "I do want to stay involved to the point where I am not bored."

"If you don't get to the point," shouted one of the dinner guests, "I'm going to be bored."

Everyone laughed at Ira's expense and he waved his

hands up and down to get their attention once again.

"All right, I'll come to the point. There are people in the outlying area who would pay a little more to not have to come to town for necessities. My proposal is that I would buy items from you, and take the items to outlying people to sell. I ask that you discount me a little to cover my expenses, and I expect that my customers will pay a little more to have the merchandise delivered to them. You and I both make a profit, and we're both happy."

One man stood up and said, "How are you going to carry all the merchandise you'll need to the outlying areas?"

"Good question. The first time through the territory, I'll collect orders. I'll come back here and buy what I need from all of you. Then I'll take the merchandise by cart to my customers, sell it to them, and collect the money. You don't have to worry about being paid—I'll do that up front." Ira paused for affect, and then said, "Wha'd'ya say?"

The courtyard was quiet. Then one man stood up and said, "I'll try it." After he primed the crowd, not one merchant left the house without shaking Ira's hand saying that this was a great idea and he wished that he had thought of it first.

When the last man left, Ira looked across the courtyard to see Sophia and Even clearing dishes off the tables.

Sophia looked up at the old man and said, "Looks like you've got a new business. Think it'll work?"

"I don't know. Seems like it should."

Collecting dishes as he crossed the room, he said, "You saved my life tonight, Sophia."

"I know," she smiled.

"Want a job?"

"My offer stands."

Even looked at his master and the thought in his mind of how Ira was going to pay for all of this was written all over his face.

"Don't worry my boy," Ira laughed. "I've been thinking this through for years."

"So, where do we go now?" Gil asked looking south along the road out of Bethlehem. "If the caravan that Ezri hooked up with was going to Bethlehem, we would have run into them on their return."

"Unless they went south," said Uri.

"Why would they do that?" John said, a sharp edge creeping into his voice.

"If the wisemen are from the east, and wanted to get home more quickly, they may have headed south to Hebron to catch the road to Gaza. From there they could save several days of travel by sailing north to Akko or Sidon."

John looked at Gil who shrugged in ambiguity.

"What do you think? Should we chance it?"

"John, if we get to Gaza and we haven't run into the caravan," Uri persuaded, "we can take the coastal highway north, along the Great Sea, back to Gischala. We'll make better time on the flat road than back through the hills. I think it's worth the try."

"All right. Let's do it, but I can't help but think that Ezri has slipped through my fingers again."

CHAPTER SIXTY-SEVEN

The caravan made camp about a third of the way to the En-gedi Oasis. Vahumisa made sure that they were well supplied with water for the journey from Hebron to the ancient oasis. The distance was only fifteen miles, but this harsh land and climate was no place to run short of water.

That night at supper, Gaspar thought that Ezri looked particularly lonely without his friend, so he took his meal over to the young man and joined him on the boulder where he sat.

"Do you miss Cassius' company?"

"Yah, I guess I do, but I wasn't thinking of that."

"Oh? What were you thinking about?"

"You will think I'm foolish if I tell you."

"Maybe I will, but why don't you tell me anyway," Gaspar smiled bumping the younger man with his shoulder.

"I was thinking how I never got to spend enough time with my father in his business. I don't know how to do what he did."

"What did he do?"

Ezri had been honestly thinking about he and his father's relationship, and how he had abused it. To tell Gaspar the truth about his father meant that he would have to admit that he had lied before. Remembering some of the talks he and John had prior to spoiling the relationship, Ezri used that information to feed to Gaspar.

"Farming is a good, honest business, Ezri. Surely your father has servants who know enough of farming to help you until you get on your feet."

"That is true, but I was given a very good offer for my father's land when he died. His best friend told me I would be a fool not to take the money, so I took it. Now, I don't know. Honestly, Gaspar, I'm not sure what I want. It would have been so easy if he wouldn't have died and I could have just fallen into what he did."

"That would have been easy, but maybe God has other plans for your life."

Gaspar's comment made Ezri very uncomfortable. With all the things that he had done in the last few months, Ezri was sure that God had no plan for him but for him to burn in hell. He tried not to think about God because he did not like thinking there might be an eternal consequence to his evil actions. Ezri

277

decided to deflect the magus' statement back on to him.

"What are God's plans for you?"

Gaspar opened his eyes wide and blew out through his mouth. "That, my friend, is a good question. Two months ago I thought I knew exactly what I wanted to do with my life, but recently things have changed drastically."

"How so?"

"I've had disturbing dreams that I think, and so do my brother magi, reveal some aspect of my future. I thought that I would never marry, but the night before I left, I all but proposed to our high priest's daughter. Our King of Kings—sort of like your emperor—turns to me more and more for counsel. My father's business that is run by one my family's servants is doing ridiculously well." Gaspar raised his hands in exasperation and let them fall on his lap. "I guess I'm overwhelmed."

"Listening to you, I'm overwhelmed," laughed Ezri placing his hands on either side of his head as if holding in its contents.

"Listen to me. I came over to console you, and now I'm dumping all of my inner turmoil on you."

"No, no, I appreciate it. Your situation is obviously different than mine, but, maybe as you work through your concerns—I'll find answers to mine."

"If nothing else, Ezri, you have a city official's tongue," Gaspar said as he grabbed the younger man by the shoulders and shook him back and forth playfully. "You may consider working toward a position in the Senate."

Ezri was good at spotting what he thought were weaknesses in others. Gaspar's was that he cared for people. As Gaspar jostled him, he realized that he was already working out in his head how he could use this to his advantage. For the first time in his life he caught himself doing so and felt ashamed.

Lachish divides the distance between Gaza and Hebron almost exactly in half. Cassius was half the distance to Lachish when John and his two friends rode up to the Roman spy. Hearing their hoofbeats coming up from behind, Cassius turned to meet them, his right hand visibly on his sword hilt.

"I want no trouble," John said raising his right hand, his two comrades staying behind him. "I want to ask a few questions, and we'll be on our way."

Cassius scanned the three young men, watching them warily and not taking his hand from his sword. "If that is all you want, I hope I have the answers you seek."

"We are looking for a man about our age who was traveling with a caravan of magi. If he went by his real name, that name is Ezri."

Cassius obviously recognized the name, but he and Ezri

had developed a friendship, and he wasn't willing to hand his friend over to a group of men he didn't know. For all he knew, their intent was to do him harm. "The name doesn't ring any bells. Why are you looking for him?"

"He stole my horse and broke his father's heart. We have come after him to bring him home to make sure that he is punished for his crime."

"Tell me his name again," Cassius said thinking that this did not sound anything like the young man he had befriended on the trail.

"Ezri."

"Wait a minute. There was a young man who joined our caravan for a little more than a day. He rode with the guards and servants. When we reached Jerusalem, he left our group and headed for Joppa. He said something about making a new life in Greece. I'm sorry I never caught his name. It could have been Ezra."

"Ezri."

"Sorry. Ezri."

"Thank you for answering my questions," John said and then looking at his friends, said, "That sounds like something Ezri would say."

Gil and Uri nodded their consent.

"Should we head back to Gischala?" asked Uri.

"I suppose so," John said. "Thank you again for talking with us," John said to Cassius. "Let's go home," he said to his friends as heeled Raven to a gallop.

Cassius watched the three riders' trail of dust. "I wonder which Ezri is the real one?"

Rachel had been standing with her back to two of the booths in the marketplace when one hand went over her mouth and another arm around her waist lifted her into the air and behind the booths. She was completely taken off of her guard. Fear coursed through her body as she strove to short-circuit its debilitating affects. As soon as her attacker set her on the ground, she had recovered enough to put Balzak's training into action. She came down hard with the edge of her heel into the man's instep which loosened his grip around her waist enough for her to slip down through his arm, roll away, and come up to her feet armed with two throwing knives. Facing her attacker, she realized she had never seen the cruel grimy face before her. He leered unsavorily as his hand moved slowly to the handle of his sword. Rachel's hand flicked the knife in her right hand deftly at the man's sword hand and raced towards the opening between the booths where she hoped to find Kahliq looking for her. Behind her she heard the man's howling pain which alerted

Kahliq to her position. The two met midway between the booths.

Kahliq hurriedly asked her, "Are you harmed?"

She shook her head that she wasn't.

Handing Rachel off to Parandis and Farrah, Kahliq bounded between the booths with his sword in hand. A few moments later, he returned saying, "The man who abducted you was nowhere to be found. I'm sorry."

"Don't worry, Kahliq. I'm just glad that you reacted as quickly as you did," said Rachel with one of her throwing knives still in her left hand.

"Is one of your knives embedded somewhere in your attacker?" he asked his mistress.

Nodding her head, she said, "As he reached for his sword, I threw my knife at his right hand. I'm assuming that that was why he yelled in pain."

"I am glad that you have been such a devoted student of Balzak's," Kahliq said, relief showing in his expression.

Kneeling down next to one of the sales booths, Rachel lifted her skirt and replaced her knife in her right calf sheath.

"Rachel, why would anyone attempt anything like that at the marketplace where there are so many people?" questioned Parandis.

"I'm guessing, but I think that horrible man was hired by Majid. My mother's and my plan to gain Gaspar's attention seemed so harmless at the time that we were planning it. Now I wish we would have come up with another strategy."

"We should go home, Rachel," Parandis said with Farrah nodding a vigorous agreement.

"No, we'll be okay now. That man won't attack again today. Besides," she looked at her friend mischievously, "I haven't seen the dresses of that dressmaker you were telling me about."

Parandis started to protest, but before she could say anything, Rachel put up her hand and said, "I came here to meet a dressmaker, and no ruffian is going to keep me from those dresses."

Smiling, Parandis said, "Come with me. Her booth is down just a bit."

Ira lost little time getting accounts from surrounding farms and villages. The day after he had met with most of the merchants in Caesarea's market, he set off with enough food for a few days. The frustration many in the outlying areas had was that when they came to town, it meant at least a whole day's work away from the fields. Coming to town was a big event for most of the landowners, but the little extra amount they could pay Ira to deliver it to them was well worth his price of doing business. Even the big landowners did not like having to take one or two of their workers away from the fields during the really busy times. Ira quickly discovered that there was going to be a natural ebb and flow to his business where there would be times of the year where he would be extremely busy, and seasons when it would not be worth his time to leave Caesarea. He realized that he could easily make enough money during the busy times to pay for his needs and have sufficient additional funds to send back to his master Matthias.

Ira had a simple life philosophy. God had placed him on planet earth to be another man's servant, and he was fortunate to discover early in life that doing that task well not only blessed his master, but also brought bliss to himself.

One of the more affluent landowners was so pleased to have someone like Ira performing this kind of service that he offered to send one of his men to town the next morning with a wagon and ox for Ira to use until he could afford to buy his own. Ira at first declined the kind offer, but after the landowner gave him his order, he realized his horse and cart would be inadequate for the task. He and the landowner came to an agreement. Ira could use the man's wagon and ox, but Ira would make deliveries for free until he could afford to buy his own.

By the time Matthias' first messenger, Tam, came to collect any information Ira might have gotten and to give him his living allowance, Ira gave the man twice the amount of money Matthias had left with Ira the first time.

"Ira, how have you had time to amass this amount of money and to collect all this information?" Tam asked in disbelief.

"I simply chose an occupation where I could do both at the same time. Traveling salesmen are supposed to ask a lot of questions. I needed something to do that I wouldn't make people suspicious of my inquiries—being a salesman was perfect. There are but a few busy times during the year where people will pay to have someone deliver supplies they need from town, so I can use the down time to promote my illusion as a retired merchant. Furthermore, I've made friends with many of these people, and it is appropriate for me to go out and visit them and have normal conversation. Normal conversation around here usually means discussing the latest news people have heard about the gold shipment disaster."

The messenger laughed shaking his head. "I think Matthias has made a mistake making you a house servant all these years. You could have been making him a lot of money."

"I've enjoyed being a house servant," Ira said matter-of-factly. "I don't see it as a mistake, Tam."

"I definitely will have some explaining to do when the

master sees that I've come back with three times the amount of money he gave me to give to you. You are a sharp businessman, Ira."

"Thank you. Now tell me, I hope you can stay the night. It would make your coming and going more commonplace if people saw you as being a visiting friend from my life as a merchant."

"I know you, you old rascal. You just want someone new to tell your old stories to."

"That's true too, but your staying wouldn't hurt my cover either."

Tam did stay that night and the next. He found that he liked spending time with the old servant. Besides, he knew that Matthias would not be angry with him for staying another day when he saw the amount of money he brought back. He also discovered Sophia's cooking.

"You really do amaze me, Ira," he said one night after one of Sophia's meals. "You're returning doubly our master's investment of your time up here in Caesarea, you make more than enough money to live off of, and you've added this incredible cook to your staff."

"A man must eat well in his old age," Ira smiled.

"You do that."

In the kitchen, Sophia overheard Tam's unconscious comment about the two men's master. "So," she thought, "Ira is not who he says that he is." She determined that she would keep her ears tuned for any other information that she could get on her employer.

CHAPTER SIXTY-EIGHT

"If the wisemen didn't come back this way, there are only two other ways they could have gone," Herod said pacing back and forth on his dais in front of two of his commanders. To one of them he said, "Send scouts to Gaza, Ashkelon, Ashdod, and Joppa to see if our holy men have taken maritime routes, or, more likely, the King's Highway west of the Dead Sea for their return to Parthia. Send a detachment of fifty soldiers to Heshbon to cut off their retreat in case they have chosen that route."

"Yes, your majesty," one said, relieved to be able to depart in the face of the king's growing irritability.

"I want you to take a detachment of one hundred cavalry to Bethlehem and kill all the male children two years old or younger," Herod said to the remaining commander.

The commander nodded his understanding turned to leave and then stopped himself, "Your majesty, may I have a word?"

Herod looked at him conveying vicious intent. "You may, only choose your words wisely, Commander."

"A few years back, we had some difficulty with the Parthians here in Palestine. If the wisemen are emissaries of the king of Parthia, might there be a chance that we could cause an international incident that could invoke Parthian reprisal if we hunt down the magi?"

"What are you suggesting?"

"Leave the wisemen alone. Let me go on the errand you have commanded. The wisemen have fulfilled their purpose in alerting you to a possible newborn king. If I kill all the children under two in a small village like Bethlehem, how many is that? Ten? fifteen? You can deal with that much more easily than an enraged king of Parthia, and Caesar will not have to get involved."

"Yes, what you say makes good sense. Go. Recall the other commander to me, and then complete your assignment."

Since the time that the magi had offered their gifts to the Christ Child, Gaspar and Melchior had wondered where Balthasar had gotten the amount of gold he had given to the child. One morning, while they were camped near Dibon, about midway up the Salt Sea, Melchior woke Gaspar in his tent.

"What is it Melchior?" Gaspar asked sitting up on his cot.

283

"What time is it?"

"I have a question for you."

Gaspar slunk back down in his covers, rolling over to go back to sleep. "It can't wait until the rest of the camp wakes up?"

"No it can't," Melchior said walking over to the side of the cot that Gaspar now faced. "Haven't you wondered where Balthasar got all that gold that he gave to the baby Jesus?"

Gaspar opened one eye. "I have wondered."

"Balthasar is a well-to-do man, but not that well-to-do."

Gaspar sat up again. "Where do you think he got it?"

"That's the question I want to ask him. Come on. Get your clothes on and let's go talk to him." While Gaspar dressed, Melchior continued. "Remember the night we looked through the Hebrew holy book together and told each other about our dreams and Balthasar said he wanted to wait until the time was right to tell us? Well now we know what he brought to give, but we don't know how he did it."

"You're right. Surely he'll tell us now," Gaspar said putting on his second sandal.

The two magi walked over to Balthasar's tent and Melchior said softly, "Are you awake, old friend."

"I am. Come in."

Walking into the old magi's tent, the two younger men saw Balthasar not only awake, but dressed.

"I've been expecting you," Balthasar said.

"You had another vision?" asked Gaspar.

"No, no," he laughed. "I know you two well enough to know that your curiosity would not let you stay away long before you had to find out how I acquired my gift for the Holy Child. Honestly, I expected you to come to me that first day we left Bethlehem."

The two gave the other looks that said, "of course."

"Well," began Melchior, "are you going to tell us?"

"Of course."

"Well?" encouraged Gaspar.

"My gift was gold."

"Don't play with us, Balthasar," said Melchior. "Where did you get the gold."

Balthasar sat down on his cot. "A few days before the king's men came to get me to escort me to Ctesiphon, I had a dream about what I should give to the Child. In the dream I kept looking to see what it was that I was giving to Him. No matter how I tried, I was unable to see what was inside the chest. Now that I'm telling you what happened, it occurs to me that I could see distinctly what your gifts were. Anyway, when I awoke, I spent time asking God what it was that I was to give. The only answer that I received was this thought in my mind: "all that you have." So I went out and sold everything I had and put the proceeds in the chest for the Child."

Rubbing the back of his neck, Gaspar asked, "But how will you live once you return to Nippur?"

"I'm not going to return to Nippur."

"Where will you go?" asked Gaspar with growing concern.

"I think I know," said Melchior.

Smiling, Balthasar said, "I think you do."

Gaspar looked to Melchior. "tell me."

"Let's just say that Balthasar has lived a full life, and he's now an old man."

"All the more reason he should hold on to his home and resources," Gaspar said.

"I don't think you're understanding," said Melchior.

Balthasar stood, walked over to the young magus, and placed his hand upon his shoulder. "I won't live to see home."

Two and a half weeks after Gaspar and the caravan left the En-gedi oasis, the travelers arrived at the gates of Damascus. The trip itself was uneventful, but Gaspar and Ezri developed a growing relationship. The magus began to experience strong feelings toward the younger man that were akin to that of an older brother. He felt that he could confide in Ezri like brothers might do with one another. Ezri, ever on the lookout for a way to advance himself, saw that Gaspar might be able to provide him with the knowledge that he would need to manage the gold that was waiting for him in Paneas.

Balzak was incredulous when he heard what had happened to Rachel in the marketplace.

"I will go to the king myself to make sure that this young narcissist does not continue with any plans he may be scheming against you. If the master were here, that pompous brat would not attempt such a bold tactic," ranted Balzak.

At any other time, Parandis and Rachel would have been stifling laughter watching Balzak's wild gesticulations as he strode first one way and then the other in Gaspar's courtyard. The gravity of Majid's sinister conniving curbed any humorous perceptions on the young women's part.

"I don't want to do anything that would place Gaspar in a bad light as far as the king is concerned," said Rachel. "We don't know how his majesty would react to your taking this matter before him. What if I stayed within the compound until Gaspar returns."

"He could be gone for another two months, dear girl," responded Balzak. "Do you really want to be confined for all that time? It hardly seems fair that you should be locked up, while Majid is free to go around as he wishes."

"Couldn't we increase the number of those who guard my mistress when she is out and about?" conjectured Kahliq.

"Maybe that is the best we can offer until the master returns," said Balzak.

"I would like to suggest that we increase the guards we have around the premises too," added Ara.

"That is a good idea," said Balzak. "I'll look into that tomorrow."

Just then something crashed against the outside wall of the house, causing stucco to rattle down the wall. Everyone jumped at the sudden commotion. Kahliq jumped up and ran towards the direction of the noise. When he came back, he carried a rock with a note tied to it.
He handed the note and the hand-sized rock to Balzak.

Balzak untied the note and read it out loud, "You who have shamed me will never know peace again until one of us has gone to be with Ahura-Mazda."

Rachel's hands covered her face as she began to sob. Parandis wrapped comforting arms around her friend, stroking her hair.

Kahliq motioned Balzak to follow him into the men's part of the house.

"I did not want to upset the women," Kahliq said, "but I want to make a recommendation."

It was clear to Balzak that Kahliq felt responsible for the abduction of his mistress whom he loved dearly. Kahliq wanted to make up for his blunder and to protect Rachel. Balzak wondered to what extent the servant was willing to go to guarantee the young woman's safety.

"What do you suggest?"

"Now hear me out before you say anything."

Balzak nodded that he should continue.

"It would be no problem to find out where Majid's room is in his father's house. At night, I could slip into his room, cut his throat, and be gone."

"Absolutely not. If you are to be a servant in this house, you must promise me that you will never entertain notions like this ever again. I will not have assassins in the house of Gaspar. Do I make myself perfectly clear? I know you want to protect your mistress, but an act like that would only hurt her and my master's reputations."

Kahliq looked like he had been whipped. "I have always taken good care of my mistress. The fear that I will let her down again eats at me day and night."

"I can understand why you would feel the way that you

286

do. Please tell me that you will not go through with your plan."

"I see the sense in what you say. You have my word that I will not carry it out."

"I hope you are telling me the truth, Kahliq."

"I am."

"Good. Let's go back out to the women before they get suspicious and start asking too many questions."

CHAPTER SIXTY-NINE

Because he worked hard and showed unbridled loyalty to his master, Matthias had always given Ira as much freedom as any servant could have. But being up in Paneas was an experience Ira had never known or ever knew to hope for. His natural compassion and kindly manner made him an easy man to like and trust. Within just a few weeks of arriving in the region, there were few people Ira did not know, and few who would not do business with him. He had been devoted to the purpose of his mission to find evidence of the gold shipment's whereabouts. Ira had laid out the region in his head and had methodically gone to every estate, farm, house, and hut searching for clues. It was a topic that the whole countryside was buzzing about and people were more than willing to discuss. Rarely did he have to bring up the topic. People knew that a person in Ira's line of business was able to pick up on the latest news, and were always keen on hearing what the old man thought or had learned.

People loved Ira because he loved them. He always made sure that he made a good income for his master, but he was generous with those who were in hardship. Before too long, the people of Paneas could not think of life without the gentle old soul. Many forgot that he was new to the area and treated him as if he had been there all of his life. Because of his line of work, he had the background and knowledge to appear that he had.

Ira was good for the people of Paneas, but after six weeks of living in the area, he had not gained any real information about the gold. He knew that Matthias would recall him to Jericho if he did not show some signs of success. It was then that he decided on a new tactic.

One evening as Ira was riding back to his home outside of Caesarea, he began going over in his head who might have come across the gold, and what they would have done with it since there were no clues leading to where it might be hidden. The only detail he was able to learn that was helpful was from Yitzhak's wife Menucha who had told him that all the donkeys that were used to transport the gold had returned to the farm a few days after the gold disappeared.

Most likely, a passerby would not have had transportation of his own to remove that much gold, so he must have used the donkeys and then released them. For the beasts to have returned in so short a time, the person must have disposed of the gold nearby. Which meant that it was either in someone's home, or was buried, or. . . at this point Ira's eyes grew wide, and he said, "Of course! The gold is hidden in one of the caves in the area."

From that time on, Ira kept visiting and talking with people, but as he traveled from home to home, he kept his eyes out for caves where the gold might have been hastily stashed. He knew that he was on to something now. He could hardly wait for Tam's next visit.

Cooking for Ira and Even had made Sophia feel respectable. It was a sensation she had not experienced since she was a young girl. Almost thirty-five now, she was never going to attract a young man, and her only opportunity was probably an old man whose wife had died. Both prospects did not appeal to her. Young men took too much work to mold into good husbands. Old men were too set in their ways. No, she would probably never marry. Ira and Even were good to her—something to which she was not accustomed. She liked cooking and the two men were easy to please. The situation she had in Ira's house was a good one, and if she had to be legitimate for awhile, this was the perfect place in which to do it.

In the week that followed, breakfasts had become disliked tasks. Most mornings, the smell of food made her nauseous. More than once, she had to run out the back door to keep from making a mess on the kitchen floor. Ira noticed her running out the back door one morning and asked her if she was feeling all right.

"I don't know what it is," she said. "I've always been quite healthy."

"There's a healer in town. I would be more than happy to pay to have her look you over."

"Thank you, Ira, I'm sure I'll be fine."

But she did not get better, and after a few weeks of her vomiting every morning, Ira insisted she go into town and be looked at.

"I'd say you're pregnant," the healer told her after she described her symptoms.

"I'm what?"

"You're pregnant."

Sophia realized that her guise of respectability just went out the door. Ira was a good man, and when he found out, she would be forced to leave her position as cook.

"You're sure it couldn't be something else?"

"You haven't been running a fever. You're only nauseas in the mornings. I don't know what else it could be. I don't mean to pry into your personal affairs, but have you had relations with anyone in the last few weeks?"

Sophia thought back to her time with Basil in the field near Hippos. She thought that they would live together forever. "Why did the Romans have to kill him?" she wondered.

"Thank you for seeing me. You've been very helpful," she said not wanting to answer the woman's question.

It would be no time at all before she started showing that she was with child. She liked working for Ira, but she knew an honest man like him would never tolerate a woman in his employ who was pregnant without a husband. She hurried home, closed the door, and collapsed on her bed sobbing for the man who would have made her his wife, and for her own miserable condition.

Everyone was anticipating getting back to Seleucia, but the setting surrounding Damascus was too magnificent for them to stay only one night. During the second night, Cyrus was at his best doing impersonations of everyone in the camp. Tears were rolling down most men's cheeks, and many were holding their sides from laughing too hard. When Vahumisa became his next victim, the men could hardly contain themselves. The soldiers who were under his charge were cautious until they saw their commander laughing harder than anyone else.

Vahumisa, barely able to speak, pointed and said, "That's me. Am I that ridiculous when I do that?" To which the rest of the camp lost even more control.

Balthasar had tried not to laugh at first, fearing he might hurt someone's feelings, but the servant's antics were so like his fellow travelers, he could not restrain himself. His laughter started a coughing fit, he got up, and stumbled to the ground. Vahumisa and Gaspar sprang off their rocks to assist the old man. When they reached him, he did not move.

Gaspar rolled the ancient magus to his back and said, "Balthasar, can you hear me?"

The magus' eyes fluttered open. Barely audible, he said, "I hear your voice, my boy."

Melchior dropped down beside Gaspar as the others crowded around the old man.

"I have something important to say before I go," rasped Balthasar.

"No," Gaspar objected.

"Listen. I don't have much time. I have seen the good God."

"A vision of Ahura-Mazda?" clarified Melchior.

"No. The Jews won't say his name out loud because it is too holy, but I tell you He is the only God—the only good God.

290

His name is Yahweh." The last word wheezed out in a final gasping effort.

Gaspar put his ear to Balthasar's chest to listen for a heartbeat. Vahumisa sat across from the the young wiseman watching Gaspar's face for an encouraging sign.

Sitting back on his haunches, Gaspar said, "There is no heartbeat. The great magus is dead."

Melchior's breath stopped as tears of deep sadness now filled his eyes where moments before had been tears of a different kind. The rest of the group stood unable to move or completely accept the truth of Gaspar's words.

"The greatest among us has passed on from life to life," croaked Melchior standing to his feet. Parting those standing in front of him with his hands, he walked out to a nearby hill to be alone in his grief.

Gaspar and Vahumisa sat on their knees facing each other on either side of the shell of the man who moments before was their friend. Vahumisa looked at the old man's eyes, and reached up with his hand to close first one eye and then the other. Gaspar, also risking contamination, grabbed Balthasar's hand and put it on the magus' chest. Vahumisa silently placed the other hand on top. Both men stared at the old hands remembering the gentleness that issued from them in life. Tears fell and wet spots appeared as libations on Balthasar's tunic as Gaspar blinked his eyes. Vahumisa rose and went to his tent. The others went to their tents as well sensing that the campfire was a place for community and stories and joking—not a place for grieving.

Gaspar stayed looking at the man whom he had known for only a few months, but had become as dear to him as anyone he knew. "What was it that he said?" Gaspar thought. "It was so important to him. What was it?"

"He is the only God. His name is Yahweh," a voice said.

Gaspar turned to see Melchior standing next to him.

"It was not Ahura-Mazda who welcomed our friend into heaven, it was Yahweh," said Melchior. "There are no gods that watch over individual countries, there is only one God he said, and His name is Yahweh. The child that we worshipped is His Son. I don't understand what that means, but the man who I know has searched for the truth more than anyone I know said: He is the the only God—the only good God—His name is Yahweh." Melchior's eyes never left the face of Balthasar.

Gaspar turned once again and gazed upon the old man's hands. "It's interesting what we think about when someone dies."

Melchior stared at the face of his friend, nodded his head and said, "We are but a breath."

Parandis understood the reluctance of Balzak and the rest of Gaspar's staff to speak to any authority concerning Majid's behavior. They were merely slaves. It would be their word against a free, wealthy man's word. When she left Gaspar's home that night, she took with her the rock and the note that was attached to it. She went directly to her room and wrote down all that she could remember concerning the whole affair involving Majid, and then she sat and waited for her father to return home.

As frequently happens when wanting to see someone, Saiar returned home late.

"Daughter, why are sitting in the courtyard? Are you waiting for someone?"

"I've been waiting for you. Have you eaten?"

"I had no time to eat. Why?"

"Let's go inside, and I will fix you something to eat while you listen to what I have to tell you."

Grinning, Saiar said, "You sound like your mother, may she be in Ahura-Mazda's care. What is so important that I can't relax first?"

Fixing him with a catty smile, she answered, "You gave up that right when you came home so late."

Mockingly, Saiar began tiptoeing around the courtyard as if looking for something.

"And what are you doing now? What I have to tell you is very important."

"I was looking to see if your mother had slipped back from the dead and was speaking for my devoted daughter. Surely my daughter would not speak to her father in this way."

With fists on her hips and no clever comeback, Parandis only whined, "Father."

Grabbing his daughter by the hand, he led her into the kitchen saying, "Come on. You talk and fix me something to eat while I relax and pretend to listen."

Shaking her head in mock anger, she said, "I want to tell you about all that has been happening in Rachel's life since the last time I saw her."

Parandis told her father how Rachel and her mother had used Majid and how he had threatened to harm her friend. After she had told him everything, he was now eating, she showed him the rock and the note.

After inspecting both items, Saiar handed them back to his daughter, saying, "This is very serious, and considering the sender, it doesn't surprise me."

"What do you mean?" Parandis said rubbing the rock with her thumbs.

"Sevent and Majid have had problems in the sister cities for years. Both are bullheaded, arrogant, and mean. Of all the people to choose from, for what they thought was an innocent scheme, Rachel and Nazli couldn't have chosen more foolishly."

"Is there nothing that you can do, father?"

"Oh, I think so, but Rachel must be very careful until Gaspar comes back. Majid knows that Gaspar will eventually return from his expedition, giving him only a few weeks to do the damage he has planned. Once Gaspar returns, he knows he will never win against all the resources the young magus has at his disposal. As long as her father Zand lived, Rachel was safe. With his death, everything has changed."

"What about Balzak's idea of going to the king?"

"Phraataces is a good administrator, but he wants nothing to do with anything that would disrupt his daily routine. Rachel was right not to let Balzak go to him. It's best if we keep this on a civic level."

"What's the next step?"

"Let me do some checking around. I will have an answer for you by tomorrow night's meal."

Parandis jumped up and hugged her father's neck. "Thank you," she said kissing him.

"You are welcome. You may thank me like that any time you wish."

At that, she kissed him again.

CHAPTER SEVENTY

A few days passed, and Sophia considered different ways she might tell Ira about her predicament. Nothing she thought of was good. When the baby came, the whole world would know that she had been with child. The best thing to do was to tell him the truth, and then live with the inevitable consequences.

That particular morning, she was going over with Even all the things she would need from the marketplace. After he left, Ira came into the kitchen and sat down to talk to Sophia as he often did while she cleaned up the breakfast dishes.

"So, I never heard what the prognosis was. Are you going to live?"

"Yes. About that. I need to talk to you."

"About your being with child?"

He said it so calmly and nonchalantly that she didn't know how to respond at first.

"Well, aren't you?"

Again, he caught her off her guard. There was no condemnation in his voice, only matter-of-factness.

"I suppose I am."

"Suppose," he said weighing the word and looking at the ceiling. "Dear woman, you either are or you aren't," he said almost playfully.

Sophia was completely nonplussed. "Are you going to fire me?"

"And then how would you take care of the child?"

"I just thought you wouldn't want all the looks and comments you're going to get when people find out. If you keep me here someone will accuse you of being its father."

"Fortunate for me. Not so fortunate for you." He was now grinning. "Even and I love your cooking and having you here to talk to. Moreover, you're just a part of things around here."

Sophia stood looking at him with the hem of her apron pulled up to her mouth. In all of her wildest imaginings, she never would have conceived the conversation she was having.

"But when the baby comes, it will make an awful racket," she said.

"This is all up to you of course, but Even and I thought we could build another room onto the kitchen where you and the child could stay during the day...or...all the time."

Sentimentality was not a characteristic that anyone would say was part of Sophia's makeup. Satanas, who had known her better than anybody, would have been surprised to see the tears brimming in her eyes.

"You don't have to say anything now. Take your time. Only, don't wait too long because we will need time to get the room built."

Sophia pulled the old man out of his chair and hugged him right there. It was now Ira's turn not to know what to say. His hands hung limply for a few seconds, and then he lifted them enough to pat Sophia's sides.

When she finally released him, he said uncomfortably, "Well, aren't you full of surprises." To which Sophia laughed so hard that she had to sit in a chair.

Ira was still standing where she had hugged him when she finally stopped laughing and wiped her eyes with her apron.

Ira slowly sat down again saying, "So, what do you think?"

"I think you're the kindest man I've ever met. If it doesn't disrupt things around here too much, I would love to take you up on your offer."

The two cities by the Tigris, Seleucia and Ctesiphon, were unique in the Parthian empire, in fact to the whole civilized world at that time, in that they had separate troops from the military to policed the city. Saiar spoke with the commander of that force for Seleucia, telling him all that his daughter had told him.

"May I see the note that was attached to the rock?" the commander said.

Saiar handed him both the note and the rock. The commander hefted the rock in his hand, noting its size and weight. He then read the note again that Saiar had read to him earlier.

The commander sat in thought for a few moments and then said, "This is a difficult situation. We have the word of women and slaves against that of an influential citizen. The note that we have doesn't point to anyone in particular, nor does it have a signature. While the high priest's daughter knows the note's intent, it could be for anyone in the house. This is all compounded by the fact that Majid's family has been a thorn in the side of many administrations. They are good at stretching the law to its fullest without stepping into illegality."

Saiar sat nodding his head in comprehension across from the commander at his desk. He himself had had to deal with the family several times in his own capacity, and it was never a pleasant affair.

"Is there anything you can suggest that we do?"

"Normally, we would send one of our soldiers to speak to Sevent and his son, telling them that we have started collecting evidence against them, and that if anything happens to the girl, they will be the first we consider. But in this case, there is more. Many of us feel that the high priest's wife and daughter were ill-treated after his death. I think that we can add to our warning by stationing guards outside Sevent's home to make our presence felt. I will also make sure that the estate of Gaspar is on a regular patrol route. Sevent and his family are despicable, that is for your ears only—and cowardly. With a little bit of pressure from the military, I think that we can keep them under control."

Saiar stood and shook the commander's hand. "What you are doing is much more than I hoped for. Thank you."

"That's our job, and Gaspar and his father have always been good to the people of Seleucia. We do want to take good care of those who have been generous with us."

Smiling, Saiar said, "I understand. Believe me, I understand."

Without a formal tower to let the elements and carrion birds do their work on Balthasar's dead body, Melchior suggested that they exhume his body in Jewish fashion. A stone vault was purchased in Damascus and was brought out by oxen to a hill overlooking the fields. It was buried three fourths of the way down into the ground with the lid above ground. Balthasar's body was wrapped in spices and burial cloths, and placed in the coffin.

The members of the caravan encircled the vault, Melchior at the head and Gaspar at the foot.

Melchior raised his hands, looking up to the sky said, "Yahweh, it is in You that Balthasar expressed his dying belief. You have made Yourself known to us by way of Your star, Your Messiah, and Your obvious involvement in our lives. We commend to You our friend and teacher, Balthasar. He was faithful as a priest to Ahura-Mazda until he became convinced there was a higher God. He has searched his whole life for the truth wherever it could be found. Ultimately, he found truth in You.

"Thank you that we knew him and lived our lives with him. His impact on all of our lives was profound. He was my true friend. May his life find bliss and fulfillment in Your presence."

Gaspar waited a moment and then spoke. "I find myself in an awkward circumstance today. I too am a priest of the god Ahura-Mazda, and have tried to be faithful in my duties to Him. Now I know that You, Yahweh, are the good God. I am new in my faith. I don't know what is appropriate to say to You. I don't know whether speaking to You as I would have Ahura-Mazda would offend You. Forgive me for my ignorance and accept my humble eulogy as it is.

"I loved Balthasar. He was a friend, a mentor, and a kind of father to me. His kindness and generosity humbles me, though I am thankful that I was one who received all that he had to give. I do not want to alienate others who are here who still worship another god, but I do know, as Melchior has said, that Balthasar's dying words revealed his faith in You. Would You tell our friend that we love him and miss him. Please tell him that our lives will be ever changed because of him, and will never be the same in his absence.

"For we who are left behind, would You guide us to truth? Would You soften the sting of our deep loss and replace it with the joy of having shared life with a great man? Jewish teachers call you Adonai. Adonai, we beseech You to mend our broken hearts."

After Gaspar, others around the group also spoke. Some were more lengthy, most said only a few words. When everyone had finished, each man laid hands on the lid that would entomb Balthasar's body for as long as the earth existed. They hoisted the stone lid and gently, as if they might disturb his body, laid it atop the vault.

Years later, a writer of the Christian Holy Book would remember him as only one of the three wisemen who visited the Christ Child bearing gifts. Legend and folklore would be the only preservers of his name.

Before he departed the ancient city, Gaspar paid a local stone carver to engrave a message on Balthasar's tomb along with his name. The engraving never took place, and the sands of ages eventually covered the unmarked tomb causing anyone who might find it to wonder who the occupant might have been.

CHAPTER SEVENTY-ONE

The members of the caravan were uncharacteristically quiet the first day out from Damascus. The picturesque landscape did little to assuage their general disconsolation. Gaspar and Melchior were constantly reminded of Balthasar's absence since they had ridden three abreast for most of the expedition. Unconsciously, they rode far enough apart for another to ride between them. Although they both would have plenty to say at some point in the future, now the soft padding of the camel's feet on the road was all the aural stimulation either man desired.

It took six days for the caravan to reach Tadmor. Almost instantly the disposition of the whole group changed once they reached the oasis. It was as if it marked the end of the grieving period for everyone. From that point onward everyone's spirits began to lift. Had Balthasar have been with them, he would have been gladdened to see them return to their old selves.

Given the sticky nature of the situation, the commander of Seleucia's military decided it would be best if he delivered the ultimatum to Sevent and his son himself. The morning after his meeting with Saiar, he went out with a detachment of five men. The six soldiers arrived at Sevent's home as father and son were having breakfast. Four soldiers remained outside the front entrance to the palatial home while one of the men accompanied the commander.

"To what do I owe the honor of having Seleucia's commander at our breakfast table?" asked Sevent, the commander noting how neither he nor his son rose to greet him as hospitality would dictate.

"I come on a personal matter concerning you and your son. Am I free to speak with all present?" the commander said levelly.

Sevent glanced to the head servant and flicked his finger for the staff to leave.

When all but the soldiers, Sevent, and Majid were present, the commander continued. "It has come to my attention that you and your son have made several menacing acts toward a young woman who is the guest of Gaspar the magus. I am here to inform you that we have initiated a list of complaints against you and we hold physical evidence."

"I never threw that rock," said Majid jumping to his feet.

Glaring and speaking through his teeth, Sevent said, "Sit down! Keep your mouth shut."

As Sevent spoke to his son, the commander spoke to his lieutenant, "Remember that statement for the record."

"You can't. . ." Began Majid, but before he could finish his sentence, Sevent had raised his hand stopping what the young man was about to blurt out.

Speaking in barely concealed rage, Sevent said, "Is there any other news we should know, Commander?"

"Only," the commander said calmly, "we will be placing a few of my men about to observe your going and coming."

Sevent's pitch rose as he said, "I am a very influential member of this city,"

"And should any harm come to Zand's daughter, Rachel, you will be the first ones we will apprehend for questioning."

"How dare you speak to me like I was some kind of a common criminal. The king will hear about this."

"Go see the king," the commander said evenly, "and see where that lands you."

The two men stared at each other until Sevent's eyes finally dropped.

"I think that concludes my duties here today, gentleman. We'll see ourselves out," the commander said motioning to his lieutenant to follow him.

When the door closed, Sevent reached over and backhanded his son across the mouth knocking him from his chair and on to the floor.

Catching a dribble of blood with his forefinger, Majid asked, "What was that for?"

"Any number of things, but more specifically that stupid comment."

"I was just trying to clear myself," Majid said getting back into his seat.

"The commander never mentioned the stone or the note, you imbecile. Now he has your statement tying you to them both."

"But what about what she did to me? And what about how Gaspar fooled me into paying for his ridiculous expedition?"

"You've closed the door for now on the only way we could really hurt him—through this woman that he loves. We're going to have to bide our time, become model citizens, and wait for the right time to get our revenge. Gaspar is too powerful for us to move openly against him. We will wait and watch and see."

"In the mean time, I'm to be made to look the fool."

"You, boy, will do as I say."

"You didn't waste any time in dealing with Gaspar's

father when he belittled you years ago."

"That was a different time, and I told you not to speak of that. If Gaspar ever learns who was behind the death of his father, your's and my life will not be worth the dust on this floor. You keep your mouth shut about that experience."

There was a knock at the door to the dining room.

"What is it," barked Sevent.

A servant appeared, bowing. "There's a man by the name of Ahmed to see you. He said you sent for him."

"Yes, yes, send him in."

The man who stepped into the doorway a few moments later was the same man who attacked Rachel. He had a bandage wrapped around his right hand where Rachel's knife had stuck.

Seeing the bandaged hand, Majid asked, "What happened to your hand?"

"You didn't tell me that the girl was handy with a knife."

"It's that human pet Gaspar keeps around his house. He's taught the girl some knife tricks, no doubt," grumbled Majid.

"A little girl with a knife should have been no obstacle for you. You guaranteed me that you could accomplish the task," Sevent said derisively.

"I had a small window of time. If I would have continued, I would have had to deal with her big servant which would have caused a big scene in the marketplace."

"Enough. Enough. I don't want you trying to attempt anymore abductions until I contact you. The girl has gone to the city commander of the guard. He was just here a few minutes ago. You need to stay out of public places until your hand heals up. I'm sure she told the commander about getting you with her knife. If a soldier sees you, they'll bring you in for questioning for sure."

Sevent took out his purse and selected a small gold coin and flipped it to Ahmed.

"This is for your trouble."

"We agreed on twice this amount."

"You weren't successful with your mission. I don't pay for people's failures. I'm being generous. Next time if you fail me, there won't be a next time, and you won't get anything."

Ahmed sneered and turned to leave through the door he had entered.

"Ahmed. Don't let the military catch you. Spend the next few weeks in Ctesiphon 'til your hand heals."

The thug nodded his head and left.

"You've made our task so much harder. You had to go and throw that rock at Gaspar's house. If you hadn't done that, and then opened your big mouth in front of the commander, we could have let things die down for a few weeks. Then we could have made another attempt to grab the girl. Now it might take years to get another opportunity."

Majid got up to leave.

"Where are you going?"

"I want to check on that hijacked silk shipment that we're buying from the bandit who works outside of Tadmor. He's supposed to be here sometime this morning."

Sevent watched his son walk out of the room. "He's got a good head for business, but not for intrigue," he thought.

Ira wasted no time securing the help of a man and his son who could build the addition on to the house. Within a few days the two builders were knocking a doorway into the kitchen that would lead into Sophia's room.

One day, Sophia's morning sickness was especially severe. Ira made her sit down while he cleaned the breakfast dishes.

"If you don't mind, Sophia, tell me about the baby's father. What kind of man is he?"

Sophia looked at the older man for a long while, so long that he stopped his work to see if she had left the room.

A resigned smile slowly appeared on her face.

"If you don't want to talk about it. That's fine with me, Sophia."

"No, I think I want to tell you. I was down in Hippos for awhile helping an old friend, when I met a man in the marketplace. He was like no one I had ever met. He was definitely the biggest man I had ever seen, and had a gruff exterior. Something about him made me think that there was a gentle, fun side to him that no one ever got to see. I helped him find food for his men—I saved him at least twice what he ended up paying. I made him laugh, and he made me feel so secure. For a woman like me who has had a rough life, security is important. He was not a good looking man by any stretch of the most creative person's imagination, but there was latent kindness about him."

As Ira heard Sophia's description of the man, his hands stopped working, and he slowly turned toward the woman. "Was the man's name Basil?"

That Ira would know Basil's name astonished her. That a man like Ira would know a man like Basil was unimaginable.

"You knew him?" she asked.

"He, ah," lying did not come easily to the old man, "he was a business associate with a client I had up in Jericho. Let me think. His name was Matthias."

Sophia looked at Ira through squinted eyes. She now

301

knew that she must not divulge any more knowledge that she had of Basil's dealings with Matthias. If Ira worked for Matthias, which she guessed he did, she didn't want to give him enough information to trace her back to Satanas. Ira's showing up in Caesarea at this time was beginning to make sense. She knew she must proceed with caution.

Shaking her head in feigned disbelief, she said, "You knew Basil. I can't believe it. I don't know this man. . . Matthias?"

"I don't know how he and Basil were connected. I only know Basil from meeting him once when I was delivering some products to Matthias. I remember the man and his name because of his great size." It pained Ira to have to lie to Sophia. She had become a good friend to him, but he couldn't let her ruin his cover.

"You did a lot of work for Matthias?"

"No more than any other client."

"I wish Basil didn't have so much to do with him."

"Where is he now?" asked Ira wincing at his feigned ignorance.

"He was killed. Whatever he was involved in with Matthias made a Roman detachment think that he was spying on them in order to rob their gold shipment. They killed him and the other men with him, buried them, and . . ." Sophia's head dropped when she told Ira this last part, unable to finish what she wanted to say.

Ira hurried over to her and knelt down and hugged her. "There, there. You don't have tell me any more." Through tear blurred eyes, she looked up to see tears in his own eyes as he said, "I'm so sorry, Sophia." Ira's gentle way knocked down the stoney wall that she had put up to protect her emotions. She could not control what happened next. All the barricaded emotions she had closed away that pertained to Basil's death, her parents abandonment of her, the numerous times she had felt used and manipulated by men, and all the senseless deaths of so many men in a scheme in which she was a key player, now came gushing out in a cascade of tears and sobbing. Ira cried with her holding her as a father holds his distraught daughter.

CHAPTER SEVENTY-TWO

Gaspar reclined on his cot, enjoying the cooling breeze that blew unimpeded through the tent's raised flaps. The emotional weight of dealing with Balthasar's death had taken a physical toll on him as well—he was exhausted. Waiting for supper, it felt good to relax and experience the healing that time gives to one's grieving. The only sounds that met his ears were the wind ruffling the the rolled flaps of his tent, and the occasional laughter coming from those who were involved in the preparation of the night's meal with Cyrus and Amehlech.

"Eminence, you are so peaceful laying there, I hate to disturb you," a vaguely familiar voice said from just beyond the head of Gaspar's cot. He turned to see a man with his keffiyeh pulled over his face so that only his eyes were showing.

Gaspar's reverie broken, he swung his legs over the side of his cot to a sitting position, looking desperately for his sword.

Before the magus could arm himself, the intruder pulled the cover from his face revealing a smiling Farshid, the bandit chieftain they had encountered on the other leg of their trip.

"I beg your forgiveness for startling you, but I was so happy to hear that you had come back to travel through my lands, that I could not restrain myself from stealing in to visit you."

Gaspar leaped up and hugged the man in genuine friendship. "You are taking such a risk to be here, but I am glad to see you. How did you know that we were here?"

"What kind of chieftain would I be if I did not know who enters my kingdom and when, huh?"

"I suppose you're right," Gaspar said the two men holding each other at arm's length now.

"I know you must be very excited to get back home, but I want to ask you if you would consider coming to my camp and staying with us a few days. All of my people want to hear about your travels. I will make sure you are treated like royalty.'

"I'm sure I can talk the others into staying. It would be a great honor to spend time with you. After all you did not rob us when you could have. We owe you a favor, and I would consider it an easy favor to grant"

This produced a great guffaw from the chieftain. "You are most wise, my friend."

Farshid had caused so much ruckus that several of the

soldiers and Melchior came to Gaspar's tent to see who was making the commotion. When they saw who it was, they greeted him with the same warmth friendship that Gaspar had. The magus told Vahumisa and Melchior of Farshid's invitation, and they heartily agreed that it was a stop that had to be made.

"May I impose on you to stay the night so that I may show you to my humble home tomorrow?"

Gaspar and the others nodded their head in happy acceptance.

"I am sorry, but I do not see the venerable Balthasar. Where is he?"

Farshid saw a shadow fall on everyone around him, and he knew immediately that the magus was dead.

"You are still grieving. My apologies. Know, too, that I am saddened by this news."

"He died seven days ago," said Gaspar. "He knew that he would die before we reached Seleucia. There was time before he left us to speak to us, and then he died. It all happened swiftly. I don't think that he felt much pain in crossing over."

Farshid touched his forehead and then placed his hand on his heart. "He was a man who won hearts easily."

"That he was," agreed Melchior.

During their supper, Melchior and Gaspar told Farshid about all that had happened with the Christ Child, Herod, and the warning from the angel to take a different route.

"Truly amazing. How I wish I could have experienced it all with you," Farshid said, his eyes wide with wonder. "I remember on your last trip through my lands that the venerable one told me that the Jews connect the birth of this king of the Jews with their deliverer. . .what was the title?"

"Messiah," said Melchior.

"Yes, messiah. Did you find that to be true?"

"We found a mother and father of very humble means with what appeared to be a normal baby boy. True greatness is often spawned in meager beginnings," said Melchior, "but we will have to wait to see if this one named Jesus is the Jew's Messiah and their king."

"What do you think, Magus?"

"I think he is their Messiah."

Tala stood at the back of the knife throwing range waiting for Balzak to finish his instruction to Rachel before she interrupted their session.

"Excuse me, Saiar, the city official, waits to see you both in the courtyard."

Rachel quickly stepped into her dress to cover her

trousers, and then led Balzak in to meet with Parandis' father.

"My dear," Saiar said bowing his head. "I have come to give news to you that I think you will find pleasing."

"Parandis just spoke with you a couple of days ago. What good news can you already possess?" She said happily.

"The commander went to Sevent's house himself yesterday and spoke with both father and son. He told them that the city military had started collecting information on the two of them concerning their relationship with you and the threats they had made. Evidently, Majid let it slip that he had thrown the rock with the note attached. Whatever mischief he may have planned has been hampered by all the information that the authorities now have in their possession. To be safe, there will be two soldiers stationed near Sevent's estate to monitor any of his comings and goings. Your house has been placed on the daily city patrol. The commander assured me that you will be safe not only in your home, but in your excursions around the city."

"Saiar, I can't tell you how happy your news has made me. Thank you so much."

"I would have done the same for anyone who came to see me in similar circumstances. The fact that the someone in this case was the daughter of one of my oldest friends may have influenced me a little," he smiled.

"I can't tell you what a relief this is to me. You honor my father's memory. Thank you."

"I was glad to do it. Now I must get back to a busy schedule." Saiar turned to leave and Balzak escorted him to the front gates.

"Sir, the house of Gaspar will not forget this kindness. If there is anything my master can ever do for you, I say with complete assurance, that it will be done."

"That is kind of you to say, but unnecessary. I will do everything I can to protect my dead friend's daughter."

The official rode off, and Balzak turned back to the courtyard with a concerned expression. Rachel, standing inside the gates, noticed his countenance and asked, "What is it, Balzak?"

"What Saiar had to say is good news, but we need to stay on our toes lest we give Majid another chance to create trouble. Remember that it was not only you who made him look foolish, but Gaspar. This expedition will cost Majid a great deal. Both of you will need to watch yourselves and make sure that you don't give him an occasion to vent his revenge."

Rachel looked at him sadly, "Will we never be rid of his reprisals?"

"The man you love is a very powerful man. Powerful men can make powerful enemies. Sevent was ever jealous of

Gaspar's father's success. It would not have taken much for Gaspar to incite either one of them to acts of vengeance. I can't help feeling that Sevent had something to do with Arioch's death, but I've never been able to prove it."

"Balzak, you're scaring me."

"I'm sorry, dear girl, but I need to impress on you how serious this business is. You must be careful in all that you do, and you must never tell Gaspar what I just told you about his father."

"Gaspar doesn't suspect the same?"

"Gaspar was young, and I have kept it from him so that he would never endanger his standing in the empire, nor his life, in a foolish act of vengeance for something which I am not completely sure myself."

Rachel nodded her understanding. "You may trust me to protect my Gaspar with this knowledge you have told me."

"You are a good woman, Rachel. You will make my master an excellent wife."

Rachel blushed.

"Come, we've been away from our knives long enough."

There were many caves around the region of Paneas near Philippi, and Ira had to be careful not to be seen so as not to appear suspicious. Unknown to him, he had walked by the cave where Ezri had buried his plunder twice. The bush Ezri had planted had taken new root and was growing well creating a very natural covering to the cave's narrow entrance. The boulder that covered most of the opening and was part of the natural outcropping of rock that surrounded the area had made the entrance difficult to find in the first place, but Ezri's simple inclusion of the bush made the entrance invisible. Ira hoped every day that he would find the right cave. He knew he was on the right track; he just had to be systematic in his efforts.

Even enjoyed having someone else around the house to keep him company when Ira was gone during the day. Sometimes, he would help Sophia with her food preparation, and sometimes she would help him with his chores. She had nothing else to do to keep her distracted, so she did not mind lending a hand to make the days pass.

The fact that Ira and Even had been so supportive in her pregnancy brought her more relief than she would have imagined. Her life prior to pregnancy had been one of con games and theft. She knew that her child would have to grow up with the stigma of not having a father, and she did not want to add to that a mother who was a known felon. Having an honest job gave her baby legitimacy. Sophia wanted to keep herself out of trouble with the authorities, and being here with Ira and Even made that desire a surety.

Returning from his rounds northwest of Caesarea, Ira stopped in town at the tanners shop to pick up a leather bag he had made to hold personal articles and those items needed for trade when out on the open road.

On his way home, a man, who was still angry with Ira because he had stopped doing business with him, stepped into the old man's path. Ira had stopped selling to the man because he habitually short-paid Ira on everything he bought from him.

"So how is that concubine you keep for a cook?"

Ira ignored the man, riding past him.

"I was just asking a friendly question. Or should I call her what she is, a whore."

Stopping his wagon, Ira said, "Look Raphael, you were dishonest in our business dealings. I harbor no contempt for you. I just choose not to argue with you every time we do business. Please don't attack the character of my cook to soothe your hurt feelings. If you would like to attack my character, then do so, but don't include the people of my household."

A small crowd had gathered when Ira had reined up his ox. One man in the crowd, Jesse, said, "Let it go, Raphael. Ira has done nothing to you that most of the merchants in town have not done. You're cantankerous and dishonest. Ira has nothing to apologize for. He's been good to everybody in this town. Leave him alone."

"You calling me dishonest? I pay everyone I owe what's due them."

The man in the crowd laughed and waved his hand. "What you consider is due them, is usually half." The rest of the people standing around laughed and nodded their head in agreement.

"Aww, to the devil with all of you," Raphael said walking away.

"You needn't have said that, Jesse. Now Raphael is going to be looking for trouble with you. But thank you just the same."

"I was on his bad side already," and then laughing, he said, "who isn't? Besides, you don't deserve that kind of harassment."

"Thank you again."

The crowd dispersed as Ira goaded the ox on with his stick.

CHAPTER SEVENTY-THREE

After Majid had left the breakfast table to check on the stolen silk shipment, Sevent had an idea of how he and his son could seek revenge on his old nemesis' son. Rushing to the family's warehouses, he sought out Majid.

"Son, I have just had a marvelous idea. Walk with me as I talk." Sevent walked away from the workers to an area where they could talk undisturbed. "We have been trying to get at Gaspar and Rachel through the woman he loves. It is too much of a risk and too difficult to try to do anything inside the walls of Seleucia. However, out in the wilds between Tadmor and Dura-Europus, we don't have to be so imaginative."

Still rumpled from their conversation at breakfast, Majid said curtly, "What are you getting at?"

"Won't you feel foolish for your impertinence when you hear my plan." Sevent said, rebuke in his tone . "To get at the rich priest of Ahura-Mazda and the dead high priest's daughter, we do what I did to his father."

Majid's face brightened with awareness, "Ambush him in the desert."

Smiling with self-satisfaction, Sevent said, "Precisely."

"How do we carry it out?"

"When Darawesh arrives with the silk shipment, have a servant come get me in my study. I'll tell you both at the same time."

With the increased danger to Rachel since the drama with Majid and his father, Balzak began more strenuous offensive training with his master's, most likely, wife-to-be. He had ordered a new calf sheath to be made for both of her legs. Instead of holding a single blade, the new one held four sheaths providing her with a total of eight small throwing knives. Slightly larger, the new sheaths were no less uncomfortable than the previous ones.

"Balzak, with a single knife on each leg, I still felt feminine though dangerous. Now, I feel like a walking arsenal. What will Gaspar think of me?"

"He will think that he is fortunate to have you around to wed."

These comments of Balzak's that made Gaspar's unspoken proposal seem to be merely a formality, always made her blush.

It was with excitement and a sense of daring that she strapped on her new calf sheaths. Balzak had made sure that the leatherworker made the sheaths loose enough for easy blade removal, but snug enough so that the knives would not work their way out and fall at an indiscreet moment.

"Today, we're going to work on a more aggressive approach. I want you to be able to run and throw your knives, moving left or right, with the same accuracy as when you're planted and throwing. Do you understand?

She nodded.

"I want you to remember not to get discouraged. You will feel like you're starting all over again until your body begins to respond to this new motion. I will demonstrate what I want you to do, and then you will practice it."

Balzak knelt down on his left knee with his right knee up. Grabbing four knives from his own sheaths, he ran parallel to the four targets he had pre-set, and stuck each of the knives in each of the targets. He stopped at the far side of the course, knelt down, grabbed four more knives and threw them at the same four targets running in the opposite direction.

Panting a little as he walked over to Rachel, he said, "did you notice how I stepped with my left foot toward each target whether I was running to my left or to my right?"

"Yes I did. We have practiced this before only the knives were not on my person."

"The secret is for you to run swiftly, step directly at your target, and not hurry yourself when you grab your knives. The procedure I want is slow, quick, then deliberate. Be slow grabbing your knives so as not to drop them, be quick as you run the course, and deliberate as you step and throw at each target."

Rachel found this practice exhilarating, but she lacked the endurance to do it for very long. That night, she excused herself early from conversation, and slept without moving or waking until Ara came in the next morning to wake her. When she went down for breakfast, Balzak was waiting for her with his knife throwing clothes on.

"Are you going to work out again today?" asked Rachel.

"Yes, and so are you."

"But why? I thought you told me it was good to let my muscles recover a day between workouts?'

"That is true, but we are not throwing knives today. We are going to run. We must build your stamina. The farther you can run, the better chance you have of escaping an assailant. Go get your clothes on. We'll eat after we run."

Gaspar, Melchior, and the rest of the caravan were met with enormous pomp and cheering when Farshid's men rode out to meet them a few miles from the bandit's camp. The oasis that had been handed down to Farshid from generation to generation for almost two hundred years was beautiful to behold. Palm and citrus trees, and lush vegetable gardens met the caravans as they entered Farshid's domain.

"This is wonderful, Farshid," gasped Melchior.

"Truly you have made an Eden in the desert," said Gaspar, the magi's praise finding happy reception on the desert bandit's ears.

"Please consider this your home while you are here. Anytime you travel through my land, you must promise me that you will make use of my humble oasis."

"You must not twist my arm so hard," teased Melchior, "you will have your wish."

"My heart is warmed."

That night, Gaspar and Melchior told story after story of their travels. Farshid's men and their families sat in spellbound attention to everything that they heard. Ezri watched all of the interaction.

"This life among these bandits," he thought, "is what life would be like if I had continued with Satanas."

He realized that a life of thievery was not all that he thought it would be. The reality of killing people was not what he had dreamt about. He wanted to live very comfortably, being able to do whatever he wanted to do, but his experience with Satanas had made him stop and think about what he was doing. While he saw in Farshid qualities that had not been present in Satanas, he would never want to willingly live the kind of lifestyle the bandit was living. He had been fortunate to break company with Satanas he now knew, and he was anxious to see what Gaspar would be able to teach him. Seeing the dead bodies of Satanas and Yitzhak in his mind, brought back the question to him: "If I were to die, would I want to be remembered as Yitzhak will be, or Satanas?"

The next morning, Gaspar, Melchior, Vahumisa, and Ezri went on a tour of the oasis with Farshid. He was excited for his guests to see what had been in his family for so many years. As they walked through the relative cool of the citrus orchards which bore oranges, lemons, and limes, Farshid's composure turned grave.

"My friends, I have invited you here for two reasons. First, I wanted you to experience my hospitality and friendship. Second, there is a band of cutthroats in this area that are ruthless and trying to cut in on my people's income source."

"I don't understand," said Gaspar.

"The merchants will allow a certain amount of pilfering of the caravans without bringing in militia to root out a troublesome group. If bandits kill and take too much, pretty soon an army is sent in to clean out the trouble makers. This competing band is led by a man named Darawesh—a most despicable man. Not long ago, he killed everyone in a caravan from the distant east and stole their whole shipment of silk. If they continue thieving in this way, the caravan routes will dry up, and my people will suffer."

"Why do you tell us?" questioned Melchior.

"For your safety and your help. They are being funded by someone in either Seleucia or Ctesiphon. When you return to your home, I would be pleased if you would ask around and see if you can help us determine who is funding them, so we can, hopefully, eliminate the problem."

"I have a man who works for me and does my family's trading business for me, while I see to my responsibilities as a priest," said Gaspar. "I will have him look into the matter as soon as we return to Seleucia."

Surprised that Gaspar was a priest who earned profit as a merchant, Farshid said, "My great apologies if my people and I have ever caused you economic hardship."

Gaspar smiled and said, "I don't think so," and then with a devious look said, "but perhaps we can work out a road-user fee in the future."

"Ah, my friend, spoken like a true man of business. Seriously, I am concerned for you and your friends. Until you reach Dura-Europus, I will send a dozen of my men with you for your protection."

"I will take you up on your offer, and pay your men well for doing so," Gaspar offered.

"No, I insist that I do this for you."

"You do not understand. This whole expedition is being underwritten by a very pompous rival of mine in Seleucia."

"Then we shall in no way interfere with his great privilege," Farshid laughed, slapping Gaspar on the shoulder.

Gaspar and company stayed three nights at the oasis. The rest and fond conversation was not only relaxing, but a soothing balm that allayed the grief felt from the death of their friend and counselor.

On the morning of their departure, Farshid sent twelve of his most trusted men, astride magnificent Arabians, with the caravan. A pair rode patrol to the left of the train, a pair to the right, and two men scouted ahead. The other six rode along side the caravan itself.

Parting was sad. Farshid had become a good and trusted friend. Gaspar planned to nurture that friendship in the

311

future to both of their advantages.

Ezri would usually split his time between riding with the comical servants, Cyrus and Amehlech, and with Gaspar on his outside shoulder. Even though it was never spoken, the space between Gaspar and Melchior was kept as the position of honor to Balthasar.

The trip back to the main road from the oasis took almost half a day. When they reached the main road that went in a northeasterly direction towards Dura-Europus, each man took out food for his noontime meal. Most had brought fresh figs, oranges, and fresh bread for the first meal on the road.

Ezri was riding along side Gaspar at this point. His silence indicated to Gaspar that the younger man wanted to ask something he was not sure how to formulate.

"You have something on your mind?" Gaspar posed.

"I do. Why did you suggest that you pay to use the public road whenever you cross the land that does not belong to Farshid?"

"Several reasons. He is my friend and I like his people. He dealt honorably with us when we were passing through before. Cities that caravans travel through charge a tax. The amount that Farshid asks is equivalent to that amount. It is an irritation to most, but in light of other taxes, it is fair. Over and above that, all the money he gets goes to the general welfare of his people. You saw how they lived in the oasis. No one had any more than anyone else. Everyone prospered—no one went without, except those who would not work. There is no such equity in the cities. I have no problem supporting his way of life. He is a fair and generous ruler."

"You think differently than most men." There was a gap of silence as Ezri tried to frame his next question. Finding no appropriate way to say it, he said, "Are you wealthy?"

Melchior had been listening to their conversation, and could not now contain himself. "Gaspar is arguably the wealthiest man in all of Parthia. Maybe even Phraataces himself has less wealth than our young magus."

Gaspar gave Melchior a disparaging glance and said, "The wise Melchior is known to dabble in hyperbole from time to time. Yes, I am wealthy, but not as much as some."

Melchior said nothing, he only rolled his eyes.

"How about you," asked Melchior, "are you wealthy?"

"I suppose I am." Looking past Gaspar to Melchior he smiled and said, "But not as much as some."

The three laughed.

Melchior liked this young man. Ezri was intelligent, good looking, and a bit of a rascal. After Ezri had warmed up to Amehlech and Cyrus, he had proven himself to be as witty as the two caravan comedians. Ezri was likeable, but there was something about his character that did not add up to what he displayed to the world. Both Melchior and Gaspar had agreed that underneath all of his personality was an air of sadness.

Watching the other two men laugh, Melchior realized something for the first time. He was now the oldest of the group, and Gaspar had taken his place as the one in the middle. The thought aroused a melancholy spirit within him causing him to think again of the man whom he had been friends with for more than a quarter of a century. He sighed to himself thinking, "Alas, life goes on, old friends die, and new ones take their place. Although new friends are always welcomed, the loss of old ones leave voids."

Breathless, and barely able to speak, a servant stopped at the open door to Sevent's study saying, "Darawesh is here, Master."

Hurrying to where his son and the bandit waited for him, Sevent arrived slightly out of breath.

"It is good to see you again, Sevent," said Darawesh rising to shake his accomplice's hand. He was a few years older than Sevent, bald with a trim of grey hair around the sides. The Syrian had brown, close set eyes that were shaded under an umbrella of grey eyebrows. His face was creviced with the wrinkles that a life in the sun creates. Wiry muscles were bundled under a clean, but well-worn tan Simlah.

Failing to acknowledge the bandit's greeting, Sevent looked beyond him to the table filled with the priceless cloth of the orient.

"The quality is excellent."

"So. You are glad to see me, too, I see," said Darawesh.

"Excuse me. I was overcome by the silk you have captured. What do you guess its worth?"

"What I have hidden, as well as what is here? Three or four million of your king's-head-coins."

Sevent and Majid said nothing. They just stood looking with foolish expressions at the valuable material before them.

"Where is the rest of it?" queried Majid.

"We have it hidden north of Dura-Europus. Several of my men are watching it. The caravan carrying the silk was a large one with many guards. Six of my men were killed in our ambush of the shipment."

"How many of theirs?" asked Majid.

"Forty. They outnumbered us, but our initial ambush killed at least two dozen of theirs."

"Did you have any trouble with the band of robbers that live in that area?" asked Sevent.

"No. That fool Farshid only asks a toll for using '*his*' road. The millions in gold coins he allows to pass through his fingers is staggering. If I had his number of men, I'd be richer than any man alive."

"What will this do to the trade route?" asked Sevent. "We must be careful that we don't interrupt the taxes that Parthian cities along the Silk Highway extract from the caravans. A calamity like this could halt the flow of the caravans and dry up the tax revenues. We don't want the kings of Parthia getting involved in hunting us down."

"We will lay low for awhile. Most who are familiar with the trade route will assume that the damage was done by Farshid and his people. If there are no other robberies, trade should not affected."

"It will be several months before we can start selling off this shipment of silk," said Majid, thinking out loud. "Whether we try to sell it here or in Rome, the authorities will want to know where such large amounts were obtained. We will have to wait and sell it off in pieces to multiple buyers to divert attention."

"You have done well, Darawesh. We all will become immeasurably richer because of your work."

"Father," said Majid, "don't you want to talk to Darawesh about that other matter we were discussing after breakfast?"

"Ah, yes. We have a troublesome competitor we would like you to eliminate for us."

"Who is it?"

"Gaspar, the magus, son of Arioch."

Darawesh's lack of response told Sevent and Majid that he had no energy for this enterprise for which they were wanting him to become involved. He walked over to one of the product tables and sat on its corner rubbing his face with both hands. When he finally spoke, there was none of the usual enthusiasm for the business in which he usually excelled.

"There is no private citizen in the empire who is more powerful and respected by the king of kings than Gaspar. On top of that, the man is a servant of the good god. What can you have against him? I have never heard an ill word spoken about him from anyone."

"He is a threat to us, and to our fencing the silk you have so competently acquired. He is right now in the process of returning from Palestine. It would be a simple matter for you to abduct him and put him out of our misery," a fiendish smile lit up Sevent's features. "If you hurried, you could do this while he is still between Tadmor and Dura-Europus, making it look like another attack by that Farshid character you spoke of."

Darawesh had started rubbing his face again. "When we ambushed the silk caravan, we did it with Farshid unaware that

314

we were in *his* territory. Knowing him, he will be looking for us now. What you ask is not as simple as you may think. Farshid is not your typical bandit, and he is a formidable foe in battle. He is the ruler of his little empire, and his people love him. His men fight like demons for him, and for what they consider their land. I am no coward, but I do not want to pit my men against his numbers and their perception of us as ones who have come to destroy their way of life."

Majid had become noticeably agitated during Darawesh's speech. Holding up his hand to his son, Sevent said to the bandit, "Look, you swoop in, kill Gaspar, and ride away. What could Farshid care about a troublesome magus from a wealthy family?"

"I don't like it, Sevent. You and your son can never spend all the wealth you have already, not to speak of the wealth you will have once we sell off the silk. Why not let this whole dispute with Gaspar settle. Listen, you can move to another city in the empire if he upsets you that much. You could move across the river to Ctesiphon. In the name of Ahura-Mazda, you could live in Rome!"

"Why should we move, when Gaspar is the perpetrator?" said Majid, his anger barely contained.

"I will pay you and your men well to bring off this request," said Sevent heading off his son's emotional response. "It will give you and your men expense money until we can sell off the silk.

"How long do I have before you need a reply?"

"Yesterday. Gaspar could be crossing the western desert right now. You will have to hurry to catch him in the window of time that we have. We may have missed it already."

"Here's what I can do. I will talk to my men. Whatever we decide, I'll be back in contact with you by this evening to tell you of our decision."

"Okay, okay. That is not what I wanted to hear, but that will have to do."

Darawesh slowly pushed away from the table saying, "I'll get as quick of an answer as I can."

Sevent only nodded his head watching the man walk out of the warehouse. He looked over at his son who was now pacing back and forth in front of the silk.

"He's going to back out of this like a coward—I know it," whined Majid.

"The man's no coward. His raids have made us both rich. Don't forget that if he wouldn't have disposed of Gaspar's father, you would have been left to roam the streets, and I would have been either executed or in prison. Arioch had found out about our illegal enterprises and was going to take that information to

315

the civil authorities. If Darawesh had not seen to Gaspar's father's death, you and I would be nothing today."

"I've heard this before, Father. I think he's gotten old and he's lost his daring."

"Would you like to be in charge of going out after Gaspar?"

"If I had Darawesh's men I would."

"You talk like a fool. You're good at business, Son. Keep to that. You let me and Darawesh take care of everything else." Saying that, Sevent left his fuming son and went back to the house.

CHAPTER SEVENTY-FOUR

Respectable was not a word most people in Caesarea would have used to describe Sophia before she became pregnant, so it was not common for people to go out of their way to speak to her now. There were a few women who looked down their noses at her, and could not believe that Ira kept her as his cook. When people found out that he was building on to his house so that she would have a place for the baby and herself, there were those who thought he had succumbed to senility. Most people saw his actions toward Sophia as what they were: the kind deeds of a compassionate old man. People eventually got used to the mateless pregnant woman, letting her go about her affairs undisturbed.

Ira and Even's excitement about having a baby around the house grew with Sophia's belly. The two bachelors could all but contain their anticipation. Every day the men would spend time thinking of new names for the child. Even hoped for a boy, and was continually offering boys' names. Ira thought it would be nice for Sophia to have a girl to keep her company, so he was always on the lookout for girls' names.

One night after supper, the two men were helping Sophia clear off the dishes offering their names-of-the-day, prompting Sophia to ask, "What if I have twins?"

"Let's hope that one is girl and one is a boy so that neither Even or I will be disappointed."

This time in her life turned out to be the best weeks of Sophia's life. Never had she had anyone care about her well being as she had with Ira. She found herself waking up everyday to expectation and happiness. It had been a long time since she entertained thoughts that maybe there really was a god who cared about the lives of mortals. She would have the thought, and then quickly brush it away as foolishness brought on by her pregnancy.

When Darawesh showed up before supper began, Sevent sent all of the servants out of the dining room. The three men all sat at one end of the table talking in hushed tones.

"What did you and your men decide?" asked Sevent.

"We'll do it, but there are stipulations."

"What are those?" Majid asked, his temper already

beginning to flare.

Sevent flashed an angry glare which contained the temper of his son.

"I will not put my men in danger. If something comes up that we don't anticipate, I'm pulling them back."

"That's understandable," Sevent said.

"If I see any lookouts that I think might be Farshid's men, we'll ride like thunder back to Seleucia."

Sevent shrugged saying, "I can't ask any more than that on short notice."

"The last point could be the deal breaker."

"And that is?"

"Each of us wants fifteen gold coins up front, and no matter what happens, we keep the money."

From his position at the head of the table, Sevent looked at his longtime partner in crime, weighing the importance of the task against the great cost.

"I don't like it at all," Majid said jumping up from his seat.

"Sit down!" Sevent commanded.

"I won't sit down. He's swindling us."

Darawesh was usually a cool negotiator, but there was a limit to how much he would endure even for an old business associate's whelp. Sevent could see the bandit's muscles flex as he struggled for control.

"Fine, I'm happy with my cut of the silk," Darawesh said rising from the table.

Grimacing more than smiling, Sevent put his hand gently on his associate's. "Wait. My son allows his wounded pride to get in the way of his reason," he said flashing Majid a look that said to get himself under control.

Darawesh did not leave, and he did not sit down as Sevent said, "Please. Sit."

Looking with disdain at Majid, Darawesh said, "I will do this last act, if you agree to my terms, and then we're done. I'm getting too old for these kinds of escapades, and I won't be denigrated by babes who have never done anything more dangerous than threatening young women." He had heard about Majid's confrontation with Rachel at the marketplace, and the reference stung the young man's sensibilities.

Patting the table twice with both hands, Sevent said, "Darawesh, I agree to your terms. When can you leave."

The fire had not fully gone out of the old thief's eyes when he said, "Tomorrow at dawn. Perhaps your brave son would like to join our party."

Sevent looked over at the boy simmering in his anger and humiliation saying, "Well?"

Majid said nothing. He stood, knocking the chair to the

floor, and stormed out of the dining room.

"I apologize for my son's behavior. His thoughts are not mine."

Cooling down a bit, Darawesh gave a forced smile saying, "When do I collect payment for my men?"

"Right now." Rising, Sevent led the way to his study.

The delay had sent the kitchen staff into a tizzy, and the serving staff stood in the hallway a long time before their master returned for his supper. For once, Sevent was gracious and said nothing about the warm, dry meal.

The thought of holding Rachel in his arms made the last few days of the trip interminable for Gaspar. Fortunately for him, he had no knowledge of all that had taken place since he left home. If he would have known, it would have made him even more impatient to run to her rescue. The smell and feel of her hair had not left him. The thought of it filled him with longing to immerse himself in her long, thick locks. The far off look in his eyes betrayed him. He happened to glance over at Melchior who was looking at him with an impish grin stamped on his face.

"What?"

"You know what," Melchior said.

"I do, but do you?"

"I may be an old man who never married, but I can still recognize the look of a man who is thinking about the woman he loves."

"Well, you're a dreamer, Melchior. I was having no such thoughts."

"What thoughts?" Ezri said as he rode up to the magi.

"Nothing," said Gaspar

Melchior smiled saying, "I don't think Rachel would appreciate being referred to as nothing."

"So, he had the look again, huh?" teased Ezri.

"He certainly did. I'm looking forward to reaching home and not having to see that cross-eyed gaze he gets."

"My eyes do not cross."

"Yah, they do," corrected Ezri.

"Can we please talk about something else?"

"As a matter of fact, we can," said Melchior. "Have you had anymore dreams?"

"Not of snow, but of something else."

"Should I leave?" offered Ezri.

"No," said Melchior. "Gaspar has had some very vivid dreams that seem to be connected with the reason behind this whole excursion of ours. Balthasar encouraged him to journal his dreams so he can keep them straight when he wants to refer back to them."

319

"This is interesting. Tell us about your new one."

"This one has more symbolism than the others," Gaspar began. "In it, there is a man sitting on a throne which sits atop the temple we saw in Jerusalem. I assume he's a king, but his scepter is a shepherd's crook, and his crown is made of thorns. There are twelve men prostrate before him. The king raises his crook waves it in a circle around him. When he does this, the men rise and go in different directions to all parts of the world. One of these men brings other men with him to Parthia. He comes to my house and tells me that he bears the truth for which I have been searching. That's pretty much the dream, though there is something strange in the dream that has caused me some concern."

"What is that?" queried Melchior.

"In the dream, the man comes to my house with these other men, and Rachel and I go to the door together to greet them. What has concerned me is that Rachel is an old woman, and I am just as I am now."

"Everyone ages, Gaspar," said Ezri.

"You said the dream felt symbolic. Maybe it's telling you that Rachel will have matured substantially by the time we return."

"I don't know, Melchior. I don't know what to think. It comforts me that Rachel and I appear to be married in the dream."

"Here comes the look," warned Ezri smiling.

"No, truly. I really only knew her for a night. Who knows if she still feels as she did that night after having only known someone for a few hours? Sometimes I think that her mind will have cleared while I've been on my trip, and I will return to find her feelings for me have changed. Seeing her in my dreams an old woman tells me that we will have many years together. I won't have wasted my time dreaming of being with her."

Gaspar looked at Melchior and then at Ezri. Both had silly smiles on their faces.

"And you tell me that I get a look. You should see your faces," Gaspar said shaking his head.

CHAPTER SEVENTY-FIVE

The men under Darawesh's command had not said that they would only work under the conditions that he had told Sevent. Those had been his terms. His men only wanted money to live on until their cut came to them for the silk heist.

There was no more ruthless man in all of the Parthian and Roman empires than he, but he always dealt fairly with his men. If a man died on one of their raids, Darawesh always made sure that the bandit's surviving widow or mother got his split. Because of the way he took care of the families of his men, Darawesh had a band who were loyal to him. He always held each man's payment until after their raid was completed, in the chance that a man might die and have his cut taken from him by someone else. He had learned that the best way to take care of his men and their families was to pay them at the end of whatever iniquitous task they were engaged.

Dura-Europus was usually a five to six day ride from Seleucia. Darawesh and his twenty men made it in three.

Setting up camp below the cliffs of the city across the Euphrates, Darawesh told his men, "I don't want you in town tonight. I'm sending Hassan and Yehyeh to determine whether the caravan we seek has arrived. I don't want any of you getting drunk tonight and not being able to function at your best tomorrow. When we've completed our business, there'll be lots of time for celebrating then."

The men cheered his last statement and then scattered to set up their individual places for the night. They were exhausted after the hard ride. It was doubtful that any of them would have gone into town even if Darawesh had told them they could.

Yehyeh and Hassan entered the fortress city, gave the caravan tax collector a small bribe to get the information they were seeking, and made it back to camp before everyone had gotten settled.

"Two silver coins made the tax collector talk like a camel seller," joked Yehyeh. "The Magi's caravan has not come through the town yet."

"Tomorrow morning we will get an early start and set up our trap," Darawesh told the two thieves. "Spread the word among the men."

As the sun went down, Darawesh, as seasoned and cautious as he was, did not notice two lone riders observing his camp from the heights below the walls of Dura-Europus. The azure sky turned to magenta, then to purple, and then the riders were gone.

"Tomorrow we will be in Dura-Europus," announced Vahumisa around the camp fire.

"By this time next week our young magi will be engaged," Melchior said boisterously causing the rest of the camp to cheer and Gaspar to blush.

One of the soldiers, who was accustomed to keeping his joking among the other soldiers, said, "Is that the look, Eminence?" causing Gaspar's face to turn red as pomegranate juice.

"All right I admit it. I've been a little distracted."

Melchior's, "A little?" sent the whole camp into spasms of laughter.

A change had slowly come over the camp during the weeks of the expedition. When it started out, there were several camp fires where like groups would sit around and talk at night. As the weeks passed, three fires became two, and now there was only one with one circle of comrades. When a group's leadership feels no superiority, vines of friendship tend to germinate. The magi's open, friendly acceptance of everyone else had allowed the bonds of friendship to extend beyond the natural social grouping that would have normally remained for the whole trip.

The joviality was cut short when the approaching hoofbeats of two horses being ridden hard put everyone on the alert. As the two riders came closer and their faces could be illuminated by the camp fire, they were recognized as two of Farshid's men. One of the men, Kiavash—Farshid's oldest son —dismounted and ran up to Gaspar and Melchior.

"Your reverences, I fear that the band that has invaded my father's territory means to do you harm. I ask that you come with me as soon as you can. My father and two hundred of his men are camped just over the hill to the south of here."

"Wait, Kiavash. How do you know this," asked Gaspar trying to make sense of the young man's words.

"Two days ago, Razi and I bribed the caravan tax collector in Dura-Europus to let us know if anything unusual passed through the city in the next few weeks. This afternoon, two men, who were with a group of riders numbering about two dozen, bribed him to tell them if a caravan carrying three magi had come through the city. We saw the men ride up and camp on the other side of Euphrates. They do not ride as a military patrol or any well organized group. I believe these are the murderers who killed everyone in the caravan last week, taking all the silk and anything else of value."

"Why would they be after us?" asked Melchior. "We have next to nothing with us. What we had of value was given to the young King in Bethlehem."

"I do not know the answer to your question, but my father told me to bring him back any news if the marauders returned, and to bring you to him if we felt the need."

Gaspar and Melchior looked at Vahumisa for advice. "Farshid knows more about this desert than I do. I say we pack up and follow Kiavash back to his father."

John, Gil, and Uri returned to their homes near Gischala to the relief of their parents. Aside from a few days of putting up with John's brooding over not catching Ezri, and another day when they had not bought enough provisions for the evening meal, the boys ended up having an enjoyable time being with one another and stopping whenever they had the notion to do so.

One day, they were riding along the Great Sea when Uri decided to run his horse into the surf. Soon the other two were doing the same thing laughing the whole time. Before long, John had taken off all of his clothes and was riding naked. He slowed Raven to a walk, waded him out into deeper water, stood on his back, and dove into the oncoming waves. The boys ended up spending most of the morning splashing around in the waves and trying to catch fish with their hands.

Another day, the threesome came upon a young woman and her mother who, upon returning from market, had their wagon wheel slip off its axel. The boys would have stopped to help anyway, but the fact that the girl was attractive made their efforts even more agreeable. The girl's mother invited the boys back to their home for a noonday meal which seemed to be a great idea to all who were present. The father and his two sons came in from their work and were surprised and a bit wary of the young travelers, but when he heard what they had done, he made sure they were well stocked with food for several days when they left.

Nevertheless, the trip had been disappointing in that they did not achieve their goal. What they did achieve was an adventure that would solder their bonds of friendship forever.

In later years, when the fire burned low, and the men had no one to disturb their talk, one of them would start the first sentence of his reminiscence with, "Do you remember when we were returning from trying to chase down that scoundrel Ezri . . ." and that would ignite story after story. After a few years

323

went by, even John looked back on that time with more of a sense of fondness than frustration.

Kiavash rode on ahead of the caravan so his father would not have to wait for the information. When the magi and their retinue arrived, they were met with a solemnity they were unaccustomed to seeing in the typically frolicsome desert people. Their survival in this land depended on their success in the next few hours, and the gravity of their situation weighed heavily on them now.

"It is good to see you again so soon, Farshid." said Gaspar, "but I can see that you have grave business to deal with."

"That is true. Our very existence. People of Dura-Europus and Tadmor are very angry about the innocent killing and silk theft. Everyone assumes that last week's murderous raid was my doing. There has been talk of the kings of Hatra, Seleucia, and Babylon joining to come against us. Although we will fight to the death to protect our people, I am afraid that that is all that will happen to us once the combined armies of the western Parthian kings attack us. This is our chance to show that it was not us, and to return the shipment to its rightful owners. I don't know why these men want you, but the fact that they do has been a blessing to my people and me."

"How so?" Melchior inquired.

"Whoever these jackals of the desert are, they would be foolish to attempt another raid on a merchant caravan in the near future. For whatever reason, they are willing to take the risk of exposing themselves to get whatever they think you have. If you would not have come into their plans, who knows how long it may have been before they would have executed their next caravan assault. More than likely, our annihilation would have taken place well before my people and I could have been vindicated.

"How can we help, outside of kismet?" offered Gaspar.

"I would like to use you as bait."

Darawesh, Yehyeh, and Hassan were up before the sun nudging the other men with their toes to wake up. Darawesh had hoped that his men would want nothing to do with the abduction and murdering of the magus, and he wished now he would have just told Sevent no. His men knew that it might be months before they saw the first income from the sale of the silk, and the chance to get a sizable remuneration this soon, was too much for them to pass up. "Oh, well," he thought, "this will be my last operation. Next week at this time, I'll be well into my retirement, living a life of ease."

"Dried meat, biscuits, and water will be our breakfast on the road today," Yehyeh told the others. Darawesh wants to leave before the sunrises. Get moving!"

For five minutes, the camp was a throng of activity while the marauders went through what had become routine for them: packing and clearing out quickly. The sky was just beginning to turn a light blue as the first few horses waded into the cool waters of the Euphrates.

Kiavash and Razi, from hidden positions in the cliffs above Dura-Europus, watched Darawesh's men exit from the Euphrates. The fording place ran deeper this time of the year, and there had been places where the water ran almost to the tops of the saddles. There was a better place to cross thirty miles south of Dura-Europus, but there was a major Parthian outpost there where Darawesh would have had to answer too many questions. That the marauder chose to cross here instead of there solidified both Kiavash's and his father's theory that these men were the same ones who attacked the silk train the week before.

Kiavash had planned to follow any scouts that the marauders sent out ahead, but none were assigned to the task.

"They are confident that no one suspects their actions," said Razi in response to the thieves' choice. "Evidently. They are making this too easy. I am surprised by their lack of foresight and caution," said Razi shaking his head.

An hour and a half after leaving the waters of the Euphrates, Darawesh reined up his men. Four were stationed on either side of the road—the rest divided—half going north with Darawesh, and the other headed south with Yehyeh. Both groups dropped over hillocks not more than a quarter of a mile from the road.

"This is where they will be waiting to ambush the magi," said Kiavash. "I will stay here and keep an eye on their movements. I want you to ride to my father and tell him of their position. Remember to tell him that there are four on the road, and nine on each side behind the nearest low lying dunes."

"I will do as you say."

"Make sure you give the group to the south a wide berth. You have plenty of time. Don't give yourself away."

Razi nodded his head, led his horse south along a wide range of sand dunes, mounted, and then slipped away.

"I hope that we don't have to wait in this sun for too many days," Darawesh said wiping his forehead with his sleeve. "We could be out here another week or two waiting for them."

"How will we know when the right caravan comes

along?" asked one of his men.

"That's why we have four of our men near the road. When they see a caravan, they'll ride up to it, and inquire as to whether Gaspar the magi from Seleucia is in their company.

"If not, they'll act like they're riding farther down the road to meet the next caravan. If it is the magi's caravan, he'll give him the note Sevent wrote for him."

"What does the note say?"

"That something bad has happened to a girl one of the magi is interested in, so he'll willfully follow our men."

"What if he doesn't go with them?"

"That's where all of us come in."

Vahumisa and his soldiers were stationed in their customary positions in the caravan. Farshid's guard had left and joined with the larger body of his men. When the four marauders saw the first sign of the caravan, they began a hurried pace towards it.

While still a hundred yards from Vahumisa, one marauder acting as the leader, held up his right hand, reining in his horse.

"We are messengers from Seleucia seeking the Magus Gaspar. Is he with your group?"

"I am Gaspar," said one of the three men directly behind Vahumisa.

"Your servant Balzak has requested your immediate return to Seleucia." Handing him the letter, he said, "This letter explains everything."

Reading the letter, a smile spread across the recipient's face. "This letter is not from Balzak."

The marauder's expression was blank. He had not expected this response and had nothing with which to come back. He stammered, and said finally, "Balzak dictated it but it comes from Balzak I assure you."

"I think not."

The four men heard the metallic sound of swords being slipped out of their scabbards. The caravan guard had ridden to the front and were now surrounding the four marauders.

"What is this?" the leader of the four cutthroats said with false indignation.

"You are going to give us the information we want," said Vahumisa speaking through clenched teeth. "But first you're going to unbuckle your swords, and drop them to the ground."

Arrogant smiles appeared on the faces of the four marauders, and the leader said, "You may want to drop your swords. Even now the rest of our group is tightening their circle around you."

Looking at the criminal with steady eyes, Vahumisa pointed with his sword behind the man and said, "Do you mean that group?"

All four men swung their heads around to see Darawesh and the rest of the marauders being herded on foot by Farshid and his two hundred men.

Reaching the caravan, Farshid's men roughly rounded Darawesh's marauders into a group away from the road.

"You did well," Farshid said to Razi as Razi handed his chieftain the note. "You make an excellent magus, don't you think, Eminence?"

"He most certainly does," said Gaspar who was sitting on a horse next to Farshid. "Thank you, Razi, for putting your life in danger for me."

"It was an honor to play your part," then smiling said, "and fun."

"What will you do with these men," asked Melchior as other members of the caravan came to the front. Farshid had insisted that his men take the places of everyone in the caravan except for Vahumisa and his men.

"We will find out where they have stashed the silk, and then turn them over to the authorities in Dura-Europus."

"Isn't that dangerous for you?" asked Ezri who had just come up with the others from the back of Farshid's host.

"No," he said with surprising calm. "Some night, very soon, we will tie them up, put them in a wooden cage, and leave them outside the city's walls. I have contacts in the city I will notify who will alert the proper authorities that the marauders and the silk are outside."

"What if the marauders won't tell you where the silk is?" Gaspar said visibly concerned.

"Oh, don't worry, young magus. They'll talk. We can be quite persuasive."

"What if they're not the same ones who stole the silk?" Melchior wondered.

"We shall find that out too, but I don't think that is the case."

That night the small caravan slept peacefully. For the first time in over two months, they laid under a Parthian sky.

CHAPTER SEVENTY-SIX

Rachel and Parandis spent many of their days together. Even though she felt confident that Saiar had made her safe from Majid, Rachel was most comfortable for the moment being at either her friend's house or her own.

One morning, Rachel was awakened by a knock at the door followed by Balzak's voice.

"My lady?"

"Yes, Balzak, what is it?"

"Ara is not feeling well, so I took the liberty of bringing you a cup of pomegranate juice. May I come in?"

Getting out of bed, she put on a robe over her night clothes saying, "Just a minute," as she did so. In the hallway she could here uneasy shuffling of feet. "You may enter, Balzak."

The bedroom door opened. There was a tall lean form of a man standing in the doorway holding a tray of juice. At first the silhouette of a man who was obviously not Balzak caused her to draw in her breath, thinking immediately of her recent trouble with Majid.

"Good morning, my lady," said the silhouette.

Recognition registered in her brain and she fell back and steadied herself on the bedpost. The silhouette strode across the distance between them and set the tray on the bedside table. Behind the form, a little man ran to the curtains and pulled them open letting sunshine spill into the room. The silhouette turned to face Rachel who was now sitting on the bed with her hands to her mouth. Kneeling down on his knees, the once silhouetted man took the hands from her face and kissed them.

"I have returned to you, beloved."

Unable to speak, she threw her arms around Gaspar's neck and sobbed into his chest. Balzak tiptoed out of the room, smiling with satisfaction, and closed the door behind him. Rachel slid from the bed into the lap of the man she loved, allowing him to hold and console her. Breathing in the scent of her hair, tears came to Gaspar's eyes.

"I have thought of little else these many weeks but holding you, dear Rachel."

"I have . . ." was all she said, unable to curb her tears.

Finally, she looked up into the eyes of the man who loved her more than life's breath. She observed strong eyebrows that tilted up slightly in benevolent yearning. "I have wondered if you missed me as I have missed you."

Gaspar hugged her more closely to his chest and kissed the top of her head. Easing his embrace, Rachel looked up at him again as she slid off his lap to face him on her knees.

Taking his hand and holding it on her lap, she said, "What do we do now? I don't want to be out of your sight."

"I am afraid," Gaspar said, his lips curling into a smile, "I shall never stand again."

Now serious, she said, "What is wrong?"

"My legs have gone to sleep, and I can't feel them any longer," he said laughing.

"Here," she said standing with her arms outstretched, "let me help you to your feet."

"No, Rachel, I think I need to stretch them out before I can stand."

Awkwardly, and comedically, Gaspar got off his knees and on to his back allowing the blood to flow to his extremities. Rachel sat next to his head and arranged her lap under his head just as there was a tapping at the door.

"My lady?" came Ara's voice through the door.

"Come in."

Ara opened the door and saw the two lovers on the floor. "Is the master okay?" she asked with concern.

"His legs fell asleep, and he couldn't get up," smiled Rachel.

"I was wondering when you would like breakfast."

Smiling, Gaspar said, "As soon as the needles leave my legs. I'm starving for a good meal."

"I will alert the kitchen," said Ara. She started to close the door behind her, stopped and turned around. "My name is Ara, sir, and I am glad that you are home."

"Thank you, Ara. I'm am glad to be home."

Ara curtsied and smiled, closing the door behind her.

Pulling her up as he got to his feet, Gaspar said, "Balzak gave me an overview of what has happened in my absence. I'm so sorry for the loss of your mother and father, Rachel."

"It has been very difficult, but Balzak has taken me under his wing and been most caring. I don't know what I would have done if I wouldn't have had him here to watch over me and to teach me."

"And what has he taught you?"

Looking up sheepishly she said, "He's been teaching me to throw knives."

Gaspar chortled, "Knife throwing?"

"What's so funny," Rachel said defensively.

"I think it's wonderful. You must show me."

"You're not angry with me?"

329

"Of course not. I'm surprised and amused that you would enjoy knife throwing, but it does add to your feminine mystery."

"You're making fun, now," she said blushing, her long lashes shading her lovely eyes.

"I promise that I am not. Balzak has always wanted to teach me to throw, but I had no interest in it. My father started teaching me to use a sword when I was barely able to walk. When he died, Cephas took over my training. I don't dislike knife throwing, I just always preferred a sword. You must show me what you can do."

Excitedly, she said, "Would you like to see, now, before breakfast?" catching Gaspar off guard.

"I, um, sure. Why not?"

Rachel pushed him out of the room telling him, "I'll meet you at the course in two minutes."

Gaspar stood outside her door scratching his head and smiling.

When Farshid began his questioning of Darawesh, he soon found that he could have tortured the marauder leader for days without getting any information out of him. Yehyeh was just as stubborn. Farshid and his men were working against time. They needed to prove that they were not involved in the theft of the silk caravan. A swift confession was needed.

Kiavash came up with the idea that got a the quick confession for which they were looking. The twenty-one men were broken into groups of three and separated by enough distance where they could not see or hear the other groups. Each group was told and offered the same bargain. Whoever told where the silk was hidden first would be released with a horse, two days of food, and enough water for three days. Three men in three different groups agreed to talk. Those three men were brought before Farshid.

"You three have been so accommodating," said Farshid. "Although you all have agreed to help us, only one can get the deal we're offering." He then held out three sticks in his hand with only the tops showing. "You will each draw a stick. Whoever draws the shortest stick will be given the opportunity to talk. If after we have checked out his story to see whether it is true or not, that man will go free."

"Wait, wait, wait," said one of the men. "I'll tell you now, only let me be the one."

"You dog," said another. "You would cheat us out of our chance to live? He's a liar. I will tell you where the silk is."

The third man said, "What about me? I want to be the one to tell."

Farshid smirked at the marauders' dishonor. "Go ahead,

you can all speak, but only one will not be turned over to the authorities to be crucified."

The three men began trying to out do the others in the clarity of their details as to the whereabouts of the silk. By the time they had finished, Farshid knew exactly where to find the stolen merchandise. Kiavash and fifty men were sent to recapture the silk. At the end of two days, the men returned with the silk and three of the four men who had been guarding it.

"What happened to the fourth?" asked Farshid.

"He tried to fight us, so I had one of our men put an arrow through him," said Kiavash. "I wasn't going to risk one of our men to try to bring him back alive. We left him on the desert floor for the birds and scorpions to feast upon."

"I would have done the same."

Farshid was good to his word. The three men who talked drew straws, and the one to draw the shortest was sent off into the desert with everything he was promised. The two others who were willing to talk were tied to the outside of the makeshift cage so they would not me harmed by the angry marauders. Razi snuck into Dura-Europus and passed along the message that the silk and the thieves were waiting outside the city walls. When the city guards found the twenty-three men tied up, in and outside the cage, a guard was set there until a sentence was passed the next day that they all would be sold to the next slave traders who came through the city. The marauders did not have to wait long for their sentence to be enacted. A slave caravan came through only three days later.

Darawesh's dreams of a restful retirement never came. He was eventually sold to work in a salt quarry in Egypt. The majority of his men were sold to work other menial jobs, while three were sold to be gladiators. Two of these died in their first gladiatorial match. The third was able to eventually win his freedom and moved to southern Gaul to live out the last year of his life.

Unfortunately for Sevent and Majid, Farshid was able to get the names of Darawesh's contact and fence in Seleucia. The match of the silk found with the marauders matched perfectly with the silk found in Sevent's warehouse. Not wanting his son to suffer his fate, Sevent lied about his son's involvement with the darker side of his business. Sevent spent the rest of his years working hard labor in a prison in the eastern part of the empire. From the fields that he worked, he saw caravans bound for Rome laden with silk from the orient.

Majid, true to form, did not object, and let his father take the full brunt of the punishment. The son did not come out of the affair unscathed, though. Sevent's holdings were confiscated by Phraataces. Majid ended up being turned out with no penny to his name.

"She's absolutely incredible," Gaspar said to Balzak watching Rachel go through her knife throwing routine.

"And deadly," Balzak said proudly.

"Look at her, Balzak. She is utterly overjoyed. I have never seen anything like it."

"She does like knife throwing, Gaspar, but I think most of the joy she's having is showing you what she can do."

Gaspar's smile widened.

"You know, Majid hired someone to abduct her."

"What?"

"You would have heard about it anyway, but I think it's best to hear it from me."

"What happened?"

"She was at the marketplace with her friend and her servant, Kahliq—who loves her as dearly as I love you, Master. Kahliq turned his head for a moment, and then she was gone. When her attacker set her on her feet behind the sales stalls, she instantly performed the defensive maneuvers I had taught her, separated from him, and when he reached for his sword, she threw her knife into his hand. She escaped back to where Kahliq and her friend were waiting for her. I don't know too many men who could have done what she did. I am very proud of my prize pupil."

"Thank you, Balzak. She told me that you have been extremely good to her. I never thought that when I told you to look in on her that you would end up doing so much. Again, thank you, old friend."

"You are welcome, Gaspar."

Rachel had stopped her demonstration and was watching master and servant as she reloaded her calf sheaths. She walked to the two men, put one arm around each of them, hugged them to her, and said, "I love you both. You can never know how dear you are to me." She pulled back to see them both hastily wipe their eyes.

"I'm hungry," she said. "Let's go eat."

Rachel put an arm around Gaspar's waist, and one around Balzak as the three walked arms around the other into the house.

CHAPTER SEVENTY- SEVEN

Melchior let the lovers have a few days together before he paid a visit to the house. Rachel and Melchior knew of each other from her father having been the high priest, and the obvious connection that was there. The pair were sitting in the shady part of the courtyard when Tala announced the magus to her master.

"What a grand couple you make," Melchior said clapping his hands together as he walked over to the two lovers.

Gaspar and Rachel stood to greet Melchior in time to be gathered up in his arms. With Gaspar on his left, and Rachel on his right, he looked from one to the other saying, "May God bless you and keep you and may He make His light to shine upon you."

Gaspar smiled, and Rachel said, "What a beautiful blessing, Melchior. I have never heard it before."

"It is not Zoroastrian. It is Hebrew."

Why would you use a Hebrew blessing when you are a priest of Ahura-Mazda?"

"I see you and Gaspar have not had time to talk about '*everything*' yet," said Melchior with concern in his eyes.

"No, in fact there is something I need to tell you both," Gaspar affirmed. "Please, let's sit down."

Rachel's confusion only became more profound.

Looking at Rachel, Gaspar said, "Remember the spiritual doubts I told you the three of us had during the trip?"

"Yes."

"When we were all visited by an angel the evening after we left the Christ Child, we became aware that we no longer believed that Ahura-Mazda was the good god. We came to believe that there is only one God, and He is Yahweh."

"Then what is Ahura-Mazda?"

"I don't know, but he's not God."

Melchior took Rachel's hand saying, "We saw a star guide us all the way to Bethlehem in Palestine. An angel visited our dreams and told us to go by a different route than what we came because Herod had lied about his intentions. Balthasar knew that he would not live to see the end of the trip, so he sold everything he had in order to present the child with a chest of gold. Ahura-Mazda did not direct us to Palestine—Yahweh did."

Rachel pulled her hand from Melchior and put her hands

333

up to her face rubbing her forehead with her finger tips. Gaspar and Melchior looked at each other wondering what the young woman was thinking.

"Neither of you can be magi," she said as a matter of fact.

"That's true," both said simultaneously.

"The bridge that my mother and father had to cross from this life to the next just became very narrow," emotion was now creeping into Rachel's voice.

Gaspar reached forward to hold Rachel's hand. Before their hands touched, Rachel stood and walked upstairs.

Looking at Melchior, Gaspar said, "What do I do?"

"I was wrong to say what I said. The time was not right. I assumed you two had talked about our change of belief. I'm sorry, Gaspar."

"If Yahweh is God, what does that say about what her father and mother believed? What comfort can I give her concerning where they are right now?"

"Comfort is hard for those who are first in their families to believe the truth. Though its reality means that everyone who came before them and believed something else, is now, most likely, in a very uncomfortable place. It also doesn't make sense for people to not believe the truth so they can join their ancestors in hell."

"No, I suppose not."

"On the other hand, once you know the truth, you get to begin a new lineage for those in your family who are going to end up in paradise. You can't save Rachel's or even your own parents, but you can save your children.

"I am looking forward to reading more of the Hebrew scriptures that Balthasar left to us. It seems strange now. I've spent my whole life following and learning about a god I thought I knew and was the true god. Now, I find myself starting all over from square one."

Gaspar was staring off at a potted plant across the courtyard and nodded his head.

Both men, lost in their thoughts, did not hear the footsteps of another entering the yard.

"I don't want our children and us to live our lives in a lie only to find at the end, everything we believed was fake," Rachel said with her nose running and her eyes swollen and red. "What I have heard you say about the miraculous happenings you have experienced in the last few months have convinced me that what you say about God is true. How foolish would I be to follow a false god just so I could feel better about where my parents are now?" She took a big breath, shuddering she said, "I love you, Gaspar. Where you go, I will follow."

Both men looked stunned. Rachel stood there in the middle of the courtyard sobbing, looking frail and abandoned. Gaspar hurried to her and held her in his arms. Melchior stood to leave.

"No, Melchior, stay," she said commandingly. "I sat at the top of the stairs," she said gulping air, "and listened to what you were saying. It's true. My parents are gone, and I loved them both dearly, but I can't sacrifice my husband and our children so I can make believe my parents are going to be fine in the afterlife. If I did that, what would become of Gaspar, of me," then in a whisper, "and our children?"

Becoming aware of all the fluid her face was producing, she excused herself.

The two men were left alone again, neither knowing what to say. Gaspar walked over to the table gong and struck it. In a few moments, Tala appeared.

"Please ask Ara to attend her lady, and then bring us some refreshment."

She bowed and left swiftly.

Rachel joined the men moments after Tala appeared with the drinks—her eyes and nose were still red.

Ezri had been out at the warehouse with Cephas and had chosen this time to see what everyone was doing. The first person he saw as he came from his room into the courtyard was Melchior. The other two had their backs to him.

"Melchior!" he said genuinely glad to see him. "I was going to ask Gaspar today when we were going to get to see you." Reaching a point where he could see the others' faces, he stopped and said, "Uh-oh, should I leave?"

"No, Ezri," Rachel said. "Sit with us. I became emotional for a few minutes, but I'm fine now."

"Uh, okay. I don't need to stay."

"I'm fine. Sit."

"How are you getting along with Cephas?" Asked Melchior.

"He's amazing. I am learning so much. I think I've discovered what I want to do with the rest of my life."

"I hope you're not learning too quickly," said Gaspar. "You just got here."

"I still have a lot to learn. I just hope I can learn it all before you two get tired of having me around."

"You are welcome in the house of Gaspar as long as you wish to stay here," Rachel said, looking at Gaspar for approval.

"Of course."

The four friends talked all afternoon. Ezri had always in the past been so focused on himself that he never noticed good relationships around him. His anger at having been born into a poor family never allowed him to see that how people live together transcends the material possessions they may acquire. What he saw on his travels with Gaspar, and what he saw once they arrived at Gaspar's home in Seleucia, was that what was really important was how people lived together, not what they have. Watching the other three interact, he began to understand that if Gaspar did not have his great wealth, what was happening before him could still take place. At one point he sat smiling as he witnessed the intimacy of the others.

Rachel observed his scrutinization and said, "What are you thinking?"

"Right now, I can't tell you, but before I go back to Perea, I want to be able to. Is that rude of me to say?"

Watching him thoughtfully, Rachel said, "No. You never have to tell us anything that you're not ready to tell. But I do know that when you do tell someone, you'll feel much better."

Melchior slapped his thighs and said, "Gaspar you have been blessed with a rare woman. She is not only beautiful, but wise."

"And don't I know it," Gaspar said squeezing Rachel's hand. "The woman I barely knew when I left has given me more reason every day to learn more about her. She is a blessing from God."

"Thank you both," Rachel said standing. "I will check to see when our evening meal will be ready. Melchior, I told Ara that you would be joining us, and I hope that you won't let me down."

"Of course not, my dear. Let it never be known that I ever turned down a good meal and gracious company."

Rachel left the men watching her as she left.

"A marvelous woman," said Melchior.

"That she is," agreed Gaspar.

"I wish she had a little sister," said Ezri, getting a chuckle out of the other two.

Nine and a half months after Sophia and Basil had joined their flesh together, Ira was chagrined and Even was euphoric that she had not one, but two baby boys. She named them Bulus and Butrus. Two days after the boys were born, Sophia died from internal bleeding. Not long after that, Matthias recalled his two servants to Jericho. Ira was convinced that he would eventually find the stolen gold—Matthias was not. Ira had been an irreplaceable house servant, and though the old servant made him a decent amount of money in Panea, it was a drop in the ocean compared to all of Matthias' wealth. Ira lived out his days in Matthias' house. The rich man was a self-centered and many times shady man of business, but he was good to those who gave him a fair day's work. Ira always gave him that.

Ira confided in Matthias that the twins that he brought with him back to Jericho were Basil's sons.

"If they end up being half the size of their father, I will have twice the prize someday," said Matthias.

Ira took care of the boys until they were ten years old. When he died, Even took over the responsibilities. Bulus and Butrus always called Ira father, and Even Uncle. At Ira's death, it was clear that the boys were definitely their father's children— they were already as big as most normal sized men.

Saiar offered to have Rachel come stay with him until she and Gaspar were married. It was an inconvenience for her to do so, but it did keep people from making false conclusions about her chastity. It also provided enough separation so Gaspar and Ezri's friendship could have space to grow. When Gaspar was not with Rachel, he was spending time with Ezri.

Balzak had offered to teach the young man to use a knife, and he did spend some time developing the skill, but what Ezri became excited about was using the Parthian bow. A Parthian, rich or poor, might know how to use different weapons, but every Parthian-born man was expert with the recurve bow. Ezri's love for bow practice was as keen as Rachel's was for knife throwing.

Gaspar and Melchior made their presentation to King Phraataces, and Daba was elated to hear that both men, especially Gaspar, had decided to leave the priesthood. Had Gaspar been a few years older, he and not Daba would have been selected as high priest. The point was moot now that Gaspar had decided to go in another direction with his faith.

Not being consumed with the responsibilities of the priesthood, Gaspar had more input into the family business. He and Cephas developed a strong bond of friendship that lasted years until the day that Gaspar found the faithful servant lying prostrate over one of the tables in the warehouse where he had been going over the books the night before.

Balzak was disappointed that his most promising pupil had changed faiths and would never be a great magus. His coming fully to grips with the Jewish faith was long in acceptance, and caused he and Gaspar to spend many nights, into the small hours, discussing theology. Balzak would finally give in to the evidence of the true faith, but not until he and Gaspar had many years of debates.

CHAPTER SEVENTY-EIGHT

Majid had disappeared from the sister city area as soon as Phraataces had confiscated his family's wealth and possessions. His absence made Rachel feel more safe and it relieved Gaspar and Balzak from having to be concerned about protecting her from him. With Majid out of the picture, life went back to normalcy for everyone who had to worry about what he might do. There was talk that he had gone to live in Susa, a city two hundred miles east of Seleucia, but no one had bothered to check to see if the rumor was true. Those who knew him were glad to be rid of him and his disagreeable temperament. The truth was that he had left the city for a few days, but he had returned disguised as an old beggar. He had followed Rachel's goings and comings, and was aware that her residence had changed until her eventual wedding with Gaspar.

One day Rachel had stayed longer than she had planned at Gaspar's. Her knife throwing practice with Balzak had gone long and there were people on the wedding invitation list that she wanted Gaspar to approve.

"I should have met with you first," she said to Gaspar. "Do not sit too close. I'm sure I'm giving off a pungent odor after my workout with Balzak."

Gaspar pulled her close in an affectionate embrace and tried to kiss her. "No odor could ever keep me away from you and your desirable lips."

Rachel pushed away from him. "No. I mean it, Gaspar. I'm embarrassed to smell this way in your presence."

"You will be my wife. Will I only be able to hold you close after you have bathed?"

"After we are wed," she said playfully, "I don't care how I smell."

"Is that true?" Gaspar asked as he pulled her tightly to himself and kissed her.

Rachel and Gaspar finished their conversation about the wedding list, but it was frequently interrupted with nestling and lovers' playful teasing.

Kahliq had accompanied Rachel to Gaspar's and returned with her to Parandis' home after she and Gaspar had finished their business.

"You were gone a long time this afternoon, Rachel," pried Parandis as she met her friend in the courtyard. "What were you doing all this time?"

Rachel smiled smugly, and said, "Just knife throwing and talk of wedding invitations."

"And?"

"Nothing else but being held in Gaspar's arms and wishing he would never have to let me go," Rachel said closing her eyes and hugging herself.

Parandis ran over and embraced her friend, drew back, and said, "Rachel, you didn't hug him smelling like that, did you?"

"I did," she responded. "He insisted, and I let him."

The girls laughed as Parandis said, "You had mentioned that you wanted to go to the marketplace tomorrow. Could we go early and plan on spending the day there?"

"I would love to do that. I will welcome the opportunity to think about something other than the wedding plans."

"Then we shall make a day of it," said Parandis walking towards the doorway. "I'm tired. I think I will go to bed early, if you will excuse me?"

"Of course, Parandis. I had supper at Gaspar's, but I am still hungry after the practice that Balzak put me through. Would you mind having one of the servants bring me a snack out here in the courtyard?"

"Not at all. Sweet or savory?

"Sweet, I think."

"I'll see you bright and early tomorrow."

Sitting back, stretching her legs out in front and her arms behind her, she let her muscles slowly relax. A hand suddenly went over her mouth, and a strong arm pulled her out of her chair—her feet dangling in mid-air.

A voice whispered, tainted with the strong scent of garlic and wine, "You have caused the destruction of my family and ruined my life."

Terror permeated Rachel's thoughts. She struggled to comprehend who might be doing this to her. For just a moment, she thought that it was someone joking with her, but the intensity of his assault conveyed a different intent.

"Not so arrogant now, are you?"

The attacker's whispering masked his voice enough that she was struggling to identify it. She kept hoping that he would set her down so she would have a chance to escape his clutches. Then she remembered Balzak sheepishly telling her once, that if there was no other way, she could grab a male attacher's soft parts and squeeze with all of her might to get him to loosen his hold of her. The thought of touching any man there who was not her husband, repulsed her. Instead, she brought the heel of her foot up sharply into the man's groin. The surprise and pain made the assailant relax his grasp of her. She dropped down through the man's arms, and rolled away to safety.

Grabbing knives from her calf sheath and turning to face her attacker, she was surprised to see Majid dressed as an old beggar. He was just now recovering and was beginning to circle her. She threw her first knife as she stood and did not get much force into the throw. Majid knocked it away, receiving only a cut on the meaty part of his left hand. Rachel was now sprinting across the courtyard, keeping Majid on her left side. She let fly the second knife which stuck in his left thigh. Majid limped to the middle of the courtyard towards his kill which meant that Rachel could continue running around him to her right, making her throws easier to execute. The next knife she threw went deep into his other thigh.

"You whore!" he screamed.

Rachel released another knife as she continued circling her attacker. That knife sliced the side of his head, and bounced away on to the ground. Majid yelled another expletive just as Kahliq and Parandis entered the courtyard. Kahliq pushed Parandis inside the doorway as Rachel bent down and armed herself with three more knives from her left leg's sheath. Movement from behind caused Majid to turn to see who was there. His exposed neck was Rachel's next target. Her fifth knife sunk deep into the man's neck. He stood up straight trying to fill his lungs with air as he inadvertently sucked in blood. Rachel ceased her circling, took careful aim, and before she could throw her knife, a sword protruded through Majid's chest. He dropped to the ground gurgling blood, dying where he lay. Kahliq stood behind the would-be assassin, somber—his stance domineering. Adrenaline completing its task in her, Rachel dropped to the ground and sobbed. Parandis ran to her friend to give her comfort. Kahliq nudged Majid with his toe to make sure he was dead.

Arriving on the scene about the time that Parandis rushed over to console Rachel, Saiar gave orders to Kahliq to remove Majid's body from the premises. By now, the whole household was looking through the door and standing in the courtyard. The big servant solicited other servants to assist him removing the body and placing it in a wagon that was taken out into the wilderness where Majid's body was dropped unceremoniously there for scavengers to feast upon.

Next day, the girls did not go to the market, but Gaspar came over as soon as the news reached him.

"I wish that I could have been here to protect you," Gaspar said.

"If you would have been here, he never would have attacked. He was a coward in every way," Rachel said. On the verge of tears, she looked at Gaspar and said, "I've never killed a man before."

"Dear Rachel," Gaspar said hugging her.

She looked up into his eyes, saying, "I feel guilty killing Majid, but at the same time, during the attack, exhilaration coursed through me." She hesitated before saying, "I almost enjoyed it."

"You were protecting your life, Rachel."

"But should I have reveled in it?"

"I think that you were using the skills that you and Balzak have worked very hard to perfect. Last night was the first time that you've had the opportunity to use them. Your senses were on alert, and you did what you were trained to do. You don't feel a need to go out looking for opportunities like that, do you?"

"No. I never want to experience anything like that again," she said, her eyes round and expressive.

Gaspar smiled, and said, "I wouldn't worry about you wanting to become an assassin."

"I love you, Gaspar."

"I love you, Rachel."

"And I am glad you have been such a serious student," said Balzak entering the courtyard. "I am ecstatic that my master's wife-to-be is here to hold him today. Have your nerves settled down, my lady?'

"Yes they have," said Rachel. "Is this a time for formality?"

Balzak gave her a questioning look.

"My lady?"

"Whenever the master is around, it's *my lady*."

Gaspar smiled looking at Balzak, "And that's as it should be. Right, Balzak?"

"Yes, Gaspar."

Gaspar did a double take and Rachel laughed as she hugged the old servant.

CHAPTER SEVENTY-NINE

It was a hot summer afternoon when Gaspar and Ezri were making their way back to the house for refreshing cups of water with limes when Ezri blurted, "I've been wanting to tell you something that I've been afraid to say. I can't let another day go by without telling you." Becoming more subdued, he continued, "I must warn you that what I have done is detestable, and after you've heard it, I will understand if you want me to leave."

Wagging his head, Gaspar said, "What could be so bad, Ezri?"

"Please don't say anything, just let me talk, or I'll lose my courage."

The two men sat in the shade of the courtyard and Gaspar ordered their drinks to be brought to them.

"Tell me, Ezri. I will listen."

It took Ezri the better part of two hours for him to tell Gaspar the truth about his past. When he was finished, Gaspar was slouched down in his chair staring at his feet stretched out in front of him.

"You have much to account for, Ezri. The burden of lies you have had to shoulder must have been unbearable."

"Would you like for me to leave?"

"No, I do want to know if you seek forgiveness."

"How could I ever receive forgiveness for all that I have done?"

"As you know, I have been reading some of the Jews' sacred scrolls Balthasar left to Melchior. One of them tells a story about an Israelite king who committed great wrongs. He lusted over the wife of one of his officers, and had an affair with her that caused her to be pregnant. When he discovered this, he had the husband placed in battle where he would most assuredly be killed, and then took the dead man's wife for his own. When God revealed to His prophet the king's great sins, the prophet confronted the king."

"Did the king kill the prophet?"

"No, the king realized what he had done and asked God for forgiveness."

"God allowed the son who was born to the soldier's wife and the king to die, but God forgave the king because he confessed it to God."

"Do you think God could forgive me for what I've done?"

"There are Jewish teachers here in Seleucia that I have started meeting with. I asked them about this story I just told to you, and one of the teachers directed me to a Psalm the king wrote after he sinned with the soldier's wife. I wrote it down. Wait here, I want you to hear it.'

Gaspar left for a few minutes leaving Ezri alone in the courtyard.

"God," Ezri said in his mind, "You know that I have blocked you out of every part of my life. If You can forgive me of my great sins, I will do my best to follow You all the days of my life. This pain that I live with is too much for me to bear. Help me to find solace in You."

Gaspar returned and said, "Listen to this, Ezri, I won't read it all, just parts," and then he read:

"Wash me throughly from mine iniquity, and cleanse me from my sin.

For I acknowledge my transgressions: and my sin is ever before me.

Against Thee, Thee only, have I sinned, and done this evil in Thy sight

Hide Thy face from my sins, and blot out all of them.

Create in me a clean heart, O God; and renew a right spirit within me.

Cast me not away from Thy presence; and take not Thy holy spirit from me.

Restore unto me the joy of Thy salvation; and uphold me with Thy free spirit.

Deliver me from bloodguiltiness, O God, Thou God of my salvation: and my tongue shall sing aloud of Thy righteousness.

The sacrifices of God are a broken spirit: a broken and a contrite heart, O God, Thou wilt not despise."

"Yahweh's holy book says that?" Ezri said in disbelief. "Those words could be my own!"

"It does," smiled Gaspar.

"I just prayed, while you were gone, that if God could forgive me, I would follow him for the rest of my days."

"It sounds to me like you might be living a changed life, my friend."

"Thanks to you and your kindness, I already have begun. But to think that I could do so with God's forgiveness is remarkable."

"It is a great gift, and not one to be taken lightly."

"I never shall."

There were no words spoken for a period as Ezri watched Gaspar trying to formulate something else he wanted to say.

"Ezri, the gold that you buried must be returned to its rightful owner."

Taking a deep breath, Ezri said, "I've thought of that a lot these weeks since the theft. Satanas once told me that Matthias, the man whose gold it was," Gaspar nodded his recognition of the name from what Ezri had told him before, "is as diabolical as was Satanas. The only difference between the two is that Matthias had wealthy, powerful political connections that gave him an air of respectability. He would kill me as soon as he received the gold from me."

"Yes, that is a problem. We should spend some time alone praying about what to do and then, in the next day or two, pray together about it."

"I would like that," Ezri said shaking his head.

"What are you thinking?"

"Only, how much better I feel thinking about what's best for someone else rather than myself all the time."

Gaspar sat up in his chair, grabbed the young man's knee, and said, "What you have done in telling me of your past sin is very courageous. You could have chosen to live with it and let it eat away at you until you became bitter and angry. Who knows what keeping that to yourself would have done to yo. You have shown wisdom in telling me about your past. Thank you for trusting me."

To be truthful, Ezri didn't feel very courageous or wise, and Gaspar's words made him squirm. Before he had to endure more awkward silence, Tala appeared.

"Excuse me, but supper will be served in a few minutes."

Slapping the younger man on his leg, Gaspar said, "Come, let's freshen up. We'll speak more of this in the days to come."

Because Parandis and Rachel were up to their chins in wedding planning, it gave Gaspar plenty of time to spend with his work and his friends. Cephas had had an idea for several years, but he and Gaspar were never quite sure how to implement it. With the addition of Ezri and his Roman citizenship, the idea had resurfaced for discussion.

The three men were conversing about a shipment that had just come in which had prompted Ezri's comment of whether Gaspar ever had a business venture that flopped.

"Not many," Cephas said scratching his head trying to

344

remember.

"That does bring up a point that I would like to talk to you about, Ezri," said Gaspar as he looked at Cephas for affirmation.

"This is perfect timing," Cephas enjoined.

"We could substantially enlarge our sales if we had a man in Damascus who could keep an eye on opportunities and business that we would run through the Roman empire."

Ezri's countenance brightened.

"This person would be a partner in all the business that channeled through Damascus, reaping a third of whatever we cleared. Cephas and I were thinking that maybe you would like to be that person."

"You're not joking with me are you? This would not be a funny joke if you were."

Gaspar and Cephas were enjoying his response.

"Do you think I'm ready?" he said looking back and forth to each man.

"I can't teach you any more, son," said Cephas.

"You will not be sorry, Cephas. I will work so hard."

"I know that you will," Gaspar smiled grabbing the younger man's shoulder.

"I'd say we have a partner," said Cephas.

Ezri had been working hard since he connected up with Cephas, but with this new revelation, there were many nights where Gaspar or Cephas had to tell him that the work would be waiting for him the next day and to go to bed.

The big day finally arrived three months and five days after Gaspar's arrival home. No one in either Seleucia or Ctesiphon could ever remember a more glamorous wedding. Gaspar was embarrassed by the grandness of it until he saw his bride the day of the wedding. From that moment on he wondered if anything could match the grace, majesty, and beauty of his bride. King Phraataces made a short appearance during the celebration that caused a predictable stir in the guests. For Gaspar and Rachel, the true royal guests were Melchior, Balzak, Ezri, Vahumisa, and the rest of the men who traveled those many weeks to glimpse together the Child Messiah.

Someone asked Gaspar at the wedding, "Do you think the Child you sought out was really the king of the Jews?"

"I believe that with every fiber of my being," he rejoined. "I will be watching with interest the life of this baby sent from God, not just to the Jews, but to all nations."

The St. Nicholas Chronicles continue in the next book of the series, *Pilate.* Due out in the summer of 2016.

God's Ear is a book of short, fictional stories about the Christian faith.

A First Century con man and his sidekick discover that their devious ways come to an end when they inadvertently swindle a more malevolent thug than themselves. The result makes blind beggars out of them, causing them to start looking at life differently than they had before.

A village positioned on a garbage heap has a door in the wall that leads its inhabitants to freedom, but none choose to challenge the mighty angel who guards it until one day a little boy makes the angel's acquaintance.

These and other stories in *God's Ear* will both challenge and encourage you in your faith.

The whole book could be easily read in an hour or two, but you might want to savor each story and its accompanying scriptures.

Characters and Story Information:

Abirami: Ezri's father. Married to Miriam. His wife's death and his
    son's, Ezri, running away break his heart.

Ahura-Mazda: The pagan god of the Parthians. MAZDA
    AHURA, meaning the Most Wise Creator, Good Lord of
    Existence.

Amehlech: Servant to Gaspar. Comic relief with Cyrus.

Ara: Female servant who follows Nazli and Rachel to Gaspar's
    home (see also Kahliq).

Arioch: Gaspar's father.

Balzak: Servant and one time guardian of Gaspar.

Basil: Mathias' giant servant (Father of Bulus and Butrus. Their
    exploits continue in the Bartimaeus short story, "Blind
    Solution", *God's Ear* on Amazon.com).

Bulus & Butrus: Sophia's and Basil's twin baby boys.

Caesarea Phillipi: Generally known as Cæsarea Panias, or
    Cæsarea Beneath Panion (Arab corruption of the name
    Panion is now Banion). The cave at Cæsarea Philippi is the
    most eastern source of the Jordan river—this alone makes
    the area important to the Jews. Earthquakes over the years
    have changed the formation of the cave forcing the water to
    emerge at the foot of the cave rather than from within it.

Cassius: Roman spy who joins up with the expedition along the
    route from Dura-Europus to Damascus. He is invited by the
    magi to join them on their quest.

Cephas: The overseer and financial manager of all Gaspar's
    holdings.

Clothes: Keffiyeh

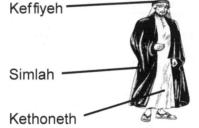

Simlah

Kethoneth

Cyrus: Comic tag team with Amehlech, servant to Gaspar.

Daba: One of Zand's close associates. His name means gold in
    Persian. He becomes high after Zand's death.

Damon: One of Satanas' henchmen left behind to let Ezri know
    that plans had changed.

Daniel: One of Melchior's servants.

Darawesh: Means wealthy. Rival bandit leader to Farshid. Plots
    with Sevent and Majid to kidnap Gaspar.

Diana: Gaspar's mother. Her life had been wholly wrapped up in
    her husband. Diana lived but one year her husband's

death.

Ethan: One of Satanas' messengers/spies who keeps Sophia and Basil's relationship a secret from Satanas.

Even: Young servant Matthias sends with Ira to be the old servant's servant in Caesarea Philippi.

Ezri: The mischievous son of Abirami who grows up to be a thief. He falls in with Sophia and Satanas helping with their criminal activities.

Farrah: Female servant to Parandis.

Farrokh: One of Zand's close associates. His name means happy/fortunate.

Farshid: Desert bandit leader. His lands are between Dura-Europus and Tadmor.

Gifts of the Magi: GOLD – Balthasar's gift. The ornamentation of the altar. FRANKINCENSE – Gaspar's gift. The incense of praise. MYRRH – Melchior's gift. The sweet aroma of the Most High God.

Gil: Friend of John's who helps retrieve Raven and hunt for Ezri. A few years older than Ezri and Uri, and known for his maturity and patience.

Gischala: A town in the mountains of upper Galilee, 12 miles NW of Capernaum. Rabbinical literature confirms that the olive oil of Gischala was excellent. Seems to have been an important settlement in Upper Galilee.

Hassan: One of two men Darawesh sends into Dura-Europus to find out whether the magi's caravan arrived. The other man was Yehyeh.

Herod (Philip): He reigned over Gaulantis, Auranitis, Batanea, Trachonitis, Paneas, and Ituraea from 4 BC to AD 34.

Hirmand: Servant of Zand who brings news of his collapse to Rachel.

Ira: Old servant of Matthias who asks to be sent to Caesarea Philippi to keep find Matthias' gold.

Jesse: Man in the crowd who defends Ira to Raphael.

John: Boyhood friend of Ezri. John's friends: see Gil and Uri.

John's Horse: Raven. Stolen by Ezri.

Judith: Wife of Levi and mother of John of Mischala.

Kahliq: Male servant of Zand who accompanies Rachel to Gaspar's home while he is in Israel (see also Ara).

Keffiyeh: Middle eastern headdress (see *Clothes*).

Kethoneth: Long robe worn under a Simlah (see *Clothes*).

Kiavash: Oldest son of Farshid.

King Phraataces: King of the Parthian Empire at the time of this story.

Laurentinus: Roman commander in charge of the detail transporting Mathias' gold from Jericho to Capernaum.

Levi: John's father. Honest. Hard working.

Majid: Nazli and Rachel use his interests in Rachel to attract Gaspar. Son of Sevent.

Matthias: Wealthy, merciless merchant in Jericho who sends his gold north to be housed in the temple of Pan near Caesarea Phillipi.

Menucha: Yitzhak's wife. Her name means tranquility.

Miriam: Wife of Abirami. Died giving birth to Ezri.

Moshen: Melchior's old servant.

Nazli: Rachel's mother and Zand's wife. Means glory; elegance; sweetheart.

Nereus: One of Satanas' henchmen. Sends him to recall the five archers to ambush Ravid's men who have been observing Satanas and his men.

Nippur: The town to which Belthasar was sent.

Noam: One of Satanas' men sent to work with Sophia in Hippos.

Omet: Lead worker for Yitzhak. He is left in charge whenever Yitzhak is away.

Parandis: Friend of Rachel's. Saiar's daughter. Name means *silk-like*.

Pesach: Man next to Gaspar at dinner party. His name is related to the Passover.

Pesha: Pesach's wife. Her name means Passover.

Podarces: Scouts with Ezri during the transportation of the gold from Capernaum to Caesarea Philippi.

Rachel: Love interest of Gaspar's. Daughter of Zand and Nazli.

Raphael: A dishonest man with whom Ira has stopped doing business.

Raven: John's horse that was stolen by Ezri. Later traded for a camel in Hazor.

Reuben: The rabbi of Tadmor, speaks with the magi and Cassius about their errant understanding of the star in Numbers 24:17.

Ravid: Becomes the leader of Bazil's group once Basil dies.

Reuben: The rabbi of Tadmor who speaks with the magi and Cassius about their errant understanding of the star in Numbers 24:17.

Saiar: Parandis' father. City official for Seleucia and close friend to Zand.

Satanas: A broker for criminal activity in Galilee, Phoenicia, and Gaulanitis. Means Satan in Greek.

Sekanjabin: Frequent drink in the story.
2 cups sugar
2 cups water
1/2 cup white vinegar
A small bunch fresh mint, washed
2 Small seedless cucumbers, washed, peeled and shredded (for the drink)

Lime rind

Sevent: Majid's father.

Simlah: A long robe worn over a Kethoneth (see *Clothes*).

Sophia: Caesarean woman who sells Pan-flutes as a cover for her pick-pocketing business. Ezri meets her when he first enters Caesarea. She is a frequent accomplice in Satanas' crimes.

Star of Bethlehem: A small star that does not behave as other stars do in the sky. It rises in the western sky. The star appears to move ahead of the wisemen.

Tadmor: An oasis city that was neutral to Parthia and Rome.

Tala: Female servant of Gaspar.

Tam: Messenger Matthias sends to give allowances to Ira and to collect news.

Uri: Friend of John's who helps retrieve Raven and hunt for Ezri.

Vahumisa: Commander of the guard that was sent along to protect the magi on their travels.

Wine goddess (Persian): Spenta Armaiti, Persian goddess of the vineyards.

Wisemen (Magi = plural of Magus):

Gaspar: Protagonist of the story. Has fantastic dreams of his future, and ages slowly. Lives in Seleucia. His gift was frankincense.

Belthasar: Lives in Nippur. The oldest of the three magi. His gift was a small chest of gold.

Melchior: Fifteen years Gaspar's senior, and a wise and trusted confidant. A wealthy man with the strong personality of a desert bandit. He lives outside Seleucia in a modest home with a high tower for observing the stars. His gift was myrrh.

Writing Material: The normal writing material used throughout the Roman Empire was the wooden writing tablet. A shallow recess was cut in a wooden board, leaving a border like a picture frame. The recess was filled with wax on which one could write with a sharp pointed stylus. (BAR; July/Aug '03)

Yacob: The old rabbi from Tadmor who spoke with the magi about the prophecies.

Yalda: Gaspar's beautiful black mare. Means longest night of the year.

Yehyeh: One of the men Darawesh sends into Dura-Europus to find out whether the magi's caravan had come in. The other man was Hassan.

Yitzhak: A wealthy man who lives in Caesarea Philippi. He is a business acquaintance of Mathias'. Sophia stole his purse and used Ezri to con him out of a reward.

Yitzhak's Map: See page 151.

<u>Zand</u>: The high priest of Ahura-Mazda. He became first concerned about Gaspar when the king showed favor toward him in his first audience in the story. He is father of Rachel and husband to Nazli.

Map of the Territory Covered in the Story:

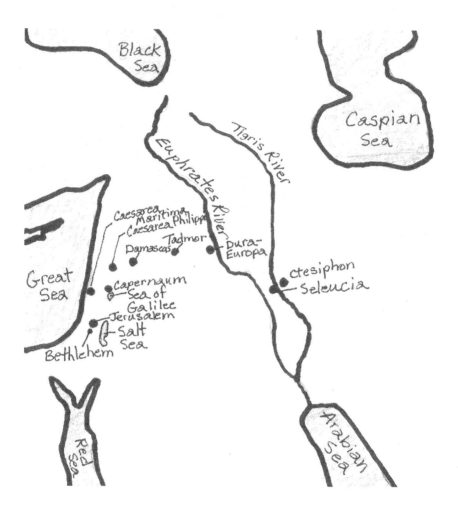